THE CASSELL BOOK OF BIBLE QUOTATIONS

THE CASSELL BOOK OF BIBLE QUOTATIONS

Edited by Jennifer Speake

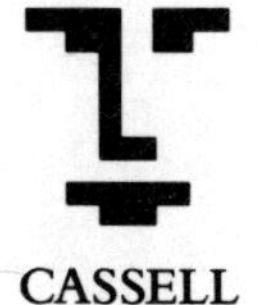

CASSELL

Cassell
Villiers House, 41/47 Strand
London WC2N 5JE

First published 1982 as *A Treasury of Biblical Quotations*
by The Hamlyn Publishing Group Limited.
Cassell edition first published 1992

British Library Cataloguing-in-Publication Data
A catalogue entry for this book is available
from the British Library.

ISBN 0-304-32052-8

Printed and bound in Great Britain by
Biddles Ltd, Guildford and King's Lynn

CONTENTS

INTRODUCTION	vii
HOW TO USE THIS BOOK	ix
THE BIBLE IN ENGLISH	xi
THE BOOKS OF THE BIBLE	xv
BIBLICAL QUOTATIONS	1
INDEX	113

INTRODUCTION

Deliberate or unconscious quotation from the Bible is a rich and significant part of the cultural heritage of all English speakers. Biblical quotation and allusion have been tellingly used in virtually every genre of English literature from the profoundly serious (T. S. Eliot) to the dazzlingly facetious (P. G. Wodehouse). The quotations in this book have been selected to show the range, beauty, and expressiveness of biblical language that has drawn not only the great literary figures of our own and past ages but also ordinary writers and speakers in search of an apt or thought-provoking phrase. In this book, readers seeking a specific passage or a text appropriate to a particular occasion will find their path smoothed by the extensive index, while browsers and those selecting topics for meditation will find that the quotations vary from the pleasantly familiar to the arrestingly unfamiliar.

Because of the long-established preeminence of the Authorized Version (*see* The Bible in English) its language has become inextricably interwoven in the fabric of our speech. The decision to use it as the basis of this book was therefore inevitable and implies no reflection on the literary or scholarly merits of other versions. The exception is the book of Psalms, where it was felt that the Authorized Version is less familiar than Coverdale's translation, used in the Psalter in the Book of Common Prayer.

The basic unit of a quotation is generally a single verse, though many well known passages extend to a number of verses and are accordingly given in full. The verse unit enables some flavour to be given of the quotation's context, and the context itself may provide a striking sidelight on an otherwise familiar phrase or saying. Because the book is not intended as a concordance, no attempt has been made to include every occurrence of particular phrases (as for instance when an Old Testament prophecy is repeated in the New Testament); such phrases are generally given in the context in which they are most likely to be familiar.

Jennifer Speake

HOW TO USE THIS BOOK

To assist the reader in finding a particular quotation, each book of the Bible from which quotations have been selected and each individual quotation has been assigned its own reference number. The books of the Old Testament, Apocrypha, and New Testament are given in their traditional order (see the list of the Books of the Bible), and the first part of the reference number relates to a particular book. Thus Exodus has been assigned the number 2, and quotations from Exodus are numbered 2.1, 2.2, 2.3, etc. These reference numbers in the index are completely independent of the chapter and verse numbers, which are printed in the form *6:9* and appear after the quotations in the main text.

Each quotation is indexed under one or more key words to enable a quotation to be traced easily. Key phrases from each quotation are listed in alphabetical order under the appropriate key word and are followed by the reference number of the full form of the quotation in the main text.

Also included in the index are certain well-known phrases which do not themselves appear in the Bible but which are derived from or allude to particular biblical passages. Thus the phrase 'Prodigal Son' does not appear in Luke's account of that parable, but **Prodigal Son** is listed in the index to direct the inquirer to the relevant passage. Such words or phrases are printed in the index in bold type.

Readers who wish to use the index to find quotations on specific topics, such as 'peace' or 'justice', will see that, in addition to the key-word listings, relevant quotations also appear under thematic headings. These headings are printed in bold type. For example, the saying 'God loveth a cheerful giver' is indexed under the key words 'loveth', 'cheerful', and 'giver', and also under the thematic heading **generosity**.

Plurals of nouns are indexed separately from the singular. Possessive forms, such as 'man's', appear under the plain form of the noun. The infinitive form of the verb, such as 'make' or 'pass', is indexed separately from the inflected forms, such as 'maketh' or 'passed'.

THE BIBLE IN ENGLISH

Before the Reformation most copies of the Bible that existed in England were written in Latin. This Latin version, the Vulgate, was compiled by St. Jerome in the late 4th century and formed the basis for the doctrine and liturgy of the Church in Europe throughout the Middle Ages. The production of Bibles in manuscript was laborious and costly, and as monks and priests were virtually the only people who could understand Latin or even read, the Bible was inaccessible to ordinary lay people.

At the end of the 9th century the West Saxon king, Alfred the Great (849–901), promoted the first drive to advance literacy in England. The first Anglo-Saxon versions of the Bible appeared under his auspices; among the sections translated were the four Gospels and the first 50 Psalms.

In the centuries following the Norman conquest more translations of individual books were made, some in prose and others as free translations in verse. It was not until the late 14th century that a more systematic programme of translation was begun at the prompting of the Lollard leader, John Wycliffe (d. 1384). The Lollards were fiercely critical of the Church and maintained the supremacy of personal faith and conscience over the dictates of the clergy; all Christians should therefore be enabled to read and interpret the Bible for themselves. As Wycliffe himself wrote, "Christ and his apostles taught the people in the tongue that was best known to the people. Why should not men do so now?" The two so-called Wycliffite versions are the first complete translations in English. They survive in many 15th-century manuscripts, thus testifying to the demand for an English Bible, despite official condemnation by the Church.

The decisive impetus towards the translation of the Bible into English was provided in the second decade of the 16th century by the Reformation. Like the Lollards, the Reformers believed in the obligation of all Christians to study the Bible. However, between the Wycliffite Bibles and the work of William Tyndale (?1494–1536), two vital changes had taken place. The first was the invention of printing, enabling books to be produced quickly and disseminated widely. The second was the revival of scholarship, which meant that scholars of international renown, like the Dutchman Desiderius Erasmus (?1466–1536), were able to make a critical study of biblical manuscripts written in Greek and Hebrew as well as in Latin and to publish authoritative texts.

Tyndale's translation, begun about 1522, was grounded in his conviction that "a boy that driveth the plough" should be as familiar with the content of the scriptures as the most learned cleric. His translation, which was made directly from the Hebrew Old Testament and the Greek New Testament texts, has remained a model in its scholarliness and clarity. It was however left incomplete at the time of Tyndale's execution for heresy, and it was Miles Coverdale (1488–1568) who produced the first complete Bible to be printed in English (1535). Like Tyndale, he was forced to live abroad on account of ecclesiastical opposition to his work, and Coverdale's Bible was probably printed at Zürich. He based his work on those parts of Tyndale's translation that were available, on the Vulgate, on the German Bible of Martin Luther, and various other sources. It is Coverdale's version of the Psalms that remains most familiar, as it was adopted for the Book of Common Prayer.

Subsequent versions of the Bible issued in Henry VIII's reign had official backing and in these Coverdale also had a hand. The Matthew's Bible (1537), edited by John Rogers (?1500–1555), recombined the work of Tyndale and Coverdale and was the first English Bible to bear the king's authorization. Coverdale himself edited the Great Bible (1539), which was printed in a large format and ordered to be placed in churches. This version was nicknamed the 'Treacle Bible' on account of its rendering of Jeremiah 8:22, 'triacle' or 'treacle' being a Middle English word meaning a 'remedy' or 'medicinal compound'. In 1540 a new edition of the Great Bible, revised by Coverdale, was issued with a preface by Archbishop Thomas Cranmer (1489–1556); this is sometimes referred to as Cranmer's Bible.

During the Roman Catholic revival of Mary's reign (1553–58), English Protestant exiles worked in Switzerland on a new biblical translation. This Geneva Bible (1560) was printed in clear roman type in a small format and for the first time the text was divided into verses. It was popularly called the 'Breeches Bible', from its version of Genesis 3:7. It achieved a wide circulation in Elizabethan England, but its marginal notes, which propounded an extreme Puritan position, made it objectionable to the queen and those of her advisers who wanted the English Church to adopt a moderate theological stance. Archbishop Matthew Parker therefore masterminded a revision of the Great Bible, which was carried out by the English bishops. The Bishops' Bible (1568) was specifically designed for public reading; in 1571 each church was ordered to obtain a copy.

The Roman Catholic Church came only slowly to the realization that it was desirable that the laity should be able to read a vernacular Bible. Scholars at the English College at Douai in Flanders produced an English New Testament, which was printed at Reims in 1582. The Old Testament appeared at Douai in 1609–10. Notable for its heavily Latinate language, the Douai-Reims Bible is the traditional version used by English Roman Catholics.

At the Hampton Court Conference (1604), chaired by James I, it was decided that a new version of the Bible was needed to accommodate both Puritan and High Church viewpoints. About 50 leading scholars, working in six groups, undertook the work, using the Bishops' Bible as their basis. They also consulted the Greek and Hebrew texts and referred to earlier English versions. The Authorized or King James Version (1611) quickly superseded all competitors, both for public reading and for private study, and retained unchallenged supremacy for over 250 years.

In 1870 it was decided that advances in the understanding of the languages and historical background of the Bible made it desirable that the Authorized Version should be revised. The panel of distinguished scholars was instructed to make as few changes as possible to the language, while incorporating the fruits of contemporary biblical scholarship in their text. Thus the cadences that make the Authorized Version preeminent for public reading were preserved, but the verbal alterations caused much criticism and the Revised Version (New Testament, 1881; Old Testament, 1885) never thoroughly displaced its predecessor.

In the 20th century numerous English versions of the Bible have been produced in both Britain and the USA. The American Standard Version (1901) was a modification of the Revised Version; the Revised Standard Version, an interdenominational project, was issued in 1952. In Britain the Roman Catholic Church sanctioned a new translation from the Vulgate made by Ronald Knox (1888–1957), which was published in 1945 (New Testament) and 1949 (Old Testament). The New Testament scholar James Moffatt (1870–1944) made a successful colloquial translation of the New Testament (1913) and a less satisfactory Old Testament (1924). In 1947 a conference of non-Roman Catholic churches in Britain set up a committee to oversee a completely new translation of the Bible. The work was carried out by three panels of scholars assisted by a panel of literary advisers, and the complete New English Bible was published in 1970.

THE BOOKS OF THE BIBLE

Books that appear in brackets are those from which no quotations have been chosen for this selection.

Old Testament

Genesis
Exodus
Leviticus
Numbers
Deuteronomy
Joshua
Judges
Ruth
I Samuel
II Samuel
I Kings
II Kings
(I Chronicles)
(II Chronicles)
Ezra
Nehemiah
Esther
Job
Psalms
Proverbs
Ecclesiastes
Song of Solomon
Isaiah
Jeremiah
Lamentations
Ezekiel
Daniel
Hosea
Joel
Amos
(Obadiah)
Jonah
Micah
(Nahum)
Habakkuk
(Zephaniah)
Haggai
Zechariah
Malachi

Apocrypha

I Esdras
II Esdras
Tobit
(Judith)
(The rest of Esther)
Wisdom
Ecclesiasticus
(Baruch, with Epistle of Jeremiah)
(Song of the Three Children)
(Susanna)
(Bel and the Dragon)
(Prayer of Manasses)
I Maccabees
II Maccabees

New Testament

Matthew
Mark
Luke
John
Acts
Romans
I Corinthians
II Corinthians
Galatians
Ephesians
Philippians
Colossians
I Thessalonians
II Thessalonians
I Timothy
II Timothy
Titus
Philemon
Hebrews
James
I Peter
II Peter
I John
II John
(III John)
Jude
Revelation

BIBLICAL QUOTATIONS

Old Testament

1 Genesis

1.1
In the beginning God created the heaven and the earth.
And the earth was without form, and void; and darkness was upon the face of the deep. And the Spirit of God moved upon the face of the waters.
And God said, Let there be light: and there was light.
And God saw the light, that it was good: and God divided the light from the darkness.
And God called the light Day, and the darkness he called Night. And the evening and the morning were the first day.

1:1–5

1.2
Fiat lux.

Vulgate 1:3

1.3
And God called the dry land Earth; and the gathering together of the waters called he Seas: and God saw that it was good.
And God said, Let the earth bring forth grass, the herb yielding seed, and the fruit tree yielding fruit after his kind, whose seed is in itself, upon the earth: and it was so.

1:10–11

1.4
And God made two great lights: the greater light to rule the day, and the lesser light to rule the night: he made the stars also.

1:16

1.5
And God created great whales, and every living creature that moveth, which the waters brought forth abundantly, after their kind, and every winged fowl after his kind: and God saw that it was good.

1:21

1.6
And God said, Let the earth bring forth the living creature after his kind, cattle, and creeping thing, and beast of the earth after his kind: and it was so.

1:24

1.7
And God said, Let us make man in our image, after our likeness: and let them have dominion over the fish of the sea, and over the fowl of the air, and over the cattle, and over all the earth, and over every creeping thing that creepeth upon the earth.
So God created man in his own image, in the image of God created he him; male and female created he them.
And God blessed them, and God said unto them, Be fruitful, and multiply, and replenish the earth, and subdue it: and have dominion over the fish of the sea, and over the fowl of the air, and over every living thing that moveth upon the earth.

1:26–28

1.8
And on the seventh day God ended his work which he had made; and he rested on the seventh day from all his work which he had made.

2:2

1.9
But there went up a mist from the earth, and watered the whole face of the ground.
And the Lord God formed man of the dust of the ground, and breathed into his nostrils the breath of life; and man became a living soul.
And the Lord God planted a garden eastward in Eden; and there he put the man whom he had formed.
And out of the ground made the Lord God to grow every tree that is pleasant to the sight, and good for food; the tree of life also in the midst of the garden, and the tree of knowledge of good and evil.
And a river went out of Eden to water the garden.

2:6–10

1.10
And the Lord God took the man, and put him into the garden of Eden to dress it and to keep it.
And the Lord God commanded the man, saying, Of every tree of the garden thou mayest freely eat:
But of the tree of the knowledge of good and evil, thou shalt not eat of it: for in the day that thou eatest thereof thou shalt surely die.

2:15–17

1.11
And the Lord God said, It is not good that the man should be alone; I will make him an help meet for him.
And out of the ground the Lord God formed every beast of the field, and every fowl of the air; and brought them unto Adam to see what he would call them: and whatsoever Adam

called every living creature, that was the name thereof.

2:18–19

1.12

And the Lord God caused a deep sleep to fall upon Adam, and he slept: and he took one of his ribs, and closed up the flesh instead thereof;

And the rib, which the Lord God had taken from man, made he a woman, and brought her unto the man.

And Adam said, This is now bone of my bones, and flesh of my flesh: she shall be called Woman, because she was taken out of Man.

Therefore shall a man leave his father and his mother, and shall cleave unto his wife: and they shall be one flesh.

And they were both naked, the man and his wife, and were not ashamed.

2:21–25

1.13

Now the serpent was more subtil than any beast of the field which the Lord God had made.

3:1

1.14

God doth know that in the day ye eat thereof, then your eyes shall be opened, and ye shall be as gods, knowing good and evil.

And when the woman saw that the tree was good for food, and that it was pleasant to the eyes, and a tree to be desired to make one wise, she took of the fruit thereof, and did eat, and gave also unto her husband with her; and he did eat.

And the eyes of them both were opened, and they knew that they were naked; and they sewed fig leaves together; and made themselves aprons.

And they heard the voice of the Lord God walking in the garden in the cool of the day: and Adam and his wife hid themselves from the presence of the Lord God amongst the trees of the garden.

3:5–8

1.15

They sewed fig leaves together and made themselves breeches.

Genevan 3:7

1.16

And he said, I heard thy voice in the garden, and I was afraid, because I was naked; and I hid myself.

And he said, Who told thee that thou wast naked?

3:10–11

1.17

And the man said, The woman whom thou gavest to be with me, she gave me of the tree, and I did eat.

And the Lord God said unto the woman, What is this that thou hast done? And the woman said, The serpent beguiled me, and I did eat.

And the Lord God said unto the serpent, Because thou hast done this, thou art cursed above all cattle, and above every beast of the field; upon thy belly shalt thou go, and dust shalt thou eat all the days of thy life:

And I will put enmity between thee and the woman, and between thy seed and her seed; it shall bruise thy head, and thou shalt bruise his heel.

Unto the woman he said, I will greatly multiply thy sorrow and thy conception; in sorrow thou shalt bring forth children; and thy desire shall be to thy husband, and he shall rule over thee.

And unto Adam he said, Because thou hast hearkened unto the voice of thy wife, and has eaten of the tree, of which I commanded thee, saying, Thou shalt not eat of it: cursed is the ground for thy sake; in sorrow shalt thou eat of it all the days of thy life.

3:12–17

1.18

In the sweat of thy face shalt thou eat bread, till thou return unto the ground; for out of it wast thou taken: for dust thou art, and unto dust shalt thou return.

And Adam called his wife's name Eve; because she was the mother of all living.

3:19–20

1.19

Abel was a keeper of sheep, but Cain was a tiller of the ground.

4:2

1.20

But unto Cain and to his offering he had not respect. And Cain was very wroth, and his countenance fell.

4:5

1.21

And the Lord said unto Cain, Where is Abel thy brother? And he said, I know not: Am I my brother's keeper?

And he said, What hast thou done? the voice of thy brother's blood crieth unto me from the ground.

4:9–10

1.22

When thou tillest the ground, it shall not henceforth yield unto thee her strength; a fugitive and a vagabond shalt thou be in the earth.

And Cain said unto the Lord, My punishment is greater than I can bear.

4:12–13

1.23
And the Lord said unto him, Therefore whosoever slayeth Cain, vengeance shall be taken on him sevenfold. And the Lord set a mark upon Cain, lest any finding him should kill him.
And Cain went out from the presence of the Lord, and dwelt in the land of Nod, on the east of Eden.

4:15–16

1.24
And Adah bare Jabal: he was the father of such as dwell in tents, and of such as have cattle.
And his brother's name was Jubal: he was the father of all such as handle the harp and organ.
And Zillah, she also bare Tubal-cain, an instructer of every artificer in brass and iron.

4:20–22

1.25
And Enoch walked with God: and he was not; for God took him.

5:24

1.26
And all the days of Methuselah were nine hundred sixty and nine years: and he died.

5:27

1.27
The sons of God saw the daughters of men that they were fair; and they took them wives of all which they chose.
And the Lord said, My spirit shall not always strive with man, for that he also is flesh: yet his days shall be an hundred and twenty years.
There were giants in the earth in those days; and also after that, when the sons of God came in unto the daughters of men, and they bare children to them, the same became mighty men which were of old, men of renown.

6:2–4

1.28
And it repented the Lord that he had made man on the earth, and it grieved him at his heart.

6:6

1.29
And they went in unto Noah into the ark, two and two of all flesh, wherein is the breath of life.
And they that went in, went in male and female of all flesh, as God had commanded him: and the Lord shut him in.
And the flood was forty days upon the earth; and the waters increased, and bare up the ark, and it was lift up above the earth.

7:15–17

1.30
But the dove found no rest for the sole of her foot, and she returned unto him into the ark, for the waters were on the face of the whole earth: then he put forth his hand, and took her, and pulled her in unto him into the ark.

8:9

1.31
And the dove came in to him in the evening; and, lo, in her mouth was an olive leaf pluckt off: so Noah knew that the waters were abated from off the earth.

8:11

1.32
And the Lord smelled a sweet savour; and the Lord said in his heart, I will not again curse the ground any more for man's sake; for the imagination of man's heart is evil from his youth; neither will I again smite any more every thing living, as I have done.
While the earth remaineth, seedtime and harvest, and cold and heat, and summer and winter, and day and night shall not cease.

8:21–22

1.33
And surely your blood of your lives will I require; at the hand of every beast will I require it, and at the hand of man; at the hand of every man's brother will I require the life of man.
Whoso sheddeth man's blood, by man shall his blood be shed: for in the image of God made he man.

9:5–6

1.34
I do set my bow in the cloud, and it shall be for a token of a covenant between me and the earth.

9:13

1.35
He was a mighty hunter before the Lord: wherefore it is said, Even as Nimrod the mighty hunter before the Lord.

10:9

1.36
And the whole earth was of one language, and of one speech.

11:1

1.37
And they said, Go to, let us build us a city and a tower, whose top may reach unto heaven; and let us make us a name, lest we be scattered abroad upon the face of the whole earth.

11:4

1.38
Therefore is the name of it called **Babel;**

because the Lord did there confound the language of all the earth: and from thence did the Lord scatter them abroad upon the face of all the earth.

11:9

1.39
Now the Lord had said unto Abram, Get thee out of thy country, and from thy kindred, and from thy father's house, unto a land that I will shew thee:
And I will make of thee a great nation, and I will bless thee, and make thy name great; and thou shalt be a blessing:
And I will bless them that bless thee, and curse him that curseth thee: and in thee shall all families of the earth be blessed.

12:1–3

1.40
But the men of Sodom were wicked and sinners before the Lord exceedingly.

13:13

1.41
After these things the word of the Lord came unto Abram in a vision, saying, Fear not, Abram: I am thy shield, and thy exceeding great reward.

15:1

1.42
And he believed in the Lord; and he counted it to him for righteousness.

15:6

1.43
And when the sun was going down, a deep sleep fell upon Abram; and, lo, an horror of great darkness fell upon him.

15:12

1.44
And thou shalt go to thy fathers in peace; thou shalt be buried in a good old age.

15:15

1.45
And he will be a wild man; his hand will be against every man, and every man's hand against him; and he shall dwell in the presence of all his brethren.

16:12

1.46
Is any thing too hard for the Lord? At the time appointed I will return unto thee, according to the time of life, and Sarah shall have a son.

18:14

1.47
That be far from thee to do after this manner, to slay the righteous with the wicked: and that the righteous should be as the wicked, that be far from thee: Shall not the Judge of all the earth do right?

18:25

1.48
Then the Lord rained upon Sodom and upon Gomorrah brimstone and fire from the Lord out of heaven.

19:24

1.49
But his wife looked back from behind him, and she became a pillar of salt.

19:26

1.50
And Abraham said, My son, God will provide himself a lamb for a burnt offering: so they went both of them together.

22:8

1.51
And Abraham lifted up his eyes, and looked, and behold behind him a ram caught in a thicket by his horns: and Abraham went and took the ram, and offered him up for a burnt offering in the stead of his son.

22:13

1.52
And Abraham was old, and well stricken in age: and the Lord had blessed Abraham in all things.

24:1

1.53
And Jacob said to Rebekah his mother, Behold, Esau my brother is a hairy man, and I am a smooth man.

27:11

1.54
And he came near, and kissed him: and he smelled the smell of his raiment, and blessed him, and said, See, the smell of my son is as the smell of a field which the Lord hath blessed:
Therefore God give thee of the dew of heaven, and the fatness of the earth, and plenty of corn and wine.

27:27–28

1.55
And he said, Thy brother came with subtilty, and hath taken away thy blessing.

27:35

1.56
And he dreamed, and behold a ladder set up on the earth, and the top of it reached to heaven: and behold the angels of God ascending and descending on it.

28:12

1.57
And Jacob awaked out of his sleep, and he said, Surely the Lord is in this place; and I knew it not.
And he was afraid, and said, How dreadful is this place! this is none other but the house of God, and this is the gate of heaven.

28:16–17

1.58
Leah was tender eyed; but Rachel was beautiful and well favoured.
29:17

1.59
And Jacob served seven years for Rachel; and they seemed unto him but a few days, for the love he had to her.
29:20

1.60
And Mizpah; for he said, The Lord watch between me and thee, when we are absent one from another.
31:49

1.61
And Jacob was left alone; and there wrestled a man with him until the breaking of the day. And when he saw that he prevailed not against him, he touched the hollow of his thigh; and the hollow of Jacob's thigh was out of joint, as he wrestled with him.
And he said, Let me go, for the day breaketh. And he said, I will not let thee go, except thou bless me.
32:24–26

1.62
And Jacob called the name of the place Peniel: for I have seen God face to face, and my life is preserved.
32:30

1.63
And his soul clave unto Dinah the daughter of Jacob, and he loved the damsel, and spake kindly unto the damsel.
34:3

1.64
Now Israel loved Joseph more than all his children, because he was the son of his old age: and he made him a coat of many colours.
37:3

1.65
And they said one to another, Behold, this dreamer cometh.
Come now therefore, and let us slay him, and cast him into some pit, and we will say, Some evil beast hath devoured him: and we shall see what will become of his dreams.
37:19–20

1.66
And all his sons and all his daughters rose up to comfort him; but he refused to be comforted; and he said, For I will go down into the grave unto my son mourning. Thus his father wept for him.
37:35

1.67
And Judah said unto Onan, Go in unto thy brother's wife, and marry her, and raise up seed to thy brother.
And Onan knew that the seed should not be his; and it came to pass, when he went in unto his brother's wife, that he spilled it on the ground, lest that he should give seed to his brother.
[*Hence onanism – coitus interruptus or masturbation*]
38:8–9

1.68
And she caught him by his garment, saying, Lie with me: and he left his garment in her hand, and fled, and got him out.
39:12

1.69
And the seven thin ears devoured the seven rank and full ears. And Pharaoh awoke, and, behold, it was a dream.
41:7

1.70
And Joseph knew his brethren, but they knew not him.
And Joseph remembered the dreams which he dreamed of them, and said unto them, Ye are spies; to see the nakedness of the land ye are come.
42:8–9

1.71
And he said, My son shall not go down with you; for his brother is dead, and he is left alone: if mischief befall him by the way in which ye go, then shall ye bring down my gray hairs with sorrow to the grave.
42:38

1.72
And the famine was sore in the land.
43:1

1.73
And take your father and your households, and come unto me: and I will give you the good of the land of Egypt, and ye shall eat the fat of the land.
45:18

1.74
So he sent his brethren away, and they departed: and he said unto them, See that ye fall not out by the way.
45:24

1.75
And Jacob said unto Pharaoh, The days of the years of my pilgrimage are an hundred and thirty years: few and evil have the days of the years of my life been, and have not attained unto the days of the years of the life of my fathers in the days of their pilgrimage.
47:9

1.76
The sceptre shall not depart from Judah, nor a lawgiver from between his feet, until Shiloh come; and unto him shall the gathering of the people be.
49:10

1.77
His eyes shall be red with wine, and his teeth white with milk.

49:12

1.78
Issachar is a strong ass couching down between two burdens:
And he saw that rest was good, and the land that it was pleasant; and bowed his shoulder to bear, and became a servant unto tribute.

49:14–15

1.79
Dan shall be a serpent by the way, an adder in the path, that biteth the horse heels, so that his rider shall fall backward.
I have waited for thy salvation, O Lord.

49:17–18

1.80
The blessings of thy father have prevailed above the blessings of my progenitors unto the utmost bound of the everlasting hills.

49:26

1.81
Benjamin shall ravin as a wolf: in the morning he shall devour the prey, and at night he shall divide the spoil.

49:27

2 Exodus

2.1
Now there arose up a new king over Egypt, which knew not Joseph.

1:8

2.2
And when she could not longer hide him, she took for him an ark of bulrushes, and daubed it with slime and with pitch, and put the child therein; and she laid it in the flags by the river's brink.

2:3

2.3
And he said, Who made thee a prince and a judge over us? intendest thou to kill me, as thou killedst the Egyptian? And Moses feared, and said, Surely this thing is known.

2:14

2.4
He called his name Gershom: for he said, I have been a stranger in a strange land.

2:22

2.5
And the angel of the Lord appeared unto him in a flame of fire out of the midst of a bush: and he looked, and, behold, the bush burned with fire, and the bush was not consumed.

3:2

2.6
And he said, Draw not nigh hither: put off thy shoes from off thy feet, for the place whereon thou standest is holy ground.
Moreover he said, I am the God of thy father, the God of Abraham, the God of Isaac, and the God of Jacob. And Moses hid his face; for he was afraid to look upon God.

3:5–6

2.7
And I am come down to deliver them out of the hand of the Egyptians, and to bring them up out of that land unto a good land and a large, unto a land flowing with milk and honey; unto the place of the Canaanites, and the Hittites, and the Amorites, and the Perizzites, and the Hivites, and the Jebusites.

3:8

2.8
And God said unto Moses, I AM THAT I AM: and he said, Thus shalt thou say unto the children of Israel, I AM hath sent me unto you.

3:14

2.9
And Moses said unto the Lord, O my Lord, I am not eloquent, neither heretofore, nor since thou hast spoken unto thy servant: but I am slow of speech, and of a slow tongue.

4:10

2.10
And Pharaoh said, Who is the Lord, that I should obey his voice to let Israel go? I know not the Lord, neither will I let Israel go.

5:2

2.11
And Pharaoh commanded the same day the taskmasters of the people, and their officers, saying,
Ye shall no more give the people straw to make brick, as heretofore: let them go and gather straw for themselves.
[*Hence the phrase 'making bricks without straw' to mean an impossible task*]

5:6–7

2.12
And Moses spake so unto the children of Israel: but they hearkened not unto Moses for anguish of spirit, and for cruel bondage.

6:9

2.13
And I will harden Pharaoh's heart, and multiply my signs and my wonders in the land of Egypt.

7:3

2.14
For they cast down every man his rod, and they became serpents: but Aaron's rod swallowed up their rods.

7:12

2.15
Then the magicians said unto Pharaoh, This is

the finger of God: and Pharaoh's heart was hardened, and he hearkened not unto them; as the Lord had said.

8:19

2.16
And Pharaoh's servants said unto him, How long shall this man be a snare unto us? let the men go, that they may serve the Lord their God: knowest thou not yet that Egypt is destroyed?

10:7

2.17
And the Lord said unto Moses, Stretch out thine hand toward heaven, that there may be darkness over the land of Egypt, even darkness which may be felt.

10:21

2.18
Your lamb shall be without blemish, a male of the first year: ye shall take it out from the sheep, or from the goats.

12:5

2.19
And thus shall ye eat it; with your loins girded, your shoes on your feet, and your staff in your hand; and ye shall eat it in haste: it is the Lord's passover.
For I will pass through the land of Egypt this night, and will smite all the firstborn in the land of Egypt, both man and beast; and against all the gods of Egypt I will execute judgment: I am the Lord.

12:11–12

2.20
And Pharaoh rose up in the night, he, and all his servants, and all the Egyptians; and there was a great cry in Egypt; for there was not a house where there was not one dead.

12:30

2.21
And the Egyptians were urgent upon the people, that they might send them out of the land in haste; for they said, We be all dead men.

12:33

2.22
And the Lord went before them by day in a pillar of a cloud, to lead them the way; and by night in a pillar of fire, to give them light; to go by day and night.

13:21

2.23
And the children of Israel went into the midst of the sea upon the dry ground: and the waters were a wall unto them on their right hand, and on their left.

14:22

2.24
Then sang Moses and the children of Israel this song unto the Lord, and spake, saying, I will sing unto the Lord, for he hath triumphed gloriously: the horse and his rider hath he thrown into the sea.

15:1

2.25
The Lord is a man of war: the Lord is his name.

15:3

2.26
And the children of Israel said unto them, Would to God we had died by the hand of the Lord in the land of Egypt, when we sat by the flesh pots, and when we did eat bread to the full; for ye have brought us forth into this wilderness, to kill this whole assembly with hunger.

16:3

2.27
And when the children of Israel saw it, they said one to another, It is manna: for they wist not what it was. And Moses said unto them, This is the bread which the Lord hath given you to eat.

16:15

2.28
And mount Sinai was altogether on a smoke, because the Lord descended upon it in fire: and the smoke thereof ascended as the smoke of a furnace, and the whole mount quaked greatly.

19:18

2.29
I am the Lord thy God, which have brought thee out of the land of Egypt, out of the house of bondage.
Thou shalt have no other gods before me.
Thou shalt not make unto thee any graven image, or any likeness of any thing that is in heaven above, or that is in the earth beneath, or that is in the water under the earth:
Thou shalt not bow down thyself to them, nor serve them: for I the Lord thy God am a jealous God, visiting the iniquity of the fathers upon the children unto the third and fourth generation of them that hate me;
And shewing mercy unto thousands of them that love me, and keep my commandments.
Thou shalt not take the name of the Lord thy God in vain; for the Lord will not hold him guiltless that taketh his name in vain.
Remember the sabbath day, to keep it holy.
Six days shalt thou labour, and do all thy work:
But the seventh day is the sabbath of the Lord thy God: in it thou shalt not do any work, thou, nor thy son, nor thy daughter, thy manservant, nor thy maidservant, nor thy cattle, nor thy stranger that is within thy gates:

For in six days the Lord made heaven and earth, the sea, and all that in them is, and rested the seventh day: wherefore the Lord blessed the sabbath day, and hallowed it.
Honour thy father and thy mother: that thy days may be long upon the land which the Lord thy God giveth thee.
Thou shalt not kill.
Thou shalt not commit adultery.
Thou shalt not steal.
Thou shalt not bear false witness against thy neighbour.
Thou shalt not covet thy neighbour's house, thou shalt not covet thy neighbour's wife, nor his manservant, nor his maidservant, nor his ox, nor his ass, nor any thing that is thy neighbour's.

20:2–17

2.30

And the people stood afar off, and Moses drew near unto the thick darkness where God was.

20:21

2.31

And if any mischief follow, then thou shalt give life for life,
Eye for eye, tooth for tooth, hand for hand, foot for foot,
Burning for burning, wound for wound, stripe for stripe.

21:23–25

2.32

Thou shalt not suffer a witch to live.

22:18

2.33

The first of the firstfruits of thy land thou shalt bring into the house of the Lord thy God. Thou shalt not seethe a kid in his mother's milk.

23:19

2.34

And the Lord said unto Moses, Come up to me into the mount, and be there: and I will give thee tables of stone, and a law, and commandments which I have written; that thou mayest teach them.

24:12

2.35

And thou shalt put in the breastplate of judgment the Urim and the Thummim; and they shall be upon Aaron's heart, when he goeth in before the Lord: and Aaron shall bear the judgment of the children of Israel upon his heart before the Lord continually.

28:30

2.36

To devise cunning works, to work in gold, and in silver, and in brass.

31:4

2.37

And he received them at their hand, and fashioned it with a graving tool, after he had made it a molten calf: and they said, These be thy gods, O Israel, which brought thee up out of the land of Egypt.

32:4

2.38

And they rose up early on the morrow, and offered burnt offerings, and brought peace offerings; and the people sat down to eat and to drink, and rose up to play.

32:6

2.39

And the Lord said unto Moses, I have seen this people, and, behold, it is a stiffnecked people.

32:9

2.40

And he said, It is not the voice of them that shout for mastery, neither is it the voice of them that cry for being overcome: but the noise of them that sing do I hear.

32:18

2.41

Then Moses stood in the gate of the camp, and said, Who is on the Lord's side? let him come unto me. And all the sons of Levi gathered themselves together unto him.

32:26

2.42

Yet now, if thou wilt forgive their sin –; and if not, blot me, I pray thee, out of thy book which thou hast written.

32:32

2.43

And he said, Thou canst not see my face: for there shall no man see me, and live.

33:20

2.44

And it shall come to pass, while my glory passeth by, that I will put thee in a clift of the rock, and will cover thee with my hand while I pass by.

33:22

3 Leviticus

3.1

Whatsoever parteth the hoof, and is cloven-footed, and cheweth the cud, among the beasts, that shall ye eat.

11:3

3.2

But the goat, on which the lot fell to be the scapegoat, shall be presented alive before the Lord, to make an atonement with him, and to let him go for a scapegoat into the wilderness.

16:10

4 Numbers

4.1
He shall separate himself from wine and strong drink, and shall drink no vinegar of wine, or vinegar of strong drink, neither shall he drink any liquor of grapes, nor eat moist grapes, or dried.

6:3

4.2
All the days of the vow of his separation there shall no razor come upon his head: until the days be fulfilled, in the which he separateth himself unto the Lord, he shall be holy, and shall let the locks of the hair of his head grow.

6:5

4.3
The Lord bless thee, and keep thee:
The Lord make his face shine upon thee, and be gracious unto thee:
The Lord lift up his countenance upon thee, and give thee peace.

6:24–26

4.4
I am not able to bear all this people alone, because it is too heavy for me.
And if thou deal thus with me, kill me, I pray thee, out of hand, if I have found favour in thy sight; and let me not see my wretchedness.

11:14–15

4.5
And Moses said unto him, Enviest thou for my sake? would God that all the Lord's people were prophets, and that the Lord would put his spirit upon them!

11:29

4.6
Now the man Moses was very meek, above all the men which were upon the face of the earth.

12:3

4.7
And they brought up an evil report of the land which they had searched unto the children of Israel, saying, The land, through which we have gone to search it, is a land that eateth up the inhabitants thereof; and all the people that we saw in it are men of a great stature.
And there we saw the giants, the sons of Anak, which come of the giants: and we were in our own sight as grasshoppers, and so we were in their sight.

13:32–33

4.8
Is it a small thing that thou hast brought us up out of a land that floweth with milk and honey, to kill us in the wilderness, except thou make thyself altogether a prince over us?

16:13

4.9
They, and all that appertained to them, went down alive into the pit, and the earth closed upon them: and they perished from among the congregation.

16:33

4.10
And it came to pass, that on the morrow Moses went into the tabernacle of witness; and, behold, the rod of Aaron for the house of Levi was budded, and brought forth buds, and bloomed blossoms, and yielded almonds.

17:8

4.11
And Moses lifted up his hand, and with his rod he smote the rock twice: and the water came out abundantly, and the congregation drank, and their beasts also.

20:11

4.12
Come now therefore, I pray thee, curse me this people; for they are too mighty for me: peradventure I shall prevail, that we may smite them, and that I may drive them out of the land: for I wot that he whom thou blessest is blessed, and he whom thou cursest is cursed.

22:6

4.13
And the Lord opened the mouth of the ass, and she said unto Balaam, What have I done unto thee, that thou hast smitten me these three times?

22:28

4.14
Who can count the dust of Jacob, and the number of the fourth part of Israel? Let me die the death of the righteous, and let my last end be like his!
And Balak said unto Balaam, What hast thou done unto me? I took thee to curse mine enemies, and, behold, thou hast blessed them together.

23:10–11

4.15
God is not a man, that he should lie, neither the son of man, that he should repent: hath he said, and shall he not do it? or hath he spoken, and shall he not make it good?

23:19

4.16
How goodly are thy tents, O Jacob, and thy tabernacles, O Israel!

24:5

4.17
But if ye will not do so, behold, ye have sinned against the Lord: and be sure your sin will find you out.

32:23

5 Deuteronomy

5.1
I call heaven and earth to witness against you this day, that ye shall soon utterly perish from off the land whereunto ye go over Jordan to possess it; ye shall not prolong your days upon it, but shall utterly be destroyed.
4:26

5.2
For the Lord thy God bringeth thee into a good land, a land of brooks of water, of fountains and depths that spring out of valleys and hills;
A land of wheat, and barley, and vines, and fig trees, and pomegranates; a land of oil olive, and honey;
A land wherein thou shalt eat bread without scarceness, thou shalt not lack any thing in it; a land whose stones are iron, and out of whose hills thou mayest dig brass.
When thou hast eaten and art full, then thou shalt bless the Lord thy God for the good land which he hath given thee.
8:7–10

5.3
My power and the might of mine hand hath gotten me this wealth.
8:17

5.4
He doth execute the judgment of the fatherless and widow, and loveth the stranger, in giving him food and raiment.
10:18

5.5
Take heed to yourselves, that your heart be not deceived, and ye turn aside, and serve other gods, and worship them.
11:16

5.6
Therefore shall ye lay up these my words in your heart and in your soul, and bind them for a sign upon your hand, that they may be as frontlets between your eyes.
11:18

5.7
Thou shalt not hearken unto the words of that prophet, or that dreamer of dreams.
13:3

5.8
If thy brother, the son of thy mother, or thy son, or thy daughter, or the wife of thy bosom, or thy friend, which is as thine own soul, entice thee secretly, saying, Let us go and serve other gods, which thou hast not known, thou, nor thy fathers.
13:6

5.9
For thou art an holy people unto the Lord thy God, and the Lord hath chosen thee to be a peculiar people unto himself, above all the nations that are upon the earth.
14:2

5.10
Thou shalt not muzzle the ox when he treadeth out the corn.
25:4

5.11
Cursed be he that removeth his neighbour's landmark. And all the people shall say, Amen.
Cursed be he that maketh the blind to wander out of the way. And all the people shall say, Amen.
Cursed be he that perverteth the judgment of the stranger, fatherless, and widow. And all the people shall say, Amen.
27:17–19

5.12
The secret things belong unto the Lord our God: but those things which are revealed belong unto us and to our children for ever, that we may do all the words of this law.
29:29

5.13
I call heaven and earth to record this day against you, that I have set before you life and death, blessing and cursing: therefore choose life, that both thou and thy seed may live.
30:19

5.14
Be strong and of a good courage, fear not, nor be afraid of them: for the Lord thy God, he it is that doth go with thee; he will not fail thee, nor forsake thee.
31:6

5.15
My doctrine shall drop as the rain, my speech shall distil as the dew, as the small rain upon the tender herb, and as the showers upon the grass.
32:2

5.16
He found him in a desert land, and in the waste howling wilderness; he led him about, he instructed him, he kept him as the apple of his eye.
32:10

5.17
But Jeshurun waxed fat, and kicked: thou art waxen fat, thou art grown thick, thou art covered with fatness; then he forsook God which made him, and lightly esteemed the Rock of his salvation.
32:15

5.18
O that they were wise, that they understood this, that they would consider their latter end!
32:29

5.19
To me belongeth vengeance, and recompence;

their foot shall slide in due time: for the day of their calamity is at hand, and the things that shall come upon them make haste.

32:35

5.20
Thy shoes shall be iron and brass; and as thy days, so shall thy strength be.

33:25

5.21
The eternal God is thy refuge, and underneath are the everlasting arms: and he shall thrust out the enemy from before thee; and shall say, Destroy them.

33:27

5.22
And he buried him in a valley in the land of Moab, over against Beth-peor: but no man knoweth of his sepulchre unto this day.

34:6

5.23
And there arose not a prophet since in Israel like unto Moses, whom the Lord knew face to face.

34:10

6 Joshua

6.1
There shall not any man be able to stand before thee all the days of thy life: as I was with Moses, so I will be with thee: I will not fail thee, nor forsake thee.

1:5

6.2
Whosoever he be that doth rebel against thy commandment, and will not hearken unto thy words in all that thou commandest him, he shall be put to death: only be strong and of a good courage.

1:18

6.3
And the priests that bare the ark of the covenant of the Lord stood firm on dry ground in the midst of Jordan, and all the Israelites passed over on dry ground, until all the people were passed clean over Jordan.

3:17

6.4
So the people shouted when the priests blew with the trumpets: and it came to pass, when the people heard the sound of the trumpet, and the people shouted with a great shout, that the wall fell down flat, so that the people went up into the city, every man straight before him, and they took the city.

6:20

6.5
And the princes said unto them, Let them live; but let them be hewers of wood and drawers of water unto all the congregation; as the princes had promised them.

9:21

6.6
Who answered, Give me a blessing; for thou hast given me a south land; give me also springs of water. And he gave her the upper springs, and the nether springs.

15:19

6.7
And, behold, this day I am going the way of all the earth: and ye know in all your hearts and in all your souls, that not one thing hath failed of all the good things which the Lord your God spake concerning you; all are come to pass unto you, and not one thing hath failed thereof.

23:14

7 Judges

7.1
And when he shewed them the entrance into the city, they smote the city with the edge of the sword; but they let go the man and all his family.

1:25

7.2
And the anger of the Lord was hot against Israel, and he delivered them into the hands of spoilers that spoiled them, and he sold them into the hands of their enemies round about, so that they could not any longer stand before their enemies.

2:14

7.3
The inhabitants of the villages ceased, they ceased in Israel, until that I Deborah arose, that I arose a mother in Israel.

5:7

7.4
Why abodest thou among the sheepfolds, to hear the bleatings of the flocks? For the divisions of Reuben there were great searchings of heart.

5:16

7.5
They fought from heaven; the stars in their courses fought against Sisera.

5:20

7.6
Blessed above women shall Jael the wife of Heber the Kenite be, blessed shall she be above women in the tent.
He asked water, and she gave him milk; she brought forth butter in a lordly dish.
She put her hand to the nail, and her right hand to the workmen's hammer; and with the hammer she smote Sisera, she smote off his

head, when she had pierced and stricken through his temples.
At her feet he bowed, he fell, he lay down: at her feet he bowed, he fell: where he bowed, there he fell down dead.
The mother of Sisera looked out at a window, and cried through the lattice, Why is his chariot so long in coming? why tarry the wheels of his chariots?

5:24–28

7.7
Have they not sped? have they not divided the prey; to every man a damsel or two; to Sisera a prey of divers colours, a prey of divers colours of needlework, of divers colours of needlework on both sides, meet for the necks of them that take the spoil?

5:30

7.8
And the angel of the Lord appeared unto him, and said unto him, The Lord is with thee, thou mighty man of valour.

6:12

7.9
When I blow with a trumpet, I and all that are with me, then blow ye the trumpets also on every side of all the camp, and say, The sword of the Lord, and of Gideon.

7:18

7.10
And Gideon came to Jordan, and passed over, he, and the three hundred men that were with him, faint, yet pursuing them.
[*Often quoted in the form* '*faint but pursuing*']

8:4

7.11
Then said they unto him, Say now Shibboleth: and he said Sibboleth: for he could not frame to pronounce it right. Then they took him, and slew him at the passages of Jordan: and there fell at that time of the Ephraimites forty and two thousand.

12:6

7.12
And he said unto them, Out of the eater came forth meat, and out of the strong came forth sweetness. And they could not in three days expound the riddle.

14:14

7.13
And the men of the city said unto him on the seventh day before the sun went down, What is sweeter than honey? and what is stronger than a lion? And he said unto them, If ye had not plowed with my heifer, ye had not found out my riddle.

14:18

7.14
And he smote them hip and thigh with a great slaughter.

15:8

7.15
And Samson said, With the jawbone of an ass, heaps upon heaps, with the jaw of an ass have I slain a thousand men.

15:16

7.16
And she said, The Philistines be upon thee, Samson. And he awoke out of his sleep, and said, I will go out as at other times before, and shake myself. And he wist not that the Lord was departed from him.

16:20

7.17
In those days there was no king in Israel, but every man did that which was right in his own eyes.

17:6

7.18
And all the people arose as one man, saying, We will not any of us go to his tent, neither will we any of us turn into his house.

20:8

8 Ruth

8.1
And Naomi said unto her two daughters in law, Go, return each to her mother's house: the Lord deal kindly with you, as ye have dealt with the dead, and with me.

1:8

8.2
And Ruth said, Intreat me not to leave thee, or to return from following after thee: for whither thou goest, I will go; and where thou lodgest, I will lodge: thy people shall be my people, and thy God my God:
Where thou diest, will I die, and there will I be buried: the Lord do so to me, and more also, if ought but death part thee and me.

1:16–17

8.3
And he shall be unto thee a restorer of thy life, and a nourisher of thine old age: for thy daughter in law, which loveth thee, which is better to thee than seven sons, hath born him.

4:15

9 I Samuel

9.1
Now the sons of Eli were sons of Belial; they knew not the Lord.

2:12

9.2
But Samuel ministered before the Lord, being a child, girded with a linen ephod.
2:18

9.3
And the man of thine, whom I shall not cut off from mine altar, shall be to consume thine eyes, and to grieve thine heart: and all the increase of thine house shall die in the flower of their age.
2:33

9.4
That the Lord called Samuel: and he answered, Here am I.
And he ran unto Eli, and said, Here am I; for thou calledst me. And he said, I called not; lie down again. And he went and lay down.
3:4–5

9.5
Therefore Eli said unto Samuel, Go, lie down: and it shall be, if he call thee, that thou shalt say, Speak, Lord; for thy servant heareth. So Samuel went and lay down in his place.
3:9

9.6
And the Lord said to Samuel, Behold, I will do a thing in Israel, at which both the ears of every one that heareth it shall tingle.
3:11

9.7
Be strong, and quit yourselves like men, O ye Philistines, that ye be not servants unto the Hebrews, as they have been to you: quit yourselves like men, and fight.
4:9

9.8
Now Eli was ninety and eight years old; and his eyes were dim, that he could not see.
4:15

9.9
And it came to pass, when he made mention of the ark of God, that he fell from off the seat backward by the side of the gate, and his neck brake, and he died: for he was an old man, and heavy.
4:18

9.10
And she named the child I-chabod, saying, The glory is departed from Israel: because the ark of God was taken, and because of her father in law and her husband.
4:21

9.11
And when they arose early on the morrow morning, behold, Dagon was fallen upon his face to the ground before the ark of the Lord; and the head of Dagon and both the palms of his hands were cut off upon the threshold; only the stump of Dagon was left to him.
5:4

9.12
And it came to pass, when all that knew him beforetime saw that, behold, he prophesied among the prophets, then the people said one to another, What is this that is come unto the son of Kish? Is Saul also among the prophets?
10:11

9.13
But now thy kingdom shall not continue: the Lord hath sought him a man after his own heart, and the Lord hath commanded him to be captain over his people, because thou hast not kept that which the Lord commanded thee.
13:14

9.14
And the people said unto Saul, Shall Jonathan die, who hath wrought this great salvation in Israel? God forbid: as the Lord liveth, there shall not one hair of his head fall to the ground; for he hath wrought with God this day. So the people rescued Jonathan, that he died not.
14:45

9.15
And Samuel said, Hath the Lord as great delight in burnt offerings and sacrifices, as in obeying the voice of the Lord? Behold, to obey is better than sacrifice, and to hearken than the fat of rams.
For rebellion is as the sin of witchcraft, and stubbornness is as iniquity and idolatry. Because thou hast rejected the word of the Lord, he hath also rejected thee from being king.
15:22–23

9.16
Then said Samuel, Bring ye hither to me Agag the king of the Amalekites. And Agag came unto him delicately. And Agag said, Surely the bitterness of death is past.
And Samuel said, As thy sword hath made women childless, so shall thy mother be childless among women. And Samuel hewed Agag in pieces before the Lord in Gilgal.
15:32–33

9.17
But the Lord said unto Samuel, Look not on his countenance, or on the height of his stature; because I have refused him: for the Lord seeth not as man seeth; for man looketh on the outward appearance, but the Lord looketh on the heart.
16:7

9.18
And he sent, and brought him in. Now he was ruddy, and withal of a beautiful countenance, and goodly to look to. And the Lord said, Arise, anoint him: for this is he.
16:12

9.19
And Eliab his eldest brother heard when he spake unto the men; and Eliab's anger was kindled against David, and he said, Why camest thou down hither? and with whom hast thou left those few sheep in the wilderness? I know thy pride, and the naughtiness of thine heart; for thou art come down that thou mightest see the battle.
And David said, What have I now done? Is there not a cause?
17:28–29

9.20
And he took his staff in his hand, and chose him five smooth stones out of the brook, and put them in a shepherd's bag which he had, even in a scrip; and his sling was in his hand: and he drew near to the Philistine.
17:40

9.21
Am I a dog, that thou comest to me with staves? And the Philistine cursed David by his gods.
17:43

9.22
And the women answered one another as they played, and said, Saul hath slain his thousands, and David his ten thousands.
18:7

9.23
Then said Saul, I have sinned: return, my son David: for I will no more do thee harm, because my soul was precious in thine eyes this day: behold, I have played the fool, and have erred exceedingly.
26:21

10 II Samuel

10.1
The beauty of Israel is slain upon thy high places: how are the mighty fallen!
Tell it not in Gath, publish it not in the streets of Askelon; lest the daughters of the Philistines rejoice, lest the daughters of the uncircumcised triumph.
1:19–20

10.2
Saul and Jonathan were lovely and pleasant in their lives, and in their death they were not divided: they were swifter than eagles, they were stronger than lions.
Ye daughters of Israel, weep over Saul, who clothed you in scarlet, with other delights, who put on ornaments of gold upon your apparel.
1:23–24

10.3
I am distressed for thee, my brother Jonathan: very pleasant hast thou been unto me: thy love to me was wonderful, passing the love of women.
How are the mighty fallen, and the weapons of war perished!
1:26–27

10.4
And David danced before the Lord with all his might; and David was girded with a linen ephod.
6:14

10.5
And he wrote in the letter, saying, Set ye Uriah in the forefront of the hottest battle, and retire ye from him, that he may be smitten, and die.
11:15

10.6
But the poor man had nothing, save one little ewe lamb, which he had bought and nourished up: and it grew up together with him, and with his children; it did eat of his own meat, and drank of his own cup, and lay in his bosom, and was unto him as a daughter.
12:3

10.7
And Nathan said to David, Thou art the man.
12:7

10.8
For we must needs die, and are as water spilt on the ground, which cannot be gathered up again; neither doth God respect any person: yet doth he devise means, that his banished be not expelled from him.
14:14

10.9
And thus said Shimei when he cursed, Come out, come out, thou bloody man, and thou man of Belial.
16:7

10.10
And a certain man saw it, and told Joab, and said, Behold, I saw Absalom hanged in an oak.
18:10

10.11
And the king was much moved, and went up to the chamber over the gate, and wept: and as he went, thus he said, O my son Absalom, my son, my son Absalom! would God I had died for thee, O Absalom, my son, my son!
18:33

10.12
And he said, Be it far from me, O Lord, that I should do this: is not this the blood of the men that went in jeopardy of their lives?
23:17

11 I Kings

11.1
Now king David was old and stricken in years; and they covered him with clothes, but he gat no heat.
Wherefore his servants said unto him, Let there be sought for my lord the king a young virgin: and let her stand before the king, and let her cherish him, and let her lie in thy bosom, that my lord the king may get heat.
1:1–2

11.2
So David slept with his fathers, and was buried in the city of David.
2:10

11.3
He said moreover, I have somewhat to say unto thee. And she said, Say on.
2:14

11.4
Give therefore thy servant an understanding heart to judge thy people, that I may discern between good and bad: for who is able to judge this thy so great a people?
3:9

11.5
Then the king answered and said, Give her the living child, and in no wise slay it: she is the mother thereof.
And all Israel heard of the judgment which the king had judged; and they feared the king: for they saw that the wisdom of God was in him, to do judgment.
3:27–28

11.6
But will God indeed dwell on the earth? behold, the heaven and heaven of heavens cannot contain thee; how much less this house that I have builded?
8:27

11.7
Then will I cut off Israel out of the land which I have given them; and this house, which I have hallowed for my name, will I cast out of my sight; and Israel shall be a proverb and a byword among all people.
9:7

11.8
And when the queen of Sheba heard of the fame of Solomon concerning the name of the Lord, she came to prove him with hard questions.
10:1

11.9
Howbeit I believed not the words, until I came, and mine eyes had seen it: and, behold, the half was not told me: thy wisdom and prosperity exceedeth the fame which I heard.
10:7

11.10
For the king had at sea a navy of Tharshish with the navy of Hiram: once in three years came the navy of Tharshish, bringing gold, and silver, ivory, and apes, and peacocks.
10:22

11.11
But king Solomon loved many strange women, together with the daughter of Pharaoh, women of the Moabites, Ammonites, Edomites, Zidonians, and Hittites.
11:1

11.12
And the young men that were grown up with him spake unto him, saying, Thus shalt thou speak unto this people that spake unto thee, saying, Thy father made our yoke heavy, but make thou it lighter unto us; thus shalt thou say unto them, My little finger shall be thicker than my father's loins.
And now whereas my father did lade you with a heavy yoke, I will add to your yoke: my father hath chastised you with whips, but I will chastise you with scorpions.
12:10–11

11.13
The rest of all the acts of Asa, and all his might, and all that he did, and the cities which he built, are they not written in the book of the chronicles of the kings of Judah? Nevertheless in the time of his old age he was diseased in his feet.
15:23

11.14
Get thee hence, and turn thee eastward, and hide thyself by the brook Cherith, that is before Jordan.
And it shall be, that thou shalt drink of the brook; and I have commanded the ravens to feed thee there.
17:3–4

11.15
And she said, As the Lord thy God liveth, I have not a cake, but an handful of meal in a barrel, and a little oil in a cruse: and, behold, I am gathering two sticks, that I may go in and dress it for me and my son, that we may eat it, and die.
[*Hence 'widow's cruse' – an unfailing source of supply*]
17:12

11.16
And the woman said to Elijah, Now by this I know that thou art a man of God, and that the word of the Lord in thy mouth is truth.
17:24

11.17
And Elijah came unto all the people, and said, How long halt ye between two opinions? if the Lord be God, follow him: but if Baal, then

follow him. And the people answered him not a word.

18:21

11.18

And it came to pass at noon, that Elijah mocked them, and said, Cry aloud: for he is a god; either he is talking, or he is pursuing, or he is in a journey, or peradventure he sleepeth, and must be awaked.

18:27

11.19

And Elijah said unto Ahab, Get thee up, eat and drink; for there is a sound of abundance of rain.

18:41

11.20

And it came to pass at the seventh time, that he said, Behold, there ariseth a little cloud out of the sea, like a man's hand. And he said, Go up, say unto Ahab, Prepare thy chariot, and get thee down, that the rain stop thee not.

18:44

11.21

But he himself went a day's journey into the wilderness, and came and sat down under a juniper tree: and he requested for himself that he might die; and said, It is enough; now, O Lord, take away my life; for I am not better than my fathers.

19:4

11.22

And the angel of the Lord came again the second time, and touched him, and said, Arise and eat; because the journey is too great for thee.

19:7

11.23

And he said, Go forth, and stand upon the mount before the Lord. And, behold, the Lord passed by, and a great and strong wind rent the mountains, and brake in pieces the rocks before the Lord; but the Lord was not in the wind: and after the wind an earthquake; but the Lord was not in the earthquake:

And after the earthquake a fire; but the Lord was not in the fire: and after the fire a still small voice.

19:11–12

11.24

So he departed thence, and found Elisha the son of Shaphat, who was plowing with twelve yoke of oxen before him, and he with the twelfth: and Elijah passed by him, and cast his mantle upon him.

19:19

11.25

And the king of Israel answered and said, Tell him, Let not him that girdeth on his harness boast himself as he that putteth it off.

20:11

11.26

And Ahab spake unto Naboth, saying, Give me thy vineyard, that I may have it for a garden of herbs, because it is near unto my house: and I will give thee for it a better vineyard than it; or, if it seem good to thee, I will give thee the worth of it in money.

[*Hence 'Naboth's vineyard' used of a piece of property that one covets and which the owner refuses to sell*]

21:2

11.27

And thou shalt speak unto him, saying, Thus saith the Lord, Hast thou killed, and also taken possession? And thou shalt speak unto him, saying, Thus saith the Lord, In the place where dogs licked the blood of Naboth shall dogs lick thy blood, even thine.

And Ahab said to Elijah, Hast thou found me, O mine enemy? And he answered, I have found thee: because thou hast sold thyself to work evil in the sight of the Lord.

21:19–20

11.28

And of Jezebel also spake the Lord, saying, The dogs shall eat Jezebel by the wall of Jezreel.

21:23

11.29

And it came to pass, when Ahab heard those words, that he rent his clothes, and put sackcloth upon his flesh, and fasted, and lay in sackcloth, and went softly.

21:27

11.30

And he said, I saw all Israel scattered upon the hills, as sheep that have not a shepherd: and the Lord said, These have no master: let them return every man to his house in peace.

22:17

11.31

Now therefore, behold, the Lord hath put a lying spirit in the mouth of all these thy prophets, and the Lord hath spoken evil concerning thee.

22:23

11.32

And say, Thus saith the king, Put this fellow in the prison, and feed him with bread of affliction and with water of affliction, until I come in peace.

22:27

11.33

And a certain man drew a bow at a venture, and smote the king of Israel between the joints of the harness: wherefore he said unto the driver of his chariot, Turn thine hand, and carry me out of the host; for I am wounded.

22:34

12 II Kings

12.1
And it came to pass, as they still went on, and talked, that, behold, there appeared a chariot of fire, and horses of fire, and parted them both asunder; and Elijah went up by a whirlwind into heaven.
And Elisha saw it, and he cried, My father, my father, the chariot of Israel, and the horsemen thereof. And he saw him no more: and he took hold of his own clothes, and rent them in two pieces.

2:11–12

12.2
And when the sons of the prophets which were to view at Jericho saw him, they said, The spirit of Elijah doth rest on Elisha. And they came to meet him, and bowed themselves to the ground before him.

2:15

12.3
And he went up from thence unto Beth-el: and as he was going up by the way, there came forth little children out of the city, and mocked him, and said unto him, Go up, thou bald head; go up, thou bald head.

2:23

12.4
Run now, I pray thee, to meet her, and say unto her, Is it well with thee? is it well with thy husband? is it well with the child? And she answered, It is well.

4:26

12.5
And it was so, when Elisha the man of God had heard that the king of Israel had rent his clothes, that he sent to the king, saying, Wherefore hast thou rent thy clothes? let him come now to me, and he shall know that there is a prophet in Israel.

5:8

12.6
But Naaman was wroth, and went away, and said, Behold, I thought, He will surely come out to me, and stand, and call on the name of the Lord his God, and strike his hand over the place, and recover the leper.
Are not Abana and Pharpar, rivers of Damascus, better than all the waters of Israel? may I not wash in them, and be clean? So he turned and went away in a rage.
And his servants came near, and spake unto him, and said, My father, if the prophet had bid thee do some great thing, wouldest thou not have done it? how much rather then, when he saith to thee, Wash, and be clean?
Then went he down, and dipped himself seven times in Jordan, according to the saying of the man of God: and his flesh came again like unto the flesh of a little child, and he was clean.

5:11–14

12.7
But he went in, and stood before his master. And Elisha said unto him, Whence comest thou, Gehazi? And he said, Thy servant went no whither.

5:25

12.8
The leprosy therefore of Naaman shall cleave unto thee, and unto thy seed for ever. And he went out from his presence a leper as white as snow.

5:27

12.9
And Hazael said, But what, is thy servant a dog, that he should do this great thing? And Elisha answered, The Lord hath shewed me that thou shalt be king over Syria.

8:13

12.10
So there went one on horseback to meet him, and said, Thus saith the king, Is it peace? And Jehu said, What hast thou to do with peace? turn thee behind me. And the watchman told, saying, The messenger came to them, but he cometh not again.

9:18

12.11
And the watchman told, saying, He came even unto them, and cometh not again: and the driving is like the driving of Jehu the son of Nimshi; for he driveth furiously.

9:20

12.12
And when Jehu was come to Jezreel, Jezebel heard of it; and she painted her face, and tired her head, and looked out at a window.

9:30

12.13
And he lifted up his face to the window, and said, Who is on my side? who? And there looked out to him two or three eunuchs.

9:32

12.14
And they went to bury her: but they found no more of her than the skull, and the feet, and the palms of her hands.

9:35

12.15
Thus saith Hezekiah, This day is a day of trouble, and of rebuke, and blasphemy: for the children are come to the birth, and there is not strength to bring forth.

19:3

12.16
In those days was Hezekiah sick unto death. And the prophet Isaiah the son of Amoz came to him, and said unto him, Thus saith the

Lord, Set thine house in order; for thou shalt die, and not live.
Then he turned his face to the wall.

20:1–2

13 Ezra

13.1

The people could not discern the noise of the shout of joy from the noise of the weeping of the people: for the people shouted with a loud shout, and the noise was heard afar off.

3:13

13.2

Blessed be the Lord God of our fathers, which hath put such a thing as this in the king's heart, to beautify the house of the Lord which is in Jerusalem.

7:27

14 Nehemiah

14.1

They which builded on the wall, and they that bare burdens, with those that laded, every one with one of his hands wrought in the work, and with the other hand held a weapon.
For the builders, every one had his sword girded by his side, and so builded. And he that sounded the trumpet was by me.

4:17–18

14.2

And I said, Should such a man as I flee? and who is there, that, being as I am, would go into the temple to save his life? I will not go in.

6:11

15 Esther

15.1

If it please the king, let there go a royal commandment from him, and let it be written among the laws of the Persians and the Medes, that it be not altered, That Vashti come no more before king Ahasuerus; and let the king give her royal estate unto another that is better than she.

1:19

15.2

And the king loved Esther above all the women, and she obtained grace and favour in his sight more than all the virgins; so that he set the royal crown upon her head, and made her queen instead of Vashti.

2:17

15.3

Go, gather together all the Jews that are present in Shushan, and fast ye for me, and neither eat nor drink three days, night or day: I also and my maidens will fast likewise; and so will I go in unto the king, which is not according to the law: and if I perish, I perish.

4:16

15.4

So Haman came in. And the king said unto him, What shall be done unto the man whom the king delighteth to honour? Now Haman thought in his heart, To whom would the king delight to do honour more than to myself?

6:6

16 Job

16.1

And the Lord said unto Satan, Whence comest thou? Then Satan answered the Lord, and said, From going to and fro in the earth, and from walking up and down in it.
And the Lord said unto Satan, Hast thou considered my servant Job, that there is none like him in the earth, a perfect and an upright man, one that feareth God, and escheweth evil?
Then Satan answered the Lord, and said, Doth Job fear God for nought?

1:7–9

16.2

Naked came I out of my mother's womb, and naked shall I return thither: the Lord gave, and the Lord hath taken away; blessed be the name of the Lord.
In all this Job sinned not, nor charged God foolishly.

1:21–22

16.3

And Satan answered the Lord, and said, Skin for skin, yea, all that a man hath will he give for his life.
But put forth thine hand now, and touch his bone and his flesh, and he will curse thee to thy face.

2:4–5

16.4

Then said his wife unto him, Dost thou still retain thine integrity? curse God, and die.

2:9

16.5

After this opened Job his mouth, and cursed his day.

3:1

16.6

Let the day perish wherein I was born, and the night in which it was said, There is a man child conceived.

3:3

16.7
For now should I have lain still and been quiet, I should have slept: then had I been at rest.

3:13

16.8
There the wicked cease from troubling; and there the weary be at rest.

3:17

16.9
Wherefore is light given to him that is in misery, and life unto the bitter in soul;
Which long for death, but it cometh not; and dig for it more than for hid treasures.

3:20–21

16.10
I was not in safety, neither had I rest, neither was I quiet; yet trouble came.

3:26

16.11
Remember, I pray thee, who ever perished, being innocent? or where were the righteous cut off?

4:7

16.12
Fear came upon me, and trembling, which made all my bones to shake.
Then a spirit passed before my face; the hair of my flesh stood up.

4:14–15

16.13
Shall mortal man be more just than God? shall a man be more pure than his maker?

4:17

16.14
Yet man is born unto trouble, as the sparks fly upward.

5:7

16.15
He taketh the wise in their own craftiness: and the counsel of the froward is carried headlong.

5:13

16.16
How forcible are right words! but what doth your arguing reprove?

6:25

16.17
Is there not an appointed time to man upon earth? are not his days also like the days of an hireling?

7:1

16.18
So am I made to possess months of vanity, and wearisome nights are appointed to me.
When I lie down, I say, When shall I arise, and the night be gone? and I am full of tossings to and fro unto the dawning of the day.

7:3–4

16.19
My days are swifter than a weaver's shuttle, and are spent without hope.

7:6

16.20
The eye of him that hath seen me shall see me no more: thine eyes are upon me, and I am not.

7:8

16.21
He shall return no more to his house, neither shall his place know him any more.

7:10

16.22
Behold, God will not cast away a perfect man, neither will he help the evil doers:
Till he fill thy mouth with laughing, and thy lips with rejoicing.

8:20–21

16.23
My soul is weary of my life; I will leave my complaint upon myself; I will speak in the bitterness of my soul.

10:1

16.24
Wherefore then hast thou brought me forth out of the womb? Oh that I had given up the ghost, and no eye had seen me!

10:18

16.25
Are not my days few? cease then, and let me alone, that I may take comfort a little,
Before I go whence I shall not return, even to the land of darkness and the shadow of death;
A land of darkness, as darkness itself; and of the shadow of death, without any order, and where the light is as darkness.

10:20–22

16.26
Canst thou by searching find out God? canst thou find out the Almighty unto perfection?

11:7

16.27
No doubt but ye are the people, and wisdom shall die with you.

12:2

16.28
With the ancient is wisdom; and in length of days understanding.

12:12

16.29
They grope in the dark without light, and he maketh them to stagger like a drunken man.

12:25

16.30
Surely I would speak to the Almighty, and I desire to reason with God.
But ye are forgers of lies, ye are all physicians of no value.

O that ye would altogether hold your peace! and it should be your wisdom.

13:3–5

16.31
Man that is born of a woman is of few days, and full of trouble.

14:1

16.32
Then Job answered and said,
I have heard many such things: miserable comforters are ye all.
[*Hence the phrase 'Job's comforters'*]

16:1–2

16.33
I have said to corruption, Thou art my father: to the worm, Thou art my mother, and my sister.

17:14

16.34
His confidence shall be rooted out of his tabernacle, and it shall bring him to the king of terrors.

18:14

16.35
His roots shall be dried up beneath, and above shall his branch be cut off.
His remembrance shall perish from the earth, and he shall have no name in the street.
He shall be driven from light into darkness, and chased out of the world.

18:16–18

16.36
My bone cleaveth to my skin and to my flesh, and I am escaped with the skin of my teeth.

19:20

16.37
Oh that my words were now written! oh that they were printed in a book!

19:23

16.38
For I know that my redeemer liveth, and that he shall stand at the latter day upon the earth:
And though after my skin worms destroy this body, yet in my flesh shall I see God.

19:25–26

16.39
But ye should say, Why persecute we him, seeing the root of the matter is found in me?
Be ye afraid of the sword: for wrath bringeth the punishments of the sword, that ye may know there is a judgment.

19:28–29

16.40
He hath swallowed down riches, and he shall vomit them up again: God shall cast them out of his belly.

20:15

16.41
Thick clouds are a covering to him, that he seeth not; and he walketh in the circuit of heaven.

22:14

16.42
But where shall wisdom be found? and where is the place of understanding?

28:12

16.43
No mention shall be made of coral, or of pearls: for the price of wisdom is above rubies.

28:18

16.44
I was eyes to the blind, and feet was I to the lame.

29:15

16.45
But now they that are younger than I have me in derision, whose fathers I would have disdained to have set with the dogs of my flock.

30:1

16.46
For I know that thou wilt bring me to death, and to the house appointed for all living.

30:23

16.47
Oh that one would hear me! behold, my desire is, that the Almighty would answer me, and that mine adversary had written a book.

31:35

16.48
I said, Days should speak, and multitude of years should teach wisdom.
But there is a spirit in man: and the inspiration of the Almighty giveth them understanding.
Great men are not always wise: neither do the aged understand judgment.

32:7–9

16.49
For I am full of matter, the spirit within me constraineth me.

32:18

16.50
What man is like Job, who drinketh up scorning like water?

34:7

16.51
Therefore hearken unto me, ye men of understanding: far be it from God, that he should do wickedness; and from the Almighty, that he should commit iniquity.

34:10

16.52
Therefore doth Job open his mouth in vain; he multiplieth words without knowledge.

35:16

16.53
Suffer me a little, and I will shew thee that I have yet to speak on God's behalf.

I will fetch my knowledge from afar, and will ascribe righteousness to my Maker.
For truly my words shall not be false: he that is perfect in knowledge is with thee.

36:2–4

16.54
Then the Lord answered Job out of the whirlwind, and said,
Who is this that darkeneth counsel by words without knowledge?
Gird up now thy loins like a man; for I will demand of thee, and answer thou me.
Where wast thou when I laid the foundations of the earth? declare, if thou hast understanding.
Who hath laid the measures thereof, if thou knowest? or who hath stretched the line upon it?
Whereupon are the foundations thereof fastened? or who laid the corner stone thereof;
When the morning stars sang together, and all the sons of God shouted for joy?

38:1–7

16.55
Hath the rain a father? or who hath begotten the drops of dew?

38:28

16.56
Canst thou bind the sweet influences of Pleiades, or loose the bands of Orion?

38:31

16.57
Hast thou given the horse strength? hast thou clothed his neck with thunder?
Canst thou make him afraid as a grasshopper? the glory of his nostrils is terrible.
He paweth in the valley, and rejoiceth in his strength: he goeth on to meet the armed men.

39:19–21

16.58
He swalloweth the ground with fierceness and rage: neither believeth he that it is the sound of the trumpet.
He saith among the trumpets, Ha, ha; and he smelleth the battle afar off, the thunder of the captains, and the shouting.

39:24–25

16.59
Deck thyself now with majesty and excellency; and array thyself with glory and beauty.

40:10

16.60
Canst thou draw out leviathan with an hook? or his tongue with a cord which thou lettest down?

41:1

16.61
His heart is as firm as a stone; yea, as hard as a piece of the nether millstone.

41:24

16.62
I know that thou canst do every thing, and that no thought can be withholden from thee.
Who is he that hideth counsel without knowledge? therefore have I uttered that I understood not; things too wonderful for me, which I knew not.

42:2–3

16.63
I have heard of thee by the hearing of the ear: but now mine eye seeth thee.
Wherefore I abhor myself, and repent in dust and ashes.

42:5–6

16.64
So the Lord blessed the latter end of Job more than his beginning: for he had fourteen thousand sheep, and six thousand camels, and a thousand yoke of oxen, and a thousand she asses.

42:12

17 Psalms

17.1
Blessed is the man that hath not walked in the counsel of the ungodly, nor stood in the way of sinners, and hath not sat in the seat of the scornful.
But his delight is in the law of the Lord; and in his law will he exercise himself day and night.
And he shall be like a tree planted by the water-side, that will bring forth his fruit in due season.
His leaf also shall not wither; and look, whatsoever he doeth, it shall prosper.

1:1–4

17.2
Why do the heathen so furiously rage together, and why do the people imagine a vain thing?

2:1

17.3
He that dwelleth in heaven shall laugh them to scorn: the Lord shall have them in derision.

2:4

17.4
Thou shalt bruise them with a rod of iron; and break them in pieces like a potter's vessel.

2:9

17.5
Kiss the Son, lest he be angry, and so ye perish from the right way; if his wrath be kindled, (yea, but a little,) blessed are all they that put their trust in him.

2:12

17.6
Lord, how are they increased that trouble me! many are they that rise against me.

3:1

17.7
Salvation belongeth unto the Lord: and thy blessing is upon thy people.

3:8

17.8
Stand in awe, and sin not: commune with your own heart, and in your chamber, and be still.

4:4

17.9
There be many that say, Who will shew us any good?
Lord, lift thou up the light of thy countenance upon us.
Thou hast put gladness in my heart since the time that their corn, and wine, and oil, increased.
I will lay me down in peace, and take my rest: for it is thou, Lord, only, that makest me dwell in safety.

4:6–9

17.10
Thou shalt destroy them that speak leasing: the Lord will abhor both the bloodthirsty and deceitful man.

5:6

17.11
For there is no faithfulness in his mouth; their inward parts are very wickedness.
Their throat is an open sepulchre; they flatter with their tongue.

5:9–10

17.12
For in death no man remembereth thee: and who will give thee thanks in the pit?
I am weary of my groaning; every night wash I my bed and water my couch with my tears.
My beauty is gone for very trouble; and worn away because of all mine enemies.
Away from me, all ye that work vanity; for the Lord hath heard the voice of my weeping.

6:5–8

17.13
All mine enemies shall be confounded, and sore vexed: they shall be turned back, and put to shame suddenly.

6:10

17.14
Out of the mouth of very babes and sucklings hast thou ordained strength, because of thine enemies, that thou mightest still the enemy, and the avenger.
For I will consider thy heavens, even the works of thy fingers, the moon and the stars, which thou hast ordained.
What is man, that thou art mindful of him? and the son of man, that thou visitest him?
Thou madest him lower than the angels, to crown him with glory and worship.

8:2–5

17.15
O thou enemy, destructions are come to a perpetual end: even as the cities which thou hast destroyed; their memorial is perished with them.

9:6

17.16
For the poor shall not alway be forgotten: the patient abiding of the meek shall not perish for ever.
Up, Lord, and let not man have the upper hand: let the heathen be judged in thy sight.
Put them in fear, O Lord: that the heathen may know themselves to be but men.

9:18–20

17.17
He sitteth lurking in the thievish corners of the streets: and privily in his lurking dens doth he murder the innocent; his eyes are set against the poor.

10:8

17.18
In the Lord put I my trust: how say ye then to my soul, that she should flee as a bird unto the hill?
For lo, the ungodly bend their bow, and make ready their arrows within the quiver that they may privily shoot at them which are true of heart.

11:1–2

17.19
Upon the ungodly he shall rain snares, fire and brimstone, storm and tempest: this shall be their portion to drink.

11:7

17.20
They talk of vanity every one with his neighbour: they do but flatter with their lips, and dissemble in their double heart.

12:2

17.21
The fool hath said in his heart, There is no God.
They are corrupt, and become abominable in their doings; there is none that doeth good, no not one.
The Lord looked down from heaven upon the children of men, to see if there were any that would understand, and seek after God.
But they are all gone out of the way, they are altogether become abominable: there is none that doeth good, no not one.

14:1–4

17.22
Their mouth is full of cursing and bitterness; their feet are swift to shed blood.
14:6

17.23
Lord, who shall dwell in thy tabernacle? or who shall rest upon thy holy hill?
Even he, that leadeth an uncorrupt life, and doeth the thing which is right, and speaketh the truth from his heart.
15:1–2

17.24
He that setteth not by himself, but is lowly in his own eyes, and maketh much of them that fear the Lord.
He that sweareth unto his neighbour, and disappointeth him not, though it were to his own hindrance.
15:4–5

17.25
The lot is fallen unto me in a fair ground; yea, I have a goodly heritage.
[*This is also familiar in the wording of the Authorised Version*]
16:7

17.26
The lines are fallen unto me in pleasant places; yea, I have a goodly heritage.
Authorised Version 16:6

17.27
For why? thou shalt not leave my soul in hell; neither shalt thou suffer thy Holy One to see corruption.
Thou shalt shew me the path of life; in thy presence is the fulness of joy; and at thy right hand there is pleasure for evermore.
16:11–12

17.28
Keep me as the apple of an eye; hide me under the shadow of thy wings.
17:8

17.29
I will love thee, O Lord, my strength; the Lord is my stony rock, and my defence; my Saviour, my God, and my might, in whom I will trust, my buckler, the horn also of my salvation, and my refuge.
18:1

17.30
The pains of hell came about me: the snares of death overtook me.
18:4

17.31
There went a smoke out in his presence, and a consuming fire out of his mouth, so that coals were kindled at it.
He bowed the heavens also, and came down: and it was dark under his feet.
He rode upon the cherubims, and did fly: he came flying upon the wings of the wind.
He made darkness his secret place; his pavilion round about him with dark water, and thick clouds to cover him.
18:8–11

17.32
Thou also shalt light my candle: the Lord my God shall make my darkness to be light.
For in thee I shall discomfit an host of men; and with the help of my God I shall leap over the wall.
18:28–29

17.33
He teacheth mine hands to fight; and mine arms shall break even a bow of steel.
18:34

17.34
A people whom I have not known shall serve me.
18:44

17.35
The heavens declare the glory of God; and the firmament sheweth his handywork.
One day telleth another; and one night certifieth another.
There is neither speech nor language, but their voices are heard among them.
Their sound is gone out into all lands, and their words into the ends of the world.
In them hath he set a tabernacle for the sun, which cometh forth as a bridegroom out of his chamber, and rejoiceth as a giant to run his course.
It goeth forth from the uttermost part of the heaven, and runneth about unto the end of it again: and there is nothing hid from the heat thereof.
The law of the Lord is an undefiled law, converting the soul: the testimony of the Lord is sure, and giveth wisdom unto the simple.
19:1–7

17.36
The fear of the Lord is clean, and endureth for ever: the judgments of the Lord are true, and righteous altogether.
More to be desired are they than gold, yea, than much fine gold: sweeter also than honey, and the honey-comb.
Moreover, by them is thy servant taught: and in keeping of them there is great reward.
Who can tell how oft he offendeth? O cleanse thou me from my secret faults.
19:9–12

17.37
Let the words of my mouth, and the meditation of my heart, be alway acceptable in thy sight,
O Lord, my strength, and my redeemer.
19:14–15

17.38
The Lord hear thee in the day of trouble; the Name of the God of Jacob defend thee;
Send thee help from the sanctuary, and strengthen thee out of Sion.
20:1–2

17.39
Some put their trust in chariots, and some in horses: but we will remember the Name of the Lord our God.
They are brought down, and fallen: but we are risen, and stand upright.
20:7–8

17.40
The King shall rejoice in thy strength, O Lord; exceeding glad shall he be of thy salvation.
Thou hast given him his heart's desire, and hast not denied him the request of his lips.
For thou shalt prevent him with the blessings of goodness: and shalt set a crown of pure gold upon his head.
He asked life of thee, and thou gavest him a long life, even for ever and ever.
21:1–4

17.41
But as for me, I am a worm, and no man: a very scorn of men, and the out-cast of the people.
All they that see me laugh me to scorn; they shoot out their lips, and shake their heads, saying,
He trusted in God, that he would deliver him: let him deliver him, if he will have him.
22:6–8

17.42
Many oxen are come about me: fat bulls of Basan close me in on every side.
22:12

17.43
I am poured out like water, and all my bones are out of joint: my heart also in the midst of my body is even like melting wax.
22:14

17.44
Deliver my soul from the sword: my darling from the power of the dog.
22:20

17.45
The Lord is my shepherd; therefore can I lack nothing.
He shall feed me in a green pasture: and lead me forth beside the waters of comfort.
He shall convert my soul: and bring me forth in the paths of righteousness, for his Name's sake.
Yea, though I walk through the valley of the shadow of death, I will fear no evil: for thou art with me; thy rod and thy staff comfort me.
Thou shalt prepare a table before me against them that trouble me: thou hast anointed my head with oil, and my cup shall be full.
But thy loving-kindness and mercy shall follow me all the days of my life: and I will dwell in the house of the Lord for ever.
23:1–6

17.46
The Lord is my shepherd; I shall not want.
He maketh me to lie down in green pastures: he leadeth me beside the still waters.
Authorised Version 23:1–2

17.47
Thou preparest a table before me in the presence of mine enemies: thou anointest my head with oil; my cup runneth over.
Surely goodness and mercy shall follow me all the days of my life: and I will dwell in the house of the Lord for ever.
Authorised Version 23:5–6

17.48
The earth is the Lord's, and all that therein is; the compass of the world, and they that dwell therein.
24:1

17.49
Lift up your heads, O ye gates, and be ye lift up, ye everlasting doors; and the King of glory shall come in.
Who is the King of glory? it is the Lord strong and mighty, even the Lord mighty in battle.
24:7–8

17.50
O remember not the sins and offences of my youth: but according to thy mercy think thou upon me, O Lord, for thy goodness.
25:6

17.51
His soul shall dwell at ease; and his seed shall inherit the land.
25:12

17.52
The sorrows of my heart are enlarged: O bring thou me out of my troubles.
25:16

17.53
Examine me, O Lord, and prove me; try out my reins and my heart.
26:2

17.54
Lord, I have loved the habitation of thy house, and the place where thine honour dwelleth.
O shut not up my soul with the sinners, nor my life with the blood-thirsty:
In whose hands is wickedness, and their right hand is full of gifts.
26:8–10

17.55
The Lord is my light, and my salvation; whom

then shall I fear? the Lord is the strength of my life; of whom then shall I be afraid?

27:1

17.56

Dominus illuminatio mea.

Vulgate 27:1

17.57

O hide not thou thy face from me; nor cast thy servant away in displeasure.

27:10

17.58

When my father and my mother forsake me, the Lord taketh me up.

27:12

17.59

O tarry thou the Lord's leisure; be strong, and he shall comfort thine heart; and put thou thy trust in the Lord.

27:16

17.60

The Lord is my strength; and he is the wholesome defence of his Anointed.

28:9

17.61

The voice of the Lord breaketh the cedar-trees; yea, the Lord breaketh the cedars of Libanus.

29:5

17.62

The voice of the Lord maketh the hinds to bring forth young, and discovereth the thick bushes: in his temple doth every man speak of his honour.

The Lord sitteth above the water-flood; and the Lord remaineth a King for ever.

29:8–9

17.63

Thou, Lord, hast brought my soul out of hell: thou hast kept my life from them that go down to the pit.

30:3

17.64

For his wrath endureth but the twinkling of an eye, and in his pleasure is life: heaviness may endure for a night, but joy cometh in the morning.

And in my prosperity I said, I shall never be removed; thou, Lord, of thy goodness hast made my hill so strong.

30:5–6

17.65

What profit is there in my blood, when I go down to the pit?

Shall the dust give thanks unto thee? or shall it declare thy truth?

30:9–10

17.66

In thee, O Lord, have I put my trust: let me never be put to confusion; deliver me in thy righteousness.

31:1

17.67

And be thou my strong rock, and house of defence, that thou mayest save me.

31:3

17.68

Into thy hands I commend my spirit: for thou hast redeemed me, O Lord, thou God of truth.

31:6

17.69

Thou hast not shut me up into the hand of the enemy: but hast set my feet in a large room.

31:9

17.70

I am clean forgotten, as a dead man out of mind: I am become like a broken vessel.

31:14

17.71

Blessed is he whose unrighteousness is forgiven, and whose sin is covered.

Blessed is the man unto whom the Lord imputeth no sin, and in whose spirit there is no guile.

For while I held my tongue, my bones consumed away through my daily complaining.

32:1–3

17.72

For this shall every one that is godly make his prayer unto thee, in a time when thou mayest be found: but in the great water-floods they shall not come nigh him.

Thou art a place to hide me in, thou shalt preserve me from trouble; thou shalt compass me about with songs of deliverance.

32:7–8

17.73

Be ye not like to horse and mule, which have no understanding: whose mouths must be held with bit and bridle, lest they fall upon thee.

32:10

17.74

Rejoice in the Lord, O ye righteous: for it becometh well the just to be thankful.

Praise the Lord with harp; sing praises unto him with the lute, and instrument of ten strings.

Sing unto the Lord a new song; sing praises lustily unto him with a good courage.

33:1–3

17.75

He loveth righteousness and judgment: the earth is full of the goodness of the Lord.

33:5

17.76

A horse is counted but a vain thing to save a

man: neither shall he deliver any man by his great strength.

33:16

17.77
I will alway give thanks unto the Lord: his praise shall ever be in my mouth.

34:1

17.78
What man is he that lusteth to live, and would fain see good days?

34:12

17.79
Eschew evil, and do good; seek peace, and ensue it.

34:14

17.80
Plead thou my cause, O Lord, with them that strive with me: and fight thou against them that fight against me.

35:1

17.81
For with thee is the well of life: and in thy light shall we see light.

36:9

17.82
Fret not thyself because of the ungodly; neither be thou envious against the evil doers.
For they shall soon be cut down like the grass, and be withered even as the green herb.

37:1–2

17.83
Delight thou in the Lord: and he shall give thee thy heart's desire.

37:4

17.84
He shall make thy righteousness as clear as the light, and thy just dealing as the noon-day.

37:6

17.85
I have been young, and now am old; and yet saw I never the righteous forsaken, nor his seed begging their bread.

37:25

17.86
I myself have seen the ungodly in great power, and flourishing like a green bay-tree.
I went by, and lo, he was gone: I sought him, but his place could no where be found.
Keep innocency, and take heed unto the thing that is right: for that shall bring a man peace at the last.

37:36–38

17.87
Lord, thou knowest all my desire; and my groaning is not hid from thee.

38:9

17.88
I said, I will take heed to my ways, that I offend not in my tongue.
I will keep my mouth as it were with a bridle, while the ungodly is in my sight.
I held my tongue, and spake nothing: I kept silence, yea, even from good words, but it was pain and grief to me.
My heart was hot within me, and while I was thus musing the fire kindled: and at the last I spake with my tongue;
Lord, let me know mine end, and the number of my days; that I may be certified how long I have to live.
Behold, thou hast made my days as it were a span long; and mine age is even as nothing in respect of thee; and verily every man living is altogether vanity.
For man walketh in a vain shadow, and disquieteth himself in vain: he heapeth up riches, and cannot tell who shall gather them.

39:1–7

17.89
When thou with rebukes dost chasten man for sin, thou makest his beauty to consume away, like as it were a moth fretting a garment: every man therefore is but vanity.

39:12

17.90
For I am a stranger with thee, and a sojourner, as all my fathers were.
O spare me a little, that I may recover my strength, before I go hence, and be no more seen.

39:14–15

17.91
I waited patiently for the Lord; and he inclined unto me, and heard my calling.
He brought me also out of the horrible pit, out of the mire and clay, and set my feet upon the rock, and ordered my goings.

40:1–2

17.92
As for me, I am poor and needy; but the Lord careth for me.
Thou art my helper and redeemer; make no long tarrying, O my God.

40:20–21

17.93
Yea, even mine own familiar friend, whom I trusted, who did also eat of my bread, hath laid great wait for me.

41:9

17.94
Like as the hart desireth the water-brooks, so longeth my soul after thee, O God.
My soul is athirst for God, yea, even for the living God: when shall I come to appear before the presence of God?

42:1–2

17.95
Why art thou so full of heaviness, O my soul? and why art thou so disquieted within me?
42:6

17.96
One deep calleth another, because of the noise of the water-pipes: all thy waves and storms are gone over me.
42:9

17.97
My bones are smitten asunder as with a sword; while mine enemies that trouble me cast me in the teeth;
Namely, while they say daily unto me: Where is now thy God?
42:12–13

17.98
For thy sake also are we killed all the day long, and are counted as sheep appointed to be slain.
44:22

17.99
My heart is inditing of a good matter: I speak of the things which I have made unto the King.
My tongue is the pen of a ready writer.
45:1–2

17.100
Kings' daughters were among thy honourable women: upon thy right hand did stand the queen in a vesture of gold, wrought about with divers colours.
Hearken, O daughter, and consider, incline thine ear; forget also thine own people, and thy father's house.
So shall the King have pleasure in thy beauty: for he is thy Lord God, and worship thou him.
45:10–12

17.101
The King's daughter is all glorious within: her clothing is of wrought gold.
She shall be brought unto the King in raiment of needle-work: the virgins that be her fellows shall bear her company, and shall be brought unto thee.
45:14–15

17.102
Instead of thy fathers thou shalt have children, whom thou mayest make princes in all lands.
45:17

17.103
God is our hope and strength, a very present help in trouble.
Therefore will we not fear, though the earth be moved, and though the hills be carried into the midst of the sea.
Though the waters thereof rage and swell, and though the mountains shake at the tempest of the same.
46:1–3

17.104
God is in the midst of her, therefore shall she not be removed: God shall help her, and that right early.
The heathen make much ado, and the kingdoms are moved: but God hath shewed his voice, and the earth shall melt away.
46:5–6

17.105
He maketh wars to cease in all the world; he breaketh the bow, and knappeth the spear in sunder, and burneth the chariots in the fire.
Be still then, and know that I am God: I will be exalted among the heathen, and I will be exalted in the earth.
The Lord of hosts is with us; the God of Jacob is our refuge.
46:9–11

17.106
God is gone up with a merry noise, and the Lord with the sound of the trump.
47:5

17.107
For God is the King of all the earth: sing ye praises with understanding.
47:7

17.108
The hill of Sion is a fair place, and the joy of the whole earth: upon the north-side lieth the city of the great King; God is well known in her palaces as a sure refuge.
For lo, the kings of the earth are gathered, and gone by together.
They marvelled to see such things; they were astonished, and suddenly cast down.
Fear came there upon them, and sorrow, as upon a woman in her travail.
Thou shalt break the ships of the sea through the east-wind.
48:2–6

17.109
Walk about Sion, and go round about her: and tell the towers thereof.
Mark well her bulwarks, set up her houses: that ye may tell them that come after.
48:11–12

17.110
And yet they think that their houses shall continue for ever, and that their dwelling-places shall endure from one generation to another; and call the lands after their own names.
49:11

17.111
Man being in honour hath no understanding: but is compared unto the beasts that perish.
49:20

17.112
Thinkest thou that I will eat bulls' flesh, and drink the blood of goats?

50:13

17.113
Wash me throughly from my wickedness, and cleanse me from my sin.
For I acknowledge my faults: and my sin is ever before me.

51:2–3

17.114
Behold, I was shapen in wickedness: and in sin hath my mother conceived me.
But lo, thou requirest truth in the inward parts: and shalt make me to understand wisdom secretly.
Thou shalt purge me with hyssop, and I shall be clean: thou shalt wash me, and I shall be whiter than snow.
Thou shalt make me hear of joy and gladness: that the bones which thou hast broken may rejoice.
Turn thy face from my sins: and put out all my misdeeds.
Make me a clean heart, O God: and renew a right spirit within me.

51:5–10

17.115
Deliver me from blood-guiltiness, O God, thou that art the God of my health: and my tongue shall sing of thy righteousness.

51:14

17.116
For thou desirest no sacrifice, else would I give it thee: but thou delightest not in burnt-offerings.
The sacrifice of God is a troubled spirit: a broken and contrite heart, O God, shalt thou not despise.

51:16–17

17.117
As for me, I am like a green olive-tree in the house of God: my trust is in the tender mercy of God for ever and ever.

52:9

17.118
They were afraid where no fear was: for God hath broken the bones of him that besieged thee; thou hast put them to confusion, because God hath despised them.

53:6

17.119
And I said, O that I had wings like a dove: for then would I flee away, and be at rest.

55:6

17.120
We took sweet counsel together, and walked in the house of God as friends.

55:15

17.121
The words of his mouth were softer than butter, having war in his heart: his words were smoother than oil, and yet be they very swords.
O cast thy burden upon the Lord, and he shall nourish thee: and shall not suffer the righteous to fall for ever.

55:22–23

17.122
They daily mistake my words: all that they imagine is to do me evil.
They hold all together, and keep themselves close, and mark my steps, when they lay wait for my soul.

56:5–6

17.123
Thou tellest my flittings; put my tears into thy bottle: are not these things noted in thy book?

56:8

17.124
For thou hast delivered my soul from death, and my feet from falling, that I may walk before God in the light of the living.

56:13

17.125
Be merciful unto me, O God, be merciful unto me, for my soul trusteth in thee: and under the shadow of thy wings shall be my refuge, until this tyranny be over-past.

57:1

17.126
God shall send forth his mercy and truth: my soul is among lions.
And I lie even among the children of men, that are set on fire: whose teeth are spears and arrows, and their tongue a sharp sword.

57:4–5

17.127
They have laid a net for my feet, and pressed down my soul: they have digged a pit before me, and are fallen into the midst of it themselves.

57:7

17.128
Awake up, my glory; awake, lute and harp: I myself will awake right early.

57:9

17.129
They are as venomous as the poison of a serpent: even like the deaf adder that stoppeth her ears;
Which refuseth to hear the voice of the charmer, charm he never so wisely.

58:4–5

17.130
They go to and fro in the evening: they grin like a dog, and run about through the city.

59:6

17.131
They will run here and there for meat, and grudge if they be not satisfied.

59:15

17.132
Thou hast shewed thy people heavy things: thou hast given us a drink of deadly wine.

60:3

17.133
O be thou our help in trouble: for vain is the help of man.

60:11

17.134
O set me up upon the rock that is higher than I: for thou hast been my hope, and a strong tower for me against the enemy.
I will dwell in thy tabernacle for ever; and my trust shall be under the covering of thy wings.

61:3–4

17.135
As for the children of men, they are but vanity: the children of men are deceitful upon the weights, they are altogether lighter than vanity itself.
O trust not in wrong and robbery, give not yourselves unto vanity: if riches increase, set not your heart upon them.

62:9–10

17.136
My soul thirsteth for thee, my flesh also longeth after thee: in a barren and dry land where no water is.

63:2

17.137
Have I not remembered thee in my bed, and thought upon thee when I was waking?

63:7

17.138
Let them fall upon the edge of the sword, that they may be a portion for foxes.

63:11

17.139
Thou, O God, art praised in Sion: and unto thee shall the vow be performed in Jerusalem. Thou that hearest the prayer, unto thee shall all flesh come.

65:1–2

17.140
Blessed is the man, whom thou choosest, and receivest unto thee: he shall dwell in thy court, and shall be satisfied with the pleasures of thy house, even of thy holy temple.
Thou shalt shew us wonderful things in thy righteousness, O God of our salvation; thou that art the hope of all the ends of the earth, and of them that remain in the broad sea.
Who in his strength setteth fast the mountains, and is girded about with power.
Who stilleth the raging of the sea, and the noise of his waves, and the madness of the people.
They also that dwell in the uttermost parts of the earth shall be afraid at thy tokens: thou that makest the outgoings of the morning and evening to praise thee.
Thou visitest the earth, and blessest it: thou makest it very plenteous.
The river of God is full of water: thou preparest their corn, for so thou providest for the earth.
Thou waterest her furrows, thou sendest rain into the little valleys thereof: thou makest it soft with the drops of rain, and blessest the increase of it.
Thou crownest the year with thy goodness; and thy clouds drop fatness.
They shall drop upon the dwellings of the wilderness; and the little hills shall rejoice on every side.
The folds shall be full of sheep; the valleys also shall stand so thick with corn, that they shall laugh and sing.

65:4–14

17.141
Then shall the earth bring forth her increase; and God, even our own God, shall give us his blessing.

67:6

17.142
O sing unto God, and sing praises unto his Name: magnify him that rideth upon the heavens, as it were upon an horse; praise him in his Name Jah, and rejoice before him.
He is a Father of the fatherless, and defendeth the cause of the widows: even God in his holy habitation.
He is the God that maketh men to be of one mind in an house, and bringeth the prisoners out of captivity; but letteth the runagates continue in scarceness.

68:4–6

17.143
As the hill of Basan, so is God's hill; even an high hill, as the hill of Basan.
Why hop ye so, ye high hills? this is God's hill, in the which it pleaseth him to dwell; yea, the Lord will abide in it for ever.
The chariots of God are twenty thousand, even thousands of angels: and the Lord is among them, as in the holy place of Sinai.
Thou art gone up on high, thou hast led captivity captive, and received gifts for men: yea, even for thine enemies, that the Lord God might dwell among them.

68:15–18

17.144
God shall wound the head of his enemies, and

the hairy scalp of such a one as goeth on still in his wickedness.

68:21

17.145
Who sitteth in the heavens over all from the beginning; lo, he doth send out his voice, yea, and that a mighty voice.

68:33

17.146
They that hate me without a cause are more than the hairs of my head: they that are mine enemies, and would destroy me guiltless, are mighty.
I paid them the things that I never took; God, thou knowest my simpleness, and my faults are not hid from thee.

69:4–5

17.147
For the zeal of thine house hath even eaten me; and the rebukes of them that rebuked thee are fallen upon me.

69:9

17.148
Thy rebuke hath broken my heart; I am full of heaviness:. I looked for some to have pity on me, but there was no man, neither found I any to comfort me.

69:21

17.149
Let them be wiped out of the book of the living, and not be written among the righteous.

69:29

17.150
Let them for their reward be soon brought to shame, that cry over me, There, there.

70:3

17.151
I am become as it were a monster unto many; but my sure trust is in thee.

71:6

17.152
Thou, O God, hast taught me from my youth up until now: therefore will I tell of thy wondrous works.
Forsake me not, O God, in mine old age, when I am gray-headed; until I have shewed thy strength unto this generation, and thy power to all them that are yet for to come.

71:15–16

17.153
He shall come down like the rain into a fleece of wool: even as the drops that water the earth.

72:6

17.154
They that dwell in the wilderness shall kneel before him; his enemies shall lick the dust.

72:9

17.155
Therefore fall the people unto them: and thereout suck they no small advantage.
Tush, say they, how should God perceive it? is there knowledge in the most High?

73:10–11

17.156
Then thought I to understand this; but it was too hard for me.

73:15

17.157
The earth is weak, and all the inhabiters thereof: I bear up the pillars of it.
I said unto the fools, Deal not so madly: and to the ungodly, Set not up your horn.
Set not up your horn on high: and speak not with a stiff neck.
For promotion cometh neither from the east, nor from the west, nor yet from the south.

75:4–7

17.158
For in the hand of the Lord there is a cup, and the wine is red; it is full mixed, and he poureth out of the same.
As for the dregs thereof, all the ungodly of the earth shall drink them, and suck them out.

75:9–10

17.159
At thy rebuke, O God of Jacob, both the chariot and horse are fallen.

76:6

17.160
I have considered the days of old, and the years that are past.
I call to remembrance my song: and in the night I commune with mine own heart, and search out my spirits.

77:5–6

17.161
Hath God forgotten to be gracious? and will he shut up his loving-kindness in displeasure?

77:9

17.162
I will open my mouth in a parable: I will declare hard sentences of old.

78:2

17.163
Like as the children of Ephraim, who being harnessed, and carrying bows, turned themselves back in the day of battle.

78:10

17.164
So man did eat angels' food: for he sent them meat enough.

78:26

17.165
So they tempted, and displeased the most high God, and kept not his testimonies;

But turned their backs, and fell away like their forefathers, starting aside like a broken bow.

78:57–58

17.166

So the Lord awaked as one out of sleep, and like a giant refreshed with wine.

78:66

17.167

Thou feedest them with the bread of tears; and givest them plenteousness of tears to drink.

80:5

17.168

Sing we merrily unto God our strength: make a cheerful noise unto the God of Jacob.

81:1

17.169

I eased his shoulder from the burden: and his hands were delivered from making the pots.

81:6

17.170

I proved thee also at the waters of strife.

81:8

17.171

So I gave them up unto their own hearts' lusts: and let them follow their own imaginations.

81:13

17.172

They will not be learned nor understand, but walk on still in darkness: all the foundations of the earth are out of course.

82:5

17.173

O how amiable are thy dwellings, thou Lord of hosts!

My soul hath a desire and longing to enter into the courts of the Lord: my heart and my flesh rejoice in the living God.

Yea, the sparrow hath found her an house, and the swallow a nest where she may lay her young, even thy altars, O Lord of hosts, my King and my God.

84:1–3

17.174

Who going through the vale of misery use it for a well; and the pools are filled with water.

They will go from strength to strength; and unto the God of gods appeareth every one of them in Sion.

84:6–7

17.175

For one day in thy courts is better than a thousand.

I had rather be a door-keeper in the house of my God, than to dwell in the tents of ungodliness.

84:10–11

17.176

Lord, thou art become gracious unto thy land: thou hast turned away the captivity of Jacob.

85:1

17.177

Mercy and truth are met together; righteousness and peace have kissed each other.

Truth shall flourish out of the earth; and righteousness hath looked down from heaven.

85:10–11

17.178

Righteousness shall go before him; and he shall direct his going in the way.

85:13

17.179

O God, the proud are risen against me; and the congregations of naughty men have sought after my soul, and have not set thee before their eyes.

86:14

17.180

Her foundations are upon the holy hills; the Lord loveth the gates of Sion more than all the dwellings of Jacob.

Very excellent things are spoken of thee, thou city of God.

87:1–2

17.181

Lord, thou hast been our refuge from one generation to another.

Before the mountains were brought forth, or ever the earth and the world were made, thou art God from everlasting, and world without end.

90:1–2

17.182

For a thousand years in thy sight are but as yesterday, seeing that is past as a watch in the night.

As soon as thou scatterest them they are even as a sleep; and fade away suddenly like the grass.

In the morning it is green, and groweth up; but in the evening it is cut down, dried up, and withered.

90:4–6

17.183

For when thou art angry all our days are gone: we bring our years to an end, as it were a tale that is told.

The days of our age are threescore years and ten; and though men be so strong that they come to fourscore years, yet is their strength then but labour and sorrow; so soon passeth it away, and we are gone.

90:9–10

17.184

And the glorious Majesty of the Lord our God be upon us: prosper thou the work of our hands upon us, O prosper thou our handy-work.

90:17

17.185
Whoso dwelleth under the defence of the most High shall abide under the shadow of the Almighty.

91:1

17.186
For he shall deliver thee from the snare of the hunter, and from the noisome pestilence.
He shall defend thee under his wings, and thou shalt be safe under his feathers: his faithfulness and truth shall be thy shield and buckler.
Thou shalt not be afraid for any terror by night; nor for the arrow that flieth by day;
For the pestilence that walketh in darkness; nor for the sickness that destroyeth in the noon-day.
A thousand shall fall beside thee, and ten thousand at thy right hand; but it shall not come nigh thee.

91:3–7

17.187
There shall no evil happen unto thee, neither shall any plague come nigh thy dwelling.
For he shall give his angels charge over thee, to keep thee in all thy ways.
They shall bear thee in their hands, that thou hurt not thy foot against a stone.
Thou shalt go upon the lion and adder: the young lion and the dragon shalt thou tread under thy feet.

91:10–13

17.188
With long life will I satisfy him; and shew him my salvation.

91:16

17.189
O Lord, how glorious are thy works: thy thoughts are very deep.
An unwise man doth not well consider this: and a fool doth not understand it.

92:5–6

17.190
The righteous shall flourish like a palm-tree: and shall spread abroad like a cedar in Libanus.

92:11

17.191
They also shall bring forth more fruit in their age, and shall be fat and well-liking.

92:13

17.192
The Lord is King, and hath put on glorious apparel: the Lord hath put on his apparel, and girded himself with strength.
He hath made the round world so sure that it cannot be moved.

93:1–2

17.193
The floods are risen, O Lord, the floods have lift up their voice; the floods lift up their waves.
The waves of the sea are mighty, and rage horribly; but yet the Lord, who dwelleth on high, is mightier.
Thy testimonies, O Lord, are very sure: holiness becometh thine house for ever.

93:4–6

17.194
He that planted the ear, shall he not hear? or he that made the eye, shall he not see?

94:9

17.195
O come, let us sing unto the Lord: let us heartily rejoice in the strength of our salvation.
Let us come before his presence with thanksgiving, and shew ourselves glad in him with psalms.
For the Lord is a great God, and a great King above all gods.
In his hand are all the corners of the earth: and the strength of the hills is his also.
The sea is his, and he made it: and his hands prepared the dry land.

95:1–5

17.196
Venite, exultemus

Vulgate 95:1

17.197
For he is the Lord our God; and we are the people of his pasture, and the sheep of his hand.
To-day if ye will hear his voice, harden not your hearts; as in the provocation, and as in the day of temptation in the wilderness.

95:7–8

17.198
The Lord is King, the earth may be glad thereof; yea, the multitude of the isles may be glad thereof.

97:1

17.199
O sing unto the Lord a new song; for he hath done marvellous things.
With his own right hand, and with his holy arm, hath he gotten himself the victory.

98:1–2

17.200
Let the sea make a noise, and all that therein is; the round world, and they that dwell therein.
Let the floods clap their hands, and let the hills be joyful together before the Lord; for he is come to judge the earth.

With righteousness shall he judge the world: and the people with equity.

98:8–10

17.201
The Lord is King, be the people never so impatient: he sitteth between the cherubims, be the earth never so unquiet.

99:1

17.202
O be joyful in the Lord, all ye lands: serve the Lord with gladness, and come before his presence with a song.
Be ye sure that the Lord he is God: it is he that hath made us, and not we ourselves; we are his people, and the sheep of his pasture.
O go your way into his gates with thanksgiving, and into his courts with praise: be thankful unto him, and speak good of his Name.
For the Lord is gracious, his mercy is everlasting; and his truth endureth from generation to generation.

100:1–4

17.203
Jubilate Deo

Vulgate 100:1

17.204
Whoso hath also a proud look and high stomach, I will not suffer him.

101:7

17.205
I am become like a pelican in the wilderness; and like an owl that is in the desert.
I have watched, and am even as it were a sparrow, that sitteth alone upon the house-top.

102:6–7

17.206
They shall perish, but thou shalt endure: they all shall wax old as doth a garment;
And as a vesture shalt thou change them, and they shall be changed: but thou art the same, and thy years shall not fail.

102:26–27

17.207
Who satisfieth thy mouth with good things, making thee young and lusty as an eagle.

103:5

17.208
He will not alway be chiding: neither keepeth he his anger for ever.

103:9

17.209
For look how high the heaven is in comparison of the earth: so great is his mercy also toward them that fear him.
Look how wide also the east is from the west: so far hath he set our sins from us.

103:11–12

17.210
The days of man are but as grass: for he flourisheth as a flower of the field.
For as soon as the wind goeth over it, it is gone; and the place thereof shall know it no more.

103:15–16

17.211
Thou deckest thyself with light as it were with a garment: and spreadest out the heavens like a curtain.
Who layeth the beams of his chambers in the waters, and maketh the clouds his chariot, and walketh upon the wings of the wind.
He maketh his angels spirits; and his ministers a flaming fire.

104:2–4

17.212
Thou coveredst it with the deep like as with a garment: the waters stand in the hills.
At thy rebuke they flee; at the voice of thy thunder they are afraid.
They go up as high as the hills, and down to the valleys beneath, even unto the place which thou hast appointed for them.
Thou hast set them their bounds which they shall not pass; neither turn again to cover the earth.
He sendeth the springs into the rivers, which run among the hills.
All beasts of the field drink thereof: and the wild asses quench their thirst.

104:6–11

17.213
He bringeth forth grass for the cattle, and green herb for the service of men;
That he may bring food out of the earth, and wine that maketh glad the heart of man, and oil to make him a cheerful countenance, and bread to strengthen man's heart.
The trees of the Lord also are full of sap: even the cedars of Libanus which he hath planted;
Wherein the birds make their nests: and the fir-trees are a dwelling for the stork.
The high hills are a refuge for the wild goats: and so are the stony rocks for the conies.

104:14–18

17.214
The lions roaring after their prey do seek their meat from God.
The sun ariseth, and they get them away together, and lay them down in their dens.
Man goeth forth to his work, and to his labour until the evening.

104:21–23

17.215
So is the great and wide sea also, wherein are things creeping innumerable, both small and great beasts.
There go the ships, and there is that Levia-

than, whom thou hast made to take his pastime therein.
These wait all upon thee; that thou mayest give them meat in due season.

104:25–27

17.216
Whose feet they hurt in the stocks: the iron entered into his soul.

105:18

17.217
O give thanks unto the Lord, for he is gracious: and his mercy endureth for ever.

106:1

17.218
Hungry and thirsty, their soul fainted in them.

107:5

17.219
He led them forth by the right way, that they might go to the city where they dwelt.

107:7

17.220
Their soul abhorred all manner of meat; and they were even hard at death's door.

107:18

17.221
They that go down to the sea in ships, and occupy their business in great waters;
These men see the works of the Lord, and his wonders in the deep.
For at his word the stormy wind ariseth, which lifteth up the waves thereof.
They are carried up to the heaven, and down again to the deep: their soul melteth away because of the trouble.
They reel to and fro, and stagger like a drunken man, and are at their wit's end.

107:23–27

17.222
Then are they glad, because they are at rest: and so he bringeth them unto the haven where they would be.

107:30

17.223
Who turneth the floods into a wilderness, and drieth up the water-springs.
A fruitful land maketh he barren, for the wickedness of them that dwell therein.
Again, he maketh the wilderness a standing water, and water-springs of a dry ground.

107:33–35

17.224
Whoso is wise will ponder these things: and they shall understand the loving-kindness of the Lord.

107:43

17.225
God hath spoken in his holiness; I will rejoice therefore, and divide Sichem, and mete out the valley of Succoth.
Gilead is mine, and Manasses is mine; Ephraim also is the strength of my head.
Judah is my law-giver, Moab is my wash-pot; over Edom will I cast out my shoe; upon Philistia will I triumph.
Who will lead me into the strong city? and who will bring me into Edom?

108:7–10

17.226
His delight was in cursing, and it shall happen unto him: he loved not blessing, therefore shall it be far from him.

109:16

17.227
The Lord said unto my Lord, Sit thou on my right hand, until I make thine enemies thy footstool.

110:1

17.228
The Lord sware, and will not repent, Thou art a Priest for ever after the order of Melchisedech.

110:4

17.229
The fear of the Lord is the beginning of wisdom; a good understanding have all they that do thereafter; the praise of it endureth for ever.

111:10

17.230
A good man is merciful, and lendeth, and will guide his words with discretion.
For he shall never be moved; and the righteous shall be had in everlasting remembrance.

112:5–6

17.231
He hath dispersed abroad, and given to the poor, and his righteousness remaineth for ever; his horn shall be exalted with honour.

112:9

17.232
He maketh the barren woman to keep house, and to be a joyful mother of children.

113:8

17.233
The sea saw that, and fled: Jordan was driven back.
The mountains skipped like rams, and the little hills like young sheep.

114:3–4

17.234
Tremble, thou earth, at the presence of the Lord, at the presence of the God of Jacob;
Who turned the hard rock into a standing water, and the flint-stone into a springing well.

114:7–8

17.235
Not unto us, O Lord, not unto us, but unto

thy Name give the praise; for thy loving mercy, and for thy truth's sake.

115:1

17.236

Non nobis, Domine

Vulgate 115:1

17.237

Their idols are silver and gold, even the work of men's hands.
They have mouths, and speak not; eyes have they, and see not.
They have ears, and hear not; noses have they, and smell not.
They have hands, and handle not; feet have they, and walk not; neither speak they through their throat.

115:4–7

17.238

The snares of death compassed me round about; and the pains of hell gat hold upon me.

116:3

17.239

And why? thou hast delivered my soul from death, mine eyes from tears, and my feet from falling.
I will walk before the Lord in the land of the living.
I believed, and therefore will I speak; but I was sore troubled: I said in my haste, All men are liars.

116:8–10

17.240

The voice of joy and health is in the dwellings of the righteous: the right hand of the Lord bringeth mighty things to pass.

118:15

17.241

I shall not die, but live, and declare the works of the Lord.
The Lord hath chastened and corrected me: but he hath not given me over unto death.

118:17–18

17.242

The same stone which the builders refused is become the head-stone in the corner.
This is the Lord's doing, and it is marvellous in our eyes.

118:22–23

17.243

Blessed be he that cometh in the Name of the Lord: we have wished you good luck, ye that are of the house of the Lord.

118:26

17.244

Blessed are those that are undefiled in the way, and walk in the law of the Lord.

119:1

17.245

Princes also did sit and speak against me: but thy servant is occupied in thy statutes.

119:23

17.246

O turn away mine eyes, lest they behold vanity, and quicken thou me in thy way.

119:37

17.247

Thy statutes have been my songs in the house of my pilgrimage.

119:54

17.248

I see that all things come to an end: but thy commandment is exceeding broad.

119:96

17.249

Thy word is a lantern unto my feet, and a light unto my paths.

119:105

17.250

My soul is alway in my hand: yet do I not forget thy law.

119:109

17.251

O stablish me according to thy word, that I may live: and let me not be disappointed of my hope.

119:116

17.252

Thy word is tried to the uttermost: and thy servant loveth it.

119:140

17.253

Princes have persecuted me without a cause: but my heart standeth in awe of thy word.

119:161

17.254

I labour for peace, but when I speak unto them thereof, they make them ready to battle.

120:6

17.255

I will lift up mine eyes unto the hills, from whence cometh my help.

121:1

17.256

He will not suffer thy foot to be moved: and he that keepeth thee will not sleep.

121:3

17.257

The Lord himself is thy keeper: the Lord is thy defence upon thy right hand;
So that the sun shall not burn thee by day, neither the moon by night.
The Lord shall preserve thee from all evil: yea, it is even he that shall keep thy soul.
The Lord shall preserve thy going out, and thy coming in, from this time forth for evermore.

121:5–8

17.258
I was glad when they said unto me, We will go into the house of the Lord.

122:1

17.259
Jerusalem is built as a city that is at unity in itself.

122:3

17.260
O pray for the peace of Jerusalem: they shall prosper that love thee.
Peace be within thy walls, and plenteousness within thy palaces.

122:6–7

17.261
The deep waters of the proud had gone even over our soul.

124:4

17.262
Our soul is escaped even as a bird out of the snare of the fowler: the snare is broken, and we are delivered.

124:6

17.263
The hills stand about Jerusalem: even so standeth the Lord round about his people, from this time forth for evermore.
For the rod of the ungodly cometh not into the lot of the righteous; lest the righteous put their hand unto wickedness.

125:2–3

17.264
Turn our captivity, O Lord, as the rivers in the south.
They that sow in tears shall reap in joy.
He that now goeth on his way weeping, and beareth forth good seed, shall doubtless come again with joy, and bring his sheaves with him.

126:5–7

17.265
Except the Lord build the house, their labour is but lost that build it.
Except the Lord keep the city, the watchman waketh but in vain.
It is but lost labour that ye haste to rise up early, and so late take rest, and eat the bread of carefulness: for so he giveth his beloved sleep.
Lo, children and the fruit of the womb are an heritage and gift that cometh of the Lord.
Like as the arrows in the hand of the giant; even so are the young children.
Happy is the man that hath his quiver full of them: they shall not be ashamed when they speak with their enemies in the gate.

127:1–6

17.266
Nisi Dominus . . . frustra.

Vulgate 127:1

17.267
Thy wife shall be as the fruitful vine upon the walls of thine house.
Thy children like the olive-branches round about thy table.

128:3–4

17.268
Yea, that thou shalt see thy children's children, and peace upon Israel.

128:7

17.269
The plowers plowed upon my back, and made long furrows.

129:3

17.270
Let them be even as the grass growing upon the house-tops, which withereth afore it be plucked up;
Whereof the mower filleth not his hand; neither he that bindeth up the sheaves his bosom.
So that they who go by say not so much as, The Lord prosper you: we wish you good luck in the Name of the Lord.

129:6–8

17.271
Out of the deep have I called unto thee, O Lord: Lord, hear my voice.
O let thine ears consider well the voice of my complaint.
If thou, Lord, wilt be extreme to mark what is done amiss, O Lord, who may abide it?

130:1–3

17.272
De profundis

Vulgate 130:1

17.273
My soul fleeth unto the Lord: before the morning watch, I say, before the morning watch.

130:6

17.274
Lord, I am not high-minded: I have no proud looks.

131:1

17.275
Behold, how good and joyful a thing it is, brethren, to dwell together in unity!

133:1

17.276
By the waters of Babylon we sat down and wept, when we remembered thee, O Sion.
As for our harps, we hanged them up upon the trees that are therein.
For they that led us away captive required of us then a song, and melody, in our heaviness: Sing us one of the songs of Sion.
How shall we sing the Lord's song in a strange land?

If I forget thee, O Jerusalem, let my right hand forget her cunning.
If I do not remember thee, let my tongue cleave to the roof of my mouth; yea, if I prefer not Jerusalem in my mirth.

137:1–6

17.277
O Lord, thou hast searched me out, and known me; thou knowest my down-sitting, and mine up-rising; thou understandest my thoughts long before.
Thou art about my path, and about my bed, and spiest out all my ways.
For lo, there is not a word in my tongue, but thou, O Lord, knowest it altogether.

139:1–3

17.278
Such knowledge is too wonderful and excellent for me: I cannot attain unto it.

139:5

17.279
If I climb up into heaven, thou art there: if I go down to hell, thou art there also.
If I take the wings of the morning, and remain in the uttermost parts of the sea;
Even there also shall thy hand lead me, and thy right hand shall hold me.
If I say, Peradventure the darkness shall cover me: then shall my night be turned to day.
Yea, the darkness is no darkness with thee, but the night is as clear as the day: the darkness and light to thee are both alike.

139:7–11

17.280
I will give thanks unto thee, for I am fearfully and wonderfully made: marvellous are thy works, and that my soul knoweth right well.

139:13

17.281
Thine eyes did see my substance, yet being imperfect, and in thy book were all my members written.

139:15

17.282
Deliver me, O Lord, from the evil man, and preserve me from the wicked man.
Who imagine mischief in their hearts, and stir up strife all the day long.
They have sharpened their tongues like a serpent: adder's poison is under their lips.

140:1–3

17.283
The proud have laid a snare for me, and spread a net abroad with cords: yea, and set traps in my way.

140:5

17.284
O Lord God, thou strength of my health, thou hast covered my head in the day of battle.

140:7

17.285
Set a watch, O Lord, before my mouth; and keep the door of my lips.

141:3

17.286
Let the righteous rather smite me friendly, and reprove me.
But let not their precious balms break my head: yea, I will pray yet against their wickedness.

141:5–6

17.287
Let the ungodly fall into their own nets together; and let me ever escape them.

141:11

17.288
Blessed be the Lord my strength, who teacheth my hands to war, and my fingers to fight.

144:1

17.289
Man is like a thing of nought: his time passeth away like a shadow.

144:4

17.290
That our oxen may be strong to labour, that there be no decay, no leading into captivity, and no complaining in our streets.

144:14

17.291
The Lord is gracious, and merciful; long-suffering, and of great goodness.

145:8

17.292
O put not your trust in princes, nor in any child of man; for there is no help in them.
For when the breath of man goeth forth he shall turn again to his earth; and then all his thoughts perish.

146:2–3

17.293
The Lord looseth men out of prison: the Lord giveth sight to the blind.
The Lord helpeth them that are fallen: the Lord careth for the righteous.
The Lord careth for the strangers: he defendeth the fatherless and widow; as for the way of the ungodly, he turneth it upside down.

146:7–9

17.294
The Lord doth build up Jerusalem, and gather together the out-casts of Israel.
He healeth those that are broken in heart, and giveth medicine to heal their sickness.
He telleth the number of the stars, and calleth them all by their names.

147:2–4

17.295
He hath no pleasure in the strength of an horse: neither delighteth he in any man's legs.
147:10

17.296
He giveth snow like wool; and scattereth the hoar-frost like ashes.
He casteth forth his ice like morsels: who is able to abide his frost?
He sendeth out his word, and melteth them; he bloweth with his wind, and the waters flow.
147:16–18

17.297
Praise the Lord upon earth, ye dragons, and all deeps;
Fire and hail, snow and vapours; wind and storm, fulfilling his word;
Mountains and all hills; fruitful trees and all cedars;
Beasts and all cattle; worms and feathered fowls;
Kings of the earth and all people; princes and all judges of the world;
Young men and maidens, old men and children, praise the Name of the Lord: for his Name only is excellent, and his praise above heaven and earth.
149:7–12

17.298
Let the saints be joyful with glory: let them rejoice in their beds.
Let the praises of God be in their mouth, and a two-edged sword in their hands.
149:5–6

17.299
To bind their kings in chains, and their nobles with links of iron.
149:8

17.300
Praise him in the cymbals and dances: praise him upon the strings and pipe.
Praise him upon the well-tuned cymbals: praise him upon the loud cymbals.
150:4–5

18 Proverbs

18.1
A wise man will hear, and will increase learning; and a man of understanding shall attain unto wise counsels:
To understand a proverb, and the interpretation; the words of the wise, and their dark sayings.
The fear of the Lord is the beginning of knowledge: but fools despise wisdom and instruction.
1:5–7

18.2
My son, if sinners entice thee, consent thou not.
1:10

18.3
Cast in thy lot among us; let us all have one purse.
1:14

18.4
Surely in vain the net is spread in the sight of any bird.
1:17

18.5
Wisdom crieth without; she uttereth her voice in the streets.
1:20

18.6
Be not wise in thine own eyes: fear the Lord, and depart from evil.
3:7

18.7
My son, despise not the chastening of the Lord; neither be weary of his correction:
For whom the Lord loveth he correcteth; even as a father the son in whom he delighteth.
3:11–12

18.8
Length of days is in her right hand: and in her left hand riches and honour.
Her ways are ways of pleasantness, and all her paths are peace.
3:16–17

18.9
Devise not evil against thy neighbour, seeing he dwelleth securely by thee.
3:29

18.10
Wisdom is the principal thing; therefore get wisdom: and with all thy getting get understanding.
4:7

18.11
But the path of the just is as the shining light, that shineth more and more unto the perfect day.
4:18

18.12
For the lips of a strange woman drop as an honeycomb, and her mouth is smoother than oil:
But her end is bitter as wormwood, sharp as a two-edged sword.
5:3–4

18.13
Let thy fountain be blessed: and rejoice with the wife of thy youth.
Let her be as the loving hind and pleasant roe; let her breasts satisfy thee at all times; and be thou ravished always with her love.
5:18–19

18.14
Go to the ant, thou sluggard; consider her ways, and be wise:
Which having no guide, overseer, or ruler,
Provideth her meat in the summer, and gathereth her food in the harvest.

6:6–8

18.15
Yet a little sleep, a little slumber, a little folding of the hands to sleep:
So shall thy poverty come as one that travelleth, and thy want as an armed man.

6:10–11

18.16
Can a man take fire in his bosom, and his clothes not be burned?

6:27

18.17
She is loud and stubborn; her feet abide not in her house:
Now is she without, now in the streets, and lieth in wait at every corner.

7:11–12

18.18
Come, let us take our fill of love until the morning: let us solace ourselves with loves.
For the goodman is not at home, he is gone a long journey.

7:18–19

18.19
He goeth after her straightway, as an ox goeth to the slaughter, or as a fool to the correction of the stocks.

7:22

18.20
For wisdom is better than rubies; and all the things that may be desired are not to be compared to it.
I wisdom dwell with prudence, and find out knowledge of witty inventions.

8:11–12

18.21
Wisdom hath builded her house, she hath hewn out her seven pillars.

9:1

18.22
Stolen waters are sweet, and bread eaten in secret is pleasant.

9:17

18.23
The proverbs of Solomon. A wise son maketh a glad father: but a foolish son is the heaviness of his mother.

10:1

18.24
The memory of the just is blessed: but the name of the wicked shall rot.

10:7

18.25
Hatred stirreth up strifes: but love covereth all sins.

10:12

18.26
The rich man's wealth is his strong city: the destruction of the poor is their poverty.

10:15

18.27
Riches profit not in the day of wrath: but righteousness delivereth from death.

11:4

18.28
Where no counsel is, the people fall: but in the multitude of counsellors there is safety.

11:14

18.29
As a jewel of gold in a swine's snout, so is a fair woman which is without discretion.

11:22

18.30
A virtuous woman is a crown to her husband: but she that maketh ashamed is as rottenness in his bones.

12:4

18.31
A righteous man regardeth the life of his beast: but the tender mercies of the wicked are cruel.

12:10

18.32
A wise son heareth his father's instruction: but a scorner heareth not rebuke.

13:1

18.33
Hope deferred maketh the heart sick: but when the desire cometh, it is a tree of life.

13:12

18.34
The desire accomplished is sweet to the soul: but it is abomination to fools to depart from evil.

13:19

18.35
He that spareth his rod hateth his son: but he that loveth him chasteneth him betimes.

13:24

18.36
The heart knoweth his own bitterness; and a stranger doth not intermeddle with his joy.

14:10

18.37
Even in laughter the heart is sorrowful; and the end of that mirth is heaviness.

14:13

18.38
In all labour there is profit: but the talk of the lips tendeth only to penury.

14:23

18.39
Righteousness exalteth a nation: but sin is a reproach to any people.
14:34

18.40
A soft answer turneth away wrath: but grievous words stir up anger.
15:1

18.41
A merry heart maketh a cheerful countenance: but by sorrow of the heart the spirit is broken.
15:13

18.42
Better is little with the fear of the Lord than great treasure and trouble therewith.
Better is a dinner of herbs where love is, than a stalled ox and hatred therewith.
15:16–17

18.43
The way of the slothful man is as an hedge of thorns: but the way of the righteous is made plain.
15:19

18.44
A man hath joy by the answer of his mouth: and a word spoken in due season, how good is it!
15:23

18.45
Pride goeth before destruction, and an haughty spirit before a fall.
[*Often quoted in the form 'Pride goeth before a fall'.*]
16:18

18.46
The hoary head is a crown of glory, if it be found in the way of righteousness.
16:31

18.47
He that is slow to anger is better than the mighty; and he that ruleth his spirit than he that taketh a city.
16:32

18.48
The lot is cast into the lap; but the whole disposing thereof is of the Lord.
16:33

18.49
Children's children are the crown of old men; and the glory of children are their fathers.
17:6

18.50
He that covereth a transgression seeketh love; but he that repeateth a matter separateth very friends.
17:9

18.51
Whoso rewardeth evil for good, evil shall not depart from his house.
17:13

18.52
He that begetteth a fool doeth it to his sorrow: and the father of a fool hath no joy.
17:21

18.53
A merry heart doeth good like a medicine: but a broken spirit drieth the bones.
17:22

18.54
He also that is slothful in his work is brother to him that is a great waster.
18:9

18.55
The spirit of a man will sustain his infirmity; but a wounded spirit who can bear?
18:14

18.56
A man that hath friends must shew himself friendly: and there is a friend that sticketh closer than a brother.
18:24

18.57
Wealth maketh many friends; but the poor is separated from his neighbour.
19:4

18.58
Wine is a mocker, strong drink is raging: and whosoever is deceived thereby is not wise.
20:1

18.59
It is an honour for a man to cease from strife: but every fool will be meddling.
20:3

18.60
Counsel in the heart of man is like deep water; but a man of understanding will draw it out.
20:5

18.61
Even a child is known by his doings, whether his work be pure, and whether it be right.
20:11

18.62
The hearing ear, and the seeing eye, the Lord hath made even both of them.
20:12

18.63
It is naught, it is naught, saith the buyer: but when he is gone his way, then he boasteth.
20:14

18.64
An inheritance may be gotten hastily at the beginning; but the end thereof shall not be blessed.
20:21

18.65
The spirit of man is the candle of the Lord, searching all the inward parts of the belly.
20:27

18.66
Every way of a man is right in his own eyes: but the Lord pondereth the hearts.
21:2

18.67
It is better to dwell in a corner of the housetop, than with a brawling woman in a wide house.
21:9

18.68
The horse is prepared against the day of battle: but safety is of the Lord.
21:31

18.69
A good name is rather to be chosen than great riches, and loving favour rather than silver and gold.
The rich and poor meet together: the Lord is the maker of them all.
22:1–2

18.70
Train up a child in the way he should go: and when he is old, he will not depart from it.
22:6

18.71
Wilt thou set thine eyes upon that which is not? for riches certainly make themselves wings; they fly away as an eagle toward heaven.
23:5

18.72
Remove not the old landmark; and enter not into the fields of the fatherless.
23:10

18.73
Apply thine heart unto instruction, and thine ears to the words of knowledge.
23:12

18.74
Be not among winebibbers; among riotous eaters of flesh:
For the drunkard and the glutton shall come to poverty: and drowsiness shall clothe a man with rags.
23:20–21

18.75
Look not thou upon the wine when it is red, when it giveth his colour in the cup, when it moveth itself aright.
At the last it biteth like a serpent, and stingeth like an adder.
23:31–32

18.76
A wise man is strong; yea, a man of knowledge increaseth strength.
24:5

18.77
If thou faint in the day of adversity, thy strength is small.
24:10

18.78
For there shall be no reward to the evil man; the candle of the wicked shall be put out.
24:20

18.79
My son, fear thou the Lord and the king: and meddle not with them that are given to change.
24:21

18.80
It is the glory of God to conceal a thing: but the honour of kings is to search out a matter.
The heaven for height, and the earth for depth, and the heart of kings is unsearchable.
25:2–3

18.81
Confidence in an unfaithful man in time of trouble is like a broken tooth, and a foot out of joint.
25:19

18.82
For thou shalt heap coals of fire upon his head, and the Lord shall reward thee.
25:22

18.83
As cold waters to a thirsty soul, so is good news from a far country.
25:25

18.84
As snow in summer, and as rain in harvest, so honour is not seemly for a fool.
As the bird by wandering, as the swallow by flying, so the curse causeless shall not come.
A whip for the horse, a bridle for the ass, and a rod for the fool's back.
26:1–3

18.85
Answer a fool according to his folly, lest he be wise in his own conceit.
26:5

18.86
As a dog returneth to his vomit, so a fool returneth to his folly.
Seest thou a man wise in his own conceit? there is more hope of a fool than of him.
26:11–12

18.87
As the door turneth upon his hinges, so doth the slothful upon his bed.
The slothful hideth his hand in his bosom; it grieveth him to bring it again to his mouth.
The sluggard is wiser in his own conceit than seven men that can render a reason.
26:14–16

18.88
He that passeth by, and meddleth with strife belonging not to him, is like one that taketh a dog by the ears.
26:17

18.89
Where no wood is, there the fire goeth out: so where there is no talebearer, the strife ceaseth.
26:20

18.90
Boast not thyself of tomorrow; for thou knowest not what a day may bring forth.
27:1

18.91
Wrath is cruel, and anger is outrageous; but who is able to stand before envy?
27:4

18.92
Open rebuke is better than secret love.
Faithful are the wounds of a friend; but the kisses of an enemy are deceitful.
27:5–6

18.93
A continual dropping in a very rainy day and a contentious woman are alike.
27:15

18.94
Iron sharpeneth iron; so a man sharpeneth the countenance of his friend.
27:17

18.95
As in water face answereth to face; so the heart of man to man.
27:19

18.96
Hell and destruction are never full; so the eyes of man are never satisfied.
27:20

18.97
Though thou shouldest bray a fool in a mortar among wheat with a pestle, yet will not his foolishness depart from him.
27:22

18.98
The wicked flee when no man pursueth: but the righteous are bold as a lion.
28:1

18.99
A poor man that oppresseth the poor is like a sweeping rain which leaveth no food.
28:3

18.100
A faithful man shall abound with blessings: but he that maketh haste to be rich shall not be innocent.
28:20

18.101
If a wise man contendeth with a foolish man, whether he rage or laugh, there is no rest.
29:9

18.102
A fool uttereth all his mind: but a wise man keepeth it in till afterwards.
29:11

18.103
Where there is no vision, the people perish: but he that keepeth the law, happy is he.
29:18

18.104
Seest thou a man that is hasty in his words? there is more hope of a fool than of him.
29:20

18.105
Remove far from me vanity and lies: give me neither poverty nor riches, feed me with food convenient for me:
30:8

18.106
The horseleach hath two daughters, crying, Give, give. There are three things that are never satisfied, yea, four things say not, It is enough:
The grave; and the barren womb; the earth that is not filled with water; and the fire that saith not, It is enough.
30:15–16

18.107
There be three things which are too wonderful for me, yea, four which I know not:
The way of an eagle in the air; the way of a serpent upon a rock; the way of a ship in the midst of the sea; and the way of a man with a maid.
30:18–19

18.108
Surely the churning of milk bringeth forth butter, and the wringing of the nose bringeth forth blood: so the forcing of wrath bringeth forth strife.
30:33

18.109
Who can find a virtuous woman? for her price is far above rubies.
The heart of her husband doth safely trust in her, so that he shall have no need of spoil.
She will do him good and not evil all the days of her life.
31:10–12

18.110
She perceiveth that her merchandise is good: her candle goeth not out by night.
31:18

18.111
Strength and honour are her clothing; and she shall rejoice in time to come.
She openeth her mouth with wisdom; and in her tongue is the law of kindness.
She looketh well to the ways of her household, and eateth not the bread of idleness.
Her children arise up, and call her blessed; her husband also, and he praiseth her.
31:25–28

19 Ecclesiastes

19.1
Vanity of vanities, saith the Preacher, vanity of vanities; all is vanity.
What profit hath a man of all his labour which he taketh under the sun?
One generation passeth away, and another generation cometh: but the earth abideth for ever.

1:2–4

19.2
All the rivers run into the sea; yet the sea is not full; unto the place from whence the rivers come, thither they return again.
All things are full of labour; man cannot utter it: the eye is not satisfied with seeing, nor the ear filled with hearing.
The thing that hath been, it is that which shall be; and that which is done is that which shall be done: and there is no new thing under the sun.

1:7–9

19.3
There is no remembrance of former things; neither shall there be any remembrance of things that are to come with those that shall come after.

1:11

19.4
And I gave my heart to seek and search out by wisdom concerning all things that are done under heaven: this sore travail hath God given to the sons of man to be exercised therewith.
I have seen all the works that are done under the sun; and, behold, all is vanity and vexation of spirit.

1:13–14

19.5
For in much wisdom is much grief: and he that increaseth knowledge increaseth sorrow.

1:18

19.6
I said of laughter, It is mad: and of mirth, What doeth it?

2:2

19.7
Then I saw that wisdom excelleth folly, as far as light excelleth darkness.
The wise man's eyes are in his head; but the fool walketh in darkness: and I myself perceived also that one event happeneth to them all.

2:13–14

19.8
Yea, I hated all my labour which I had taken under the sun: because I should leave it unto the man that shall be after me.
And who knoweth whether he shall be a wise man or a fool? yet shall he have rule over all my labour wherein I have laboured, and wherein I have shewed myself wise under the sun. This is also vanity.

2:18–19

19.9
To every thing there is a season, and a time to every purpose under the heaven:
A time to be born, and a time to die; a time to plant, and a time to pluck up that which is planted;
A time to kill, and a time to heal; a time to break down, and a time to build up;
A time to weep, and a time to laugh; a time to mourn, and a time to dance;
A time to cast away stones, and a time to gather stones together; a time to embrace, and a time to refrain from embracing;
A time to get, and a time to lose; a time to keep, and a time to cast away;
A time to rend, and a time to sew; a time to keep silence, and a time to speak;
A time to love, and a time to hate; a time of war, and a time of peace.

3:1–8

19.10
Wherefore I praised the dead which are already dead more than the living which are yet alive.
Yea, better is he than both they, which hath not yet been, who hath not seen the evil work that is done under the sun.

4:2–3

19.11
Better is an handful with quietness, than both the hands full with travail and vexation of spirit.

4:6

19.12
Two are better than one; because they have a good reward for their labour.
For if they fall, the one will lift up his fellow: but woe to him that is alone when he falleth; for he hath not another to help him up.

4:9–10

19.13
And if one prevail against him, two shall withstand him; and a threefold cord is not quickly broken.

4:12

19.14
Better is a poor and a wise child than an old and foolish king, who will no more be admonished.

4:13

19.15
Better is it that thou shouldest not vow, than that thou shouldest vow and not pay.

5:5

19.16
The sleep of a labouring man is sweet,

whether he eat little or much: but the abundance of the rich will not suffer him to sleep.

5:12

19.17

Better is the sight of the eyes than the wandering of the desire: this is also vanity and vexation of spirit.

6:9

19.18

A good name is better than precious ointment; and the day of death than the day of one's birth.

It is better to go to the house of mourning, than to go to the house of feasting: for that is the end of all men; and the living will lay it to his heart.

7:1–2

19.19

For as the crackling of thorns under a pot, so is the laughter of the fool: this also is vanity.

7:6

19.20

Better is the end of a thing than the beginning thereof: and the patient in spirit is better than the proud in spirit.

7:8

19.21

Wisdom is good with an inheritance: and by it there is profit to them that see the sun.

7:11

19.22

In the day of prosperity be joyful, but in the day of adversity consider: God also hath set the one over against the other, to the end that man should find nothing after him.

All things have I seen in the days of my vanity: there is a just man that perisheth in his righteousness, and there is a wicked man that prolongeth his life in his wickedness.

Be not righteous over much; neither make thyself over wise: why shouldest thou destroy thyself?

7:14–16

19.23

Lo, this only have I found, that God hath made man upright; but they have sought out many inventions.

7:29

19.24

There is no man that hath power over the spirit to retain the spirit; neither hath he power in the day of death: and there is no discharge in that war; neither shall wickedness deliver those that are given to it.

8:8

19.25

Then I commended mirth, because a man hath no better thing under the sun, than to eat, and to drink, and to be merry: for that shall abide with him of his labour the days of his life, which God giveth him under the sun.

8:15

19.26

For to him that is joined to all the living there is hope: for a living dog is better than a dead lion.

For the living know that they shall die: but the dead know not any thing, neither have they any more a reward; for the memory of them is forgotten.

Also their love, and their hatred, and their envy, is now perished; neither have they any more a portion for ever in any thing that is done under the sun.

9:4–6

19.27

Go thy way, eat thy bread with joy, and drink thy wine with a merry heart; for God now accepteth thy works.

9:7

19.28

Whatsoever thy hand findeth to do, do it with thy might; for there is no work, nor device, nor knowledge, nor wisdom, in the grave, whither thou goest.

9:10

19.29

I returned, and saw under the sun, that the race is not to the swift, nor the battle to the strong, neither yet bread to the wise, nor yet riches to men of understanding, nor yet favour to men of skill; but time and chance happeneth to them all.

For man also knoweth not his time: as the fishes that are taken in an evil net, and as the birds that are caught in the snare; so are the sons of men snared in an evil time, when it falleth suddenly upon them.

9:11–12

19.30

The words of wise men are heard in quiet more than the cry of him that ruleth among fools.

9:17

19.31

Dead flies cause the ointment of the apothecary to send forth a stinking savour: so doth a little folly him that is in reputation for wisdom and honour.

10:1

19.32

He that diggeth a pit shall fall into it; and whoso breaketh an hedge, a serpent shall bite him.

10:8

19.33

By much slothfulness the building decayeth;

and through idleness of the hands the house droppeth through.

10:18

19.34

A feast is made for laughter, and wine maketh merry: but money answereth all things.

10:19

19.35

Curse not the king, no not in thy thought; and curse not the rich in thy bedchamber: for a bird of the air shall carry the voice, and that which hath wings shall tell the matter.

10:20

19.36

Cast thy bread upon the waters: for thou shalt find it after many days.

11:1

19.37

If the clouds be full of rain, they empty themselves upon the earth: and if the tree fall toward the south, or toward the north, in the place where the tree falleth, there it shall be.

11:3

19.38

He that observeth the wind shall not sow; and he that regardeth the clouds shall not reap.

11:4

19.39

In the morning sow thy seed, and in the evening withhold not thine hand: for thou knowest not whether shall prosper, either this or that, or whether they both shall be alike good.

11:6

19.40

Remember now thy Creator in the days of thy youth, while the evil days come not, nor the years draw nigh, when thou shalt say, I have no pleasure in them;
While the sun, or the light, or the moon, or the stars, be not darkened, nor the clouds return after the rain:
In the day when the keepers of the house shall tremble, and the strong men shall bow themselves, and the grinders cease because they are few, and those that look out of the windows be darkened,
And the doors shall be shut in the streets, when the sound of the grinding is low, and he shall rise up at the voice of the bird, and all the daughters of musick shall be brought low;
Also when they shall be afraid of that which is high, and fears shall be in the way, and the almond tree shall flourish, and the grasshopper shall be a burden, and desire shall fail: because man goeth to his long home, and the mourners go about the streets:
Or ever the silver cord be loosed, or the golden bowl be broken, or the pitcher be broken at the fountain, or the wheel broken at the cistern.
Then shall the dust return to the earth as it was: and the spirit shall return unto God who gave it.

12:1–7

19.41

And further, by these, my son, be admonished: of making many books there is no end; and much study is a weariness of the flesh.

12:12

19.42

Let us hear the conclusion of the whole matter: Fear God, and keep his commandments: for this is the whole duty of man.

12:13

20 Song of Solomon

20.1

The song of songs, which is Solomon's.
Let him kiss me with the kisses of his mouth: for thy love is better than wine.
Because of the savour of thy good ointments thy name is as ointment poured forth, therefore do the virgins love thee.
Draw me, we will run after thee: the king hath brought me into his chambers: we will be glad and rejoice in thee, we will remember thy love more than wine: the upright love thee.
I am black, but comely, O ye daughters of Jerusalem, as the tents of Kedar, as the curtains of Solomon.
Look not upon me, because I am black, because the sun hath looked upon me: my mother's children were angry with me; they made me the keeper of the vineyards; but mine own vineyard have I not kept.
Tell me, O thou whom my soul loveth, where thou feedest, where thou makest thy flock to rest at noon: for why should I be as one that turneth aside by the flocks of thy companions?
If thou know not, O thou fairest among women, go thy way forth by the footsteps of the flock, and feed thy kids beside the shepherds' tents.
I have compared thee, O my love, to a company of horses in Pharaoh's chariots.

1:1–9

20.2

A bundle of myrrh is my wellbeloved unto me; he shall lie all night betwixt my breasts.

1:13

20.3

I am the rose of Sharon, and the lily of the valleys.
As the lily among thorns, so is my love among the daughters.

2:1–2

20.4
He brought me to the banqueting house, and his banner over me was love.
Stay me with flagons, comfort me with apples: for I am sick of love.
His left hand is under my head, and his right hand doth embrace me.

2:4–6

20.5
The voice of my beloved! behold, he cometh leaping upon the mountains, skipping upon the hills.

2:8

20.6
My beloved spake, and said unto me, Rise up, my love, my fair one, and come away.
For, lo, the winter is past, the rain is over and gone;
The flowers appear on the earth; the time of the singing of birds is come, and the voice of the turtle is heard in our land.

2:10–12

20.7
Take us the foxes, the little foxes, that spoil the vines: for our vines have tender grapes.

2:15

20.8
My beloved is mine, and I am his: he feedeth among the lilies.
Until the day break, and the shadows flee away, turn, my beloved, and be thou like a roe or a young hart upon the mountains of Bether.

2:16–17

20.9
By night on my bed I sought him whom my soul loveth: I sought him, but I found him not.

3:1

20.10
They all hold swords, being expert in war: every man hath his sword upon his thigh because of fear in the night.

3:8

20.11
Behold, thou art fair, my love, behold, thou art fair; thou hast doves' eyes within thy locks; thy hair is as a flock of goats, that appear from mount Gilead.
Thy teeth are like a flock of sheep that are even shorn, which came up from the washing; whereof every one bear twins, and none is barren among them.
Thy lips are like a thread of scarlet, and thy speech is comely: thy temples are like a piece of a pomegranate within thy locks.
Thy neck is like the tower of David builded for an armoury, whereon there hang a thousand bucklers, all shields of mighty men.
Thy two breasts are like two young roes that are twins, which feed among the lilies.
Until the day break, and the shadows flee away, I will get me to the mountain of myrrh, and to the hill of frankincense.
Thou art all fair, my love; there is no spot in thee.

4:1–7

20.12
A garden inclosed is my sister, my spouse; a spring shut up, a fountain sealed.

4:12

20.13
A fountain of gardens, a well of living waters, and streams from Lebanon.

4:15

20.14
Awake, O north wind; and come, thou south; blow upon my garden, that the spices thereof may flow out. Let my beloved come into his garden, and eat his pleasant fruits.

4:16

20.15
I am come into my garden, my sister, my spouse: I have gathered my myrrh with my spice; I have eaten my honeycomb with my honey; I have drunk my wine with my milk: eat, O friends; drink, yea, drink abundantly, O beloved.
I sleep, but my heart waketh: it is the voice of my beloved that knocketh, saying, Open to me, my sister, my love, my dove, my undefiled: for my head is filled with dew, and my locks with the drops of the night.

5:1–2

20.16
My beloved put in his hand by the hole of the door, and my bowels were moved for him.

5:4

20.17
My beloved is white and ruddy, the chiefest among ten thousand.

5:10

20.18
My beloved is gone down into his garden, to the beds of spices, to feed in the gardens, and to gather lilies.
I am my beloved's, and my beloved is mine: he feedeth among the lilies.

6:2–3

20.19
Who is she that looketh forth as the morning, fair as the moon, clear as the sun, and terrible as an army with banners?

6:10

20.20
Return, return, O Shulamite; return, return, that we may look upon thee. What will ye see

in the Shulamite? As it were the company of two armies.

6:13

20.21
How beautiful are thy feet with shoes, O prince's daughter! the joints of thy thighs are like jewels, the work of the hands of a cunning workman.
Thy navel is like a round goblet, which wanteth not liquor: thy belly is like an heap of wheat set about with lilies.

7:1–2

20.22
How fair and how pleasant art thou, O love, for delights!

7:6

20.23
I am my beloved's, and his desire is toward me.

7:10

20.24
I charge you, O daughters of Jerusalem, that ye stir not up, nor awake my love, until he please.

8:4

20.25
Who is this that cometh up from the wilderness, leaning upon her beloved? I raised thee up under the apple tree: there thy mother brought thee forth: there she brought thee forth that bare thee.

8:5

20.26
Set me as a seal upon thine heart, as a seal upon thine arm: for love is strong as death; jealousy is cruel as the grave: the coals thereof are coals of fire, which hath a most vehement flame.
Many waters cannot quench love, neither can the floods drown it: if a man would give all the substance of his house for love, it would utterly be contemned.

8:6–7

20.27
Make haste, my beloved, and be thou like to a roe or to a young hart upon the mountains of spices.

8:14

21 Isaiah

21.1
The ox knoweth his owner, and the ass his master's crib: but Israel doth not know, my people doth not consider.

1:3

21.2
And the daughter of Zion is left as a cottage in a vineyard, as a lodge in a garden of cucumbers, as a besieged city.

1:8

21.3
Bring no more vain oblations; incense is an abomination unto me; the new moons and sabbaths, the calling of assemblies, I cannot away with; it is iniquity, even the solemn meeting.

1:13

21.4
Come now, and let us reason together, saith the Lord: though your sins be as scarlet, they shall be as white as snow; though they be red like crimson, they shall be as wool.

1:18

21.5
How is the faithful city become an harlot! it was full of judgment; righteousness lodged in it; but now murderers.

1:21

21.6
And it shall come to pass in the last days, that the mountain of the Lord's house shall be established in the top of the mountains, and shall be exalted above the hills; and all nations shall flow unto it.

2:2

21.7
And he shall judge among the nations, and shall rebuke many people: and they shall beat their swords into plowshares, and their spears into pruning-hooks: nation shall not lift up sword against nation, neither shall they learn war any more.

2:4

21.8
And they shall go into the holes of the rocks, and into the caves of the earth, for fear of the Lord, and for the glory of his majesty, when he ariseth to shake terribly the earth.

2:19

21.9
Cease ye from man, whose breath is in his nostrils: for wherein is he to be accounted of?

2:22

21.10
For, behold, the Lord, the Lord of hosts, doth take away from Jerusalem and from Judah the stay and the staff, the whole stay of bread, and the whole stay of water,
The mighty man, and the man of war, the judge, and the prophet, and the prudent, and the ancient,
The captain of fifty, and the honourable man, and the counsellor, and the cunning artificer, and the eloquent orator.
And I will give children to be their princes, and babes shall rule over them.
And the people shall be oppressed, every one

by another, and every one by his neighbour: the child shall behave himself proudly against the ancient, and the base against the honourable.

3:1–5

21.11
What mean ye that ye beat my people to pieces, and grind the faces of the poor? saith the Lord God of hosts.

3:15

21.12
And in that day seven women shall take hold of one man, saying, We will eat our own bread, and wear our own apparel: only let us be called by thy name, to take away our reproach.

4:1

21.13
Now will I sing to my wellbeloved a song of my beloved touching his vineyard. My wellbeloved hath a vineyard in a very fruitful hill:
And he fenced it, and gathered out the stones thereof, and planted it with the choicest vine, and built a tower in the midst of it, and also made a winepress therein: and he looked that it should bring forth grapes, and it brought forth wild grapes.

5:1–2

21.14
For the vineyard of the Lord of hosts is the house of Israel, and the men of Judah his pleasant plant: and he looked for judgment, but behold oppression; for righteousness, but behold a cry.
Woe unto them that join house to house, that lay field to field, till there be no place, that they may be placed alone in the midst of the earth!

5:7–8

21.15
Woe unto them that rise up early in the morning, that they may follow strong drink; that continue until night, till wine inflame them!

5:11

21.16
Woe unto them that call evil good, and good evil; that put darkness for light, and light for darkness; that put bitter for sweet, and sweet for bitter!

5:20

21.17
In the year that king Uzziah died I saw also the Lord sitting upon a throne, high and lifted up, and his train filled the temple.
Above it stood the seraphims: each one had six wings; with twain he covered his face, and with twain he covered his feet, and with twain he did fly.
And one cried unto another, and said, Holy, holy, holy, is the Lord of hosts: the whole earth is full of his glory.
And the posts of the door moved at the voice of him that cried, and the house was filled with smoke.
Then said I, Woe is me! for I am undone; because I am a man of unclean lips, and I dwell in the midst of a people of unclean lips: for mine eyes have seen the King, the Lord of hosts.
Then flew one of the seraphims unto me, having a live coal in his hand, which he had taken with the tongs from off the altar:
And he laid it upon my mouth, and said, Lo, this hath touched thy lips; and thine iniquity is taken away, and thy sin purged.
Also I heard the voice of the Lord, saying, Whom shall I send, and who will go for us? Then said I, Here am I; send me.

6:1–8

21.18
Make the heart of this people fat, and make their ears heavy, and shut their eyes; lest they see with their eyes, and hear with their ears, and understand with their heart, and convert, and be healed.
Then said I, Lord, how long? And he answered, Until the cities be wasted without inhabitant, and the houses without man, and the land be utterly desolate.

6:10–11

21.19
Therefore the Lord himself shall give you a sign; Behold, a virgin shall conceive, and bear a son, and shall call his name Immanuel.
Butter and honey shall he eat, that he may know to refuse the evil, and choose the good.

7:14–15

21.20
And he shall be for a sanctuary; but for a stone of stumbling and for a rock of offence to both the houses of Israel, for a gin and for a snare to the inhabitants of Jerusalem.

8:14

21.21
And when they shall say unto you, Seek unto them that have familiar spirits, and unto wizards that peep, and that mutter: should not a people seek unto their God? for the living to the dead?

8:19

21.22
The people that walked in darkness have seen a great light: they that dwell in the land of the shadow of death, upon them hath the light shined.
Thou hast multiplied the nation, and not increased the joy: they joy before thee accord-

ing to the joy in harvest, and as men rejoice when they divide the spoil.
For thou hast broken the yoke of his burden, and the staff of his shoulder, the rod of his oppressor, as in the day of Midian.

9:2–4

21.23
For unto us a child is born, unto us a son is given: and the government shall be upon his shoulder: and his name shall be called Wonderful, Counsellor, The mighty God, The everlasting Father, The Prince of Peace.
Of the increase of his government and peace there shall be no end, upon the throne of David, and upon his kingdom, to order it, and to establish it with judgment and with justice from henceforth even for ever. The zeal of the Lord of hosts will perform this.

9:6–7

21.24
Shall the axe boast itself against him that heweth therewith? or shall the saw magnify itself against him that shaketh it? as if the rod should shake itself against them that lift it up, or as if the staff should lift up itself, as if it were no wood.

10:15

21.25
And there shall come forth a rod out of the stem of Jesse, and a Branch shall grow out of his roots:
And the spirit of the Lord shall rest upon him, the spirit of wisdom and understanding, the spirit of counsel and might, the spirit of knowledge and of the fear of the Lord.

11:1–2

21.26
The wolf also shall dwell with the lamb, and the leopard shall lie down with the kid; and the calf and the young lion and the fatling together: and a little child shall lead them.
And the cow and the bear shall feed; their young ones shall lie down together: and the lion shall eat straw like the ox.
And the sucking child shall play on the hole of the asp, and the weaned child shall put his hand on the cockatrice' den.
They shall not hurt nor destroy in all my holy mountain: for the earth shall be full of the knowledge of the Lord, as the waters cover the sea.

11:6–9

21.27
Therefore with joy shall ye draw water out of the wells of salvation.

12:3

21.28
But wild beasts of the desert shall lie there; and their houses shall be full of doleful creatures; and owls shall dwell there, and satyrs shall dance there.
And the wild beasts of the islands shall cry in their desolate houses, and dragons in their pleasant palaces: and her time is near to come, and her days shall not be prolonged.

13:21–22

21.29
That thou shalt take up this proverb against the king of Babylon, and say, How hath the oppressor ceased! the golden city ceased!

14:4

21.30
Thy pomp is brought down to the grave, and the noise of thy viols: the worm is spread under thee, and the worms cover thee.
How art thou fallen from heaven, O Lucifer, son of the morning! how art thou cut down to the ground, which didst weaken the nations!

14:11–12

21.31
I will also make it a possession for the bittern, and pools of water: and I will sweep it with the besom of destruction, saith the Lord of hosts.

14:23

21.32
And in mercy shall the throne be established: and he shall sit upon it in truth in the tabernacle of David, judging, and seeking judgment, and hasting righteousness.

16:5

21.33
At that day shall a man look to his Maker, and his eyes shall have respect to the Holy One of Israel.

17:7

21.34
He calleth to me out of Seir, Watchman, what of the night? Watchman, what of the night?
The watchman said, The morning cometh, and also the night: if ye will enquire, enquire ye: return, come.

21:11–12

21.35
And behold joy and gladness, slaying oxen, and killing sheep, eating flesh, and drinking wine: let us eat and drink; for tomorrow we shall die.

22:13

21.36
And the key of the house of David will I lay upon his shoulder; so he shall open, and none shall shut; and he shall shut, and none shall open.
And I will fasten him as a nail in a sure place; and he shall be for a glorious throne to his father's house.

22:22–23

21.37
Who hath taken this counsel against Tyre, the crowning city, whose merchants are princes, whose traffickers are the honourable of the earth?

23:8

21.38
Take an harp, go about the city, thou harlot that hast been forgotten; make sweet melody, sing many songs, that thou mayest be remembered.

23:16

21.39
They shall not drink wine with a song; strong drink shall be bitter to them that drink it.

24:9

21.40
In that day the Lord with his sore and great and strong sword shall punish leviathan the piercing serpent, even leviathan that crooked serpent; and he shall slay the dragon that is in the sea.

27:1

21.41
For precept must be upon precept, precept upon precept; line upon line, line upon line; here a little, and there a little.

28:10

21.42
Therefore thus saith the Lord God, Behold, I lay in Zion for a foundation a stone, a tried stone, a precious corner stone, a sure foundation: he that believeth shall not make haste.
Judgment also will I lay to the line, and righteousness to the plummet: and the hail shall sweep away the refuge of lies, and the waters shall overflow the hiding place.
And your covenant with death shall be disannulled, and your agreement with hell shall not stand; when the overflowing scourge shall pass through, then ye shall be trodden down by it.

28:16–18

21.43
Stay yourselves, and wonder; cry ye out, and cry: they are drunken, but not with wine; they stagger, but not with strong drink.

29:9

21.44
For the Egyptians shall help in vain, and to no purpose: therefore have I cried concerning this, Their strength is to sit still.

30:7

21.45
Which say to the seers, See not; and to the prophets, Prophesy not unto us right things, speak unto us smooth things, prophesy deceits.

30:10

21.46
And he shall break it as the breaking of the potters' vessel that is broken in pieces; he shall not spare: so that there shall not be found in the bursting of it a sherd to take fire from the hearth, or to take water withal out of the pit.

30:14

21.47
One thousand shall flee at the rebuke of one; at the rebuke of five shall ye flee: till ye be left as a beacon upon the top of a mountain, and as an ensign on an hill.

30:17

21.48
And though the Lord give you the bread of adversity, and the water of affliction, yet shall not thy teachers be removed into a corner any more, but thine eyes shall see thy teachers.

30:20

21.49
And thine ears shall hear a word behind thee, saying, This is the way, walk ye in it, when ye turn to the right hand, and when ye turn to the left.

30:21

21.50
And a man shall be as an hiding place from the wind, and a covert from the tempest; as rivers of water in a dry place, as the shadow of a great rock in a weary land.

32:2

21.51
And thorns shall come up in her palaces, nettles and brambles in the fortresses thereof: and it shall be an habitation of dragons, and a court for owls.
The wild beasts of the desert shall also meet with the wild beasts of the island, and the satyr shall cry to his fellow; the screech owl also shall rest there, and find for herself a place of rest.
There shall the great owl make her nest, and lay, and hatch, and gather under her shadow: there shall the vultures also be gathered, every one with her mate.

34:13–15

21.52
The wilderness and the solitary place shall be glad for them; and the desert shall rejoice, and blossom as the rose.

35:1

21.53
Strengthen ye the weak hands, and confirm the feeble knees.

35:3

21.54
Then the eyes of the blind shall be opened, and the ears of the deaf shall be unstopped.
Then shall the lame man leap as an hart, and the tongue of the dumb sing: for in the

wilderness shall waters break out, and streams in the desert.
And the parched ground shall become a pool, and the thirsty land springs of water: in the habitation of dragons, where each lay, shall be grass with reeds and rushes.

35:5–7

21.55
And the ransomed of the Lord shall return, and come to Zion with songs and everlasting joy upon their heads: they shall obtain joy and gladness, and sorrow and sighing shall flee away.

35:10

21.56
Lo, thou trustest in the staff of this broken reed, on Egypt; whereon if a man lean, it will go into his hand, and pierce it: so is Pharaoh king of Egypt to all that trust in him.

36:6

21.57
Like a crane or a swallow, so did I chatter: I did mourn as a dove: mine eyes fail with looking upward: O Lord, I am oppressed; undertake for me.
What shall I say? he hath both spoken unto me, and himself hath done it: I shall go softly all my years in the bitterness of my soul.

38:14–15

21.58
For the grave cannot praise thee, death cannot celebrate thee: they that go down into the pit cannot hope for thy truth.

38:18

21.59
Comfort ye, comfort ye my people, saith your God.
Speak ye comfortably to Jerusalem, and cry unto her, that her warfare is accomplished, that her iniquity is pardoned: for she hath received of the Lord's hand double for all her sins.
The voice of him that crieth in the wilderness, Prepare ye the way of the Lord, make straight in the desert a highway for our God.
Every valley shall be exalted, and every mountain and hill shall be made low: and the crooked shall be made straight, and the rough places plain:
And the glory of the Lord shall be revealed, and all flesh shall see it together: for the mouth of the Lord hath spoken it.
The voice said, Cry. And he said, What shall I cry? All flesh is grass, and all the goodliness thereof is as the flower of the field:
The grass withereth, the flower fadeth: because the spirit of the Lord bloweth upon it: surely the people is grass.
The grass withereth, the flower fadeth: but the word of our God shall stand for ever.
O Zion, that bringest good tidings, get thee up into the high mountain; O Jerusalem, that bringest good tidings, lift up thy voice with strength; lift it up, be not afraid; say unto the cities of Judah, Behold your God!

40:1–9

21.60
He shall feed his flock like a shepherd: he shall gather the lambs with his arm, and carry them in his bosom, and shall gently lead those that are with young.

40:11

21.61
Behold, the nations are as a drop of a bucket, and are counted as the small dust of the balance: behold, he taketh up the isles as a very little thing.

40:15

21.62
Have ye not known? have ye not heard? hath it not been told you from the beginning? have ye not understood from the foundations of the earth?
It is he that sitteth upon the circle of the earth, and the inhabitants thereof are as grasshoppers; that stretcheth out the heavens as a curtain, and spreadeth them out as a tent to dwell in.

40:21–22

21.63
Yea, they shall not be planted; yea, they shall not be sown: yea, their stock shall not take root in the earth: and he shall also blow upon them, and they shall wither, and the whirlwind shall take them away as stubble.

40:24

21.64
But they that wait upon the Lord shall renew their strength; they shall mount up with wings as eagles; they shall run, and not be weary; and they shall walk, and not faint.

40:31

21.65
The isles saw it, and feared; the ends of the earth were afraid, drew near, and came.
They helped every one his neighbour; and every one said to his brother, Be of good courage.

41:5–6

21.66
A bruised reed shall he not break, and the smoking flax shall he not quench: he shall bring forth judgment unto truth.
He shall not fail nor be discouraged, till he have set judgment in the earth: and the isles shall wait for his law.

42:3–4

21.67
Fear not: for I am with thee: I will bring thy seed from the east, and gather thee from the west;
I will say to the north, Give up; and to the south, Keep not back: bring my sons from far, and my daughters from the ends of the earth.
43:5–6

21.68
He burneth part thereof in the fire; with part thereof he eateth flesh; he roasteth roast, and is satisfied: yea, he warmeth himself, and saith, Aha, I am warm, I have seen the fire.
44:16

21.69
Woe unto him that striveth with his Maker! Let the potsherd strive with the potsherds of the earth. Shall the clay say to him that fashioneth it, What makest thou? or thy work, He hath no hands?
45:9

21.70
Verily thou art a God that hidest thyself, O God of Israel, the Saviour.
45:15

21.71
Come down, and sit in the dust, O virgin daughter of Babylon, sit on the ground: there is no throne, O daughter of the Chaldeans: for thou shalt no more be called tender and delicate.
47:1

21.72
Behold, I have refined thee, but not with silver; I have chosen thee in the furnace of affliction.
48:10

21.73
O that thou hadst hearkened to my commandments! then had thy peace been as a river, and thy righteousness as the waves of the sea.
48:18

21.74
There is no peace, saith the Lord, unto the wicked.
48:22

21.75
Can a woman forget her sucking child, that she should not have compassion on the son of her womb? yea, they may forget, yet will I not forget thee.
49:15

21.76
And kings shall be thy nursing fathers, and their queens thy nursing mothers: they shall bow down to thee with their face toward the earth, and lick up the dust of thy feet; and thou shalt know that I am the Lord: for they shall not be ashamed that wait for me.
49:23

21.77
The Lord God hath given me the tongue of the learned, that I should know how to speak a word in season to him that is weary: he wakeneth morning by morning, he wakeneth mine ear to hear as the learned.
50:4

21.78
I gave my back to the smiters, and my cheeks to them that plucked off the hair: I hid not my face from shame and spitting.
50:6

21.79
For the Lord shall comfort Zion: he will comfort all her waste places; and he will make her wilderness like Eden, and her desert like the garden of the Lord; joy and gladness shall be found therein, thanksgiving, and the voice of melody.
51:3

21.80
How beautiful upon the mountains are the feet of him that bringeth good tidings, that publisheth peace; that bringeth good tidings of good, that publisheth salvation; that saith unto Zion, Thy God reigneth!
Thy watchmen shall lift up the voice; with the voice together shall they sing: for they shall see eye to eye, when the Lord shall bring again Zion.
52:7–8

21.81
Who hath believed our report? and to whom is the arm of the Lord revealed?
For he shall grow up before him as a tender plant, and as a root out of a dry ground: he hath no form nor comeliness; and when we shall see him, there is no beauty that we should desire him.
He is despised and rejected of men: a man of sorrows, and acquainted with grief: and we hid as it were our faces from him; he was despised, and we esteemed him not.
Surely he hath borne our griefs, and carried our sorrows: yet we did esteem him stricken, smitten of God, and afflicted.
But he was wounded for our transgressions, he was bruised for our iniquities: the chastisement of our peace was upon him; and with his stripes we are healed.
All we like sheep have gone astray; we have turned every one to his own way; and the Lord hath laid on him the iniquity of us all.
He was oppressed, and he was afflicted, yet he opened not his mouth: he is brought as a lamb to the slaughter, and as a sheep before her shearers is dumb, so he openeth not his mouth.
He was taken from prison and from judgment: and who shall declare his generation?

for he was cut off out of the land of the living: for the transgression of my people was he stricken.

53:1–8

21.82

He shall see of the travail of his soul, and shall be satisfied: by his knowledge shall my righteous servant justify many; for he shall bear their iniquities.

Therefore will I divide him a portion with the great, and he shall divide the spoil with the strong; because he hath poured out his soul unto death: and he was numbered with the transgressors; and he bare the sin of many, and made intercession for the transgressors.

53:11–12

21.83

For a small moment have I forsaken thee; but with great mercies will I gather thee.

In a little wrath I hid my face from thee for a moment; but with everlasting kindness will I have mercy on thee, saith the Lord thy Redeemer.

54:7–8

21.84

Ho, every one that thirsteth, come ye to the waters, and he that hath no money; come ye, buy, and eat; yea, come, buy wine and milk without money and without price.

Wherefore do ye spend money for that which is not bread? and your labour for that which satisfieth not? hearken diligently unto me, and eat ye that which is good, and let your soul delight itself in fatness.

55:1–2

21.85

Seek ye the Lord while he may be found, call ye upon him while he is near.

55:6

21.86

For my thoughts are not your thoughts, neither are your ways my ways, saith the Lord.

For as the heavens are higher than the earth, so are my ways higher than your ways, and my thoughts than your thoughts.

55:8–9

21.87

Instead of the thorn shall come up the fir tree, and instead of the brier shall come up the myrtle tree: and it shall be to the Lord for a name, for an everlasting sign that shall not be cut off.

55:13

21.88

Even unto them will I give in mine house and within my walls a place and a name better than of sons and of daughters: I will give them an everlasting name, that shall not be cut off.

56:5

21.89

The righteous perisheth, and no man layeth it to heart: and merciful men are taken away, none considering that the righteous is taken away from the evil to come.

57:1

21.90

I create the fruit of the lips; Peace, peace to him that is far off, and to him that is near, saith the Lord; and I will heal him.

57:19

21.91

Then shall thy light break forth as the morning, and thine health shall spring forth speedily: and thy righteousness shall go before thee; the glory of the Lord shall be thy rereward.

58:8

21.92

And if thou draw out thy soul to the hungry, and satisfy the afflicted soul; then shall thy light rise in obscurity, and thy darkness be as the noonday.

58:10

21.93

Their feet run to evil, and they make haste to shed innocent blood: their thoughts are thoughts of iniquity; wasting and destruction are in their paths.

59:7

21.94

Arise, shine; for thy light is come, and the glory of the Lord is risen upon thee.

For, behold, the darkness shall cover the earth, and gross darkness the people: but the Lord shall arise upon thee, and his glory shall be seen upon thee.

And the Gentiles shall come to thy light, and kings to the brightness of thy rising.

60:1–3

21.95

A little one shall become a thousand, and a small one a strong nation: I the Lord will hasten it in his time.

60:22

21.96

The Spirit of the Lord God is upon me; because the Lord hath anointed me to preach good tidings unto the meek; he hath sent me to bind up the brokenhearted, to proclaim liberty to the captives, and the opening of the prison to them that are bound;

To proclaim the acceptable year of the Lord, and the day of vengeance of our God; to comfort all that mourn;

To appoint unto them that mourn in Zion, to give unto them beauty for ashes, the oil of joy for mourning, the garment of praise for the spirit of heaviness; that they might be called trees of righteousness, the planting of the Lord, that he might be glorified.

61:1–3

21.97

I have trodden the winepress alone; and of the people there was none with me: for I will tread them in mine anger, and trample them in my fury; and their blood shall be sprinkled upon my garments, and I will stain all my raiment.

63:3

21.98

In all their affliction he was afflicted, and the angel of his presence saved them: in his love and in his pity he redeemed them; and he bare them, and carried them all the days of old.

63:9

21.99

Oh that thou wouldest rend the heavens, that thou wouldest come down, that the mountains might flow down at thy presence.

64:1

21.100

But we are all as an unclean thing, and all our righteousnesses are as filthy rags; and we all do fade as a leaf; and our iniquities, like the wind, have taken us away.

64:6

21.101

Which say, Stand by thyself, come not near to me; for I am holier than thou. These are a smoke in my nose, a fire that burneth all the day.

65:5

21.102

And they shall build houses, and inhabit them; and they shall plant vineyards, and eat the fruit of them.

They shall not build, and another inhabit; they shall not plant, and another eat: for as the days of a tree are the days of my people, and mine elect shall long enjoy the work of their hands.

65:21–22

21.103

For, behold, I create new heavens and a new earth: and the former shall not be remembered, nor come into mind.

65:17

22 Jeremiah

22.1

They were as fed horses in the morning: every one neighed after his neighbour's wife.

5:8

22.2

But this people hath a revolting and a rebellious heart; they are revolted and gone.

5:23

22.3

As a cage is full of birds, so are their houses full of deceit: therefore they are become great, and waxen rich.

5:27

22.4

They have healed also the hurt of the daughter of my people slightly, saying, Peace, peace; when there is no peace.

6:14

22.5

We looked for peace, but no good came; and for a time of health, and behold trouble!

8:15

22.6

The harvest is past, the summer is ended, and we are not saved.

8:20

22.7

Is there no balm in Gilead: is there no physician there? why then is not the health of the daughter of my people recovered?

8:22

22.8

There is no more triacle [treacle] in Gilead.

Great Bible 8:22

22.9

Can the Ethiopian change his skin, or the leopard his spots? then may ye also do good, that are accustomed to do evil.

13:23

22.10

Then the Lord said unto me, The prophets prophesy lies in my name: I sent them not, neither have I commanded them, neither spake unto them: they prophesy unto you a false vision and divination, and a thing of nought, and the deceit of their heart.

14:14

22.11

And it shall come to pass, if they say unto thee, Whither shall we go forth? then thou shalt tell them, Thus saith the Lord; Such as are for death, to death; and such as are for the sword, to the sword; and such as are for the famine, to the famine; and such as are for the captivity, to the captivity.

15:2

22.12

Woe is me, my mother, that thou hast borne me a man of strife and a man of contention to the whole earth! I have neither lent on usury, nor men have lent to me on usury; yet every one of them doth curse me.

15:10

22.13
The heart is deceitful above all things, and desperately wicked: who can know it?
17:9

22.14
As the partridge sitteth on eggs, and hatcheth them not, so he that getteth riches, and not by right, shall leave them in the midst of his days, and at his end shall be a fool.
17:11

22.15
Woe be unto the pastors that destroy and scatter the sheep of my pasture! saith the Lord.
23:1

22.16
Am I a God at hand, saith the Lord, and not a God afar off?
23:23

22.17
As for me, behold, I am in your hand: do with me as seemeth good and meet unto you.
26:14

22.18
And I set before the sons of the house of the Rechabites pots full of wine, and cups, and I said unto them, Drink ye wine.
But they said, We will drink no wine: for Jonadab the son of Rechab our father commanded us, saying, Ye shall drink no wine, neither ye, nor your sons for ever.
35:5–6

22.19
And seekest thou great things for thyself? seek them not: for, behold, I will bring evil upon all flesh, saith the Lord: but thy life will I give unto thee for a prey in all places whither thou goest.
45:5

22.20
How say ye, We are mighty and strong men for the war?
48:14

22.21
Arise, get you up unto the wealthy nation, that dwelleth without care, saith the Lord, which have neither gates nor bars, which dwell alone.
49:31

22.22
In their heat I will make their feasts, and I will make them drunken, that they may rejoice, and sleep a perpetual sleep, and not wake, saith the Lord.
51:39

23 Lamentations

23.1
How doth the city sit solitary, that was full of people! how is she become as a widow! she that was great among the nations, and princess among the provinces, how is she become tributary!
1:1

23.2
Is it nothing to you, all ye that pass by? behold, and see if there be any sorrow like unto my sorrow, which is done unto me, wherewith the Lord hath afflicted me in the day of his fierce anger.
1:12

23.3
And I said, My strength and my hope is perished from the Lord:
Remembering mine affliction and my misery, the wormwood and the gall.
3:18–19

23.4
It is of the Lord's mercies that we are not consumed, because his compassions fail not.
They are new every morning: great is thy faithfulness.
3:22–23

23.5
It is good for a man that he bear the yoke in his youth.
3:27

23.6
Waters flowed over mine head; then I said, I am cut off.
3:54

24 Ezekiel

24.1
And thou, son of man, be not afraid of them, neither be afraid of their words, though briers and thorns be with thee, and thou dost dwell among scorpions: be not afraid of their words, nor be dismayed at their looks, though they be a rebellious house.
2:6

24.2
And I will give them one heart, and I will put a new spirit within you; and I will take the stony heart out of their flesh, and will give them an heart of flesh.
11:19

24.3
Son of man, thou dwellest in the midst of a rebellious house, which have eyes to see, and see not; they have ears to hear, and hear not: for they are a rebellious house.
12:2

24.4
Son of man, what is that proverb that ye have

in the land of Israel, saying, The days are prolonged, and every vision faileth?

12:22

24.5

Behold, every one that useth proverbs shall use this proverb against thee, saying, As is the mother, so is her daughter.

Thou are thy mother's daughter, that lotheth her husband and her children; and thou art the sister of thy sisters, which lothed their husbands and their children: your mother was an Hittite, and your father an Amorite.

16:44–45

24.6

What mean ye, that ye use this proverb concerning the land of Israel, saying, The fathers have eaten sour grapes, and the children's teeth are set on edge?

18:2

24.7

Again, when the wicked man turneth away from his wickedness that he hath committed, and doeth that which is lawful and right, he shall save his soul alive.

18:27

24.8

For the king of Babylon stood at the parting of the way, at the head of the two ways, to use divination: he made his arrows bright, he consulted with images, he looked in the liver.

21:21

24.9

And Aholah played the harlot when she was mine; and she doted on her lovers, on the Assyrians her neighbours,

Which were clothed with blue, captains and rulers, all of them desirable young men, horsemen riding upon horses.

23:5–6

24.10

It shall be a place for the spreading of nets in the midst of the sea: for I have spoken it, saith the Lord God: and it shall become a spoil to the nations.

26:5

24.11

The hand of the Lord was upon me, and carried me out in the spirit of the Lord, and set me down in the midst of the valley which was full of bones,

And caused me to pass by them round about: and, behold, there were very many in the open valley; and, lo, they were very dry.

And he said unto me, Son of man, can these bones live? And I answered, O Lord God, thou knowest.

Again he said unto me, Prophesy upon these bones, and say unto them, O ye dry bones, hear the word of the Lord.

37:1–4

24.12

So I prophesied as I was commanded: and as I prophesied, there was a noise, and behold a shaking, and the bones came together, bone to his bone.

37:7

24.13

And the man said unto me, Son of man, behold with thine eyes, and hear with thine ears, and set thine heart upon all that I shall shew thee; for to the intent that I might shew them unto thee art thou brought hither: declare all that thou seest to the house of Israel.

40:4

25 Daniel

25.1

Children in whom was no blemish, but well favoured, and skilful in all wisdom, and cunning in knowledge, and understanding science, and such as had ability in them to stand in the king's palace, and whom they might teach the learning and the tongue of the Chaldeans.

1:4

25.2

And he changeth the times and the seasons: he removeth kings, and setteth up kings: he giveth wisdom unto the wise, and knowledge to them that know understanding:

He revealeth the deep and secret things: he knoweth what is in the darkness, and the light dwelleth with him.

2:21–22

25.3

This image's head was of fine gold, his breast and his arms of silver, his belly and his thighs of brass,

His legs of iron, his feet part of iron and part of clay.

Thou sawest till that a stone was cut out without hands, which smote the image upon his feet that were of iron and clay, and brake them to pieces.

2:32–34

25.4

That at what time ye hear the sound of the cornet, flute, harp, sackbut, psaltery, dulcimer, and all kinds of musick, ye fall down and worship the golden image that Nebuchadnezzar the king hath set up:

And whoso falleth not down and worshippeth shall the same hour be cast into the midst of a burning fiery furnace.

3:5–6

25.5

Shadrach, Meshach, and Abed-nego, answered

and said to the king, O Nebuchadnezzar, we are not careful to answer thee in this matter.

3:16

25.6

Then was Nebuchadnezzar full of fury, and the form of his visage was changed against Shadrach, Meshach, and Abed-nego: therefore he spake, and commanded that they should heat the furnace one seven times more than it was wont to be heated.

3:19

25.7

He answered and said, Lo, I see four men loose, walking in the midst of the fire, and they have no hurt; and the form of the fourth is like the Son of God.

3:25

25.8

The same hour was the thing fulfilled upon Nebuchadnezzar: and he was driven from men, and did eat grass as oxen, and his body was wet with the dew of heaven, till his hairs were grown like eagles' feathers, and his nails like birds' claws.

4:33

25.9

In the same hour came forth fingers of a man's hand, and wrote over against the candlestick upon the plaister of the wall of the king's palace: and the king saw the part of the hand that wrote.

[*Hence the phrase the 'writing on the wall'*]

5:5

25.10

And this is the writing that was written, MENE, MENE, TEKEL, UPHARSIN.

This is the interpretation of the thing: MENE; God hath numbered thy kingdom, and finished it.

TEKEL; Thou art weighed in the balances, and art found wanting.

PERES; Thy kingdom is divided, and given to the Medes and Persians.

5:25–28

25.11

Then the king commanded, and they brought Daniel, and cast him into the den of lions. Now the king spake and said unto Daniel, Thy God whom thou servest continually, he will deliver thee.

6:16

25.12

My God hath sent his angel, and hath shut the lions' mouths, that they have not hurt me: forasmuch as before him innocency was found in me; and also before thee, O king, have I done no hurt.

6:22

25.13

I beheld till the thrones were cast down, and the Ancient of days did sit, whose garment was white as snow, and the hair of his head like the pure wool: his throne was like the fiery flame, and his wheels as burning fire.

7:9

25.14

But thou, O Daniel, shut up the words, and seal the book, even to the time of the end: many shall run to and fro, and knowledge shall be increased.

12:4

26 Hosea

26.1

For they have sown the wind, and they shall reap the whirlwind: it hath no stalk: the bud shall yield no meal: if so be it yield, the strangers shall swallow it up.

8:7

26.2

Sow to yourselves in righteousness, reap in mercy; break up your fallow ground: for it is time to seek the Lord, till he come and rain righteousness upon you.

Ye have plowed wickedness, ye have reaped iniquity; ye have eaten the fruit of lies: because thou didst trust in thy way, in the multitude of thy mighty men.

10:12–13

26.3

I drew them with cords of a man, with bands of love: and I was to them as they that take off the yoke on their jaws, and I laid meat unto them.

11:4

27 Joel

27.1

That which the palmerworm hath left hath the locust eaten; and that which the locust hath left hath the cankerworm eaten; and that which the cankerworm hath left hath the caterpiller eaten.

1:4

27.2

Blow ye the trumpet in Zion, and sound an alarm in my holy mountain: let all the inhabitants of the land tremble: for the day of the Lord cometh, for it is nigh at hand.

2:1

27.3

And the Lord shall utter his voice before his army: for his camp is very great: for he is strong that executeth his word: for the day of the Lord is great and very terrible: and who can abide it?

2:11

27.4
And I will restore to you the years that the locust hath eaten, the cankerworm, and the caterpiller, and the palmerworm, my great army which I sent among you.

2:25

27.5
And it shall come to pass afterward, that I will pour out my spirit upon all flesh; and your sons and your daughters shall prophesy, your old men shall dream dreams, your young men shall see visions.

2:28

27.6
Beat your plowshares into swords, and your pruninghooks into spears: let the weak say, I am strong.

3:10

27.7
Put ye in the sickle, for the harvest is ripe: come, get you down; for the press is full, the fats overflow; for their wickedness is great.
Multitudes, multitudes in the valley of decision: for the day of the Lord is near in the valley of decision.
The sun and the moon shall be darkened, and the stars shall withdraw their shining.

3:13–15

28 Amos

28.1
Can two walk together, except they be agreed? Will a lion roar in the forest, when he hath no prey? will a young lion cry out of his den, if he have taken nothing?

3:3–4

28.2
Shall a trumpet be blown in the city, and the people not be afraid? shall there be evil in a city, and the Lord hath not done it?

3:6

28.3
I have overthrown some of you, as God overthrew Sodom and Gomorrah, and ye were as a firebrand plucked out of the burning: yet have ye not returned unto me, saith the Lord.

4:11

28.4
Seek him that maketh the seven stars and Orion, and turneth the shadow of death into the morning, and maketh the day dark with night: that calleth for the waters of the sea, and poureth them out upon the face of the earth: The Lord is his name.

5:8

28.5
Ye that put far away the evil day, and cause the seat of violence to come near;
That lie upon beds of ivory, and stretch themselves upon their couches, and eat the lambs out of the flock, and the calves out of the midst of the stall.

6:3–4

28.6
Thus he shewed me: and, behold, the Lord stood upon a wall made by a plumbline, with a plumbline in his hand.
And the Lord said unto me, Amos, what seest thou? And I said, A plumbline. Then said the Lord, Behold, I will set a plumbline in the midst of my people Israel: I will not again pass by them any more.

7:7–8

29 Jonah

29.1
So the shipmaster came to him, and said unto him, What meanest thou, O sleeper? arise, call upon thy God, if so be that God will think upon us, that we perish not.
And they said every one to his fellow, Come, and let us cast lots, that we may know for whose cause this evil is upon us. So they cast lots, and the lot fell upon Jonah.

1:6–7

29.2
Now the Lord had prepared a great fish to swallow up Jonah. And Jonah was in the belly of the fish three days and three nights.

1:17

29.3
But I will sacrifice unto thee with the voice of thanksgiving; I will pay that that I have vowed. Salvation is of the Lord.

2:9

29.4
And the Lord God prepared a gourd, and made it to come up over Jonah, that it might be a shadow over his head, to deliver him from his grief. So Jonah was exceeding glad of the gourd.
But God prepared a worm when the morning rose the next day, and it smote the gourd that it withered.

4:6–7

30 Micah

30.1
But they shall sit every man under his vine and under his fig tree; and none shall make them afraid: for the mouth of the Lord of hosts hath spoken it.

4:4

30.2
But thou, Beth-lehem Ephratah, though thou

be little among the thousands of Judah, yet out of thee shall he come forth unto me that is to be ruler in Israel; whose goings forth have been from of old, from everlasting.

5:2

30.3
And the remnant of Jacob shall be in the midst of many people as a dew from the Lord, as the showers upon the grass, that tarrieth not for man, nor waiteth for the sons of men.

5:7

30.4
He hath shewed thee, O man, what is good; and what doth the Lord require of thee, but to do justly, and to love mercy, and to walk humbly with thy God?

6:8

30.5
Trust ye not in a friend, put ye not confidence in a guide: keep the doors of thy mouth from her that lieth in thy bosom.

7:5

31 Habakkuk

31.1
And the Lord answered me, and said, Write the vision, and make it plain upon tables, that he may run that readeth it.

2:2

31.2
But the Lord is in his holy temple: let all the earth keep silence before him.

2:20

32 Haggai

32.1
Now therefore thus saith the Lord of hosts; Consider your ways.
Ye have sown much, and bring in little; ye eat, but ye have not enough; ye drink, but ye are not filled with drink; ye clothe you, but there is none warm; and he that earneth wages earneth wages to put it into a bag with holes.

1:5–6

33 Zechariah

33.1
Your fathers, where are they? and the prophets, do they live for ever?

1:5

33.2
And they answered the angel of the Lord that stood among the myrtle trees, and said, We have walked to and fro through the earth, and, behold, all the earth sitteth still, and is at rest.

1:11

33.3
And the Lord said unto Satan, The Lord rebuke thee, O Satan; even the Lord that hath chosen Jerusalem rebuke thee: is not this a brand plucked out of the fire?

3:2

33.4
For who hath despised the day of small things? for they shall rejoice, and shall see the plummet in the hand of Zerubbabel with those seven; they are the eyes of the Lord, which run to and fro through the whole earth.

4:10

33.5
Turn you to the strong hold, ye prisoners of hope: even to day do I declare that I will render double unto thee.

9:12

33.6
And one shall say unto him, What are these wounds in thine hands? Then he shall answer, Those with which I was wounded in the house of my friends.

13:6

34 Malachi

34.1
Have we not all one father? hath not one God created us? why do we deal treacherously every man against his brother, by profaning the covenant of our fathers?

2:10

34.2
Behold, I will send my messenger, and he shall prepare the way before me: and the Lord, whom ye seek, shall suddenly come to his temple, even the messenger of the covenant, whom ye delight in: behold, he shall come, saith the Lord of hosts.
But who may abide the day of his coming? and who shall stand when he appeareth? for he is like a refiner's fire, and like fullers' soap.

3:1–2

34.3
For, behold, the day cometh, that shall burn as an oven; and all the proud, yea, and all that do wickedly, shall be stubble: and the day that cometh shall burn them up, saith the Lord of hosts, that it shall leave them neither root nor branch.
But unto you that fear my name shall the Sun of righteousness arise with healing in his wings; and ye shall go forth, and grow up as calves of the stall.

4:1–2

Apocrypha

35 I Esdras

35.1

And he said thus, O ye men, how exceeding strong is wine! it causeth all men to err that drink it:
It maketh the mind of the king and of the fatherless child to be all one; of the bondman and of the freeman, of the poor man and of the rich:
It turneth also every thought into jollity and mirth, so that a man remembereth neither sorrow nor debt.

3:18–20

35.2

And when they are in their cups, they forget their love both to friends and brethren, and a little after draw out swords:
But when they are from the wine, they remember not what they have done.

3:22–23

35.3

O ye men, do not men excel in strength, that bear rule over sea and land, and all things in them?

4:2

35.4

These also make garments for men; these bring glory unto men; and without women cannot men be.
Yea, and if men have gathered together gold and silver, or any other goodly thing, do they not love a woman which is comely in favour and beauty?

4:17–18

35.5

By this also ye must know that women have dominion over you: do ye not labour and toil, and give and bring all to the woman?
Yea, a man taketh his sword, and goeth his way to rob and to steal, to sail upon the sea and upon rivers;
And looketh upon a lion, and goeth in the darkness; and when he hath stolen, spoiled, and robbed, he bringeth it to his love.

4:22–24

35.6

And all the people then shouted, and said, Great is Truth, and mighty above all things.

4:41

35.7

Magna est veritas et praevalet.

Vulgate 4:41

35.8

And by their secret plots, and popular persuasions and commotions, they hindered the finishing of the building all the time that king Cyrus lived: so they were hindered from building for the space of two years, until the reign of Darius.

5:73

35.9

Go then, and eat the fat, and drink the sweet, and send part to them that have nothing;
For this day is holy unto the Lord: and be not sorrowful; for the Lord will bring you to honour.

9:51–52

36 II Esdras

36.1

Then had I pity upon your mournings, and gave you manna to eat; so ye did eat angels' bread.

1:19

36.2

He answered and said unto me, These be they that have put off the mortal clothing, and put on the immortal, and have confessed the name of God: now are they crowned, and receive palms.
Then said I unto the angel, What young person is it that crowneth them, and giveth them palms in their hands?
So he answered and said unto me, It is the Son of God, whom they have confessed in the world. Then began I greatly to commend them that stood so stiffly for the name of the Lord.

2:45–47

36.3

And he said unto me, If I should ask thee how great dwellings are in the midst of the sea, or how many springs are in the beginning of the deep, or how many springs are above the firmament, or which are the outgoings of paradise:
Peradventure thou wouldest say unto me, I never went down into the deep, nor as yet into hell, neither did I ever climb up into heaven.

4:7–8

36.4

He answered me, and said, I went into a forest into a plain, and the trees took counsel,
And said, Come, let us go and make war against the sea, that it may depart away before us, and that we may make us more woods.
The floods of the sea also in like manner took counsel, and said, Come, let us go up and subdue the woods of the plain, that there also we may make us another country.
The thought of the wood was in vain, for the fire came and consumed it.
The thought of the floods of the sea came

likewise to nought, for the sand stood up and stopped them.

4:13–17

36.5

Then were the entrances of this world made narrow, full of sorrow and travail: they are but few and evil, full of perils, and very painful.
For the entrances of the elder world were wide and sure, and brought immortal fruit.

7:12–13

36.6

For the world hath lost his youth, and the times begin to wax old.

14:10

36.7

And come hither, and I shall light a candle of understanding in thine heart, which shall not be put out, till the things be performed which thou shalt begin to write.

14:25

37 Tobit

37.1

Be not greedy to add money to money: but let it be as refuse in respect of our child.

5:18

37.2

Be of good comfort, my daughter; the Lord of heaven and earth give thee joy for this thy sorrow: be of good comfort, my daughter.

7:18

38 Wisdom

38.1

For the holy spirit of discipline will flee deceit, and remove from thoughts that are without understanding, and will not abide when unrighteousness cometh in.
For wisdom is a loving spirit; and will not acquit a blasphemer of his words: for God is witness of his reins, and a true beholder of his heart, and a hearer of his tongue.

1:5–6

38.2

For the ear of jealousy heareth all things: and the noise of murmurings is not hid.

1:10

38.3

But the souls of the righteous are in the hand of God, and there shall no torment touch them.
In the sight of the unwise they seemed to die: and their departure is taken for misery,
And their going from us to be utter destruction: but they are in peace.
For though they be punished in the sight of men, yet is their hope full of immortality.
And having been a little chastised, they shall be greatly rewarded: for God proved them, and found them worthy for himself.

3:1–5

38.4

And in the time of their visitation they shall shine, and run to and fro like sparks among the stubble.

3:7

38.5

For the bewitching of naughtiness doth obscure things that are honest; and the wandering of concupiscence doth undermine the simple mind.
He, being made perfect in a short time, fulfilled a long time.

4:12–13

38.6

And as a ship that passeth over the waves of the water, which when it is gone by, the trace thereof cannot be found, neither the pathway of the keel in the waves;
Or as when a bird hath flown through the air, there is no token of her way to be found, but the light air being beaten with the stroke of her wings, and parted with the violent noise and motion of them, is passed through, and therein afterwards no sign where she went is to be found;
Or like as when an arrow is shot at a mark, it parteth the air, which immediately cometh together again, so that a man cannot know where it went through:
Even so we in like manner, as soon as we were born, began to draw to our end, and had no sign of virtue to shew; but were consumed in our own wickedness.

5:10–13

38.7

For all men have one entrance into life, and the like going out.

7:6

38.8

For wisdom is more moving than any motion: she passeth and goeth through all things by reason of her pureness.
For she is the breath of the power of God, and a pure influence flowing from the glory of the Almighty: therefore can no defiled thing fall into her.
For she is the brightness of the everlasting light, the unspotted mirror of the power of God, and the image of his goodness.
And being but one, she can do all things: and remaining in herself, she maketh all things new: and in all ages entering into holy souls,

she maketh them friends of God, and prophets.
For God loveth none but him that dwelleth with wisdom.

7:24–28

38.9
Wisdom reacheth from one end to another mightily: and sweetly doth she order all things.

8:1

38.10
But thou sparest all: for they are thine, O Lord, thou lover of souls.

11:26

38.11
For thine incorruptible Spirit is in all things.

12:1

38.12
And so the multitude, allured by the grace of the work, took him now for a god, which a little before was but honoured as a man.
And this was an occasion to deceive the world: for men, serving either calamity or tyranny, did ascribe unto stones and stocks the incommunicable name.

14:20–21

38.13
For thou hast power of life and death: thou leadest to the gates of hell, and bringest up again.

16:13

39 Ecclesiasticus

39.1
My son, if thou come to serve the Lord, prepare thy soul for temptation.

2:1

39.2
For gold is tried in the fire, and acceptable men in the furnace of adversity.

2:5

39.3
Saying, We will fall into the hands of the Lord, and not into the hands of men: for as his majesty is, so is his mercy.

2:18

39.4
Be not curious in unnecessary matters: for more things are shewed unto thee than men understand.

3:23

39.5
Winnow not with every wind, and go not into every way: for so doth the sinner that hath a double tongue.

5:9

39.6
Be not ignorant of any thing in a great matter or a small.

5:15

39.7
A faithful friend is the medicine of life; and they that fear the Lord shall find him.

6:16

39.8
Miss not the discourse of the elders: for they also learned of their fathers, and of them thou shalt learn understanding, and to give answer as need requireth.

8:9

39.9
Forsake not an old friend; for the new is not comparable to him: a new friend is as new wine; when it is old, thou shalt drink it with pleasure.

9:10

39.10
The physician cutteth off a long disease; and he that is to day a king to morrow shall die.

10:10

39.11
Many kings have sat down upon the ground; and one that was never thought of hath worn the crown.

11:5

39.12
Judge none blessed before his death: for a man shall be known in his children.

11:28

39.13
He that toucheth pitch shall be defiled therewith; and he that hath fellowship with a proud man shall be like unto him.

13:1

39.14
All flesh waxeth old as a garment: for the covenant from the beginning is, Thou shalt die the death.

14:17

39.15
Desire not a multitude of unprofitable children, neither delight in ungodly sons.

16:1

39.16
Be not made a beggar by banqueting upon borrowing, when thou hast nothing in thy purse: for thou shalt lie in wait for thine own life, and be talked on.

18:33

39.17
A labouring man that is given to drunkenness shall not be rich: and he that contemneth small things shall fall by little and little.

19:1

39.18
If thou hast heard a word, let it die with thee; and be bold, it will not burst thee.

19:10

39.19
If thou hast gathered nothing in thy youth, how canst thou find any thing in thine age?

25:3

39.20
As the climbing up a sandy way is to the feet of the aged, so is a wife full of words to a quiet man.

25:20

39.21
Leave off first for manners' sake: and be not unsatiable, lest thou offend.

31:17

39.22
Let thy speech be short, comprehending much in few words; be as one that knoweth and yet holdeth his tongue.

32:8

39.23
For a man's mind is sometime wont to tell him more than seven watchmen, that sit above in an high tower.

37:14

39.24
Honour a physician with the honour due unto him for the uses which ye may have of him: for the Lord hath created him.
For of the most High cometh healing, and he shall receive honour of the king.

38:1–2

39.25
The wisdom of a learned man cometh by opportunity of leisure: and he that hath little business shall become wise.
How can he get wisdom that holdeth the plough, and that glorieth in the goad, that driveth oxen, and is occupied in their labours, and whose talk is of bullocks?

38:24–25

39.26
O death, how bitter is the remembrance of thee to a man that liveth at rest in his possessions, unto the man that hath nothing to vex him, and that hath prosperity in all things: yea, unto him that is yet able to receive meat!
O death, acceptable is thy sentence unto the needy, and unto him whose strength faileth, that is now in the last age, and is vexed with all things, and to him that despaireth, and hath lost patience!

41:1–2

39.27
Let us now praise famous men, and our fathers that begat us.

44:1

39.28
Such as did bear rule in their kingdoms, men renowned for their power, giving counsel by their understanding, and declaring prophecies:
Leaders of the people by their counsels, and by their knowledge of learning meet for the people, wise and eloquent in their instructions:
Such as found out musical tunes and recited verses in writing:
Rich men furnished with ability living peaceably in their habitations:
All these were honoured in their generations, and were the glory of their times.
There be of them, that have left a name behind them, that their praises might be reported.
And some there be, which have no memorial; who are perished, as though they had never been; and are become as though they had never been born; and their children after them.

44:3–9

39.29
Their bodies are buried in peace; but their name liveth for evermore.

44:14

40 I Maccabees

40.1
I perceive therefore that for this cause these troubles are come upon me, and, behold, I perish through great grief in a strange land.

6:13

40.2
Then Judas said, God forbid that I should do this thing, and flee away from them: if our time be come, let us die manfully for our brethren, and let us not stain our honour.

9:10

41 II Maccabees

41.1
For if he had not hoped that they that were slain should have risen again, it had been superfluous and vain to pray for the dead.
And also in that he perceived that there was great favour laid up for those that died godly, it was an holy and good thought. Whereupon he made a reconciliation for the dead, that they might be delivered from sin.

12:44–45

New Testament

42 Matthew

42.1
Then Joseph her husband, being a just man, and not willing to make her a publick example, was minded to put her away privily.
1:19

42.2
Now when Jesus was born in Bethlehem of Judaea in the days of Herod the king, behold, there came wise men from the east to Jerusalem,
Saying, Where is he that is born King of the Jews? for we have seen his star in the east, and are come to worship him.
When Herod the king had heard these things, he was troubled, and all Jerusalem with him.
2:1–3

42.3
And when they were come into the house, they saw the young child with Mary his mother, and fell down, and worshipped him: and when they had opened their treasures, they presented unto him gifts; gold, and frankincense, and myrrh.
And being warned of God in a dream that they should not return to Herod, they departed into their own country another way.
2:11–12

42.4
In Rama was there a voice heard, lamentation, and weeping, and great mourning, Rachel weeping for her children, and would not be comforted, because they are not.
2:18

42.5
For this is he that was spoken of by the prophet Esaias, saying, The voice of one crying in the wilderness, Prepare ye the way of the Lord, make his paths straight.
And the same John had his raiment of camel's hair, and a leathern girdle about his loins; and his meat was locusts and wild honey.
3:3–4

42.6
But when he saw many of the Pharisees and Sadducees come to his baptism, he said unto them, O generation of vipers, who hath warned you to flee from the wrath to come?
3:7

42.7
And think not to say within yourselves, We have Abraham to our father: for I say unto you, that God is able of these stones to raise up children unto Abraham.
And now also the axe is laid unto the root of the trees: therefore every tree which bringeth not forth good fruit is hewn down, and cast into the fire.
I indeed baptize you with water unto repentance: but he that cometh after me is mightier than I, whose shoes I am not worthy to bear: he shall baptize you with the Holy Ghost, and with fire:
Whose fan is in his hand, and he will throughly purge his floor, and gather his wheat into the garner; but he will burn up the chaff with unquenchable fire.
3:9–12

42.8
And Jesus answering said unto him, Suffer it to be so now: for thus it becometh us to fulfil all righteousness. Then he suffered him.
And Jesus, when he was baptized, went up straightway out of the water: and, lo, the heavens were opened unto him, and he saw the Spirit of God descending like a dove, and lighting upon him:
And lo a voice from heaven, saying, This is my beloved Son, in whom I am well pleased.
3:15–17

42.9
Then was Jesus led up of the Spirit into the wilderness to be tempted of the devil.
And when he had fasted forty days and forty nights, he was afterward an hungred.
And when the tempter came to him, he said, If thou be the Son of God, command that these stones be made bread.
But he answered and said, It is written, Man shall not live by bread alone, but by every word that proceedeth out of the mouth of God.
4:1–4

42.10
Jesus said unto him, It is written again, Thou shalt not tempt the Lord thy God.
Again, the devil taketh him up into an exceeding high mountain, and sheweth him all the kingdoms of the world, and the glory of them.
4:7–8

42.11
Then the devil leaveth him, and, behold, angels came and ministered unto him.
4:11

42.12
From that time Jesus began to preach, and to say, Repent: for the kingdom of heaven is at hand.
4:17

42.13
And he saith unto them, Follow me, and I will make you fishers of men.
4:19

42.14
And Jesus went about all Galilee, teaching in

their synagogues, and preaching the gospel of the kingdom, and healing all manner of sickness and all manner of disease among the people.

4:23

42.15

Blessed are the poor in spirit: for theirs is the kingdom of heaven.
Blessed are they that mourn: for they shall be comforted.
Blessed are the meek: for they shall inherit the earth.
Blessed are they which do hunger and thirst after righteousness: for they shall be filled.
Blessed are the merciful: for they shall obtain mercy.
Blessed are the pure in heart: for they shall see God.
Blessed are the peacemakers: for they shall be called the children of God.
Blessed are they which are persecuted for righteousness' sake: for theirs is the kingdom of heaven.

5:3–10

42.16

Ye are the salt of the earth: but if the salt have lost his savour, wherewith shall it be salted? it is thenceforth good for nothing, but to be cast out, and to be trodden under foot of men.
Ye are the light of the world. A city that is set on an hill cannot be hid.
Neither do men light a candle, and put it under a bushel, but on a candlestick; and it giveth light unto all that are in the house.
Let your light so shine before men, that they may see your good works, and glorify your Father which is in heaven.

5:13–16

42.17

For verily I say unto you, Till heaven and earth pass, one jot or one tittle shall in no wise pass from the law, till all be fulfilled.

5:18

42.18

For I say unto you, That except your righteousness shall exceed the righteousness of the scribes and Pharisees, ye shall in no case enter into the kingdom of heaven.

5:20

42.19

But I say unto you, That whosoever is angry with his brother without a cause shall be in danger of the judgment: and whosoever shall say to his brother, Raca, shall be in danger of the council: but whosoever shall say, Thou fool, shall be in danger of hell fire.

5:22

42.20

Agree with thine adversary quickly, whiles thou art in the way with him; lest at any time the adversary deliver thee to the judge, and the judge deliver thee to the officer, and thou be cast into prison.
Verily I say unto thee, Thou shalt by no means come out thence, till thou hast paid the uttermost farthing.

5:25–26

42.21

And if thy right eye offend thee, pluck it out, and cast it from thee: for it is profitable for thee that one of thy members should perish, and not that thy whole body should be cast into hell.

5:29

42.22

But I say unto you, Swear not at all; neither by heaven; for it is God's throne:
Nor by the earth; for it is his footstool: neither by Jerusalem; for it is the city of the great King.
Neither shalt thou swear by thy head, because thou canst not make one hair white or black.
But let your communication be, Yea, yea; Nay, nay: for whatsoever is more than these cometh of evil.

5:34–37

42.23

But I say unto you, That ye resist not evil: but whosoever shall smite thee on thy right cheek, turn to him the other also.
And if any man will sue thee at the law, and take away thy coat, let him have thy cloke also.
And whosoever shall compel thee to go a mile, go with him twain.

5:39–41

42.24

But I say unto you, Love your enemies, bless them that curse you, do good to them that hate you, and pray for them which despitefully use you, and persecute you;
That ye may be the children of your Father which is in heaven: for he maketh his sun to rise on the evil and on the good, and sendeth rain on the just and on the unjust.
For if ye love them which love you, what reward have ye? do not even the publicans the same?

5:44–46

42.25

Be ye therefore perfect, even as your Father which is in heaven is perfect.

5:48

42.26

Therefore when thou doest thine alms, do not sound a trumpet before thee, as the hypocrites do in the synagogues and in the streets, that they may have glory of men. Verily I say unto you, They have their reward.
But when thou doest alms, let not thy left hand know what thy right hand doeth:

That thine alms may be in secret: and thy Father which seeth in secret himself shall reward thee openly.

6:2–4

42.27

But when ye pray, use not vain repetitions, as the heathen do: for they think that they shall be heard for their much speaking.
Be not ye therefore like unto them: for your Father knoweth what things ye have need of, before ye ask him.
After this manner therefore pray ye: Our Father which art in heaven, Hallowed be thy name.
Thy kingdom come. Thy will be done in earth, as it is in heaven.
Give us this day our daily bread.
And forgive us our debts, as we forgive our debtors.
And lead us not into temptation, but deliver us from evil: For thine is the kingdom, and the power, and the glory, for ever. Amen.

6:7–13

42.28

Lay not up for yourselves treasures upon earth, where moth and rust doth corrupt, and where thieves break through and steal:
But lay up for yourselves treasures in heaven, where neither moth nor rust doth corrupt, and where thieves do not break through nor steal:
For where your treasure is, there will your heart be also.

6:19–21

42.29

The light of the body is the eye: if therefore thine eye be single, thy whole body shall be full of light.
But if thine eye be evil, thy whole body shall be full of darkness. If therefore the light that is in thee be darkness, how great is that darkness!

6:22–23

42.30

No man can serve two masters: for either he will hate the one, and love the other; or else he will hold to the one, and despise the other. Ye cannot serve God and mammon.
Therefore I say unto you, Take no thought for your life, what ye shall eat, or what ye shall drink; nor yet for your body, what ye shall put on. Is not the life more than meat, and the body than raiment?

6:24–25

42.31

Behold the fowls of the air: for they sow not, neither do they reap, nor gather into barns; yet your heavenly Father feedeth them. Are ye not much better than they?
Which of you by taking thought can add one cubit unto his stature?
And why take ye thought for raiment? Consider the lilies of the field, how they grow; they toil not, neither do they spin:
And yet I say unto you, That even Solomon in all his glory was not arrayed like one of these.
Wherefore, if God so clothe the grass of the field, which to day is, and to morrow is cast into the oven, shall he not much more clothe you, O ye of little faith?
Therefore take no thought, saying, What shall we eat? or, What shall we drink? or, Wherewithal shall we be clothed?

6:26–31

42.32

But seek ye first the kingdom of God, and his righteousness; and all these things shall be added unto you.
Take therefore no thought for the morrow: for the morrow shall take thought for the things of itself. Sufficient unto the day is the evil thereof.

6:33–34

42.33

Judge not, that ye be not judged.

7:1

42.34

And why beholdest thou the mote that is in thy brother's eye, but considerest not the beam that is in thine own eye?

7:3

42.35

Give not that which is holy unto the dogs, neither cast ye your pearls before swine, lest they trample them under their feet, and turn again and rend you.

7:6

42.36

Ask, and it shall be given you; seek, and ye shall find; knock, and it shall be opened unto you:
For every one that asketh receiveth; and he that seeketh findeth; and to him that knocketh it shall be opened.

7:7–8

42.37

Or what man is there of you, whom if his son ask bread, will he give him a stone?

7:9

42.38

If ye then, being evil, know how to give good gifts unto your children, how much more shall your Father which is in heaven give good things to them that ask him?
Therefore all things whatsoever ye would that men should do to you, do ye even so to them: for this is the law and the prophets.

7:11–12

42.39
Enter ye in at the strait gate: for wide is the gate, and broad is the way, that leadeth to destruction, and many there be which go in thereat:
Because strait is the gate, and narrow is the way, which leadeth unto life, and few there be that find it.

7:13–14

42.40
Beware of false prophets, which come to you in sheep's clothing, but inwardly they are ravening wolves.

7:15

42.41
Ye shall know them by their fruits. Do men gather grapes of thorns, or figs of thistles?
Even so every good tree bringeth forth good fruit; but a corrupt tree bringeth forth evil fruit.
A good tree cannot bring forth evil fruit, neither can a corrupt tree bring forth good fruit.
Every tree that bringeth not forth good fruit is hewn down, and cast into the fire.
Wherefore by their fruits ye shall know them.

7:16–20

42.42
Not every one that saith unto me, Lord, Lord, shall enter into the kingdom of heaven; but he that doeth the will of my Father which is in heaven.

7:21

42.43
And then will I profess unto them, I never knew you: depart from me, ye that work iniquity.

7:23

42.44
Therefore whosoever heareth these sayings of mine, and doeth them, I will liken him unto a wise man, which built his house upon a rock:
And the rain descended, and the floods came, and the winds blew, and beat upon that house; and it fell not: for it was founded upon a rock.
And every one that heareth these sayings of mine, and doeth them not, shall be likened unto a foolish man, which built his house upon the sand:
And the rain descended, and the floods came, and the winds blew, and beat upon that house; and it fell: and great was the fall of it.

7:24–27

42.45
For he taught them as one having authority, and not as the scribes.

7:29

42.46
The centurion answered and said, Lord, I am not worthy that thou shouldest come under my roof: but speak the word only, and my servant shall be healed.
For I am a man under authority, having soldiers under me: and I say to this man, Go, and he goeth; and to another, Come, and he cometh; and to my servant, Do this, and he doeth it.
When Jesus heard it, he marvelled, and said to them that followed, Verily I say unto you, I have not found so great faith, no, not in Israel.

8:8–10

42.47
But the children of the kingdom shall be cast out into outer darkness: there shall be weeping and gnashing of teeth.

8:12

42.48
And Jesus saith unto him, The foxes have holes, and the birds of the air have nests; but the Son of man hath not where to lay his head.

8:20

42.49
But Jesus said unto him, Follow me; and let the dead bury their dead.

8:22

42.50
And his disciples came to him, and awoke him, saying, Lord, save us: we perish.
And he saith unto them, Why are ye fearful, O ye of little faith? Then he arose, and rebuked the winds and the sea; and there was a great calm.
But the men marvelled, saying, What manner of man is this, that even the winds and the sea obey him!

8:25–27

42.51
And as Jesus passed forth from thence, he saw a man, named Matthew, sitting at the receipt of custom: and he saith unto him, Follow me. And he arose, and followed him.

9:9

42.52
But when Jesus heard that, he said unto them, They that be whole need not a physician, but they that are sick.
But go ye and learn what that meaneth, I will have mercy, and not sacrifice: for I am not come to call the righteous, but sinners to repentance.

9:12–13

42.53
And Jesus said unto them, Can the children of the bridechamber mourn, as long as the bridegroom is with them? but the days will come,

when the bridegroom shall be taken from them, and then shall they fast.

9:15

42.54
Neither do men put new wine into old bottles: else the bottles break, and the wine runneth out, and the bottles perish: but they put new wine into new bottles, and both are preserved.

9:17

42.55
He said unto them, Give place: for the maid is not dead, but sleepeth. And they laughed him to scorn.

9:24

42.56
But the Pharisees said, He casteth out devils through the prince of the devils.

9:34

42.57
But when he saw the multitudes, he was moved with compassion on them, because they fainted, and were scattered abroad, as sheep having no shepherd.
Then saith he unto his disciples, The harvest truly is plenteous, but the labourers are few;
Pray ye therefore the Lord of the harvest, that he will send forth labourers into his harvest.

9:36–38

42.58
But go rather to the lost sheep of the house of Israel.

10:6

42.59
Heal the sick, cleanse the lepers, raise the dead, cast out devils: freely ye have received, freely give.

10:8

42.60
And whosoever shall not receive you, nor hear your words, when ye depart out of that house or city, shake off the dust of your feet.

10:14

42.61
Behold, I send you forth as sheep in the midst of wolves: be ye therefore wise as serpents, and harmless as doves.

10:16

42.62
And ye shall be hated of all men for my name's sake: but he that endureth to the end shall be saved.

10:22

42.63
The disciple is not above his master, nor the servant above his lord.

10:24

42.64
Fear them not therefore: for there is nothing covered, that shall not be revealed; and hid, that shall not be known.
What I tell you in darkness, that speak ye in light: and what ye hear in the ear, that preach ye upon the housetops.
And fear not them which kill the body, but are not able to kill the soul: but rather fear him which is able to destroy both soul and body in hell.

10:26–28

42.65
Are not two sparrows sold for a farthing? and one of them shall not fall on the ground without your Father.
But the very hairs of your head are all numbered.
Fear ye not therefore, ye are of more value than many sparrows.

10:29–31

42.66
Think not that I am come to send peace on earth: I came not to send peace, but a sword.

10:34

42.67
And a man's foes shall be they of his own household.

10:36

42.68
He that findeth his life shall lose it: and he that loseth his life for my sake shall find it.

10:39

42.69
And whosoever shall give to drink unto one of these little ones a cup of cold water only in the name of a disciple, verily I say unto you, he shall in no wise lose his reward.

10:42

42.70
And said unto him, Art thou he that should come, or do we look for another?

11:3

42.71
And as they departed, Jesus began to say unto the multitudes concerning John, What went ye out into the wilderness to see? A reed shaken with the wind?
But what went ye out for to see? A man clothed in soft raiment? behold, they that wear soft clothing are in kings' houses.
But what went ye out for to see? A prophet? yea, I say unto you, and more than a prophet.

11:7–9

42.72
He that hath ears to hear, let him hear.

11:15

42.73
And saying, We have piped unto you, and ye have not danced; we have mourned unto you, and ye have not lamented.

11:17

42.74
For John came neither eating nor drinking, and they say, He hath a devil.
The Son of man came eating and drinking, and they say, Behold a man gluttonous, and a winebibber, a friend of publicans and sinners. But wisdom is justified of her children.
11:18–19

42.75
At that time Jesus answered and said, I thank thee, O Father, Lord of heaven and earth, because thou hast hid these things from the wise and prudent, and hast revealed them unto babes.
11:25

42.76
Come unto me, all ye that labour and are heavy laden, and I will give you rest.
Take my yoke upon you, and learn of me; for I am meek and lowly in heart: and ye shall find rest unto your souls.
For my yoke is easy, and my burden is light.
11:28–30

42.77
He that is not with me is against me; and he that gathereth not with me scattereth abroad.
12:30

42.78
Wherefore I say unto you, All manner of sin and blasphemy shall be forgiven unto men: but the blasphemy against the Holy Ghost shall not be forgiven unto men.
And whosoever speaketh a word against the Son of man, it shall be forgiven him: but whosoever speaketh against the Holy Ghost, it shall not be forgiven him, neither in this world, neither in the world to come.
12:31–32

42.79
O generation of vipers, how can ye, being evil, speak good things? for out of the abundance of the heart the mouth speaketh.
12:34

42.80
But I say unto you, That every idle word that men shall speak, they shall give account thereof in the day of judgment.
For by thy words thou shalt be justified, and by thy words thou shalt be condemned.
12:36–37

42.81
But he answered and said unto them, An evil and adulterous generation seeketh after a sign; and there shall no sign be given to it, but the sign of the prophet Jonas:
For as Jonas was three days and three nights in the whale's belly; so shall the Son of man be three days and three nights in the heart of the earth.
12:39–40

42.82
The queen of the south shall rise up in the judgment with this generation, and shall condemn it: for she came from the uttermost parts of the earth to hear the wisdom of Solomon; and, behold, a greater than Solomon is here.
12:42

42.83
When the unclean spirit is gone out of a man, he walketh through dry places, seeking rest, and findeth none.
Then he saith, I will return into my house from whence I came out; and when he is come, he findeth it empty, swept, and garnished.
Then goeth he, and taketh with himself seven other spirits more wicked than himself, and they enter in and dwell there: and the last state of that man is worse than the first. Even so shall it be also unto this wicked generation.
12:43–45

42.84
For whosoever shall do the will of my Father which is in heaven, the same is my brother, and sister, and mother.
12:50

42.85
And he spake many things unto them in parables, saying, Behold, a sower went forth to sow;
And when he sowed, some seeds fell by the way side, and the fowls came and devoured them up:
Some fell upon stony places, where they had not much earth: and forthwith they sprung up, because they had no deepness of earth:
And when the sun was up, they were scorched; and because they had no root, they withered away.
And some fell among thorns; and the thorns sprung up, and choked them:
But other fell into good ground, and brought forth fruit, some an hundredfold, some sixtyfold, some thirtyfold.
13:3–8

42.86
And in them is fulfilled the prophecy of Esaias, which saith, By hearing ye shall hear, and shall not understand; and seeing ye shall see, and shall not perceive:
For this people's heart is waxed gross, and their ears are dull of hearing, and their eyes they have closed; lest at any time they should see with their eyes, and hear with their ears, and should understand with their heart, and should be converted, and I should heal them.
But blessed are your eyes, for they see: and your ears, for they hear.
13:14–16

42.87
When any one heareth the word of the kingdom, and understandeth it not, then cometh the wicked one, and catcheth away that which was sown in his heart. This is he which received seed by the way side.
13:19

42.88
He also that received seed among the thorns is he that heareth the word; and the care of this world, and the deceitfulness of riches, choke the word, and he becometh unfruitful.
13:22

42.89
But while men slept, his enemy came and sowed tares among the wheat, and went his way.
13:25

42.90
He said unto them, An enemy hath done this. The servants said unto him, Wilt thou then that we go and gather them up?
But he said, Nay; lest while ye gather up the tares, ye root up also the wheat with them.
Let both grow together until the harvest: and in the time of harvest I will say to the reapers, Gather ye together first the tares, and bind them in bundles to burn them: but gather the wheat into my barn.
13:28–30

42.91
Another parable put he forth unto them, saying, The kingdom of heaven is like to a grain of mustard seed, which a man took, and sowed in his field:
Which indeed is the least of all seeds: but when it is grown, it is the greatest among herbs, and becometh a tree, so that the birds of the air come and lodge in the branches thereof.
13:31–32

42.92
The field is the world; the good seed are the children of the kingdom; but the tares are the children of the wicked one;
The enemy that sowed them is the devil; the harvest is the end of the world; and the reapers are the angels.
13:38–39

42.93
Again, the kingdom of heaven is like unto a merchant man, seeking goodly pearls:
Who, when he had found one pearl of great price, went and sold all that he had, and bought it.
13:45–46

42.94
Then said he unto them, Therefore every scribe which is instructed unto the kingdom of heaven is like unto a man that is an householder, which bringeth forth out of his treasure things new and old.
13:52

42.95
And they were offended in him. But Jesus said unto them, A prophet is not without honour, save in his own country, and in his own house.
13:57

42.96
But when Herod's birthday was kept, the daughter of Herodias danced before them, and pleased Herod.
Whereupon he promised with an oath to give her whatsoever she would ask.
And she, being before instructed of her mother, said, Give me here John Baptist's head in a charger.
14:6–8

42.97
And in the fourth watch of the night Jesus went unto them, walking on the sea.
And when the disciples saw him walking on the sea, they were troubled, saying, It is a spirit; and they cried out for fear.
But straightway Jesus spake unto them, saying, Be of good cheer; it is I; be not afraid.
14:25–27

42.98
And immediately Jesus stretched forth his hand, and caught him, and said unto him, O thou of little faith, wherefore didst thou doubt?
14:31

42.99
And besought him that they might only touch the hem of his garment: and as many as touched were made perfectly whole.
14:36

42.100
This people draweth nigh unto me with their mouth, and honoureth me with their lips; but their heart is far from me.
15:8

42.101
Not that which goeth into the mouth defileth a man; but that which cometh out of the mouth, this defileth a man.
15:11

42.102
But he answered and said, Every plant, which my heavenly Father hath not planted, shall be rooted up.
Let them alone: they be blind leaders of the blind. And if the blind lead the blind, both shall fall into the ditch.
15:13–14

42.103
But he answered and said, It is not meet to take the children's bread, and to cast it to dogs.

And she said, Truth, Lord: yet the dogs eat of the crumbs which fall from their masters' table.

15:26–27

42.104
He answered and said unto them, When it is evening, ye say, It will be fair weather: for the sky is red.
And in the morning, It will be foul weather to day: for the sky is red and lowring. O ye hypocrites, ye can discern the face of the sky; but can ye not discern the signs of the times?

16:2–3

42.105
And I say also unto thee, That thou art Peter, and upon this rock I will build my church; and the gates of hell shall not prevail against it.
And I will give unto thee the keys of the kingdom of heaven: and whatsoever thou shalt bind on earth shall be bound in heaven: and whatsoever thou shalt loose on earth shall be loosed in heaven.

16:18–19

42.106
Then said Jesus unto his disciples, If any man will come after me, let him deny himself, and take up his cross, and follow me.

16:24

42.107
Then answered Peter, and said unto Jesus, Lord, it is good for us to be here: if thou wilt, let us make here three tabernacles; one for thee, and one for Moses, and one for Elias.

17:4

42.108
And Jesus answered and said unto them, Elias truly shall first come, and restore all things.

17:11

42.109
And Jesus said unto them, Because of your unbelief: for verily I say unto you, If ye have faith as a grain of mustard seed, ye shall say unto this mountain, Remove hence to yonder place; and it shall remove; and nothing shall be impossible unto you.

17:20

42.110
He saith, Yes. And when he was come into the house, Jesus prevented him, saying, What thinkest thou, Simon? of whom do the kings of the earth take custom or tribute? of their own children, or of strangers?
Peter saith unto him, Of strangers. Jesus saith unto him, Then are the children free.

17:25–26

42.111
And said, Verily I say unto you, Except ye be converted, and become as little children, ye shall not enter into the kingdom of heaven.

18:3

42.112
And whoso shall receive one such little child in my name receiveth me.
But whoso shall offend one of these little ones which believe in me, it were better for him that a millstone were hanged about his neck, and that he were drowned in the depth of the sea.

18:5–6

42.113
Woe unto the world because of offences! for it must needs be that offences come; but woe to that man by whom the offence cometh!

18:7

42.114
Take heed that ye despise not one of these little ones; for I say unto you, That in heaven their angels do always behold the face of my Father which is in heaven.

18:10

42.115
For where two or three are gathered together in my name, there am I in the midst of them.

18:20

42.116
Then came Peter to him, and said, Lord, how oft shall my brother sin against me, and I forgive him? till seven times?
Jesus saith unto him, I say not unto thee, Until seven times: but, Until seventy times seven.

18:21–22

42.117
The servant therefore fell down, and worshipped him, saying, Lord, have patience with me, and I will pay thee all.

18:26

42.118
But the same servant went out, and found one of his fellowservants, which owed him an hundred pence: and he laid hands on him, and took him by the throat, saying, Pay me that thou owest.

18:28

42.119
Wherefore they are no more twain, but one flesh. What therefore God hath joined together, let not man put asunder.

19:6

42.120
His disciples say unto him, If the case of the man be so with his wife, it is not good to marry.

19:10

42.121
Jesus said unto him, If thou wilt be perfect, go and sell that thou hast, and give to the poor,

and thou shalt have treasure in heaven: and come and follow me.
But when the young man heard that saying, he went away sorrowful: for he had great possessions.

19:21–22

42.122
Then said Jesus unto his disciples, Verily I say unto you, That a rich man shall hardly enter into the kingdom of heaven.
And again I say unto you, It is easier for a camel to go through the eye of a needle, than for a rich man to enter into the kingdom of God.

19:23–24

42.123
But many that are first shall be last; and the last shall be first.

19:30

42.124
And he went out about the third hour, and saw others standing idle in the marketplace.

20:3

42.125
Saying, These last have wrought but one hour, and thou hast made them equal unto us, which have borne the burden and heat of the day.

20:12

42.126
Is it not lawful for me to do what I will with mine own? Is thine eye evil, because I am good?

20:15

42.127
But Jesus answered and said, Ye know not what ye ask. Are ye able to drink of the cup that I shall drink of, and to be baptized with the baptism that I am baptized with? They say unto him, We are able.
And he saith unto them, Ye shall drink indeed of my cup, and be baptized with the baptism that I am baptized with: but to sit on my right hand, and on my left, is not mine to give, but it shall be given to them for whom it is prepared of my Father.

20:22–23

42.128
Tell ye the daughters of Sion, Behold, thy King cometh unto thee, meek, and sitting upon an ass, and a colt the foal of an ass.

21:5

42.129
And a very great multitude spread their garments in the way; others cut down branches from the trees, and strawed them in the way.
And the multitudes that went before, and that followed, cried, saying, Hosanna to the Son of David: Blessed is he that cometh in the name of the Lord; Hosanna in the highest.

21:8–9

42.130
And said unto them, It is written, My house shall be called the house of prayer; but ye have made it a den of thieves.

21:13

42.131
And all things, whatsoever ye shall ask in prayer, believing, ye shall receive.

21:22

42.132
Then saith he to his servants, The wedding is ready, but they which were bidden were not worthy.

22:8

42.133
For many are called, but few are chosen.

22:14

42.134
And he saith unto them, Whose is this image and superscription?
They say unto him, Caesar's. Then saith he unto them, Render therefore unto Caesar the things which are Caesar's; and unto God the things that are God's.

22:20–21

42.135
For in the resurrection they neither marry, nor are given in marriage, but are as the angels of God in heaven.

22:30

42.136
Jesus said unto him, Thou shalt love the Lord thy God with all thy heart, and with all thy soul, and with all thy mind.
This is the first and great commandment.
And the second is like unto it, Thou shalt love thy neighbour as thyself.
On these two commandments hang all the law and the prophets.

22:37–40

42.137
But all their works they do for to be seen of men: they make broad their phylacteries, and enlarge the borders of their garments,
And love the uppermost rooms at feasts, and the chief seats in the synagogues,
And greetings in the markets, and to be called of men, Rabbi, Rabbi.

23:5–7

42.138
But he that is greatest among you shall be your servant.
And whosoever shall exalt himself shall be abased; and he that shall humble himself shall be exalted.

23:11–12

42.139
Woe unto you, scribes and Pharisees, hypocrites! for ye compass sea and land to make one proselyte, and when he is made, ye make him twofold more the child of hell than yourselves.
23:15

42.140
Ye blind guides, which strain at a gnat, and swallow a camel.
23:24

42.141
Woe unto you, scribes and Pharisees, hypocrites! for ye are like unto whited sepulchres, which indeed appear beautiful outward, but are within full of dead men's bones, and of all uncleanness.
23:27

42.142
O Jerusalem, Jerusalem, thou that killest the prophets, and stonest them which are sent unto thee, how often would I have gathered thy children together, even as a hen gathereth her chickens under her wings, and ye would not!
23:37

42.143
And Jesus said unto them, See ye not all these things? verily I say unto you, There shall not be left here one stone upon another, that shall not be thrown down.
24:2

42.144
And ye shall hear of wars and rumours of wars: see that ye be not troubled: for all these things must come to pass, but the end is not yet.
For nation shall rise against nation, and kingdom against kingdom: and there shall be famines, and pestilences, and earthquakes, in divers places.
All these are the beginning of sorrows.
24:6–8

42.145
And because iniquity shall abound, the love of many shall wax cold.
24:12

42.146
When ye therefore shall see the abomination of desolation, spoken of by Daniel the prophet, stand in the holy place, (whoso readeth, let him understand).
24:15

42.147
For as the lightning cometh out of the east, and shineth even unto the west; so shall also the coming of the Son of man be.
For wheresoever the carcase is, there will the eagles be gathered together.
24:27–28

42.148
Immediately after the tribulation of those days shall the sun be darkened, and the moon shall not give her light, and the stars shall fall from heaven, and the powers of the heavens shall be shaken:
And then shall appear the sign of the Son of man in heaven: and then shall all the tribes of the earth mourn, and they shall see the Son of man coming in the clouds of heaven with power and great glory.
And he shall send his angels with a great sound of a trumpet, and they shall gather together his elect from the four winds, from one end of heaven to the other.
24:29–31

42.149
Heaven and earth shall pass away, but my words shall not pass away.
24:35

42.150
For as in the days that were before the flood they were eating and drinking, marrying and giving in marriage, until the day that Noe entered into the ark,
And knew not until the flood came, and took them all away; so shall also the coming of the Son of man be.
24:38–39

42.151
Then shall two be in the field; the one shall be taken, and the other left.
24:40

42.152
And at midnight there was a cry made, Behold, the bridegroom cometh; go ye out to meet him.
Then all those virgins arose, and trimmed their lamps.
And the foolish said unto the wise, Give us of your oil; for our lamps are gone out.
25:6–8

42.153
And unto one he gave five talents, to another two, and to another one; to every man according to his several ability; and straightway took his journey.
25:15

42.154
His lord said unto him, Well done, thou good and faithful servant: thou hast been faithful over a few things, I will make thee ruler over many things: enter thou into the joy of thy lord.
25:21

42.155
Then he which had received the one talent came and said, Lord, I knew thee that thou art an hard man, reaping where thou has not

sown, and gathering where thou hast not strawed.

25:24

42.156
For unto every one that hath shall be given, and he shall have abundance: but from him that hath not shall be taken away even that which he hath.
And cast ye the unprofitable servant into outer darkness: there shall be weeping and gnashing of teeth.

25:29–30

42.157
And before him shall be gathered all nations: and he shall separate them one from another, as a shepherd divideth his sheep from the goats:
And he shall set the sheep on his right hand, but the goats on the left.

25:32–33

42.158
Then shall the King say unto them on his right hand, Come, ye blessed of my Father, inherit the kingdom prepared for you from the foundation of the world:
For I was an hungred, and ye gave me meat: I was thirsty, and ye gave me drink: I was a stranger, and ye took me in:
Naked, and ye clothed me: I was sick, and ye visited me: I was in prison, and ye came unto me.

25:34–36

42.159
And the King shall answer and say unto them, Verily I say unto you, Inasmuch as ye have done it unto one of the least of these my brethren, ye have done it unto me.

25:40

42.160
There came unto him a woman having an alabaster box of very precious ointment, and poured it on his head, as he sat at meat.
But when his disciples saw it, they had indignation, saying, To what purpose is this waste?

26:7–8

42.161
For ye have the poor always with you; but me ye have not always.

26:11

42.162
And he answered and said, He that dippeth his hand with me in the dish, the same shall betray me.
The Son of man goeth as it is written of him: but woe unto that man by whom the Son of man is betrayed! it had been good for that man if he had not been born.
Then Judas, which betrayed him, answered and said, Master, is it I? He said unto him, Thou hast said.

26:23–25

42.163
And as they were eating, Jesus took bread, and blessed it, and brake it, and gave it to the disciples, and said, Take, eat; this is my body.
And he took the cup, and gave thanks, and gave it to them, saying, Drink ye all of it;
For this is my blood of the new testament, which is shed for many for the remission of sins.

26:26–28

42.164
Jesus said unto him, Verily I say unto thee, That this night, before the cock crow, thou shalt deny me thrice.
Peter said unto him, Though I should die with thee, yet will I not deny thee. Likewise also said all the disciples.

26:34–35

42.165
Then saith he unto them, My soul is exceeding sorrowful, even unto death: tarry ye here, and watch with me.

26:38

42.166
And he went a little further, and fell on his face, and prayed, saying, O my Father, if it be possible, let this cup pass from me: nevertheless not as I will, but as thou wilt.

26:39

42.167
Watch and pray, that ye enter not into temptation: the spirit indeed is willing, but the flesh is weak.

26:41

42.168
And forthwith he came to Jesus, and said, Hail, master; and kissed him.
And Jesus said unto him, Friend, wherefore art thou come? Then came they, and laid hands on Jesus, and took him.

26:49–50

42.169
Then said Jesus unto him, Put up again thy sword into his place: for all they that take the sword shall perish with the sword.

26:52

42.170
Then Judas, which had betrayed him, when he saw that he was condemned, repented himself, and brought again the thirty pieces of silver to the chief priests and elders,
Saying, I have sinned in that I have betrayed the innocent blood. And they said, What is that to us? see thou to that.

27:3–4

42.171
When he was set down on the judgment seat,

his wife sent unto him, saying, Have thou nothing to do with that just man: for I have suffered many things this day in a dream because of him.

27:19

42.172
When Pilate saw that he could prevail nothing, but that rather a tumult was made, he took water, and washed his hands before the multitude, saying, I am innocent of the blood of this just person: see ye to it.
Then answered all the people, and said, His blood be on us, and on our children.

27:24–25

42.173
He saved others; himself he cannot save. If he be the King of Israel, let him now come down from the cross, and we will believe him.

27:42

42.174
And about the ninth hour Jesus cried with a loud voice, saying, Eli, Eli, lama sabachthani? that is to say, My God, my God, why hast thou forsaken me?

27:46

42.175
Jesus, when he had cried again with a loud voice, yielded up the ghost.
And, behold, the veil of the temple was rent in twain from the top to the bottom; and the earth did quake, and the rocks rent;
And the graves were opened; and many bodies of the saints which slept arose.

27:50–52

42.176
Command therefore that the sepulchre be made sure until the third day, lest his disciples come by night, and steal him away, and say unto the people, He is risen from the dead: so the last error shall be worse than the first.

27:64

42.177
Teaching them to observe all things whatsoever I have commanded you: and, lo, I am with you alway, even unto the end of the world. Amen.

28:20

43 Mark

43.1
And at even, when the sun did set, they brought unto him all that were diseased, and them that were possessed with devils.

1:32

43.2
But he went out, and began to publish it much, and to blaze abroad the matter, insomuch that Jesus could no more openly enter into the city, but was without in desert places: and they came to him from every quarter.

1:45

43.3
Whether is it easier to say to the sick of the palsy, Thy sins be forgiven thee; or to say, Arise, and take up thy bed, and walk?

2:9

43.4
And he said unto them, The sabbath was made for man, and not man for the sabbath: Therefore the Son of man is Lord also of the sabbath.

2:27–28

43.5
And James the son of Zebedee, and John the brother of James; and he surnamed them Boanerges, which is, The sons of thunder.

3:17

43.6
And he called them unto him, and said unto them in parables, How can Satan cast out Satan?
And if a kingdom be divided against itself, that kingdom cannot stand.
And if a house be divided against itself, that house cannot stand.
And if Satan rise up against himself, and be divided, he cannot stand, but hath an end.
No man can enter into a strong man's house, and spoil his goods, except he will first bind the strong man; and then he will spoil his house.

3:23–27

43.7
And he asked him, What is thy name? And he answered, saying, My name is Legion: for we are many.

5:9

43.8
And forthwith Jesus gave them leave. And the unclean spirits went out, and entered into the swine: and the herd ran violently down a steep place into the sea, (they were about two thousand;) and were choked in the sea.

5:13

43.9
And they come to Jesus, and see him that was possessed with the devil, and had the legion, sitting, and clothed, and in his right mind: and they were afraid.

5:15

43.10
And besought him greatly, saying, My little daughter lieth at the point of death: I pray thee, come and lay thy hands on her, that she may be healed; and she shall live.

5:23

43.11
And had suffered many things of many physi-

cians, and had spent all that she had, and was nothing bettered, but rather grew worse.

5:26

43.12
And Jesus, immediately knowing in himself that virtue had gone out of him, turned him about in the press, and said, Who touched my clothes?

5:30

43.13
And straightway his ears were opened, and the string of his tongue was loosed, and he spake plain.

7:35

43.14
And he looked up, and said, I see men as trees, walking.

8:24

43.15
For what shall it profit a man, if he shall gain the whole world, and lose his own soul?
Or what shall a man give in exchange for his soul?

8:36–37

43.16
And straightway the father of the child cried out, and said with tears, Lord, I believe; help thou mine unbelief.

9:24

43.17
Where their worm dieth not, and the fire is not quenched.

9:44

43.18
But when Jesus saw it, he was much displeased, and said unto them, Suffer the little children to come unto me, and forbid them not: for of such is the kingdom of God.

10:14

43.19
And they were astonished out of measure, saying among themselves, Who then can be saved?
And Jesus looking upon them saith, With men it is impossible, but not with God: for with God all things are possible.

10:26–27

43.20
Which devour widows' houses, and for a pretence make long prayers: these shall receive greater damnation.

12:40

43.21
And there came a certain poor widow, and she threw in two mites, which make a farthing.
And he called unto him his disciples, and saith unto them, Verily I say unto you, That this poor widow hath cast more in, than all they which have cast into the treasury:
For all they did cast in of their abundance; but she of her want did cast in all that she had, even all her living.

12:42–44

43.22
Watch ye therefore: for ye know not when the master of the house cometh, at even, or at midnight, or at the cockcrowing, or in the morning:
Lest coming suddenly he find you sleeping.

13:35–36

43.23
And he said unto them, Go ye into all the world, and preach the gospel to every creature.

16:15

44 Luke

44.1
And the angel came in unto her, and said, Hail, thou that art highly favoured, the Lord is with thee: blessed art thou among women.
And when she saw him, she was troubled at his saying, and cast in her mind what manner of salutation this should be.

1:28–29

44.2
And Mary said, My soul doth magnify the Lord,
And my spirit hath rejoiced in God my Saviour.
For he hath regarded the low estate of his handmaiden: for, behold, from henceforth all generations shall call me blessed.

1:46–48

44.3
He hath shewed strength with his arm; he hath scattered the proud in the imagination of their hearts.
He hath put down the mighty from their seats, and exalted them of low degree.
He hath filled the hungry with good things; and the rich he hath sent empty away.

1:51–53

44.4
Blessed be the Lord God of Israel; for he hath visited and redeemed his people.

1:68

44.5
Through the tender mercy of our God; whereby the dayspring from on high hath visited us,
To give light to them that sit in darkness and in the shadow of death, to guide our feet into the way of peace.

1:78–79

44.6
And the child grew, and waxed strong in

spirit, and was in the deserts till the day of his shewing unto Israel.

1:80

44.7
And it came to pass in those days, that there went out a decree from Caesar Augustus, that all the world should be taxed.

2:1

44.8
And she brought forth her firstborn son, and wrapped him in swaddling clothes, and laid him in a manger; because there was no room for them in the inn.

2:7

44.9
And there were in the same country shepherds abiding in the field, keeping watch over their flock by night.
And, lo, the angel of the Lord came upon them, and the glory of the Lord shone round about them: and they were sore afraid.
And the angel said unto them, Fear not: for, behold, I bring you good tidings of great joy, which shall be to all people.

2:8–10

44.10
Glory to God in the highest, and on earth peace, good will toward men.

2:14

44.11
But Mary kept all these things, and pondered them in her heart.

2:19

44.12
Lord, now lettest thou thy servant depart in peace, according to thy word:
For mine eyes have seen thy salvation,
Which thou hast prepared before the face of all people;
A light to lighten the Gentiles, and the glory of thy people Israel.

2:29–32

44.13
And it came to pass, that after three days they found him in the temple, sitting in the midst of the doctors, both hearing them, and asking them questions.
And all that heard him were astonished at his understanding and answers.

2:46–47

44.14
And he said unto them, How is it that ye sought me? wist ye not that I must be about my Father's business?

2:49

44.15
And Jesus increased in wisdom and stature, and in favour with God and man.

2:52

44.16
And the soldiers likewise demanded of him, saying, And what shall we do? And he said unto them, Do violence to no man, neither accuse any falsely; and be content with your wages.

3:14

44.17
And the devil, taking him up into an high mountain, shewed unto him all the kingdoms of the world in a moment of time.

4:5

44.18
And he said unto them, Ye will surely say unto me this proverb, Physician, heal thyself: whatsoever we have heard done in Capernaum, do also here in thy country.

4:23

44.19
And Simon answering said unto him, Master, we have toiled all the night, and have taken nothing: nevertheless at thy word I will let down the net.
And when they had this done, they inclosed a great multitude of fishes: and their net brake.

5:5–6

44.20
No man also having drunk old wine straightway desireth new: for he saith, The old is better.

5:39

44.21
But woe unto you that are rich! for ye have received your consolation.
Woe unto you that are full! for ye shall hunger. Woe unto you that laugh now! for ye shall mourn and weep.
Woe unto you, when all men shall speak well of you! for so did their fathers to the false prophets.

6:24–26

44.22
Give, and it shall be given unto you; good measure, pressed down, and shaken together, and running over, shall men give into your bosom. For with the same measure that ye mete withal it shall be measured to you again.

6:38

44.23
Now when he came nigh to the gate of the city, behold, there was a dead man carried out, the only son of his mother, and she was a widow: and much people of the city was with her.

7:12

44.24
And stood at his feet behind him weeping, and began to wash his feet with tears, and did wipe them with the hairs of her head, and

kissed his feet, and anointed them with the ointment.

7:38

44.25
Wherefore I say unto thee, Her sins, which are many, are forgiven; for she loved much: but to whom little is forgiven, the same loveth little.

7:47

44.26
And he said to the woman, Thy faith hath saved thee; go in peace.

7:50

44.27
And Jesus said unto him, No man, having put his hand to the plough, and looking back is fit for the kingdom of God.

9:62

44.28
Go your ways: behold, I send you forth as lambs among wolves.
Carry neither purse, nor scrip, nor shoes: and salute no man by the way.
And into whatsoever house ye enter, first say, Peace be to this house.
And if the son of peace be there, your peace shall rest upon it: if not, it shall turn to you again.
And in the same house remain, eating and drinking such things as they give: for the labourer is worthy of his hire. Go not from house to house.

10:3–7

44.29
And he said unto them, I beheld Satan as lightning fall from heaven.

10:18

44.30
For I tell you, that many prophets and kings have desired to see those things which ye see, and have not seen them; and to hear those things which ye hear, and have not heard them.

10:24

44.31
And Jesus answering said, A certain man went down from Jerusalem to Jericho, and fell among thieves, which stripped him of his raiment, and wounded him, and departed, leaving him half dead.
And by chance there came down a certain priest that way: and when he saw him, he passed by on the other side.

10:30–31

44.32
But a certain Samaritan, as he journeyed, came where he was: and when he saw him, he had compassion on him,
And went to him, and bound up his wounds, pouring in oil and wine, and set him on his own beast, and brought him to an inn, and took care of him.
And on the morrow when he departed, he took out two pence, and gave them to the host, and said unto him, Take care of him; and whatsoever thou spendest more, when I come again, I will repay thee.

10:33–35

44.33
And he said, He that shewed mercy on him. Then said Jesus unto him, Go, and do thou likewise.

10:37

44.34
But Martha was cumbered about much serving, and came to him, and said, Lord, dost thou not care that my sister hath left me to serve alone? bid her therefore that she help me.
And Jesus answered and said unto her, Martha, Martha, thou art careful and troubled about many things:
But one thing is needful: and Mary hath chosen that good part, which shall not be taken away from her.

10:40–42

44.35
When a strong man armed keepeth his palace, his goods are in peace.

11:21

44.36
Woe unto you, lawyers! for ye have taken away the key of knowledge: ye entered not in yourselves, and them that were entering in ye hindered.

11:52

44.37
Are not five sparrows sold for two farthings, and not one of them is forgotten before God?

12:6

44.38
And I will say to my soul, Soul, thou hast much goods laid up for many years; take thine ease, eat, drink, and be merry.
But God said unto him, Thou fool, this night thy soul shall be required of thee: then whose shall those things be, which thou hast provided?
So is he that layeth up treasure for himself, and is not rich toward God.

12:19–21

44.39
Fear not, little flock; for it is your Father's good pleasure to give you the kingdom.

12:32

44.40
Let your loins be girded about, and your lights burning.

12:35

44.41
For from henceforth there shall be five in one house divided, three against two, and two against three.
The father shall be divided against the son, and the son against the father; the mother against the daughter, and the daughter against the mother; the mother in law against her daughter in law, and the daughter in law against her mother in law.
12:52–53

44.42
Then said he unto the dresser of his vineyard, Behold, these three years I come seeking fruit on this fig tree, and find none: cut it down; why cumbereth it the ground?
13:7

44.43
When thou art bidden of any man to a wedding, sit not down in the highest room; lest a more honourable man than thou be bidden of him;
And he that bade thee and him come and say to thee, Give this man place; and thou begin with shame to take the lowest room.
But when thou art bidden, go and sit down in the lowest room; that when he that bade thee cometh, he may say unto thee, Friend, go up higher: then shalt thou have worship in the presence of them that sit at meat with thee.
14:8–10

44.44
And they all with one consent began to make excuse. The first said unto him, I have bought a piece of ground, and I must needs go and see it: I pray thee have me excused.
And another said, I have bought five yoke of oxen, and I go to prove them: I pray thee have me excused.
And another said, I have married a wife, and therefore I cannot come.
So that servant came, and shewed his lord these things. Then the master of the house being angry said to his servant, Go out quickly into the streets and lanes of the city, and bring in hither the poor, and the maimed, and the halt, and the blind.
14:18–21

44.45
And the lord said unto the servant, Go out into the highways and hedges, and compel them to come in, that my house may be filled.
14:23

44.46
For which of you, intending to build a tower, sitteth not down first, and counteth the cost, whether he have sufficient to finish it?
14:28

44.47
What man of you, having an hundred sheep, if he lose one of them, doth not leave the ninety and nine in the wilderness, and go after that which is lost until he find it?
And when he hath found it, he layeth it on his shoulders, rejoicing.
And when he cometh home, he calleth together his friends and neighbours, saying unto them, Rejoice with me; for I have found my sheep which was lost.
I say unto you, that likewise joy shall be in heaven over one sinner that repenteth, more than over ninety and nine just persons, which need no repentance.
15:4–7

44.48
And not many days after the younger son gathered all together, and took his journey into a far country, and there wasted his substance with riotous living.
15:13

44.49
And he would fain have filled his belly with the husks that the swine did eat: and no man gave unto him.
And when he came to himself, he said, How many hired servants of my father's have bread enough and to spare, and I perish with hunger!
I will arise and go to my father, and will say unto him, Father, I have sinned against heaven, and before thee,
And am no more worthy to be called thy son: make me as one of thy hired servants.
And he arose, and came to his father. But when he was yet a great way off, his father saw him, and had compassion, and ran, and fell on his neck, and kissed him.
15:16–20

44.50
And bring hither the fatted calf, and kill it; and let us eat, and be merry:
For this my son was dead, and is alive again; he was lost, and is found. And they began to be merry.
15:23–24

44.51
And he said unto him, Thy brother is come; and thy father hath killed the fatted calf, because he hath received him safe and sound.
15:27

44.52
And he said unto him, Son, thou art ever with me, and all that I have is thine.
15:31

44.53
Then the steward said within himself, What shall I do? for my lord taketh away from me the stewardship: I cannot dig; to beg I am ashamed.
16:3

44.54
And the lord commended the unjust steward, because he had done wisely: for the children of this world are in their generation wiser than the children of light.
And I say unto you, Make to yourselves friends of the mammon of unrighteousness; that, when ye fail, they may receive you into everlasting habitations.
He that is faithful in that which is least is faithful also in much: and he that is unjust in the least is unjust also in much.
16:8–10

44.55
There was a certain rich man, which was clothed in purple and fine linen, and fared sumptuously every day:
And there was a certain beggar named Lazarus, which was laid at his gate, full of sores,
And desiring to be fed with the crumbs which fell from the rich man's table: moreover the dogs came and licked his sores.
And it came to pass, that the beggar died, and was carried by the angels into Abraham's bosom: the rich man also died, and was buried;
16:19–22

44.56
And beside all this, between us and you there is a great gulf fixed: so that they which would pass from hence to you cannot; neither can they pass to us, that would come from thence.
16:26

44.57
And he said unto him, If they hear not Moses and the prophets, neither will they be persuaded, though one rose from the dead.
16:31

44.58
And Jesus answering said, Were there not ten cleansed? but where are the nine?
There are not found that returned to give glory to God, save this stranger.
17:17–18

44.59
And when he was demanded of the Pharisees, when the kingdom of God should come, he answered them and said, The kingdom of God cometh not with observation:
Neither shall they say, Lo here! or, lo there! for, behold, the kingdom of God is within you.
17:20–21

44.60
Remember Lot's wife.
17:32

44.61
The Pharisee stood and prayed thus with himself, God, I thank thee, that I am not as other men are, extortioners, unjust, adulterers, or even as this publican.
18:11

44.62
And the publican, standing afar off, would not lift up so much as his eyes unto heaven, but smote upon his breast, saying, God be merciful to me a sinner.
18:13

44.63
And he saith unto him, Out of thine own mouth will I judge thee, thou wicked servant. Thou knewest that I was an austere man, taking up that I laid not down, and reaping that I did not sow.
19:22

44.64
And he answered and said unto them, I tell you that, if these should hold their peace, the stones would immediately cry out.
19:40

44.65
Saying, If thou hadst known, even thou, at least in this thy day, the things which belong unto thy peace! but now they are hid from thine eyes.
19:42

44.66
Settle it therefore in your hearts, not to meditate before what ye shall answer:
For I will give you a mouth and wisdom, which all your adversaries shall not be able to gainsay nor resist.
21:14–15

44.67
In your patience possess ye your souls.
21:19

44.68
And there shall be signs in the sun, and in the moon, and in the stars; and upon the earth distress of nations, with perplexity; the sea and the waves roaring.
21:25

44.69
For whether is greater, he that sitteth at meat, or he that serveth? is not he that sitteth at meat? but I am among you as he that serveth.
22:27

44.70
Saying, Father, if thou be willing, remove this cup from me: nevertheless not my will, but thine, be done.
22:42

44.71
But Jesus turning unto them said, Daughters of Jerusalem, weep not for me, but weep for yourselves, and for your children.
For, behold, the days are coming, in the which they shall say, Blessed are the barren, and the

wombs that never bare, and the paps which never gave suck.
Then shall they begin to say to the mountains, Fall on us; and to the hills, Cover us.
For if they do these things in a green tree, what shall be done in the dry?

23:28–31

44.72

And when they were come to the place, which is called Calvary, there they crucified him, and the malefactors, one on the right hand, and the other on the left.

23:33

44.73

Then said Jesus, Father, forgive them; for they know not what they do. And they parted his raiment, and cast lots.

23:34

44.74

But the other answering rebuked him, saying, Dost not thou fear God, seeing thou art in the same condemnation?
And we indeed justly; for we receive the due reward of our deeds: but this man hath done nothing amiss.
And he said unto Jesus, Lord, remember me when thou comest into thy kingdom.
And Jesus said unto him, Verily I say unto thee, To day shalt thou be with me in paradise.

23:40–43

44.75

And when Jesus had cried with a loud voice, he said, Father, into thy hands I commend my spirit: and having said thus, he gave up the ghost.

23:46

44.76

And, behold, there was a man named Joseph, a counsellor; and he was a good man, and a just.

23:50

44.77

And as they were afraid, and bowed down their faces to the earth, they said unto them, Why seek ye the living among the dead?

24:5

44.78

And their words seemed to them as idle tales, and they believed them not.

24:11

44.79

But they constrained him, saying, Abide with us: for it is toward evening, and the day is far spent. And he went in to tarry with them.

24:29

44.80

And they said one to another, Did not our heart burn within us, while he talked with us by the way, and while he opened to us the scriptures?

24:32

44.81

Saying, The Lord is risen indeed, and hath appeared to Simon.
And they told what things were done in the way, and how he was known of them in breaking of bread.

24:34–35

44.82

And, behold, I send the promise of my Father upon you: but tarry ye in the city of Jerusalem, until ye be endued with power from on high.

24:49

45 John

45.1

In the beginning was the Word, and the Word was with God, and the Word was God.
The same was in the beginning with God.
All things were made by him; and without him was not any thing made that was made.
In him was life; and the life was the light of men.
And the light shineth in darkness; and the darkness comprehended it not.
There was a man sent from God, whose name was John.
The same came for a witness, to bear witness of the Light, that all men through him might believe.
He was not that Light, but was sent to bear witness of that Light.
That was the true Light, which lighteth every man that cometh into the world.
He was in the world, and the world was made by him, and the world knew him not.
He came unto his own, and his own received him not.
But as many as received him, to them gave he power to become the sons of God, even to them that believe on his name:
Which were born, not of blood, nor of the will of the flesh, nor of the will of man, but of God.
And the Word was made flesh, and dwelt among us, (and we beheld his glory, the glory as of the only begotten of the Father,) full of grace and truth.

1:1–14

45.2

No man hath seen God at any time, the only begotten Son, which is in the bosom of the Father, he hath declared him.

1:18

45.3
He it is, who coming after me is preferred before me, whose shoe's latchet I am not worthy to unloose.

1:27

45.4
The next day John seeth Jesus coming unto him, and saith, Behold the Lamb of God, which taketh away the sin of the world.

1:29

45.5
And Nathanael said unto him, Can there any good thing come out of Nazareth? Philip saith unto him, Come and see.
Jesus saw Nathanael coming to him, and saith of him, Behold an Israelite indeed, in whom is no guile!
Nathanael saith unto him, Whence knowest thou me? Jesus answered and said unto him, Before that Philip called thee, when thou wast under the fig tree, I saw thee.

1:46–48

45.6
Jesus saith unto her, Woman, what have I to do with thee? mine hour is not yet come.

2:4

45.7
When the ruler of the feast had tasted the water that was made wine, and knew not whence it was: (but the servants which drew the water knew;) the governor of the feast called the bridegroom,
And saith unto him, Every man at the beginning doth set forth good wine; and when men have well drunk, then that which is worse: but thou hast kept the good wine until now.

2:9–10

45.8
Jesus answered and said unto him, Verily, verily, I say unto thee, Except a man be born again, he cannot see the kingdom of God.

3:3

45.9
Jesus answered, Verily, verily, I say unto thee, Except a man be born of water and of the Spirit, he cannot enter into the kingdom of God.
That which is born of the flesh is flesh; and that which is born of the Spirit is spirit.

3:5–6

45.10
The wind bloweth where it listeth, and thou hearest the sound thereof, but canst not tell whence it cometh, and whither it goeth: so is every one that is born of the Spirit.
Nicodemus answered and said unto him, How can these things be?
Jesus answered and said unto him, Art thou a master of Israel, and knowest not these things?
Verily, verily, I say unto thee, We speak that we do know, and testify that we have seen; and ye receive not our witness.
If I have told you earthly things, and ye believe not, how shall ye believe, if I tell you of heavenly things?

3:8–12

45.11
And as Moses lifted up the serpent in the wilderness, even so must the Son of man be lifted up.

3:14

45.12
For God so loved the world, that he gave his only begotten Son, that whosoever believeth in him should not perish, but have everlasting life.

3:16

45.13
And this is the condemnation, that light is come into the world, and men loved darkness rather than light, because their deeds were evil.

3:19

45.14
He that hath the bride is the bridegroom: but the friend of the bridegroom, which standeth and heareth him, rejoiceth greatly because of the bridegroom's voice: this my joy therefore is fulfilled.
He must increase, but I must decrease.

3:29–30

45.15
The Father loveth the Son, and hath given all things into his hand.
He that believeth on the Son hath everlasting life: and he that believeth not the Son shall not see life; but the wrath of God abideth on him.

3:35–36

45.16
Jesus answered and said unto her, Whosoever drinketh of this water shall thirst again:
But whosoever drinketh of the water that I shall give him shall never thirst; but the water that I shall give him shall be in him a well of water springing up into everlasting life.

4:13–14

45.17
For thou hast had five husbands; and he whom thou now hast is not thy husband: in that saidst thou truly.

4:18

45.18
But the hour cometh, and now is, when the true worshippers shall worship the Father in spirit and in truth: for the Father seeketh such to worship him.

God is a Spirit: and they that worship him must worship him in spirit and in truth.

4:23–24

45.19

Jesus saith unto them, My meat is to do the will of him that sent me, and to finish his work.

Say not ye, There are yet four months, and then cometh harvest? behold, I say unto you, Lift up your eyes, and look on the fields; for they are white already to harvest.

4:34–35

45.20

I sent you to reap that whereon ye bestowed no labour: other men laboured, and ye are entered into their labours.

4:38

45.21

For an angel went down at a certain season into the pool, and troubled the water: whosoever then first after the troubling of the water stepped in was made whole of whatsoever disease he had.

5:4

45.22

Afterward Jesus findeth him in the temple, and said unto him, Behold, thou art made whole: sin no more, lest a worse thing come unto thee.

5:14

45.23

Verily, verily, I say unto you, He that heareth my word, and believeth on him that sent me, hath everlasting life, and shall not come into condemnation; but is passed from death unto life.

Verily, verily, I say unto you, The hour is coming, and now is, when the dead shall hear the voice of the Son of God: and they that hear shall live.

5:24–25

45.24

He was a burning and a shining light: and ye were willing for a season to rejoice in his light.

5:35

45.25

Search the scriptures; for in them ye think ye have eternal life: and they are they which testify of me.

5:39

45.26

There is a lad here, which hath five barley loaves, and two small fishes: but what are they among so many?

And Jesus said, Make the men sit down. Now there was much grass in the place. So the men sat down, in number about five thousand.

6:9–10

45.27

When they were filled, he said unto his disciples, Gather up the fragments that remain, that nothing be lost.

6:12

45.28

Then said they unto him, What shall we do, that we might work the works of God?

6:28

45.29

And Jesus said unto them, I am the bread of life: he that cometh to me shall never hunger; and he that believeth on me shall never thirst.

6:35

45.30

All that the Father giveth me shall come to me; and him that cometh to me I will in no wise cast out.

6:37

45.31

No man can come to me, except the Father which hath sent me draw him: and I will raise him up at the last day.

6:44

45.32

Your fathers did eat manna in the wilderness, and are dead.

This is the bread which cometh down from heaven, that a man may eat thereof, and not die.

I am the living bread which came down from heaven: if any man eat of this bread, he shall live for ever: and the bread that I will give is my flesh, which I will give for the life of the world.

6:49–51

45.33

It is the spirit that quickeneth; the flesh profiteth nothing: the words that I speak unto you, they are spirit, and they are life.

6:63

45.34

Judge not according to the appearance, but judge righteous judgment.

7:24

45.35

The officers answered, Never man spake like this man.

7:46

45.36

So when they continued asking him, he lifted up himself, and said unto them, He that is without sin among you, let him first cast a stone at her.

8:7

45.37

She said, No man, Lord. And Jesus said unto her, Neither do I condemn thee: go, and sin no more.

8:11

45.38

Then spake Jesus again unto them, saying, I

am the light of the world: he that followeth me shall not walk in darkness, but shall have the light of life.

8:12

45.39

And ye shall know the truth, and the truth shall make you free.

8:32

45.40

Ye are of your father the devil, and the lusts of your father ye will do. He was a murderer from the beginning, and abode not in the truth, because there is no truth in him. When he speaketh a lie, he speaketh of his own: for he is a liar, and the father of it.

[*Hence 'father of lies' as a term for the Devil*]

8:44

45.41

Then answered the Jews, and said unto him, Say we not well that thou art a Samaritan, and hast a devil?

8:48

45.42

Verily, verily, I say unto you, If a man keep my saying, he shall never see death.

8:51

45.43

I must work the works of him that sent me, while it is day: the night cometh, when no man can work.

9:4

45.44

But by what means he now seeth, we know not; or who hath opened his eyes, we know not: he is of age; ask him: he shall speak for himself.

9:21

45.45

He answered and said, Whether he be a sinner or no, I know not: one thing I know, that, whereas I was blind, now I see.

9:25

45.46

Verily, verily, I say unto you, He that entereth not by the door into the sheepfold, but climbeth up some other way the same is a thief and a robber.

But he that entereth in by the door is the shepherd of the sheep.

To him the porter openeth, and the sheep hear his voice: and he calleth his own sheep by name, and leadeth them out.

And when he putteth forth his own sheep, he goeth before them, and the sheep follow him: for they know his voice.

10:1–4

45.47

I am the door: by me if any man enter in, he shall be saved, and shall go in and out, and find pasture.

10:9

45.48

I am the good shepherd: the good shepherd giveth his life for the sheep.

But he that is an hireling, and not the shepherd, whose own the sheep are not, seeth the wolf coming, and leaveth the sheep, and fleeth: and the wolf catcheth them, and scattereth the sheep.

The hireling fleeth, because he is an hireling, and careth not for the sheep.

10:11–13

45.49

And other sheep I have, which are not of this fold: them also I must bring, and they shall hear my voice; and there shall be one fold, and one shepherd.

10:16

45.50

Jesus said unto her, I am the resurrection, and the life: he that believeth in me, though he were dead, yet shall he live.

11:25

45.51

When Jesus therefore saw her weeping, and the Jews also weeping which came with her, he groaned in the spirit, and was troubled,

And said, Where have ye laid him? They said unto him, Lord, come and see.

Jesus wept.

11:33–35

45.52

Verily, verily, I say unto you, Except a corn of wheat fall into the ground and die, it abideth alone: but if it die, it bringeth forth much fruit.

12:24

45.53

Now is the judgment of this world: now shall the prince of this world be cast out.

And I, if I be lifted up from the earth, will draw all men unto me.

12:31–32

45.54

Then Jesus said unto them, Yet a little while is the light with you. Walk while ye have the light, lest darkness come upon you: for he that walketh in darkness knoweth not whither he goeth.

12:35

45.55

Now there was leaning on Jesus' bosom one of his disciples, whom Jesus loved.

13:23

45.56

In my Father's house are many mansions: if it

were not so, I would have told you. I go to prepare a place for you.

14:2

45.57
Jesus saith unto him, I am the way, the truth, and the life: no man cometh unto the Father, but by me.

14:6

45.58
Jesus saith unto him, Have I been so long time with you, and yet hast thou not known me, Philip? he that hath seen me hath seen the Father; and how sayest thou then, Shew us the Father?

14:9

45.59
If ye love me, keep my commandments.
And I will pray the Father, and he shall give you another Comforter, that he may abide with you for ever;
Even the Spirit of truth; whom the world cannot receive, because it seeth him not, neither knoweth him: but ye know him; for he dwelleth with you, and shall be in you.

14:15–17

45.60
Yet a little while, and the world seeth me no more; but ye see me: because I live, ye shall live also.

14:19

45.61
Peace I leave with you, my peace I give unto you: not as the world giveth, give I unto you. Let not your heart be troubled, neither let it be afraid.

14:27

45.62
I am the true vine, and my Father is the husbandman.

15:1

45.63
Greater love hath no man than this, that a man lay down his life for his friends.

15:13

45.64
Ye have not chosen me, but I have chosen you, and ordained you, that ye should go and bring forth fruit, and that your fruit should remain: that whatsoever ye shall ask of the Father in my name, he may give it you.

15:16

45.65
They shall put you out of the synagogues: yea, the time cometh, that whosoever killeth you will think that he doeth God service.

16:2

45.66
But now I go my way to him that sent me; and none of you asketh me, Whither goest thou?

16:5

45.67
Quo vadis?

Vulgate 16:5

45.68
Nevertheless I tell you the truth; It is expedient for you that I go away: for if I go not away, the Comforter will not come unto you; but if I depart, I will send him unto you.

16:7

45.69
I have yet many things to say unto you, but ye cannot bear them now.

16:12

45.70
A little while, and ye shall not see me: and again, a little while, and ye shall see me, because I go to the Father.

16:16

45.71
A woman when she is in travail hath sorrow, because her hour is come: but as soon as she is delivered of the child, she remembereth no more the anguish, for joy that a man is born into the world.

16:21

45.72
These things I have spoken unto you, that in me ye might have peace. In the world ye shall have tribulation: but be of good cheer; I have overcome the world.

16:33

45.73
Then said Jesus unto Peter, Put up thy sword into the sheath: the cup which my Father hath given me, shall I not drink it?

18:11

45.74
Now Caiaphas was he, which gave counsel to the Jews, that it was expedient that one man should die for the people.

18:14

45.75
And when he had thus spoken, one of the officers which stood by struck Jesus with the palm of his hand, saying, Answerest thou the high priest so?

18:22

45.76
Pilate saith unto him, What is truth? And when he had said this, he went out again unto the Jews, and saith unto them, I find in him no fault at all.

18:38

45.77
Then cried they all again, saying, Not this

man, but Barabbas. Now Barabbas was a robber.

18:40

45.78
Then came Jesus forth, wearing the crown of thorns, and the purple robe. And Pilate saith unto them, Behold the man!

19:5

45.79
Ecce homo.

Vulgate 19:5

45.80
Pilate answered, What I have written I have written.

19:22

45.81
When Jesus therefore saw his mother, and the disciple standing by, whom he loved, he saith unto his mother, Woman, behold thy son!
Then saith he to the disciple, Behold thy mother! And from that hour that disciple took her unto his own home.

19:26–27

45.82
When Jesus therefore had received the vinegar, he said, It is finished: and he bowed his head, and gave up the ghost.

19:30

45.83
Consummatum est.

Vulgate 19:30

45.84
But one of the soldiers with a spear pierced his side, and forthwith came there out blood and water.

19:34

45.85
And after this Joseph of Arimathaea, being a disciple of Jesus, but secretly for fear of the Jews, besought Pilate that he might take away the body of Jesus: and Pilate gave him leave. He came therefore, and took the body of Jesus.

19:38

45.86
Now in the place where he was crucified there was a garden; and in the garden a new sepulchre, wherein was never man yet laid.

19:41

45.87
The first day of the week cometh Mary Magdalene early, when it was yet dark, unto the sepulchre, and seeth the stone taken away from the sepulchre.
Then she runneth, and cometh to Simon Peter, and to the other disciple, whom Jesus loved, and saith unto them, They have taken away the Lord out of the sepulchre, and we know not where they have laid him.

20:1–2

45.88
So they ran both together: and the other disciple did outrun Peter, and came first to the sepulchre.

20:4

45.89
Jesus saith unto her, Woman, why weepest thou? whom seekest thou? She, supposing him to be the gardener, saith unto him, Sir, if thou have borne him hence, tell me where thou hast laid him, and I will take him away.
Jesus saith unto her, Mary. She turned herself, and saith unto him, Rabboni; which is to say, Master.
Jesus saith unto her, Touch me not; for I am not yet ascended to my Father: but go to my brethren, and say unto them, I ascend unto my Father, and your Father; and to my God, and your God.

20:15–17

45.90
Noli me tangere.

Vulgate 20:17

45.91
The other disciples therefore said unto him, We have seen the Lord. But he said unto them, Except I shall see in his hands the print of the nails, and put my finger into the print of the nails, and thrust my hand into his side, I will not believe.

20:25

45.92
Then saith he to Thomas, Reach hither thy finger, and behold my hands; and reach hither thy hand, and thrust it into my side: and be not faithless, but believing.
And Thomas answered and said unto him, My Lord and my God.
Jesus saith unto him, Thomas, because thou hast seen me, thou hast believed: blessed are they that have not seen, and yet have believed.

20:27–29

45.93
Simon Peter saith unto them, I go a fishing. They say unto him, We also go with thee. They went forth, and entered into a ship immediately; and that night they caught nothing.

21:3

45.94
So when they had dined, Jesus saith to Simon Peter, Simon, son of Jonas, lovest thou me more than these? He saith unto him, Yea, Lord; thou knowest that I love thee. He saith unto him, Feed my lambs.

21:15

45.95
He saith unto him the third time, Simon, son of Jonas, lovest thou me? Peter was grieved because he said unto him the third time,

Lovest thou me? And he said unto him, Lord, thou knowest all things; thou knowest that I love thee. Jesus saith unto him, Feed my sheep.

21:17

45.96

Peter seeing him saith to Jesus, Lord, and what shall this man do?
Jesus saith unto him, If I will that he tarry till I come, what is that to thee? follow thou me.

21:21–22

46 Acts

46.1

And he said unto them, It is not for you to know the times or the seasons, which the Father hath put in his own power.

1:7

46.2

And when he had spoken these things, while they beheld, he was taken up; and a cloud received him out of their sight.

1:9

46.3

Which also said, Ye men of Galilee, why stand ye gazing up into heaven? this same Jesus, which is taken up from you into heaven, shall so come in like manner as ye have seen him go into heaven.
Then returned they unto Jerusalem from the mount called Olivet, which is from Jerusalem a sabbath day's journey.

1:11–12

46.4

Now this man purchased a field with the reward of iniquity; and falling headlong, he burst asunder in the midst, and all his bowels gushed out.

1:18

46.5

For it is written in the book of Psalms, Let his habitation be desolate, and let no man dwell therein: and his bishoprick let another take.

1:20

46.6

And when the day of Pentecost was fully come, they were all with one accord in one place.
And suddenly there came a sound from heaven as of a rushing mighty wind, and it filled all the house where they were sitting.
And there appeared unto them cloven tongues like as of fire, and it sat upon each of them.
And they were all filled with the Holy Ghost, and began to speak with other tongues, as the Spirit gave them utterance.

2:1–4

46.7

Others mocking said, These men are full of new wine.

2:13

46.8

Men and brethren, let me freely speak unto you of the patriarch David, that he is both dead and buried, and his sepulchre is with us unto this day.

2:29

46.9

And all that believed were together, and had all things common.

2:44

46.10

Then Peter said, Silver and gold have I none; but such as I have give I thee: In the name of Jesus Christ of Nazareth rise up and walk.

3:6

46.11

But ye denied the Holy One and the Just, and desired a murderer to be granted unto you;
And killed the Prince of life, whom God hath raised from the dead; whereof we are witnesses.

3:14–15

46.12

Now when they saw the boldness of Peter and John, and perceived that they were unlearned and ignorant men, they marvelled; and they took knowledge of them, that they had been with Jesus.

4:13

46.13

And Joses, who by the apostles was surnamed Barnabas, (which is, being interpreted, The son of consolation,) a Levite, and of the country of Cyprus.

4:36

46.14

Then Peter and the other apostles answered and said, We ought to obey God rather than men.

5:29

46.15

And now I say unto you, Refrain from these men, and let them alone: for if this counsel or this work be of men, it will come to nought:
But if it be of God, ye cannot overthrow it; lest haply ye be found even to fight against God.

5:38–39

46.16

Then the twelve called the multitude of the disciples unto them, and said, It is not reason that we should leave the word of God, and serve tables.
Wherefore, brethren, look ye out among you seven men of honest report, full of the Holy

Ghost and wisdom, whom we may appoint over this business.
But we will give ourselves continually to prayer, and to the ministry of the word.

6:2–4

46.17
And all that sat in the council, looking stedfastly on him, saw his face as it had been the face of an angel.

6:15

46.18
When they heard these things, they were cut to the heart, and they gnashed on him with their teeth.

7:54

46.19
Then they cried out with a loud voice, and stopped their ears, and ran upon him with one accord,
And cast him out of the city, and stoned him: and the witnesses laid down their clothes at a young man's feet, whose name was Saul.

7:57–58

46.20
And he kneeled down, and cried with a loud voice, Lord, lay not this sin to their charge. And when he had said this, he fell asleep.

7:60

46.21
And Saul was consenting unto his death. And at that time there was a great persecution against the church which was at Jerusalem; and they were all scattered abroad throughout the regions of Judaea and Samaria, except the apostles.

8:1

46.22
But Peter said unto him, Thy money perish with thee, because thou hast thought that the gift of God may be purchased with money.
Thou hast neither part nor lot in this matter: for thy heart is not right in the sight of God.

8:20–21

46.23
And Philip ran thither to him, and heard him read the prophet Esaias, and said, Understandest thou what thou readest?
And he said, How can I, except some man should guide me? And he desired Philip that he would come up and sit with him.

8:30–31

46.24
And Saul, yet breathing out threatenings and slaughter against the disciples of the Lord, went unto the high priest.

9:1

46.25
And as he journeyed, he came near Damascus: and suddenly there shined round about him a light from heaven:
And he fell to the earth, and heard a voice saying unto him, Saul, Saul, why persecutest thou me?
And he said, Who art thou, Lord? And the Lord said, I am Jesus whom thou persecutest: it is hard for thee to kick against the pricks.

9:3–5

46.26
And the Lord said unto him, Arise, and go into the street which is called Straight, and enquire in the house of Judas for one called Saul, of Tarsus: for, behold, he prayeth.

9:11

46.27
But the Lord said unto him, Go thy way: for he is a chosen vessel unto me, to bear my name before the Gentiles, and kings, and the children of Israel.

9:15

46.28
Now there was at Joppa a certain disciple named Tabitha, which by interpretation is called Dorcas: this woman was full of good works and almsdeeds which she did.

9:36

46.29
And the voice spake unto him again the second time, What God hath cleansed, that call not thou common.

10:15

46.30
But Peter took him up, saying, Stand up; I myself also am a man.

10:26

46.31
Then Peter opened his mouth, and said, Of a truth I perceive that God is no respecter of persons.

10:34

46.32
And the Spirit bade me go with them, nothing doubting. Moreover these six brethren accompanied me, and we entered into the man's house.

11:12

46.33
And the people gave a shout, saying, It is the voice of a god, and not of a man.
And immediately the angel of the Lord smote him, because he gave not God the glory: and he was eaten of worms, and gave up the ghost.

12:22–23

46.34
And when the people saw what Paul had done, they lifted up their voices, saying in the speech of Lycaonia, The gods are come down to us in the likeness of men.

14:11

46.35
Now therefore why tempt ye God, to put a

yoke upon the neck of the disciples, which neither our fathers nor we were able to bear? But we believe that through the grace of the Lord Jesus Christ we shall be saved, even as they.

15:10–11

46.36

But the Jews which believed not, moved with envy, took unto them certain lewd fellows of the baser sort, and gathered a company, and set all the city on an uproar, and assaulted the house of Jason, and sought to bring them out to the people.
And when they found them not, they drew Jason and certain brethren unto the rulers of the city, crying, These that have turned the world upside down are come hither also.

17:5–6

46.37

Then certain philosophers of the Epicureans, and of the Stoicks, encountered him. And some said, What will this babbler say? other some, He seemeth to be a setter forth of strange gods: because he preached unto them Jesus, and the resurrection.

17:18

46.38

(For all the Athenians and strangers which were there spent their time in nothing else, but either to tell, or to hear some new thing.)
Then Paul stood in the midst of Mars' hill, and said, Ye men of Athens, I perceive that in all things ye are too superstitious.
For as I passed by, and beheld your devotions, I found an altar with this inscription, TO THE UNKNOWN GOD. Whom therefore ye ignorantly worship, him declare I unto you.
God that made the world and all things therein, seeing that he is Lord of heaven and earth, dwelleth not in temples made with hands.

17:21–24

46.39

For in him we live, and move, and have our being; as certain also of your own poets have said, For we are also his offspring.

17:28

46.40

Then all the Greeks took Sosthenes, the chief ruler of the synagogue, and beat him before the judgment seat. And Gallio cared for none of those things.

18:17

46.41

He said unto them, Have ye received the Holy Ghost since ye believed? And they said unto him, We have not so much as heard whether there be any Holy Ghost.

19:2

46.42

And the evil spirit answered and said, Jesus I know, and Paul I know; but who are ye?

19:15

46.43

And when they heard these sayings, they were full of wrath, and cried out, saying, Great is Diana of the Ephesians.

19:28

46.44

Some therefore cried one thing, and some another: for the assembly was confused; and the more part knew not wherefore they were come together.

19:32

46.45

Seeing then that these things cannot be spoken against, ye ought to be quiet, and to do nothing rashly.

19:36

46.46

For we are in danger to be called in question for this day's uproar, there being no cause whereby we may give an account of this concourse.

19:40

46.47

And when they were come to him, he said unto them, Ye know, from the first day that I came into Asia, after what manner I have been with you at all seasons.
Serving the Lord with all humility of mind, and with many tears, and temptations, which befell me by the lying in wait of the Jews.

20:18–19

46.48

And now, behold, I go bound in the spirit unto Jerusalem, not knowing the things that shall befall me there.

20:22

46.49

But none of these things move me, neither count I my life dear unto myself, so that I might finish my course with joy, and the ministry, which I have received of the Lord Jesus, to testify the gospel of the grace of God.

20:24

46.50

I have shewed you all things, how that so labouring ye ought to support the weak, and to remember the words of the Lord Jesus, how he said, It is more blessed to give than to receive.

20:35

46.51

But Paul said, I am a man which am a Jew of Tarsus, a city in Cilicia, a citizen of no mean city: and, I beseech thee, suffer me to speak unto the people.

21:39

46.52
And the chief captain answered, With a great sum obtained I this freedom. And Paul said, But I was free born.

22:28

46.53
Then said Paul unto him, God shall smite thee, thou whited wall: for sittest thou to judge me after the law, and commandest me to be smitten contrary to the law?

23:3

46.54
But when Paul perceived that the one part were Sadducees, and the other Pharisees, he cried out in the council, Men and brethren, I am a Pharisee, the son of a Pharisee: of the hope and resurrection of the dead I am called in question.

23:6

46.55
For we have found this man a pestilent fellow, and a mover of sedition among all the Jews throughout the world, and a ringleader of the sect of the Nazarenes.

24:5

46.56
And herein do I exercise myself, to have always a conscience void of offence toward God, and toward men.

24:16

46.57
Then Festus, when he had conferred with the council, answered, Hast thou appealed unto Caesar? unto Caesar shalt thou go.

25:12

46.58
Then Agrippa said unto Paul, Thou art permitted to speak for thyself. Then Paul stretched forth the hand, and answered for himself.

26:1

46.59
Which knew me from the beginning, if they would testify, that after the most straitest sect of our religion I lived a Pharisee.

26:5

46.60
And as he thus spake for himself, Festus said with a loud voice, Paul, thou art beside thyself; much learning doth make thee mad.
But he said, I am not mad, most noble Festus; but speak forth the words of truth and soberness.
For the king knoweth of these things, before whom also I speak freely: for I am persuaded that none of these things are hidden from him; for this thing was not done in a corner.

26:24–26

46.61
Then Agrippa said unto Paul, Almost thou persuadest me to be a Christian.
And Paul said, I would to God, that not only thou, but also all that hear me this day, were both almost, and altogether such as I am, except these bonds.

26:28–29

46.62
And the barbarous people shewed us no little kindness: for they kindled a fire, and received us every one, because of the present rain, and because of the cold.

28:2

46.63
But we desire to hear of thee what thou thinkest: for as concerning this sect, we know that every where it is spoken against.

28:22

47 Romans

47.1
Paul, a servant of Jesus Christ, called to be an apostle, separated unto the gospel of God.

1:1

47.2
For God is my witness, whom I serve with my spirit in the gospel of his Son, that without ceasing I make mention of you always in my prayers.

1:9

47.3
For I long to see you, that I may impart unto you some spiritual gift, to the end ye may be established.

1:11

47.4
I am debtor both to the Greeks, and to the Barbarians; both to the wise, and to the unwise.

1:14

47.5
For therein is the righteousness of God revealed from faith to faith: as it is written, The just shall live by faith.

1:17

47.6
Professing themselves to be wise, they became fools.

1:22

47.7
Who changed the truth of God into a lie, and worshipped and served the creature more than the Creator, who is blessed for ever. Amen.

1:25

47.8
To them who by patient continuance in well

doing seek for glory and honour and immortality, eternal life.

2:7

47.9
For there is no respect of persons with God.

2:11

47.10
For when the Gentiles, which have not the law, do by nature the things contained in the law, these, having not the law, are a law unto themselves.

2:14

47.11
God forbid: yea, let God be true, but every man a liar; as it is written, That thou mightest be justified in thy sayings, and mightest overcome when thou art judged.

3:4

47.12
And not rather, (as we be slanderously reported, and as some affirm that we say,) Let us do evil, that good may come? whose damnation is just.

3:8

47.13
For all have sinned, and come short of the glory of God.

3:23

47.14
Where is boasting then? It is excluded. By what law? of works? Nay: but by the law of faith.

3:27

47.15
Because the law worketh wrath: for where no law is, there is no transgression.

4:15

47.16
Who against hope believed in hope, that he might become the father of many nations, according to that which was spoken, So shall thy seed be.

4:18

47.17
And not only so, but we glory in tribulations also: knowing that tribulation worketh patience;
And patience, experience; and experience, hope:
And hope maketh not ashamed; because the love of God is shed abroad in our hearts by the Holy Ghost which is given unto us.

5:3–5

47.18
Moreover the law entered, that the offence might abound. But where sin abounded, grace did much more abound.

5:20

47.19
Therefore we are buried with him by baptism into death: that like as Christ was raised up from the dead by the glory of the Father, even so we also should walk in newness of life.

6:4

47.20
Knowing that Christ being raised from the dead dieth no more; death hath no more dominion over him.
For in that he died, he died unto sin once: but in that he liveth, he liveth unto God.
Likewise reckon ye also yourselves to be dead indeed unto sin, but alive unto God through Jesus Christ our Lord.

6:9–11

47.21
For the wages of sin is death; but the gift of God is eternal life through Jesus Christ our Lord.

6:23

47.22
For the good that I would I do not: but the evil which I would not, that I do.
Now if I do that I would not, it is no more I that do it, but sin that dwelleth in me.
I find then a law, that, when I would do good, evil is present with me.

7:19–21

47.23
O wretched man that I am! who shall deliver me from the body of this death?

7:24

47.24
For they that are after the flesh do mind the things of the flesh; but they that are after the Spirit the things of the Spirit.
For to be carnally minded is death; but to be spiritually minded is life and peace.

8:5–6

47.25
For as many as are led by the Spirit of God, they are the sons of God.
For ye have not received the spirit of bondage again to fear; but ye have received the Spirit of adoption, whereby we cry, Abba, Father.
The Spirit itself beareth witness with our spirit, that we are the children of God:
And if children, then heirs; heirs of God, and joint-heirs with Christ; if so be that we suffer with him, that we may be also glorified together.

8:14–17

47.26
For the earnest expectation of the creature waiteth for the manifestation of the sons of God.
For the creature was made subject to vanity, not willingly, but by reason of him who hath subjected the same in hope,
Because the creature itself also shall be deliv-

ered from the bondage of corruption into the glorious liberty of the children of God.
For we know that the whole creation groaneth and travaileth in pain together until now.

8:19–22

47.27
Likewise the Spirit also helpeth our infirmities: for we know not what we should pray for as we ought: but the Spirit itself maketh intercession for us with groanings which cannot be uttered.

8:26

47.28
And we know that all things work together for good to them that love God, to them who are the called according to his purpose.

8:28

47.29
What shall we then say to these things? If God be for us, who can be against us?

8:31

47.30
Who shall lay any thing to the charge of God's elect? It is God that justifieth.

8:33

47.31
Nay, in all these things we are more than conquerors through him that loved us.
For I am persuaded, that neither death, nor life, nor angels, nor principalities, nor powers, nor things present, nor things to come,
Nor height, nor depth, nor any other creature, shall be able to separate us from the love of God, which is in Christ Jesus our Lord.

8:37–39

47.32
So then it is not of him that willeth, nor of him that runneth, but of God that sheweth mercy.

9:16

47.33
Hath not the potter power over the clay, of the same lump to make one vessel unto honour, and another unto dishonour?

9:21

47.34
For I bear them record that they have a zeal of God, but not according to knowledge.

10:2

47.35
So then faith cometh by hearing, and hearing by the word of God.

10:17

47.36
I beseech you therefore, brethren, by the mercies of God, that ye present your bodies a living sacrifice, holy, acceptable unto God, which is your reasonable service.

12:1

47.37
Let love be without dissimulation. Abhor that which is evil; cleave to that which is good.
By kindly affectioned one to another with brotherly love; in honour preferring one another;
Not slothful in business; fervent in spirit; serving the Lord;
Rejoicing in hope; patient in tribulation; continuing instant in prayer;
Distributing to the necessity of saints; given to hospitality.
Bless them which persecute you: bless, and curse not.
Rejoice with them that do rejoice, and weep with them that weep.
Be of the same mind one toward another. Mind not high things, but condescend to men of low estate. Be not wise in your own conceits.
Recompense to no man evil for evil. Provide things honest in the sight of all men.
If it be possible, as much as lieth in you, live peaceably with all men.
Dearly beloved, avenge not yourselves, but rather give place unto wrath: for it is written, Vengeance is mine; I will repay, saith the Lord.

12:9–19

47.38
Be not overcome of evil, but overcome evil with good.

12:21

47.39
Let every soul be subject unto the higher powers. For there is no power but of God: the powers that be are ordained of God.

13:1

47.40
For rulers are not a terror to good works, but to the evil. Wilt thou then not be afraid of the power? do that which is good, and thou shalt have praise of the same.

13:3

47.41
Wherefore ye must needs be subject, not only for wrath, but also for conscience sake.

13:5

47.42
Render therefore to all their dues: tribute to whom tribute is due; custom to whom custom; fear to whom fear; honour to whom honour.
Owe no man any thing, but to love one another: for he that loveth another hath fulfilled the law.

13:7–8

47.43
Love worketh no ill to his neighbour: therefore love is the fulfilling of the law.

And that, knowing the time, that now it is high time to awake out of sleep: for now is our salvation nearer than when we believed.
The night is far spent, the day is at hand: let us therefore cast off the works of darkness, and let us put on the armour of light.
Let us walk honestly, as in the day; not in rioting and drunkenness, not in chambering and wantonness, not in strife and envying.
But put ye on the Lord Jesus Christ, and make not provision for the flesh, to fulfil the lusts thereof.

13:10–14

47.44
Him that is weak in the faith receive ye, but not to doubtful disputations.
For one believeth that he may eat all things: another, who is weak, eateth herbs.

14:1–2

47.45
One man esteemeth one day above another: another esteemeth every day alike. Let every man be fully persuaded in his own mind.
He that regardeth the day, regardeth it unto the Lord; and he that regardeth not the day, to the Lord he doth not regard it. He that eateth, eateth to the Lord, for he giveth God thanks; and he that eateth not, to the Lord he eateth not, and giveth God thanks.

14:5–6

47.46
We then that are strong ought to bear the infirmities of the weak, and not to please ourselves.

15:1

47.47
Now the God of patience and consolation grant you to be likeminded one toward another according to Christ Jesus.

15:5

47.48
Salute one another with an holy kiss. The churches of Christ salute you.

16:16

48 I Corinthians

48.1
For the preaching of the cross is to them that perish foolishness; but unto us which are saved it is the power of God.

1:18

48.2
For after that in the wisdom of God the world by wisdom knew not God, it pleased God by the foolishness of preaching to save them that believe.
For the Jews require a sign, and the Greeks seek after wisdom:
But we preach Christ crucified, unto the Jews a stumblingblock, and unto the Greeks foolishness.

1:21–23

48.3
But God hath chosen the foolish things of the world to confound the wise; and God hath chosen the weak things of the world to confound the things which are mighty.

1:27

48.4
For I determined not to know any thing among you, save Jesus Christ, and him crucified.

2:2

48.5
But as it is written, Eye hath not seen, nor ear heard, neither have entered into the heart of man, the things which God hath prepared for them that love him.

2:9

48.6
I have planted, Apollos watered; but God gave the increase.

3:6

48.7
Every man's work shall be made manifest: for the day shall declare it, because it shall be revealed by fire; and the fire shall try every man's work of what sort it is.

3:13

48.8
For the wisdom of this world is foolishness with God. For it is written, He taketh the wise in their own craftiness.

3:19

48.9
Let a man so account of us, as of the ministers of Christ, and stewards of the mysteries of God.

4:1

48.10
For I think that God hath set forth us the apostles last, as it were appointed to death: for we are made a spectacle unto the world, and to angels, and to men.
We are fools for Christ's sake, but ye are wise in Christ; we are weak, but ye are strong; ye are honourable, but we are despised.
Even unto this present hour we both hunger, and thirst, and are naked, and are buffeted, and have no certain dwellingplace:
And labour, working with our own hands: being reviled, we bless; being persecuted, we suffer it:
Being defamed, we intreat: we are made as the filth of the world, and are the offscouring of all things unto this day.

4:9–13

48.11
For the kingdom of God is not in word, but in power.

4:20

48.12
For I verily, as absent in body, but present in spirit, have judged already, as though I were present, concerning him that hath so done this deed.

5:3

48.13
Your glorying is not good. Know ye not that a little leaven leaveneth the whole lump?
Purge out therefore the old leaven, that ye may be a new lump as ye are unleavened. For even Christ our passover is sacrificed for us:
Therefore let us keep the feast, not with old leaven, neither with the leaven of malice and wickedness; but with the unleavened bread of sincerity and truth.

5:6–8

48.14
Meats for the belly, and the belly for meats: but God shall destroy both it and them. Now the body is not for fornication, but for the Lord; and the Lord for the body.

6:13

48.15
What? know ye not that your body is the temple of the Holy Ghost which is in you, which ye have of God, and ye are not your own?

6:19

48.16
Let the husband render unto the wife due benevolence: and likewise also the wife unto the husband.

7:3

48.17
But I speak this by permission, and not of commandment.

7:6

48.18
But if they cannot contain, let them marry: for it is better to marry than to burn.

7:9

48.19
Circumcision is nothing, and uncircumcision is nothing, but the keeping of the commandments of God.
Let every man abide in the same calling wherein he was called.

7:19–20

48.20
I suppose therefore that this is good for the present distress, I say, that it is good for a man so to be.
Art thou bound unto a wife? seek not to be loosed. Art thou loosed from a wife? seek not a wife.
But and if thou marry, thou hast not sinned; and if a virgin marry, she hath not sinned. Nevertheless such shall have trouble in the flesh: but I spare you.

7:26–28

48.21
And they that use this world, as not abusing it: for the fashion of this world passeth away.

7:31

48.22
But he that is married careth for the things that are of the world, how he may please his wife.

7:33

48.23
Now as touching things offered unto idols, we know that we all have knowledge. Knowledge puffeth up, but charity edifieth.

8:1

48.24
But take heed lest by any means this liberty of yours become a stumblingblock to them that are weak.

8:9

48.25
Who goeth a warfare any time at his own charges? who planteth a vineyard, and eateth not of the fruit thereof? or who feedeth a flock, and eateth not of the milk of the flock?

9:7

48.26
To the weak became I as weak, that I might gain the weak: I am made all things to all men, that I might by all means save some.

9:22

48.27
Know ye not that they which run in a race run all, but one receiveth the prize? So run, that ye may obtain.
And every man that striveth for the mastery is temperate in all things. Now they do it to obtain a corruptible crown; but we an incorruptible.
I therefore so run, not as uncertainly; so fight I, not as one that beateth the air:
But I keep under my body, and bring it into subjection: lest that by any means, when I have preached to others, I myself should be a castaway.

9:24–27

48.28
Wherefore let him that thinketh he standeth take heed lest he fall.
There hath no temptation taken you but such as is common to man: but God is faithful, who will not suffer you to be tempted above that ye are able; but will with the temptation also make a way to escape, that ye may be able to bear it.

10:12–13

48.29
All things are lawful for me, but all things are not expedient: all things are lawful for me, but all things edify not.
10:23

48.30
For the earth is the Lord's, and the fulness thereof.
10:26

48.31
Conscience, I say, not thine own, but of the other: for why is my liberty judged of another man's conscience?
10:29

48.32
Whether therefore ye eat, or drink, or whatsoever ye do, do all to the glory of God.
10:31

48.33
But if a woman have long hair, it is a glory to her: for her hair is given her for a covering.
11:15

48.34
Now there are diversities of gifts, but the same Spirit.
12:4

48.35
Though I speak with the tongues of men and of angels, and have not charity, I am become as sounding brass, or a tinkling cymbal.
And though I have the gift of prophecy, and understand all mysteries, and all knowledge; and though I have all faith, so that I could remove mountains, and have not charity, I am nothing.
And though I bestow all my goods to feed the poor, and though I give my body to be burned, and have not charity, it profiteth me nothing.
Charity suffereth long, and is kind; charity envieth not; charity vaunteth not itself, is not puffed up,
Doth not behave itself unseemly, seeketh not her own, is not easily provoked, thinketh no evil;
Rejoiceth not in iniquity, but rejoiceth in the truth;
Beareth all things, believeth all things, hopeth all things, endureth all things.
Charity never faileth: but whether there be prophecies, they shall fail; whether there be tongues, they shall cease; whether there be knowledge, it shall vanish away.
For we know in part, and we prophesy in part.
But when that which is perfect is come, then that which is in part shall be done away.
When I was a child, I spake as a child, I understood as a child, I thought as a child: but when I became a man, I put away childish things.
For now we see through a glass, darkly; but then face to face: now I know in part; but then shall I know even as also I am known.
And now abideth faith, hope, charity, these three; but the greatest of these is charity.
13:1–13

48.36
For if the trumpet give an uncertain sound, who shall prepare himself to the battle?
14:8

48.37
Brethren, be not children in understanding: howbeit in malice be ye children, but in understanding be men.
14:20

48.38
Let all things be done decently and in order.
14:40

48.39
And last of all he was seen of me also, as of one born out of due time.
For I am the least of the apostles, that am not meet to be called an apostle, because I persecuted the church of God.
But by the grace of God I am what I am: and his grace which was bestowed upon me was not in vain; but I laboured more abundantly than they all: yet not I, but the grace of God which was with me.
15:8–10

48.40
If in this life only we have hope in Christ, we are of all men most miserable.
But now is Christ risen from the dead, and become the firstfruits of them that slept.
For since by man came death, by man came also the resurrection of the dead.
For as in Adam all die, even so in Christ shall all be made alive.
15:19–22

48.41
Then cometh the end, when he shall have delivered up the kingdom to God, even the Father; when he shall have put down all rule and all authority and power.
For he must reign, till he hath put all enemies under his feet.
The last enemy that shall be destroyed is death.
15:24–26

48.42
If after the manner of men I have fought with beasts at Ephesus, what advantageth it me, if the dead rise not? let us eat and drink; for to morrow we die.
Be not deceived: evil communications corrupt good manners.
15:32–33

48.43
There is one glory of the sun, and another glory of the moon, and another glory of the stars: for one star differeth from another star in glory.
So also is the resurrection of the dead. It is sown in corruption; it is raised in incorruption.

15:41–42

48.44
The first man is of the earth, earthy: the second man is the Lord from heaven.

15:47

48.45
Behold, I shew you a mystery; We shall not all sleep, but we shall all be changed,
In a moment, in the twinkling of an eye, at the last trump: for the trumpet shall sound, and the dead shall be raised incorruptible, and we shall be changed.
For this corruptible must put on incorruption, and this mortal must put on immortality.
So when this corruptible shall have put on incorruption, and this mortal shall have put on immortality, then shall be brought to pass the saying that is written, Death is swallowed up in victory.
O death, where is thy sting? O grave, where is thy victory?

15:51–55

48.46
If any man love not the Lord Jesus Christ, let him be Anathema Maranatha.
The grace of our Lord Jesus Christ be with you.

16:22–23

49 II Corinthians

49.1
For our rejoicing is this, the testimony of our conscience, that in simplicity and godly sincerity, not with fleshly wisdom, but by the grace of God, we have had our conversation in the world, and more abundantly to you-ward.

1:12

49.2
Not for that we have dominion over your faith, but are helpers of your joy: for by faith ye stand.

1:24

49.3
Forasmuch as ye are manifestly declared to be the epistle of Christ ministered by us, written not with ink, but with the Spirit of the living God; not in tables of stone, but in fleshy tables of the heart.

3:3

49.4
Who also hath made us able ministers of the new testament; not of the letter, but of the spirit; for the letter killeth, but the spirit giveth life.

3:6

49.5
For if that which is done away was glorious, much more that which remaineth is glorious.

3:11

49.6
But we have this treasure in earthen vessels, that the excellency of the power may be of God, and not of us.

4:7

49.7
For our light affliction, which is but for a moment, worketh for us a far more exceeding and eternal weight of glory.

4:17

49.8
For we know that if our earthly house of this tabernacle were dissolved, we have a building of God, an house not made with hands, eternal in the heavens.

5:1

49.9
For we walk by faith, not by sight.

5:7

49.10
For the love of Christ constraineth us; because we thus judge, that if one died for all, then were all dead.

5:14

49.11
Therefore if any man be in Christ, he is a new creature: old things are passed away; behold, all things are become new.

5:17

49.12
For he saith, I have heard thee in a time accepted, and in the day of salvation have I succoured thee: behold, now is the accepted time: behold now is the day of salvation.

6:2

49.13
By the word of truth, by the power of God, by the armour of righteousness on the right hand and on the left,
By honour and dishonour, by evil report and good report: as deceivers, and yet true;
As unknown, and yet well known; as dying, and, behold, we live; as chastened, and not killed;
As sorrowful, yet alway rejoicing; as poor, yet making many rich; as having nothing, and yet possessing all things.

6:7–10

49.14
For, when we were come into Macedonia, our

flesh had no rest, but we were troubled on every side; without were fightings, within were fears.

7:5

49.15
Every man according as he purposeth in his heart, so let him give; not grudgingly, or of necessity: for God loveth a cheerful giver.

9:7

49.16
For though we walk in the flesh, we do not war after the flesh:
For the weapons of our warfare are not carnal, but mighty through God to the pulling down of strong holds.

10:3–4

49.17
For ye suffer fools gladly, seeing ye yourselves are wise.

11:19

49.18
Are they Hebrews? so am I. Are they Israelites? so am I. Are they the seed of Abraham? so am I.
Are they ministers of Christ? (I speak as a fool) I am more; in labours more abundant, in stripes above measure, in prisons more frequent, in deaths oft.
Of the Jews five times received I forty stripes save one.
Thrice was I beaten with rods, once was I stoned, thrice I suffered shipwreck, a night and a day I have been in the deep;
In journeyings often, in perils of waters, in perils of robbers, in perils by mine own countrymen, in perils by the heathen, in perils in the city, in perils in the wilderness, in perils in the sea, in perils among false brethren;
In weariness and painfulness, in watchings often, in hunger and thirst, in fastings often, in cold and nakedness.

11:22–27

49.19
I knew a man in Christ above fourteen years ago, (whether in the body, I cannot tell; or whether out of the body, I cannot tell: God knoweth;) such an one caught up to the third heaven.

12:2

49.20
And lest I should be exalted above measure through the abundance of the revelations, there was given to me a thorn in the flesh, the messenger of Satan to buffet me, lest I should be exalted above measure.

12:7

49.21
And he said unto me, My grace is sufficient for thee: for my strength is made perfect in weakness. Most gladly therefore will I rather glory in my infirmities, that the power of Christ may rest upon me.

12:9

49.22
This is the third time I am coming to you. In the mouth of two or three witnesses shall every word be established.

13:1

50 Galatians

50.1
But of these who seemed to be somewhat, (whatsoever they were, it maketh no matter to me: God accepteth no man's person:) for they who seemed to be somewhat in conference added nothing to me.

2:6

50.2
And when James, Cephas, and John, who seemed to be pillars, perceived the grace that was given unto me, they gave to me and Barnabas the right hands of fellowship; that we should go unto the heathen, and they unto the circumcision.

2:9

50.3
O foolish Galatians, who hath bewitched you, that ye should not obey the truth, before whose eyes Jesus Christ hath been evidently set forth, crucified among you?

3:1

50.4
Wherefore the law was our schoolmaster to bring us unto Christ, that we might be justified by faith.
But after that faith is come, we are no longer under a schoolmaster.

3:24–25

50.5
There is neither Jew nor Greek, there is neither bond nor free, there is neither male nor female: for ye are all one in Christ Jesus.

3:28

50.6
But now, after that ye have known God, or rather are known of God, how turn ye again to the weak and beggarly elements, whereunto ye desire again to be in bondage?

4:9

50.7
Which things are an allegory: for these are the two covenants; the one from the mount Sinai, which gendereth to bondage, which is Agar.

4:24

50.8
But Jerusalem which is above is free, which is the mother of us all.

4:26

50.9
For, brethren, ye have been called unto liberty; only use not liberty for an occasion to the flesh, but by love serve one another.

5:13

50.10
For the flesh lusteth against the Spirit, and the Spirit against the flesh: and these are contrary the one to the other: so that ye cannot do the things that ye would.

5:17

50.11
But the fruit of the Spirit is love, joy, peace, longsuffering, gentleness, goodness, faith,
Meekness, temperance: against such there is no law.

5:22–23

50.12
Bear ye one another's burdens, and so fulfil the law of Christ.
For if a man think himself to be something, when he is nothing, he deceiveth himself.

6:2–3

50.13
Be not deceived: God is not mocked: for whatsoever a man soweth, that shall he also reap.
For he that soweth to his flesh shall of the flesh reap corruption; but he that soweth to the Spirit shall of the Spirit reap life everlasting.
And let us not be weary in well doing: for in due season we shall reap, if we faint not.

6:7–9

50.14
Ye see how large a letter I have written unto you with mine own hand.

6:11

51 Ephesians

51.1
The eyes of your understanding being enlightened; that ye may know what is the hope of his calling, and what the riches of the glory of his inheritance in the saints.

1:18

51.2
And you hath he quickened, who were dead in trespasses and sins;
Wherein in time past ye walked according to the course of this world, according to the prince of the power of the air, the spirit that now worketh in the children of disobedience.

2:1–2

51.3
And came and preached peace to you which were afar off, and to them that were nigh.

2:17

51.4
Unto me, who am less than the least of all saints, is this grace given, that I should preach among the Gentiles the unsearchable riches of Christ.

3:8

51.5
That he would grant you, according to the riches of his glory, to be strengthened with might by his Spirit in the inner man;
That Christ may dwell in your hearts by faith; that ye, being rooted and grounded in love,
May be able to comprehend with all saints what is the breadth, and length, and depth, and height;
And to know the love of Christ, which passeth knowledge, that ye might be filled with all the fulness of God.
Now unto him that is able to do exceeding abundantly above all that we ask or think, according to the power that worketh in us,
Unto him be glory in the church by Christ Jesus throughout all ages, world without end. Amen.

3:16–21

51.6
I therefore, the prisoner of the Lord, beseech you that ye walk worthy of the vocation wherewith ye are called,
With all lowliness and meekness, with longsuffering, forbearing one another in love;
Endeavouring to keep the unity of the Spirit in the bond of peace.

4:1–3

51.7
That we henceforth be no more children, tossed to and fro, and carried about with every wind of doctrine, by the sleight of men, and cunning craftiness, whereby they lie in wait to deceive.

4:14

51.8
Wherefore putting away lying, speak every man truth with his neighbour: for we are members one of another.
Be ye angry, and sin not: let not the sun go down upon your wrath:
Neither give place to the devil.
Let him that stole steal no more: but rather let him labour, working with his hands the thing which is good, that he may have to give to him that needeth.

4:25–28

51.9
And grieve not the holy Spirit of God, whereby ye are sealed unto the day of redemption.

4:30

51.10
Let no man deceive you with vain words: for

because of these things cometh the wrath of God upon the children of disobedience.

5:6

51.11

See then that ye walk circumspectly, not as fools, but as wise,
Redeeming the time, because the days are evil.

5:15–16

51.12

Nevertheless let every one of you in particular so love his wife even as himself; and the wife see that she reverence her husband.

5:33

51.13

Children, obey your parents in the Lord: for this is right.

6:1

51.14

Finally, my brethren, be strong in the Lord, and in the power of his might.
Put on the whole armour of God, that ye may be able to stand against the wiles of the devil.
For we wrestle not against flesh and blood, but against principalities, against powers, against the rulers of the darkness of this world, against spiritual wickedness in high places.
Wherefore take unto you the whole armour of God, that ye may be able to withstand in the evil day, and having done all, to stand.
Stand therefore, having your loins girt about with truth, and having on the breastplate of righteousness;
And your feet shod with the preparation of the gospel of peace;
Above all, taking the shield of faith, wherewith ye shall be able to quench all the fiery darts of the wicked.
And take the helmet of salvation, and the sword of the Spirit, which is the word of God.

6:10–17

51.15

For which I am an ambassador in bonds: that therein I may speak boldly, as I ought to speak.

6:20

52 Philippians

52.1

I thank my God upon every remembrance of you,
Always in every prayer of mine for you all making request with joy.

1:3–4

52.2

For to me to live is Christ, and to die is gain.

1:21

52.3

For I am in a strait betwixt two, having a desire to depart, and to be with Christ; which is far better:
Nevertheless to abide in the flesh is more needful for you.

1:23–24

52.4

But made himself of no reputation, and took upon him the form of a servant, and was made in the likeness of men:
And being found in fashion as a man, he humbled himself, and became obedient unto death, even the death of the cross.
Wherefore God also hath highly exalted him, and given him a name which is above every name:
That at the name of Jesus every knee should bow, of things in heaven, and things in earth, and things under the earth.
And that every tongue should confess that Jesus Christ is Lord, to the glory of God the Father.

2:7–11

52.5

Wherefore, my beloved, as ye have always obeyed, not as in my presence only, but now much more in my absence, work out your own salvation with fear and trembling.

2:12

52.6

Circumcised the eighth day, of the stock of Israel, of the tribe of Benjamin, an Hebrew of the Hebrews; as touching the law, a Pharisee.

3:5

52.7

But what things were gain to me, those I counted loss for Christ.

3:7

52.8

Brethren, I count not myself to have apprehended: but this one thing I do, forgetting those things which are behind, and reaching forth unto those things which are before,
I press toward the mark for the prize of the high calling of God in Christ Jesus.

3:13–14

52.9

Whose end is destruction, whose God is their belly, and whose glory is in their shame, who mind earthly things.

3:19

52.10

Rejoice in the Lord alway: and again I say, Rejoice.

4:4

52.11

And the peace of God, which passeth all

understanding, shall keep your hearts and minds through Christ Jesus.

4:7

52.12
Finally, brethren, whatsoever things are true, whatsoever things are honest, whatsoever things are just, whatsoever things are pure, whatsoever things are lovely, whatsoever things are of good report; if there be any virtue; and if there be any praise, think on these things.

4:8

52.13
I can do all things through Christ which strengtheneth me.

4:13

53 Colossians

53.1
Beware lest any man spoil you through philosophy and vain deceit, after the tradition of men, after the rudiments of the world, and not after Christ.

2:8

53.2
Touch not; taste not; handle not.

2:21

53.3
Set your affection on things above, not on things on the earth.
For ye are dead, and your life is hid with Christ in God.

3:2–3

53.4
Where there is neither Greek nor Jew, circumcision nor uncircumcision, Barbarian, Scythian, bond nor free; but Christ is all, and in all.

3:11

53.5
Husbands, love your wives, and be not bitter against them.

3:19

53.6
Fathers, provoke not your children to anger, lest they be discouraged.

3:21

53.7
And whatsoever ye do, do it heartily, as to the Lord, and not unto men.

3:23

53.8
Let your speech be alway with grace, seasoned with salt, that ye may know how ye ought to answer every man.

4:6

53.9
Luke, the beloved physician, and Demas, greet you.

4:14

54 I Thessalonians

54.1
Remembering without ceasing your work of faith, and labour of love, and patience of hope in our Lord Jesus Christ, in the sight of God and our Father.

1:3

54.2
And that ye study to be quiet, and to do your own business, and to work with your own hands, as we commanded you.

4:11

54.3
But I would not have you to be ignorant, brethren, concerning them which are asleep, that ye sorrow not, even as others which have no hope.

4:13

54.4
For yourselves know perfectly that the day of the Lord so cometh as a thief in the night.

5:2

54.5
Prove all things; hold fast that which is good.

5:21

55 II Thessalonians

55.1
Let no man deceive you by any means: for that day shall not come, except there come a falling away first, and that man of sin be revealed, the son of perdition.

2:3

55.2
For even when we were with you, this we commanded you, that if any would not work, neither should he eat.

3:10

56 I Timothy

56.1
Neither give heed to fables and endless genealogies, which minister questions, rather than godly edifying which is in faith: so do.

1:4

56.2
This is a faithful saying, and worthy of all acceptation, that Christ Jesus came into the world to save sinners; of whom I am chief.

1:15

56.3
Holding faith, and a good conscience; which some having put away concerning faith have made shipwreck.

1:19

56.4
This is a true saying, If a man desire the office of a bishop, he desireth a good work.
A bishop then must be blameless, the husband of one wife, vigilant, sober, of good behaviour, given to hospitality, apt to teach;
Not given to wine, no striker, not greedy of filthy lucre; but patient, not a brawler, not covetous.

3:1–3

56.5
For every creature of God is good, and nothing to be refused, if it be received with thanksgiving.

4:4

56.6
But refuse profane and old wives' fables, and exercise thyself rather unto godliness.
For bodily exercise profiteth little: but godliness is profitable unto all things, having promise of the life that now is, and of that which is to come.

4:7–8

56.7
Rebuke not an elder, but intreat him as a father; and the younger men as brethren.

5:1

56.8
And withal they learn to be idle, wandering about from house to house; and not only idle, but tattlers also and busybodies, speaking things which they ought not.

5:13

56.9
Drink no longer water, but use a little wine for thy stomach's sake and thine often infirmities.

5:23

56.10
For we brought nothing into this world, and it is certain we can carry nothing out.

6:7

56.11
For the love of money is the root of all evil: which while some coveted after, they have erred from the faith, and pierced themselves through with many sorrows.

6:10

56.12
Fight the good fight of faith, lay hold on eternal life, whereunto thou art also called, and hast professed a good profession before many witnesses.

6:12

56.13
Who only hath immortality, dwelling in the light which no man can approach unto; whom no man hath seen, nor can see: to whom be honour and power everlasting. Amen.

6:16

56.14
That they do good, that they be rich in good works, ready to distribute, willing to communicate.

6:18

56.15
O Timothy, keep that which is committed to thy trust, avoiding profane and vain babblings, and oppositions of science falsely so called.

6:20

57 II Timothy

57.1
For God hath not given us the spirit of fear; but of power, and of love, and of a sound mind.

1:7

57.2
Hold fast the form of sound words, which thou hast heard of me, in faith and love which is in Christ Jesus.

1:13

57.3
Thou therefore endure hardness, as a good soldier of Jesus Christ.
No man that warreth entangleth himself with the affairs of this life; that he may please him who hath chosen him to be a soldier.
And if a man also strive for masteries, yet is he not crowned, except he strive lawfully.

2:3–5

57.4
But evil men and seducers shall wax worse and worse, deceiving, and being deceived.

3:13

57.5
That the man of God may be perfect, throughly furnished unto all good works.

3:17

57.6
Preach the word; be instant in season, out of season; reprove, rebuke, exhort with all longsuffering and doctrine.

4:2

57.7
For I am now ready to be offered, and the time of my departure is at hand.
I have fought a good fight, I have finished my course, I have kept the faith:
Henceforth there is laid up for me a crown of righteousness, which the Lord, the righteous judge, shall give me at that day: and not to me only, but unto all them also that love his appearing.

4:6–8

57.8
For Demas hath forsaken me, having loved this present world, and is departed unto Thes-

salonica; Crescens to Galatia, Titus unto Dalmatia.

4:10

57.9
At my first answer no man stood with me, but all men forsook me: I pray God that it may not be laid to their charge.
Notwithstanding the Lord stood with me, and strengthened me; that by me the preaching might be fully known, and that all the Gentiles might hear: and I was delivered out of the mouth of the lion.

4:16–17

58 Titus

58.1
One of themselves, even a prophet of their own, said, The Cretians are alway liars, evil beasts, slow bellies.

1:12

58.2
Unto the pure all things are pure: but unto them that are defiled and unbelieving is nothing pure; but even their mind and conscience is defiled.

1:15

59 Philemon

59.1
Yet for love's sake I rather beseech thee, being such an one as Paul the aged, and now also a prisoner of Jesus Christ.

9

60 Hebrews

60.1
God, who at sundry times and in divers manners spake in time past unto the fathers by the prophets,
Hath in these last days spoken unto us by his Son, whom he hath appointed heir of all things, by whom also he made the worlds;
Who being the brightness of his glory, and the express image of his person, and upholding all things by the word of his power, when he had by himself purged our sins, sat down on the right hand of the Majesty on high;
Being made so much better than the angels, as he hath by inheritance obtained a more excellent name than they.

1:1–4

60.2
And of the angels he saith, Who maketh his angels spirits, and his ministers a flame of fire.

1:7

60.3
Are they not all ministering spirits, sent forth to minister for them who shall be heirs of salvation?

1:14

60.4
But exhort one another daily, while it is called To day; lest any of you be hardened through the deceitfulness of sin.

3:13

60.5
For the word of God is quick, and powerful, and sharper than any two-edged sword, piercing even to the dividing asunder of soul and spirit, and of the joints and marrow, and is a discerner of the thoughts and intents of the heart.

4:12

60.6
Seeing then that we have a great high priest, that is passed into the heavens, Jesus the Son of God, let us hold fast our profession.

4:14

60.7
For when for the time ye ought to be teachers, ye have need that one teach you again which be the first principles of the oracles of God; and are become such as have need of milk, and not of strong meat.

5:12

60.8
And without all contradiction the less is blessed of the better.

7:7

60.9
And almost all things are by the law purged with blood; and without shedding of blood is no remission.

9:22

60.10
It is a fearful thing to fall into the hands of the living God.

10:31

60.11
Now faith is the substance of things hoped for, the evidence of things not seen.

11:1

60.12
These all died in faith, not having received the promises, but having seen them afar off, and were persuaded of them, and embraced them, and confessed that they were strangers and pilgrims on the earth.

11:13

60.13
Esteeming the reproach of Christ greater riches than the treasures in Egypt: for he had respect unto the recompence of the reward.

11:26

60.14
By faith the walls of Jericho fell down, after they were compassed about seven days.
11:30

60.15
(Of whom the world was not worthy:) they wandered in deserts, and in mountains, and in dens and caves of the earth.
11:38

60.16
Wherefore seeing we also are compassed about with so great a cloud of witnesses, let us lay aside every weight, and the sin which doth so easily beset us, and let us run with patience the race that is set before us,
Looking unto Jesus the author and finisher of our faith; who for the joy that was set before him endured the cross, despising the shame, and is set down at the right hand of the throne of God.
12:1–2

60.17
For whom the Lord loveth he chasteneth, and scourgeth every son whom he receiveth.
12:6

60.18
For ye know how that afterward, when he would have inherited the blessing, he was rejected: for he found no place of repentance, though he sought it carefully with tears.
12:17

60.19
To the general assembly and church of the firstborn, which are written in heaven, and to God the Judge of all, and to the spirits of just men made perfect.
12:23

60.20
Let brotherly love continue.
Be not forgetful to entertain strangers: for thereby some have entertained angels unawares.
13:1–2

60.21
Jesus Christ the same yesterday, and to day, and for ever.
13:8

60.22
For here have we no continuing city but we seek one to come.
13:14

61 James

61.1
But let patience have her perfect work, that ye may be perfect and entire, wanting nothing.
If any of you lack wisdom, let him ask of God, that giveth to all men liberally, and upbraideth not; and it shall be given him.
But let him ask in faith, nothing wavering. For he that wavereth is like a wave of the sea driven with the wind and tossed.
1:4–6

61.2
Blessed is the man that endureth temptation: for when he is tried, he shall receive the crown of life, which the Lord hath promised to them that love him.
1:12

61.3
Every good gift and every perfect gift is from above, and cometh down from the Father of lights, with whom is no variableness, neither shadow of turning.
1:17

61.4
Wherefore, my beloved brethren, let every man be swift to hear, slow to speak, slow to wrath:
For the wrath of man worketh not the righteousness of God.
Wherefore lay apart all filthiness and superfluity of naughtiness, and receive with meekness the engrafted word, which is able to save your souls.
But be ye doers of the word, and not hearers only, deceiving your own selves.
For if any be a hearer of the word, and not a doer, he is like unto a man beholding his natural face in a glass:
For he beholdeth himself, and goeth his way, and straightway forgetteth what manner of man he was.
But whoso looketh into the perfect law of liberty, and continueth therein, he being not a forgetful hearer, but a doer of the work, this man shall be blessed in his deed.
1:19–25

61.5
Pure religion and undefiled before God and the Father is this, To visit the fatherless and widows in their affliction, and to keep himself unspotted from the world.
1:27

61.6
Even so faith, if it hath not works, is dead, being alone.
2:17

61.7
Even so the tongue is a little member, and boasteth great things. Behold, how great a matter a little fire kindleth!
3:5

61.8
But the tongue can no man tame; it is an unruly evil, full of deadly poison.
3:8

61.9
Out of the same mouth proceedeth blessing

and cursing. My brethren, these things ought not so to be.

Doth a fountain send forth at the same place sweet water and bitter?

3:10–11

61.10

This wisdom descendeth not from above, but is earthly, sensual, devilish.

3:15

61.11

But the wisdom that is from above is first pure, then peaceable, gentle, and easy to be intreated, full of mercy and good fruits, without partiality, and without hypocrisy.

3:17

61.12

Submit yourselves therefore to God. Resist the devil, and he will flee from you.

Draw nigh to God, and he will draw nigh to you. Cleanse your hands, ye sinners; and purify your hearts, ye double minded.

4:7–8

61.13

Whereas ye know not what shall be on the morrow. For what is your life? It is even a vapour, that appeareth for a little time, and then vanisheth away.

4:14

61.14

Grudge not one against another, brethren, lest ye be condemned: behold, the judge standeth before the door.

5:9

61.15

Behold, we count them happy which endure. Ye have heard of the patience of Job, and have seen the end of the Lord; that the Lord is very pitiful, and of tender mercy.

But above all things, my brethren, swear not, neither by heaven, neither by the earth, neither by any other oath: but let your yea be yea; and your nay, nay; lest ye fall into condemnation.

5:11–12

61.16

Confess your faults one to another, and pray one for another, that ye may be healed. The effectual fervent prayer of a righteous man availeth much.

5:16

61.17

Let him know, that he which converteth the sinner from the error of his way shall save a soul from death, and shall hide a multitude of sins.

5:20

62 I Peter

62.1

Wherein ye greatly rejoice, though now for a season, if need be, ye are in heaviness through manifold temptations.

1:6

62.2

Whom having not seen, ye love; in whom, though now ye see him not, yet believing, ye rejoice with joy unspeakable and full of glory.

1:8

62.3

Wherefore gird up the loins of your mind, be sober, and hope to the end for the grace that is to be brought unto you at the revelation of Jesus Christ.

1:13

62.4

Being born again, not of corruptible seed, but of incorruptible, by the word of God, which liveth and abideth for ever.

For all flesh is as grass, and all the glory of man as the flower of grass. The grass withereth, and the flower thereof falleth away.

1:23–24

62.5

As newborn babes, desire the sincere milk of the word, that ye may grow thereby.

2:2

62.6

Dearly beloved, I beseech you as strangers and pilgrims, abstain from fleshly lusts, which war against the soul.

2:11

62.7

Honour all men. Love the brotherhood. Fear God. Honour the king.

2:17

62.8

For what glory is it, if, when ye be buffeted for your faults, ye shall take it patiently? but if, when ye do well, and suffer for it, ye take it patiently, this is acceptable with God.

2:20

62.9

Who did no sin, neither was guile found in his mouth.

2:22

62.10

For ye were as sheep going astray; but are now returned unto the Shepherd and Bishop of your souls.

2:25

62.11

But let it be the hidden man of the heart, in that which is not corruptible, even the ornament of a meek and quiet spirit, which is in the sight of God of great price.

3:4

62.12
Even as Sara obeyed Abraham, calling him lord: whose daughters ye are, as long as ye do well, and are not afraid with any amazement.
Likewise, ye husbands, dwell with them according to knowledge, giving honour unto the wife, as unto the weaker vessel, and as being heirs together of the grace of life; that your prayers be not hindered.

3:6–7

62.13
Not rendering evil for evil, or railing for railing: but contrariwise blessing; knowing that ye are thereunto called, that ye should inherit a blessing.
For he that will love life, and see good days, let him refrain his tongue from evil, and his lips that they speak no guile.

3:9–10

62.14
But the end of all things is at hand: be ye therefore sober, and watch unto prayer.

4:7

62.15
Use hospitality one to another without grudging.

4:9

62.16
Humble yourselves therefore under the mighty hand of God, that he may exalt you in due time:
Casting all your care upon him; for he careth for you.
Be sober, be vigilant; because your adversary the devil, as a roaring lion, walketh about, seeking whom he may devour:
Whom resist stedfast in the faith, knowing that the same afflictions are accomplished in your brethren that are in the world.

5:6–9

63 II Peter

63.1
We have also a more sure word of prophecy; whereunto ye do well that ye take heed, as unto a light that shineth in a dark place, until the day dawn, and the day star arise in your hearts.

1:19

63.2
But chiefly them that walk after the flesh in the lust of uncleanness, and despise government. Presumptuous are they, selfwilled, they are not afraid to speak evil of dignities.

2:10

63.3
The Lord is not slack concerning his promise, as some men count slackness; but is longsuffering to us-ward, not willing that any should perish, but that all should come to repentance.

3:9

64 I John

64.1
And these things write we unto you, that your joy may be full.

1:4

64.2
If we say that we have no sin, we deceive ourselves, and the truth is not in us.
If we confess our sins, he is faithful and just to forgive us our sins, and to cleanse us from all unrighteousness.

1:8–9

64.3
My little children, these things write I unto you, that ye sin not. And if any man sin, we have an advocate with the Father, Jesus Christ the righteous:
And he is the propitiation for our sins: and not for ours only, but also for the sins of the whole world.

2:1–2

64.4
For all that is in the world, the lust of the flesh, and the lust of the eyes, and the pride of life, is not of the Father, but is of the world.

2:16

64.5
But whoso hath this world's good, and seeth his brother have need, and shutteth up his bowels of compassion from him, how dwelleth the love of God in him?

3:17

64.6
Beloved, believe not every spirit, but try the spirits whether they are of God: because many false prophets are gone out into the world.

4:1

64.7
Beloved, let us love one another: for love is of God; and every one that loveth is born of God, and knoweth God.
He that loveth not knoweth not God; for God is love.

4:7–8

64.8
There is no fear in love; but perfect love casteth out fear: because fear hath torment. He that feareth is not made perfect in love.

4:18

64.9
If a man say, I love God, and hateth his brother, he is a liar: for he that loveth not his

brother whom he hath seen, how can he love God whom he hath not seen?

4:20

64.10
Little children, keep yourselves from idols.

5:21

65 II John

65.1
The elder unto the elect lady and her children, whom I love in the truth; and not I only, but also all they that have known the truth.

1:1

66 Jude

66.1
Mercy unto you, and peace, and love, be multiplied.

2

66.2
Likewise also these filthy dreamers defile the flesh, despise dominion, and speak evil of dignities.
Yet Michael the archangel, when contending with the devil he disputed about the body of Moses, durst not bring against him a railing accusation, but said, The Lord rebuke thee.

8–9

66.3
These are spots in your feasts of charity, when they feast with you, feeding themselves without fear: clouds they are without water, carried about of winds; trees whose fruit withereth, without fruit, twice dead, plucked up by the roots;
Raging waves of the sea, foaming out their own shame; wandering stars, to whom is reserved the blackness of darkness for ever.

12–13

66.4
These are murmurers, complainers, walking after their own lusts; and their mouth speaketh great swelling words, having men's persons in admiration because of advantage.

16

67 Revelations

67.1
John to the seven churches which are in Asia: Grace be unto you, and peace, from him which is, and which was, and which is to come; and from the seven Spirits which are before his throne.

1:4

67.2
Behold, he cometh with clouds; and every eye shall see him, and they also which pierced him: and all kindreds of the earth shall wail because of him. Even so, Amen.

I am Alpha and Omega, the beginning and the ending, saith the Lord, which is, and which was, and which is to come, the Almighty.

I John, who also am your brother, and companion in tribulation, and in the kingdom and patience of Jesus Christ, was in the isle that is called Patmos, for the word of God, and for the testimony of Jesus Christ.

I was in the Spirit on the Lord's day, and heard behind me a great voice, as of a trumpet,
Saying, I am Alpha and Omega, the first and the last: and, What thou seest, write in a book, and send it unto the seven churches which are in Asia; unto Ephesus, and unto Smyrna, and unto Pergamos, and unto Thyatira, and unto Sardis, and unto Philadelphia, and unto Laodicea.

And I turned to see the voice that spake with me. And being turned, I saw seven golden candlesticks;

And in the midst of the seven candlesticks one like unto the Son of man, clothed with a garment down to the foot, and girt about the paps with a golden girdle.

His head and his hairs were white like wool, as white as snow; and his eyes were as a flame of fire;
And his feet like unto fine brass, as if they burned in a furnace; and his voice as the sound of many waters.
And he had in his right hand seven stars: and out of his mouth went a sharp twoedged sword: and his countenance was as the sun shineth in his strength.

1:7–16

67.3
I am he that liveth, and was dead; and, behold, I am alive for evermore, Amen; and have the keys of hell and of death.

1:18

67.4
The mystery of the seven stars which thou sawest in my right hand, and the seven golden candlesticks. The seven stars are the angels of the seven churches: and the seven candlesticks which thou sawest are the seven churches.

1:20

67.5
And hast borne, and hast patience, and for my name's sake hast laboured, and hast not fainted.

Nevertheless I have somewhat against thee, because thou hast left thy first love.

2:3–4

67.6

He that hath an ear, let him hear what the Spirit saith unto the churches; To him that overcometh will I give to eat of the tree of life, which is in the midst of the paradise of God.

2:7

67.7

Fear none of those things which thou shalt suffer: behold, the devil shall cast some of you into prison, that ye may be tried; and ye shall have tribulation ten days: be thou faithful unto death, and I will give thee a crown of life.

2:10

67.8

He that hath an ear, let him hear what the Spirit saith unto the churches; To him that overcometh will I give to eat of the hidden manna, and will give him a white stone, and in the stone a new name written, which no man knoweth saving he that receiveth it.

2:17

67.9

But that which ye have already hold fast till I come.

2:25

67.10

And he shall rule them with a rod of iron; as the vessels of a potter shall they be broken to shivers: even as I received of my Father.

2:27

67.11

He that overcometh, the same shall be clothed in white raiment; and I will not blot out his name out of the book of life, but I will confess his name before my Father, and before his angels.

3:5

67.12

I know thy works: behold, I have set before thee an open door, and no man can shut it: for thou hast a little strength, and hast kept my word, and hast not denied my name.

3:8

67.13

Him that overcometh will I make a pillar in the temple of my God, and he shall go no more out: and I will write upon him the name of my God, and the name of the city of my God, which is new Jerusalem, which cometh down out of heaven from my God: and I will write upon him my new name.

3:12

67.14

I know thy works, that thou art neither cold nor hot: I would thou wert cold or hot.
So then because thou art lukewarm, and neither cold nor hot, I will spue thee out of my mouth.

[*This rebuke, addressed to the Christians of Laodicea in Asia Minor, gave rise to the term 'Laodicean' for anyone who is indifferent or lukewarm about religious or political affiliations*]

3:15–16

67.15

Behold, I stand at the door, and knock: if any man hear my voice, and open the door, I will come in to him, and will sup with him, and he with me.

3:20

67.16

After this I looked, and, behold, a door was opened in heaven: and the first voice which I heard was as it were of a trumpet talking with me; which said, Come up hither, and I will shew thee things which must be hereafter.
And immediately I was in the spirit: and, behold, a throne was set in heaven, and one sat on the throne.
And he that sat was to look upon like a jasper and a sardine stone: and there was a rainbow round about the throne, in sight like unto an emerald.
And round about the throne were four and twenty seats: and upon the seats I saw four and twenty elders sitting, clothed in white raiment; and they had on their heads crowns of gold.
And out of the throne proceeded lightnings and thunderings and voices: and there were seven lamps of fire burning before the throne, which are the seven Spirits of God.
And before the throne there was a sea of glass like unto crystal: and in the midst of the throne, and round about the throne, were four beasts full of eyes before and behind.
And the first beast was like a lion, and the second beast like a calf, and the third beast had a face as a man, and the fourth beast was like a flying eagle.
And the four beasts had each of them six wings about him; and they were full of eyes within: and they rest not day and night, saying, Holy, holy, holy, Lord God Almighty, which was, and is, and is to come.

[*The traditional symbols of the four evangelists are based on 4:7; Matthew is represented by the man, Mark by the lion, Luke by the calf, and John by the eagle*]

4:1–8

67.17

The four and twenty elders fall down before him that sat on the throne, and worship him that liveth for ever and ever, and cast their crowns before the throne, saying,
Thou art worthy, O Lord, to receive glory and honour and power: for thou hast created all

things, and for thy pleasure they are and were created.

4:10–11

67.18

And I saw in the right hand of him that sat on the throne a book written within and on the backside, sealed with seven seals.
And I saw a strong angel proclaiming with a loud voice, Who is worthy to open the book, and to loose the seals thereof?

5:1–2

67.19

And I beheld, and, lo, in the midst of the throne and of the four beasts, and in the midst of the elders, stood a Lamb as it had been slain, having seven horns and seven eyes, which are the seven Spirits of God sent forth into all the earth.

5:6

67.20

And when he had taken the book, the four beasts and four and twenty elders fell down before the Lamb, having every one of them harps, and golden vials full of odours, which are the prayers of saints.

5:8

67.21

Saying with a loud voice, Worthy is the Lamb that was slain to receive power, and riches, and wisdom, and strength, and honour, and glory, and blessing.

5:12

67.22

And I saw, and behold a white horse: and he that sat on him had a bow; and a crown was given unto him: and he went forth conquering, and to conquer.

6:2

67.23

And I heard a voice in the midst of the four beasts say, A measure of wheat for a penny, and three measures of barley for a penny; and see thou hurt not the oil and the wine.

6:6

67.24

And I looked, and behold a pale horse: and his name that sat on him was Death, and Hell followed with him. And power was given unto them over the fourth part of the earth, to kill with sword, and with hunger, and with death, and with the beasts of the earth.

6:8

67.25

And they cried with a loud voice, saying, How long, O Lord, holy and true, dost thou not judge and avenge our blood on them that dwell on the earth?

6:10

67.26

And I beheld when he had opened the sixth seal, and, lo, there was a great earthquake; and the sun became black as sackcloth of hair, and the moon became as blood;
And the stars of heaven fell unto the earth, even as a fig tree casteth her untimely figs, when she is shaken of a mighty wind.
And the heaven departed as a scroll when it is rolled together; and every mountain and island were moved out of their places.

6:12–14

67.27

After this I beheld, and, lo, a great multitude, which no man could number, of all nations, and kindreds, and people, and tongues, stood before the throne, and before the Lamb, clothed with white robes, and palms in their hands.

7:9

67.28

And one of the elders answered, saying unto me, What are these which are arrayed in white robes? and whence came they?
And I said unto him, Sir, thou knowest. And he said to me, These are they which came out of great tribulation, and have washed their robes, and made them white in the blood of the Lamb.
Therefore are they before the throne of God, and serve him day and night in his temple: and he that sitteth on the throne shall dwell among them.
They shall hunger no more, neither thirst any more; neither shall the sun light on them, nor any heat.
For the Lamb which is in the midst of the throne shall feed them, and shall lead them unto living fountains of waters: and God shall wipe away all tears from their eyes.

7:13–17

67.29

And when he had opened the seventh seal, there was silence in heaven about the space of half an hour.

8:1

67.30

And the smoke of the incense, which came with the prayers of the saints, ascended up before God out of the angel's hand.

8:4

67.31

And the name of the star is called Wormwood: and the third part of the waters became wormwood; and many men died of the waters, because they were made bitter.

8:11

67.32

And the fifth angel sounded, and I saw a star fall from heaven unto the earth: and to him was given the key of the bottomless pit.

9:1

67.33
And it was commanded them that they should not hurt the grass of the earth, neither any green thing, neither any tree; but only those men which have not the seal of God in their foreheads.

9:4

67.34
And in those days shall men seek death, and shall not find it; and shall desire to die, and death shall flee from them.

9:6

67.35
And they had tails like unto scorpions, and there were stings in their tails: and their power was to hurt men five months.

9:10

67.36
And I went unto the angel, and said unto him, Give me the little book. And he said unto me, Take it, and eat it up; and it shall make thy belly bitter, but it shall be in thy mouth sweet as honey.

10:9

67.37
And there appeared a great wonder in heaven; a woman clothed with the sun, and the moon under her feet, and upon her head a crown of twelve stars.

12:1

67.38
And there was war in heaven: Michael and his angels fought against the dragon; and the dragon fought and his angels,
And prevailed not; neither was their place found any more in heaven.
And the great dragon was cast out, that old serpent, called the Devil, and Satan, which deceiveth the whole world: he was cast out into the earth, and his angels were cast out with him.

12:7–9

67.39
Therefore rejoice, ye heavens, and ye that dwell in them. Woe to the inhabiters of the earth and of the sea! for the devil is come down unto you, having great wrath, because he knoweth that he hath but a short time.

12:12

67.40
And they worshipped the dragon which gave power unto the beast: and they worshipped the beast, saying, Who is like unto the beast? who is able to make war with him?

13:4

67.41
And all that dwell upon the earth shall worship him, whose names are not written in the book of life of the Lamb slain from the foundation of the world.

13:8

67.42
And that no man might buy or sell, save he that had the mark, or the name of the beast, or the number of his name.
Here is wisdom. Let him that hath understanding count the number of the beast: for it is the number of a man; and his number is Six hundred threescore and six.

13:17–18

67.43
And I heard a voice from heaven, as the voice of many waters, and as the voice of a great thunder: and I heard the voice of harpers harping with their harps:
And they sung as it were a new song before the throne, and before the four beasts, and the elders: and no man could learn that song but the hundred and forty and four thousand, which were redeemed from the earth.

14:2–3

67.44
And in their mouth was found no guile: for they are without fault before the throne of God.

14:5

67.45
And there followed another angel, saying, Babylon is fallen, is fallen, that great city, because she made all nations drink of the wine of the wrath of her fornication.

14:8

67.46
The same shall drink of the wine of the wrath of God, which is poured out without mixture into the cup of his indignation; and he shall be tormented with fire and brimstone in the presence of the holy angels, and in the presence of the Lamb:
And the smoke of their torment ascendeth up for ever and ever: and they have no rest day nor night, who worship the beast and his image, and whosoever receiveth the mark of his name.

14:10–11

67.47
And I heard a voice from heaven saying unto me, Write, Blessed are the dead which die in the Lord from henceforth: Yea, saith the Spirit, that they may rest from their labours; and their works do follow them.

14:13

67.48
And another angel came out of the temple, crying with a loud voice to him that sat on the cloud, Thrust in thy sickle, and reap: for the

time is come for thee to reap; for the harvest of the earth is ripe.

14:15

67.49

And the angel thrust in his sickle into the earth, and gathered the vine of the earth, and cast it into the great winepress of the wrath of God.

14:19

67.50

And I saw another sign in heaven, great and marvellous, seven angels having the seven last plagues; for in them is filled up the wrath of God.

And I saw as it were a sea of glass mingled with fire: and them that had gotten the victory over the beast, and over his image, and over his mark, and over the number of his name, stand on the sea of glass, having the harps of God.

15:1–2

67.51

And I heard a great voice out of the temple saying to the seven angels, Go your ways, and pour out the vials of the wrath of God upon the earth.

16:1

67.52

Behold, I come as a thief. Blessed is he that watcheth, and keepeth his garments, lest he walk naked, and they see his shame.

And he gathered them together into a place called in the Hebrew tongue Armageddon.

16:15–16

67.53

And there came one of the seven angels which had the seven vials, and talked with me, saying unto me, Come hither; I will shew unto thee the judgment of the great whore that sitteth upon many waters.

17:1

67.54

And the woman was arrayed in purple and scarlet colour, and decked with gold and precious stones and pearls, having a golden cup in her hand full of abominations and filthiness of her fornication:

And upon her forehead was a name written, MYSTERY, BABYLON THE GREAT, THE MOTHER OF HARLOTS AND ABOMINATIONS OF THE EARTH.

And I saw the woman drunken with the blood of the saints, and with the blood of the martyrs of Jesus: and when I saw her, I wondered with great admiration.

17:4–6

67.55

How much she hath glorified herself, and lived deliciously, so much torment and sorrow give her: for she saith in her heart, I sit a queen, and am no widow, and shall see no sorrow.

18:7

67.56

For in one hour so great riches is come to nought.

18:17

67.57

And a mighty angel took up a stone like a great millstone, and cast it into the sea, saying, Thus with violence shall that great city Babylon be thrown down, and shall be found no more at all.

18:21

67.58

And I heard as it were the voice of a great multitude, and as the voice of many waters, and as the voice of mighty thunderings, saying, Alleluia: for the Lord God omnipotent reigneth.

Let us be glad and rejoice, and give honour to him: for the marriage of the Lamb is come, and his wife hath made herself ready.

19:6–7

67.59

And he saith unto me, Write, Blessed are they which are called unto the marriage supper of the Lamb. And he saith unto me, These are the true sayings of God.

19:9

67.60

And I saw heaven opened, and behold a white horse; and he that sat upon him was called Faithful and True, and in righteousness he doth judge and make war.

19:11

67.61

And he hath on his vesture and on his thigh a name written, KING OF KINGS, AND LORD OF LORDS.

19:16

67.62

And he laid hold on the dragon, that old serpent, which is the Devil, and Satan, and bound him a thousand years.

20:2

67.63

Blessed and holy is he that hath part in the first resurrection: on such the second death hath no power, but they shall be priests of God and of Christ, and shall reign with him a thousand years.

And when the thousand years are expired, Satan shall be loosed out of his prison,

And shall go out to deceive the nations which are in the four quarters of the earth, Gog and Magog, to gather them together to battle: the number of whom is as the sand of the sea.

20:6–8

67.64
And I saw a great white throne, and him that sat on it, from whose face the earth and the heaven fled away; and there was found no place for them.
And I saw the dead, small and great, stand before God; and the books were opened: and another book was opened, which is the book of life: and the dead were judged out of those things which were written in the books, according to their works.
And the sea gave up the dead which were in it; and death and hell delivered up the dead which were in them: and they were judged every man according to their works.

20:11–13

67.65
And I saw a new heaven and a new earth: for the first heaven and the first earth were passed away; and there was no more sea.
And I John saw the holy city, new Jerusalem, coming down from God out of heaven, prepared as a bride adorned for her husband.
And I heard a great voice out of heaven saying, Behold, the tabernacle of God is with men, and he will dwell with them, and they shall be his people, and God himself shall be with them, and be their God.
And God shall wipe away all tears from their eyes; and there shall be no more death, neither sorrow, nor crying, neither shall there be any more pain: for the former things are passed away.
And he that sat upon the throne said, Behold, I make all things new. And he said unto me, Write: for these words are true and faithful.

21:1–5

67.66
And he carried me away in the spirit to a great and high mountain, and shewed me that great city, the holy Jerusalem, descending out of heaven from God.
Having the glory of God: and her light was like unto a stone most precious, even like a jasper stone, clear as crystal.

21:10–11

67.67
And the building of the wall of it was of jasper: and the city was pure gold, like unto clear glass.
And the foundations of the wall of the city were garnished with all manner of precious stones. The first foundation was jasper; the second, sapphire; the third, a chalcedony; the fourth, an emerald;
The fifth, sardonyx; the sixth, sardius; the seventh, chrysolite; the eighth, beryl; the ninth, a topaz; the tenth, a chrysoprasus; the eleventh, a jacinth; the twelfth, an amethyst.
And the twelve gates were twelve pearls; every several gate was of one pearl: and the street of the city was pure gold, as it were transparent glass.
And I saw no temple therein: for the Lord God Almighty and the Lamb are the temple of it.
And the city had no need of the sun, neither of the moon, to shine in it: for the glory of God did lighten it, and the Lamb is the light thereof.

21:18–23

67.68
And he shewed me a pure river of water of life, clear as crystal, proceeding out of the throne of God and of the Lamb.
In the midst of the street of it, and on either side of the river, was there the tree of life, which bare twelve manner of fruits, and yielded her fruit every month: and the leaves of the tree were for the healing of the nations.

22:1–2

67.69
And they shall see his face; and his name shall be in their foreheads.
And there shall be no night there; and they need no candle, neither light of the sun; for the Lord God giveth them light: and they shall reign for ever and ever.

22:4–5

67.70
He that is unjust, let him be unjust still: and he which is filthy, let him be filthy still: and he that is righteous, let him be righteous still: and he that is holy, let him be holy still.
And, behold, I come quickly; and my reward is with me, to give every man according as his work shall be.

22:11–12

67.71
Blessed are they that do his commandments, that they may have right to the tree of life, and may enter in through the gates into the city.
For without are dogs, and sorcerers, and whoremongers, and murderers, and idolaters, and whosoever loveth and maketh a lie.
I Jesus have sent mine angel to testify unto you these things in the churches. I am the root and the offspring of David, and the bright and morning star.
And the Spirit and the bride say, Come. And let him that heareth say, Come. And let him that is athirst come. And whosoever will, let him take the water of life freely.

22:14–17

INDEX

A

Aaron's Rod 2.14, 4.10
abased whosoever shall exalt himself shall be a. 42.138
abated the waters were a. 1.31
Abba A., Father 47.25
abide a. under the shadow of the Almighty 17.185
who may a. it? 17.271
who is able to a. his frost? 17.296
the day of the Lord ... who can a. it? 27.3
who may a. the day of his coming? 34.2
a. with us: for ... the day is far spent 44.79
another Comforter, that he may a. ... for ever 45.59
let every man a. in the same calling 48.19
to a. in the flesh is more needful for you 52.3
abideth the wrath of God a. on him 45.15
now a. faith, hope, charity 48.35
the word of God, which liveth and a. 62.4
ability rich men furnished with a. 39.28
to every man according to his several a. 42.153
able God ... will not suffer you to be tempted above that ye are a. 48.28
abomination incense is an a. 21.3
a. of desolation 42.146
abominations full of a. 67.54
abound grace did much more a. 47.18
above Jerusalem which is a. is free 50.8
a name which is a. every name 52.4
Abraham the God of A. 2.6
A.'s bosom 44.55
are they the seed of A.? so am I 49.18
abroad blaze a. the matter 43.2
Absalom A. hanged in an oak 10.10
O A., my son 10.11
absent a. in body 48.12
abstain a. from fleshly lusts 62.6
abstention we will drink no wine 22.18
abundance sound of a. of rain 11.19
out of the a. of the heart the mouth speaketh 42.79
they did cast in of their a. 43.21
abundant in labours more a. 49.18
abundantly laboured more a. 48.39
more a. to you-ward 49.1
able to do exceeding a. 51.5
acceptable let the words of my mouth ... be alway a. in thy sight 17.37
to proclaim the a. year of the Lord 21.96
a. men in the furnace of adversity 39.2
O death, a. is thy sentence 39.26
a living sacrifice, holy, a. 47.36
accepted now is the a. time 49.12
accepteth God a. no man's person 50.1
accord they were all with one a. in one place 46.6
ran upon him with one a. 46.19
account every idle word ... they shall give a. thereof 42.80
accusation a railing a. 66.2
accuse neither a. any falsely 44.16
acquainted a. with grief 21.81
Adam as in A. all die 48.40
added all these things shall be a. unto you 42.32
adder an a. in the path 1.79
the deaf a. that stoppeth her ears 17.129
thou shalt go upon the lion and a. 17.187
a.'s poison is under their lips 17.282
wine ... stingeth like an a. 18.75
admiration having men's persons in a. because of advantage 66.4
ado the heathen make much a. 17.104
adoption the Spirit of a. 47.25
adorned as a bride a. for her husband 67.65
adulterous an evil and a. generation 42.81
adultery lie with me 1.68
thou shalt not commit a. 2.29
let us take our fill of love 18.18
neighed after his neighbour's wife 22.1
he ... is not thy husband 45.17
advantage no small a. 17.155
having men's persons in admiration because of a. 66.4
adversary agree with thine a. quickly 42.20
your a. the devil 62.16
adversity if thou faint in ... a., thy strength is small 18.77
in the day of a. consider 19.22
the bread of a. 21.48
the furnace of a. 39.2
advocate an a. with the Father 64.3
afar peace to you which were a. off 51.3
affairs no man that warreth entangleth himself with the a. of this life 57.3
affection set your a. on things above 53.3
affectioned be kindly a. 47.37
afflicted smitten of God, and a. 21.81
affliction feed him with bread of a. 11.32
the water of a. 21.48
the furnace of a. 21.72
in all their a. he was afflicted 21.98
our light a. ... is but for a moment 49.7
afraid I was a., because I was naked 1.16
a. to look upon God 2.6
a. where no fear was 17.118
thou shalt not be a. for any terror by night 17.186
shall a trumpet be blown ... and the people not be a.? 28.2

let not your heart be troubled, neither let it be a. 45.61
not a. with any amazement 62.12
not a. to speak evil of dignities 63.2
Agag A. came unto him delicately 9.16
against if God be for us, who can be a. us? 47.29
age buried in a good old a. 1.44
the son of his old a. 1.64
multitude of years should teach wisdom 16.48
mine a. is even as nothing in respect of thee 17.88
forsake me not . . . in mine old a. 17.152
the hoary head is a crown of glory 18.46
nothing in thy youth, how canst thou find any thing in thine a.? 39.19
he is of a. . . . he shall speak for himself 45.44
aged Paul the a. 59.1
agree a. with thine adversary quickly 42.20
agreed can two walk together, except they be a.? 28.1
agreement your a. with hell shall not stand 21.42
aid if they fall, the one will lift up his fellow 19.12
they helped every one his neighbour 21.65
air so fight I, not as one that beateth the a. 48.27
the prince of the power of the a. 51.2
alarm sound an a. in my holy mountain 27.2
alive a. into the pit 4.9
he shall save his soul a. 24.7
this my son was dead, and is a. again 44.50
dead . . . unto sin, but a. unto God 47.20
in Christ shall all be made a. 48.40
I am a. for evermore 67.3
all the earth is the Lord's, and a. that therein is 17.48
thine incorruptible spirit is in a. things 38.11
Elias truly shall . . . restore a. things 42.108
a. that I have is thine 44.52
above a. that we ask or think 51.5
Christ is a., and in all 53.4
upholding a. things by the word of his power 60.1
allegory which things are an a. 50.7
alleluia a.: for the Lord God omnipotent reigneth 67.58
almost a., and altogether such as I am 46.61
alone it is not good that man should be a. 1.11
let me a., that I may take comfort 16.25
a sparrow . . . a. upon the house-top 17.205
woe to him that is a. when he falleth 19.12
I have trodden the winepress a. 21.97
refrain from these men, and let them a. 46.15
faith, if it hath not works, is dead, being a. 61.6
Alpha A. and Omega 67.2
altered among the laws of the Persians . . . that it be not a. 15.1
altogether almost, and a. such as I am 46.61
alway lo, I am with you a. 42.177
am I a. that I am 2.8
I a. what I am 48.39
amazement not afraid with any a. 62.12
ambassador an a. in bonds 51.15
amiable how a. are thy dwellings 17.173
amiss to mark what is done a. 17.271
Anathema A. Maranatha 48.46
ancient with the a. is wisdom 16.28
the prudent, and the a. 21.10
Ancient the A. of days 25.13
angel the a. of the Lord . . . in a flame of fire 2.5
the a. of his presence 21.98
the a. of the Lord that stood among the myrtle trees 33.2
the a. of the Lord came upon them 44.9
an a. . . . troubled the water 45.21
as it had been the face of an a. 46.17
angels a. of God ascending and descending 1.56
thou madest him lower than the a. 17.14
man did eat a.' food 17.164
he shall give his a. charge over thee 17.187
he maketh his a. spirits 17.211
gave you manna . . . a.' bread 36.1
a. came and ministered unto him 42.11
the reapers are the a. 42.92
their a. do always behold the face of my Father 42.114
neither death, nor life, nor a. 47.31
the tongues of men and of a. 48.35
made so much better than the a. 60.1
who maketh his a. spirits 60.2
entertained a. unawares 60.20
the a. of the seven churches 67.4
anger neither keepeth he his a. for ever 17.208
he that is slow to a. is better than the mighty 18.47
wrath is cruel, and a. is outrageous 18.91
–See also wrath.
angry kiss the Son, lest he be a. 17.5
a. with his brother without a cause 42.19
be ye a., and sin not 51.8
anguish a. of spirit 2.12
Annunciation 44.1
Anointed the Lord . . . is the wholesome defence of his A. 17.60
another do we look for a.? 42.70
answer a soft a. turneth away wrath 18.40
a. a fool according to his folly 18.85
we are not careful to a. thee in this matter 25.5
give a. as need requireth 39.8
answered the Lord a. . . . out of the whirlwind 16.54
answerest a. thou the high priest so? 45.75
ant go to the a., thou sluggard 18.14
apes ivory, and a., and peacocks 11.10
apostle Paul . . . called to be an a. 47.1
apostles the a. . . . as it were appointed to death 48.10
the least of the a. 48.39

apparel the Lord ... hath put on glorious a. 17.192
appealed hast thou a. unto Caesar? 46.57
appearance man looketh on the outward a. 9.17
judge not according to the a. 45.34
appeareth who shall stand when he a.? 34.2
apple as the a. of his eye 5.16
keep me as the a. of an eye 17.28
I raised thee up under the a. tree 20.25
apples comfort me with a. 20.4
appointed is there not an a. time to man upon earth? 16.17
to the house a. for all living 16.46
the apostles ... as it were a. to death 48.10
approach the light which no man can a. 56.13
aprons they ... made themselves a. 1.14
arguing what doth your a. reprove? 16.16
arise a., shine 21.94
a., call upon thy God 29.1
shall ... a. with healing in his wings 34.3
a., and take up thy bed 43.3
I will a. and go to my father 44.49
until ... the day star a. in your hearts 63.1
ark into the a., two and two 1.29
an a. of bulrushes 2.2
arm with his holy a., hath he gotten himself the victory 17.199
he shall gather the lambs with his a. 21.60
Armageddon a place called ... A. 67.52
armed he goeth on to meet the a. men 16.57
a strong man a. keepeth his palace 44.35
armour put on the a. of light 47.43
the a. of righteousness 49.13
put on the whole a. of God 51.14
arms underneath are the everlasting a. 5.21
army terrible as an a. with banners 20.19
arrayed a. in white robes 67.28
arrow the a. that flieth by day 17.186
as when an a. is shot 38.6
arrows a. in the hand of the giant ... are the young children 17.265
artificer every a. in brass and iron 1.24
the cunning a. 21.10
ascend I a. unto my Father, and your Father 45.89
ascended the smoke ... a. up before God 67.30
ascending angels of God a. and descending 1.56
ashamed naked ... and were not a. 1.12
to beg I am a. 44.53
hope maketh not a. 47.17
ashes beauty for a. 21.96
ask your Father knoweth ... before ye a. him 42.27
a., and it shall be given 42.36
whatsoever ye shall a. in prayer, believing 42.131
above all that we a. or think 51.5
if any ... lack wisdom, let him a. of God 61.1
Askelon publish it not in the streets of A. 10.1
asking both hearing them, and a. them questions 44.13
asleep he fell a. 46.20
ignorant ... concerning them which are a. 54.3
ass a strong a. 1.78
the Lord opened the mouth of the a. 4.13
with the jawbone of an a. 7.15
a bridle for the a. 18.84
the ox knoweth his owner, and the a. his master's crib 21.1
meek, and sitting upon an a. 42.128
astonished they were a., and suddenly cast down 17.108
a. out of measure 43.19
a. at his understanding 44.13
astray all we like sheep have gone a. 21.81
asunder what ... God hath joined together, let not man put a. 42.119
Athens men of A. ... ye are too superstitious 46.38
athirst my soul is a. for God 17.94
author Jesus the a. and finisher of our faith 60.16
authority he taught them as one having a. 42.45
a man under a. 42.46
the powers that be are ordained of God 47.39
put down all rule and all a. 48.41
avenge judge and a. our blood 67.25
awake I myself will a. right early 17.128
a., O north wind 20.14
stir not up, nor a. my love 20.24
high time to a. out of sleep 47.43
awaked peradventure he sleepeth, and must be a. 11.18
awe stand in a., and sin not 17.8
axe shall the a. boast itself? 21.24
the a. is laid unto the root of the trees 42.7

B

babbler what will this b. say? 46.37
babblings vain b. 56.15
Babel B.; because the Lord did there confound the language 1.38
babes out of the mouth of ... b. and sucklings 17.14
b. shall rule over them 21.10
things ... revealed ... unto b. 42.75
Babylon by the waters of B. we sat down and wept 17.276
O virgin daughter of B., sit on the ground 21.71
B. is fallen 67.45
B. the great 67.54
thus with violence shall ... B. be thrown down 67.57
back the plowers ... upon my b. ... made long furrows 17.269
I gave my b. to the smiters 21.78

Balaam's Ass 4.13
balance the small dust of the b. 21.61
balances thou art weighed in the b., and art found wanting 25.10
bald go up, thou b. head 12.3
balm is there no b. in Gilead? 22.7
bands I drew them ... with b. of love 26.3
banner his b. over me was love 20.4
banners terrible as an army with b. 20.19
baptize b. ... with water unto repentance 42.7
b. ... with the Holy Ghost, and with fire 42.7
Barabbas now B. was a robber 45.77
Barbarians debtor both to the Greeks, and to the B. 47.4
barbarous the b. people shewed us no little kindness 46.62
barn gather the wheat into my b. 42.90
Barnabas B. ... the son of consolation 46.13
barren a fruitful land maketh he b. 17.223
he maketh the b. woman to keep house 17.232
blessed are the b. 44.71
Basan the hill of B. 17.143
baser certain lewd fellows of the b. sort 46.36
battle the forefront of the hottest b. 10.5
he smelleth the b. afar off 16.58
the children of Ephraim, who ... turned themselves back in the day of b. 17.163
I labour for peace, but ... they make them ready for b. 17.254
thou hast covered my head in the day of b. 17.284
the horse is prepared against ... b. 18.68
nor the b. to the strong 19.29
who shall prepare himself to the b.? 48.36
bay-tree the ungodly ... flourishing like a green b. 17.86
beam the b. that is in thine own eye 42.34
bear I have yet many things to say ... but ye cannot b. them 45.69
a yoke ... which neither our fathers nor we were able to b. 46.35
strong ought to b. the infirmities of the weak 47.46
b. ye one another's burdens 50.12
beareth b. all things, believeth all things 48.35
beast b. of the earth 1.6
some evil b. hath devoured him 1.65
a righteous man regardeth the life of his b. 18.31
who is like unto the b.? 67.40
the mark ... of the b. 67.42
beasts all the b. of the field drink thereof 17.212
b. and all cattle 17.297
wild b. of the desert shall lie there 21.28
after the manner of men I have fought with b. 48.42
evil b., slow bellies 58.1
four b. full of eyes 67.16
beat b. your plowshares into swords 27.6
beateth so fight I, not as one that b. the air 48.27
Beatitudes 42.15.
beautiful Rachel was b. 1.58
how b. are thy feet with shoes 20.21
how b. upon the mountains are the feet 21.80
beautify to b. the house of the Lord 13.2
beauty the b. of Israel is slain 10.1
array thyself with glory and b. 16.59
my b. is gone for very trouble 17.12
so shall the King have pleasure in thy b. 17.100
no b. that we should desire him 21.81
b. for ashes 21.96
bed have I not remembered thee in my b.? 17.137
thou art ... about my b. 17.277
by night on my b. I sought him whom my soul loveth 20.9
take up thy b., and walk 43.3
beds let the saints ... rejoice in their b. 17.298
before reaching forth unto those things which are b. 52.8
beg to b. I am ashamed 44.53
beggar be not made a b. by banqueting upon borrowing 39.16
beggarly the weak and b. elements 50.6
beginning in the b. God 1.1
more than his b. 16.64
the fear of the Lord is the b. of wisdom 17.229
better ... the end of a thing than the b. 19.20
hath it not been told you from the b.? 21.62
the b. of sorrows 42.144
in the b. was the word 45.1
every man at the b. doth set forth good wine 45.7
a murderer from the b. 45.40
the b. and the ending 67.2
behind forgetting those things which are b. 52.8
behold b. your God 21.59
b. trouble 22.5
b. with thine eyes 24.13
b. the fowls of the air 42.31
b. the man 45.78
beholding a man b. his natural face in a glass 61.4
being in him we live, and move, and have our b. 46.39
Belial sons of B. 9.1
man of B. 10.9
believe that all men through him might b. 45.1
I have told you earthly things, and ye b. not 45.10
how shall ye b., if I tell you of heavenly things? 45.10
except I ... thrust my hand into his side, I will not b. 45.91
b. not every spirit 64.6
believed who hath b. our report? 21.81

seemed ... idle tales, and they b. them not 44.78
blessed are they that have not seen, and yet have b. 45.92
all that b. ... had all things common 46.9
who against hope b. in hope 47.16
believeth that whosoever b. ... should not perish 45.12
he that b. not the Son shall not see life 45.15
beareth all things, b. all things 48.35
believing whatsoever ye shall ask in prayer, b. 42.131
be not faithless, but b. 45.92
bellies evil beasts, slow b. 58.1
belly upon thy b. shalt thou go 1.17
thy b. is like an heap of wheat 20.21
Jonah was in the b. of the fish 29.2
the b. for meats 48.14
whose God is their b. 52.9
make thy b. bitter 67.36
belong the things which b. unto thy peace 44.65
beloved the voice of my b. 20.5
my b. is mine, and I am his 20.8
let my b. come into his garden 20.14
my b. is white and ruddy 20.17
my b. is gone down ... to the beds of spices 20.18
I am my b.'s, and my beloved is mine 20.18
I am my b.'s, and his desire is toward me 20.23
who is this ... leaning upon her b.? 20.25
make haste, my b. 20.27
this is my b. Son 42.8
Luke, the b. physician 53.9
b., let us love one another 64.7
benevolence due b. 48.16
Bethlehem B. Ephratah, though thou be little 30.2
when Jesus was born in B. of Judaea 42.2
betrayed woe unto that man by whom the Son of man is b. 42.162
better take away my life; for I am not b. than my fathers 11.21
b. is little with the fear of the Lord 18.42
b. to dwell in a corner of the housetop, than with a brawling woman 18.67
open rebuke is b. than secret love 18.92
b. is he ... who hath not seen the evil work 19.10
b. is an handful with quietness 19.11
two are b. than one 19.12
a place and a name b. than of sons and of daughters 21.88
b. ... that a millstone were hanged about his neck 42.112
the old is b. 44.20
b. to marry than to burn 48.18
to be with Christ; which is far b. 52.3
made so much b. than the angels 60.1
the less is blessed of the b. 60.8
beware b. lest any man spoil you through philosophy 53.1
bewitched O foolish Galatians, who hath b. you? 50.3
bewitching the b. of naughtiness 38.5
bidden they which were b. were not worthy 42.132
bind canst thou b. the sweet influences of Pleiades? 16.56
to b. their kings in chains 17.299
to b. up the brokenhearted 21.96
whatsoever thou shalt b. on earth shall be bound in heaven 42.105
except he ... first b. the strong man 43.6
bird my soul ... should flee as a b. 17.18
as a b. out of the snare of the fowler 17.262
in vain the net is spread in the sight of any b. 18.4
a b. of the air shall carry the voice 19.35
he shall rise up at the voice of the b. 19.40
as when a b. hath flown through the air 38.6
birds b. ... caught in the snare 19.29
the time of the singing of b. 20.6
as a cage ... full of b. ... their houses full of deceit 22.3
the b. of the air have nests 42.48
birth children are come to the b., and there is not strength to bring forth 12.15
bishop if a man desire the office of a b. 56.4
a b. ... must be blameless 56.4
the shepherd and b. of your souls 62.10
bishoprick his b. let another take 46.5
bitter the b. in soul 16.9
her end is b. as wormwood 18.12
that put b. for sweet 21.16
O death, how b. is the remembrance of thee 39.26
be not b. against them 53.5
sweet water and b. 61.9
make thy belly b. 67.36
bittern make it a possession for the b. 21.31
bitterness surely the b. of death is past 9.16
I will speak in the b. of my soul 16.23
their mouth is full of ... b. 17.22
the heart knoweth his own b. 18.36
I shall go softly ... in the b. of my soul 21.57
black I am b., but comely 20.1
b., because the sun hath looked upon me 20.1
blasphemer wisdom ... will not acquit a b. 38.1
blasphemy b. against the Holy Ghost shall not be forgiven 42.78
blaze b. abroad the matter 43.2
blemish lamb ... without b. 2.18
children in whom was no b. 25.1
bless I will b. them that bless thee 1.39
I will not let thee go, except thou b. me 1.61
the Lord b. thee, and keep thee 4.3
b. them that curse you 42.24
b. them which persecute you 47.37
being reviled, we b. 48.10
blessed he whom thou blessest is b. 4.12
thou hast b. them together 4.14
b. ... above women in the tent 7.6
the Lord b. the latter end of Job 16.64

b. is he whose unrighteousness is forgiven 17.71
b. is the man, whom thou choosest 17.140
b. be he that cometh in the name of the Lord 17.243
b. are those that are undefiled in the way 17.244
the memory of the just is b. 18.24
her children arise up, and call her b. 18.111
judge none b. before his death 39.12
b. are the poor in spirit 42.15
b. are they that mourn 42.15
b. are the meek 42.15
b. are they which do hunger and thirst after righteousness 42.15
b. are the merciful 42.15
b. are the pure in heart 42.15
b. are the peacemakers 42.15
b. are they which are persecuted for righteousness' sake 42.15
b. are your eyes, for they see 42.86
b. is he that cometh in the name of the Lord 42.129
ye b. of my Father 42.158
Jesus took bread, and b. it 42.163
all generations shall call me b. 44.2
b. are the barren 44.71
b. are they that have not seen, and yet have believed 45.92
more b. to give than to receive 46.50
the less is b. of the better 60.8
b. is the man that endureth temptation 61.2
b. in his deed 61.4
b. are the dead which die in the Lord 67.47
b. are they . . . called unto the marriage supper of the lamb 67.59
b. and holy is he that hath part in the first resurrection 67.63
b. are they that do his commandments 67.71

blessest thou visitest the earth, and b. it 17.140

blessing all families of the earth be blessed 1.39
thy brother . . . hath taken away thy b. 1.55
b. and cursing 5.13
give me a b. 6.6
he loved not b., therefore shall it be far from him 17.226
out of the same mouth proceedeth b. and cursing 61.9
inherit a b. 62.13
–*See also* blessed.

blessings the b. of thy father have prevailed 1.80
the b. of goodness 17.40
a faithful man shall abound with b. 18.100

blind cursed be he that maketh the b. to wander 5.11
I was eyes to the b. 16.44
the Lord giveth sight to the b. 17.293
b. leaders of the blind 42.102
b. guides 42.140
the halt, and the b. 44.44
whereas I was b., now I see 45.45

blood thy brother's b. crieth unto me 1.21
your b. of your lives will I require 1.33
by man shall his b. be shed 1.33
their feet are swift to shed b. 17.22
what profit is there in my b.? 17.65
the wringing of the nose bringeth forth b. 18.108
they make haste to shed innocent b. 21.93
my b. of the new testament 42.163
his b. be on us 42.172
born, not of b. . . . but of God 45.1
forthwith came there out b. and water 45.84
without shedding of b. is no remission 60.9
judge and avenge our b. 67.25
washed their robes . . . in the b. of the Lamb 67.28
drunken with the b. of the saints 67.54

blood-guiltiness deliver me from b. 17.115

bloodthirsty the Lord will abhor . . . the b. and deceitful man 17.10

bloody thou b. man 10.9

blossom the desert shall . . . b. as the rose 21.52

blot b. me . . . out of thy book 2.42
not b. out his name out of the book of life 67.11

bloweth the wind b. where it listeth 45.10

Boanerges B. . . . sons of thunder 43.5

boast let not him that girdeth on his harness b. . . . as he that putteth it off 11.25
b. not thyself of tomorrow 18.90
shall the axe b. itself? 21.24

boasteth the buyer . . . when he is gone his way, then he b. 18.63
the tongue is a little member, and b. 61.7

boasting where is b. then? 47.14

bodies many b. of the saints which slept arose 42.175
your b. a living sacrifice 47.36

bodily b. exercise profiteth little 56.6

body his b. was wet with the dew of heaven 25.8
the b. than raiment 42.30
destroy both b. and soul in hell 42.64
take, eat; this is my b. 42.163
who shall deliver me from the b. of this death? 47.23
absent in b. 48.12
your b. is the temple of the Holy Ghost 48.15
keep under my b., and bring it into subjection 48.27

bold the righteous are b. as a lion 18.98

boldly I may speak b., as I ought 51.15

bond neither b. nor free 50.5
the b. of peace 51.6

bondage cruel b. 2.12
the house of b. 2.29
the spirit of b. 47.25
the b. of corruption 47.26

bonds an ambassador in b. 51.15
bone b. of my bones 1.12
b. to his bone 24.12
bones all my b. are out of joint 17.43
my b. consumed away 17.71
the b. which thou hast broken 17.114
the valley which was full of b. 24.11
can these b. live? 24.11
O ye dry b. 24.11
the b. came together 24.12
book blot me ... out of thy b. 2.42
oh that they were printed in a b. 16.37
my desire is ... that mine adversary had written a b. 16.47
the b. of the living 17.149
in thy b. were all my members written 17.281
shut up the words, and seal the b. 25.14
out of the b. of life 67.11
a b. ... sealed with seven seals 67.18
give me the little b. 67.36
books of making many b. there is no end 19.41
born let the day perish wherein I was b. 16.6
a time to be b., and a time to die 19.9
we ... as soon as we were b., began to draw to our end 38.6
become as though they had never been b. 39.28
where is he that is b. King of the Jews? 42.2
b., not of blood ... but of God 45.1
except a man be b. again 45.8
b. of water and of the Spirit 45.9
that which is b. of the flesh is flesh 45.9
that which is b. of the Spirit is spirit 45.9
joy that a man is b. into the world 45.71
I was free b. 46.52
one b. out of due time 48.39
b. again, not of corruptible seed 62.4
borne b. the burden and heat of the day 42.125
hast b., and hast patience 67.5
borrowing be not made a beggar by banqueting upon b. 39.16
bosom Abraham's b. 44.55
bottle put my tears into thy b. 17.123
bottles new wine into old b. 42.54
bottomless the b. pit 67.32
bound unto the utmost b. of the everlasting hills 1.80
b. up his wounds 44.32
I go b. in the spirit 46.48
art thou b. unto a wife? 48.20
b. him a thousand years 67.62
bounds thou hast set them their b. which they shall not pass 17.212
bow my b. in the cloud 1.34
a certain man drew a b. at a venture 11.33
starting aside like a broken b. 17.165
bow thou shalt not b. down 2.29
at the name of Jesus every knee should b. 52.4
bowed he ... b. his shoulder to bear 1.78
at her feet he b., he fell 7.6
bowels my b. were moved for him 20.16
all his b. gushed out 46.4
shutteth up his b. of compassion 64.5
bowl or ever ... the golden b. be broken 19.40
box an alabaster b. of very precious ointment 42.160
branch above shall his b. be cut off 16.35
a b. shall grow out of his roots 21.25
leave them neither root nor b. 34.3
brand a b. plucked out of the fire 33.3
brass out of whose hills thou mayest dig b. 5.2
sounding b. 48.35
bread b. of affliction 11.32
the b. of tears 17.167
b. to strengthen man's heart 17.213
the b. of carefulness 17.265
b. eaten in secret is pleasant 18.22
she ... eateth not the b. of idleness 18.111
eat thy b. with joy 19.27
cast thy b. upon the waters 19.36
the whole stay of b. 21.10
the b. of adversity 21.48
wherefore ... spend money for that which is not b.? 21.84
gave you manna ... angels' b. 36.1
command that these stones be made b. 42.9
man shall not live by b. alone 42.9
give us this day our daily b. 42.27
if his son ask b., will he give him a stone? 42.37
the children's b., and to cast it to dogs 42.103
Jesus took b., and blessed it 42.163
b. enough and to spare 44.49
known of them in breaking of b. 44.81
I am the b. of life 45.29
the b. which cometh down from heaven 45.32
the living b. 45.32
the unleavened b. of sincerity and truth 48.13
breadth the b., and length, and depth 51.5
break b. them ... like a potter's vessel 17.4
thou shalt b. the ships of the sea 17.108
let not their precious balms b. my head 17.286
a time to b. down, and a time to build up 19.9
b. it as ... the potter's vessel 21.46
a bruised reed shall he not b. 21.66
then shall thy light b. forth 21.91
breaketh whoso b. an hedge, a serpent shall bite 19.32
breaking until the b. of the day 1.61
known of them in b. of bread 44.81
breastplate the b. of righteousness 51.14
breasts let her b. satisfy thee 18.13
he shall lie all night betwixt my b. 20.2
thy two b. are like two young roes 20.11
breath the b. of life 1.9
when the b. of man goeth forth 17.292
cease ye from man, whose b. is in his nostrils 21.9
wisdom ... the b. of the power of God 38.8
breathed God ... b. into his nostrils 1.9

breathing yet b. out threatenings and slaughter 46.24
breeches sewed fig leaves ... and made ... b. 1.15
brethren Joseph knew his b. 1.70
how good and joyful ... b., to dwell together in unity 17.275
let us die manfully for our b. 40.2
the least of these my b. 42.159
brick straw to make b. 2.11
bride as a b. adorned for her husband 67.65
the Spirit and the b. say, come 67.71
bridegroom the sun ... cometh forth as a b. 17.35
the b. shall be taken from them 42.53
behold, the b. cometh 42.152
the friend of the b. ... rejoiceth 45.14
bridle I will keep my mouth as it were with a b. 17.88
bright the b. and morning star 67.71
brightness kings to the b. of thy rising 21.94
brimstone b. and fire 1.48
tormented with fire and b. 67.46
bring b. down my gray hairs with sorrow to the grave 1.71
thou knowest not what a day may b. forth 18.90
b. my sons from far 21.67
when the Lord shall b. again Zion 21.80
bringest that b. good tidings 21.59
bringeth the feet of him that b. good tidings 21.80
which b. forth out of his treasure things new and old 42.94
broad thy commandment is exceeding b. 17.248
b. is the way, that leadeth to destruction 42.39
broken I am become like a b. vessel 17.70
the bones which thou hast b. 17.114
starting aside like a b. bow 17.165
those that are b. in heart 17.294
a threefold cord is not quickly b. 19.13
thou trustest in ... this b. reed 21.56
b. to shivers 67.10
brokenhearted to bind up the b. 21.96
brook the b. Cherith 11.14
brother a friend that sticketh closer than a b. 18.56
every one said to his b., be of good courage 21.65
the same is my b. 42.84
how oft shall my b. sin against me? 42.116
love God, and hateth his b. 64.9
b., and companion in tribulation 67.2
brotherhood love the b. 62.7
brotherly let b. love continue 60.20
brought b. nothing into this world 56.10
bruise it shall b. thy head 1.17
thou shalt b. his heel 1.17
b. them with a rod of iron 17.4
bruised a b. reed shall he not break 21.66
b. for our iniquities 21.81
bucket a drop of a b. 21.61
buckler his faithfulness and truth shall be thy shield and b. 17.186
buffeted b., and have no certain dwellingplace 48.10
b. for your faults ... take it patiently 62.8
build a time to break down, and a time to b. up 19.9
they shall b. houses, and inhabit them 21.102
they shall not b., and another inhabit 21.102
upon this rock I will b. my church 42.105
builders the b., every one had his sword girded by his side 14.1
the same stone which the b. refused 17.242
building by much slothfulness the b. decayeth 19.33
built a wise man, which b. his house upon a rock 42.44
bullocks how can he get wisdom ... whose talk is of b.? 39.25
bulls fat b. of Basan 17.42
bulrushes an ark of b. 2.2
bulwarks mark well her b. 17.109
burden cast thy b. upon the Lord 17.121
I eased his shoulder from the b. 17.169
the grasshopper shall be a b. 19.40
broken the yoke of his b. 21.22
my b. is light 42.76
borne the b. and heat of the day 42.125
burdens bear ye one another's b. 50.12
buried their bodies are b. in peace 39.29
the patriarch David ... is both dead and b. 46.8
burn the sun shall not b. thee by day 17.257
the day cometh, that shall b. as an oven 34.3
b. up the chaff 42.7
bind them in bundles to b. them 42.90
did not our heart b. within us? 44.80
better to marry than to b. 48.18
burned can a man take fire in his bosom ... and ... not be b.? 18.16
burning b. for burning 2.31
a b. fiery furnace 25.4
a firebrand plucked out of the b. 28.3
your lights b. 44.40
a b. and a shining light 45.24
Burning Bush 2.5
bury let the dead b. their dead 42.49
bush the b. was not consumed 2.5
bushel light a candle, and put it under a b. 42.16
bushes the voice of the Lord ... discovereth the thick b. 17.62
business they ... occupy their b. in great waters 17.221
wist ye not that I must be about my Father's b.? 44.14
not slothful in b. 47.37
busybodies tattlers ... and b. 56.8
butter b. in a lordly dish 7.6
the words of his mouth were softer than b. 17.121
the churning of milk bringeth forth b. 18.108
b. and honey shall he eat 21.19

buy b. . . . without money and without price 21.84
buyer it is naught, saith the b. 18.63
the b. . . . when he is gone his way, then he boasteth 18.63
byword a proverb and a b. 11.7

C

Caesar render . . . unto C. the things which are Caesar's 42.134
hast thou appealed unto C.? 46.57
Cain the Lord set a mark upon C. 1.23
calamity the day of their c. is at hand 5.19
serving either c. or tyranny 38.12
calf a molten c. 2.37
the fatted c. 44.50
call not come to c. the righteous 42.52
called whatsoever Adam c. every living creature 1.11
I c. not; lie down again 9.4
out of the deep have I c. unto thee 17.271
many are c. 42.133
c. in question for this day's uproar 46.46
abide in the same calling wherein he was c. 48.19
science falsely so c. 56.15
calling abide in the same c. wherein he was called 48.19
the hope of his c. 51.1
the prize of the high c. of God 52.8
Calvary the place, which is called C. 44.72
calves c. out of the midst of the stall 28.5
came Christ Jesus c. into the world to save sinners 56.2
camel raiment of c.'s hair 42.5
easier for a c. to go through the eye of a needle 42.122
strain at a gnat, and swallow a c. 42.140
candle thou . . . shalt light my c. 17.32
the spirit of man is the c. of the Lord 18.65
the c. of the wicked shall be put out 18.78
her c. goeth not out by night 18.110
a c. of understanding 36.7
light a c., and put it under a bushel 42.16
they need no c. 67.69
candlesticks seven golden c. 67.2
captain the c. of fifty 21.10
captive they that led us away c. required . . . a song 17.276
captives to proclaim liberty to the c. 21.96
captivity God that . . . bringeth the prisoners out of c. 17.142
thou hast led c. captive 17.143
thou hast turned away the c. of Jacob 17.176
turn our c., O Lord 17.264
no decay, no leading into c. 17.290
such as are for the c., to the captivity 22.11
carcase wheresoever the c. is, there will the eagles be gathered 42.147
care the wealthy nation, that dwelleth without c. 22.21
the c. of this world 42.88
casting all your c. upon him 62.16
cared Gallio c. for none of those things 46.40
careful we are not c. to answer thee in this matter 25.5
c. and troubled about many things 44.34
carefully sought it c. with tears 60.18
carefulness the bread of c. 17.265
careth an hireling . . . c. not for the sheep 45.48
he that is married c. . . . how he may please his wife 48.22
carnal the weapons of our warfare are not c. 49.16
carnally to be c. minded is death 47.24
carried he hath . . . c. our sorrows 21.81
c. about with every wind of doctrine 51.7
c. me away in the spirit 67.66
carry c. neither purse, nor scrip 44.28
certain we can c. nothing out 56.10
cast mine enemies . . . c. me in the teeth 17.97
they were astonished, and suddenly c. down 17.108
c. thy burden upon the Lord 17.121
c. in thy lot among us 18.3
a time to keep, and a time to c. away 19.9
c. thy bread upon the waters 19.36
neither c. ye your pearls before swine 42.35
c. out into outer darkness 42.47
not meet to . . . c. it to dogs 42.103
she of her want did c. in all that she had 43.21
him that cometh to me I will in no wise c. out 45.30
he that is without sin . . . let him first c. a stone 45.36
c. off the works of darkness 47.43
c. their crowns before the throne 67.17
the great dragon was c. out 67.38
castaway lest . . . I myself should be a c. 48.27
casteth c. out devils through the prince of the devils 42.56
perfect love c. out fear 64.8
casting c. all your care upon him 62.16
catcheth c. away that which was sown in his heart 42.87
cattle c. and creeping thing 1.6
beasts and all c. 17.297
caught c. up to the third heaven 49.19
cause is there not a c.? 9.19
plead thou my c., O Lord 17.80
princes have persecuted me without a c. 17.253
angry with his brother without a c. 42.19
causeless the curse c. shall not come 18.84
caves go . . . into the c. of the earth 21.8
cease he maketh wars to c. in all the world 17.105
c. ye from man, whose breath is in his nostrils 21.9
tongues, they shall c. 48.35

ceased how hath the oppressor c. 21.29
ceasing without c. I make mention of you always in my prayers 47.2
cedar spread abroad like a c. in Libanus 17.190
cedars the c. of Libanus 17.61
the c. of Libanus which he hath planted 17.213
fruitful trees and all c. 17.297
chaff burn up the c. 42.7
chains to bind their kings in c. 17.299
chambering not in c. and wantonness 47.43
chance time and c. happeneth to them all 19.29
change as a vesture shalt thou c. them 17.206
meddle not with them that are given to c. 18.79
can the Ethiopian c. his skin? 22.9
the fashion of this world passeth away 48.21
no continuing city 60.22
changed and they shall be c. 17.206
who c. the truth of God into a lie 47.7
we shall all be c. 48.45
changeth he c. the times and the seasons 25.2
charge lay not this sin to their c. 46.20
who shall lay any thing to the c. of God's elect? 47.30
charger John Baptist's head in a c. 42.96
charges who goeth a warfare . . . at his own c.?
chariot why is his c. so long in coming? 7.6
the c. of Israel, and the horsemen thereof 12.1
at thy rebuke . . . both the c. and horse are fallen 17.159
who . . . maketh the clouds his c. 17.211
chariots some put their trust in c. 17.39
the c. of God are twenty thousand 17.143
a company of horses in Pharaoh's c. 20.1
charity knowledge puffeth up, but c. edifieth 48.23
though I speak with the tongues . . . of angels, and have not c. 48.35
c. suffereth long, and is kind 48.35
c. never faileth 48.35
the greatest of these is c. 48.35
spots in your feasts of c. 66.3
charm c. he never so wisely 17.129
chased he shall be . . . c. out of the world 16.35
chasteneth he that loveth him c. him betimes 18.35
whom the Lord loveth he c. 60.17
chastening despise not the c. of the Lord 18.7
chastise I will c. you with scorpions 11.12
chastised my father hath c. you with whips 11.12
having been a little c., they shall be greatly rewarded 38.3
chastisement the c. of our peace was upon him 21.81
chatter like a crane . . . so did I c. 21.57
cheek whosoever shall smite thee on thy right c. 42.23
cheer be of good c.; it is I 42.97
cheerful make a c. noise unto . . . God 17.168
a merry heart maketh a c. countenance 18.41
God loveth a c. giver 49.15
cherish let her c. him, and . . . lie in thy bosom 11.1
Cherith the brook C. 11.14
cherubims he rode upon the c. 17.31
chickens as a hen gathereth her c. under her wings 42.142
chiding he will not alway be c. 17.208
child Samuel ministered . . . being a c. 9.2
give her the living c. 11.5
even a c. is known by his doings 18.61
train up a c. in the way he should go 18.70
better . . . a poor and a wise c. than an old and foolish king 19.14
the c. shall behave himself proudly 21.10
unto us a c. is born 21.23
and a little c. shall lead them 21.26
the sucking c. shall play on the hole of the asp 21.26
can a woman forget her sucking c.? 21.75
money . . . be as refuse in respect of our c. 37.1
the young c. with Mary his mother 42.3
receive one such little c. in my name 42.112
twofold more the c. of hell 42.139
when I was a c., I spake as a child 48.35
childish I put away c. things 48.35
childless thy sword hath made women c. 9.16
children in sorrow thou shalt bring forth c. 1.17
instead of thy fathers thou shalt have c. 17.102
a joyful mother of c. 17.232
c. . . . are an heritage and gift . . . of the Lord 17.265
arrows in the hand of the giant . . . are the young c. 17.265
thy c. like the olive-branches 17.267
thou shalt see thy children's c. 17.268
children's c. are the crown of old men 18.49
her c. arise up, and call her blessed 18.111
give c. to be their princes 21.10
the c.'s teeth are set on edge 24.6
c. in whom was no blemish 25.1
a man shall be known in his c. 39.12
desire not a multitude of unprofitable c. 39.15
Rachel weeping for her c. 42.4
God is able of these stones to raise up c. unto Abraham 42.7
peacemakers . . . shall be called the c. of God 42.15
give good gifts unto your c. 42.38
wisdom is justified of her c. 42.74
not meet to take the c.'s bread 42.103
then are the c. free 42.110
except ye . . . become as little c. 42.111
their angels . . . behold . . . my Father 42.114
suffer the little c. 43.18
the c. of this world 44.54
and if c., then heirs 47.25
the glorious liberty of the c. of God 47.26
be not c. in understanding 48.37
c., obey your parents 51.13
provoke not your c. 53.6

little c., keep yourselves from idols 64.10
–*See also* child
choose refuse the evil, and c. the good 21.19
chosen I have c. thee in the furnace of affliction 21.72
but few are c. 42.133
Mary hath c. that good part 44.34
ye have not c. me, but I have chosen you 45.64
a c. vessel 46.27
Christ save Jesus C., and him crucified 48.4
fools for C.'s sake 48.10
C. our passover is sacrificed for us 48.13
now is C. risen from the dead 48.40
the love of C. constraineth us 49.10
the unsearchable riches of C. 51.4
to live is C. 52.2
a desire to depart, and to be with C. 52.3
gain ... I counted loss for C. 52.7
do all things through C. 52.13
your life is hid with C. in God 53.3
C. is all, and in all 53.4
C. Jesus came into the world to save sinners 56.2
Jesus C. the same yesterday, and to day 60.21
Christian almost thou persuadest me to be a C. 46.61
church upon this rock I will build my c. 42.105
churches the seven c. which are in Asia 67.1
the angels of the seven c. 67.4
circle he that sitteth upon the c. of the earth 21.62
circuit he walketh in the c. of heaven 16.41
circumcision c. is nothing 48.19
circumspectly walk c. 51.11
cities until the c. be wasted without inhabitant 21.18
citizen a c. of no mean city 46.51
city very excellent things are spoken of thee, thou c. of God 17.180
the c. where they dwelt 17.219
who will lead me into the strong c.? 17.225
Jerusalem is built as a c. ... at unity 17.259
except the Lord keep the c. 17.265
how is the faithful c. become an harlot 21.5
how hath ... the golden c. ceased 21.29
Tyre, the crowning c. 21.37
how doth the c. sit solitary 23.1
shall there be evil in a c.? 28.2
a c. ... set on an hill cannot be hid 42.16
no mean c. 46.51
no continuing c. 60.22
Babylon ... that great c. 67.45
the holy c., new Jerusalem 67.65
the c. was pure gold 67.67
the c. had no need of the sun 67.67
clay shall the c. say to him that fashioneth it, what makest thou? 21.69
his feet ... part of c. 25.3
hath not the potter power over the c.? 47.33
clean wash, and be c. 12.6
cleanse to c. us from all unrighteousness 64.2
cleansed were there not ten c.? 44.58
what God hath c., that call not thou common 46.29
clear c. as the sun 20.19
cleave c. to that which is good 47.37
clothe ye c. you, but there is none warm 32.1
clothed hast thou c. his neck with thunder? 16.57
wherewithal shall we be c.? 42.31
naked, and ye c. me 42.158
c., and in his right mind 43.9
c. with white robes 67.27
a woman c. with the sun 67.37
clothes wrapped him in swaddling c. 44.8
laid down their c. at a young man's feet 46.19
clothing they that have put off the mortal c. 36.2
sheep's c. 42.40
wear soft c. ... in kings' houses 42.71
cloud my bow in the c. 1.34
a pillar of a c. 2.22
a little c. ... like a man's hand 11.20
a c. received him out of their sight 46.2
so great a c. of witnesses 60.16
clouds thy c. drop fatness 17.140
he that regardeth the c. shall not reap 19.38
the Son of man coming in the c. 42.148
c. ... without water 66.3
clovenfooted c., and cheweth the cud 3.1
coal having a live c. in his hand 21.17
coals heap c. of fire upon his head 18.82
coat a c. of many colours 1.64
if any man ... take away thy c., let him have thy cloak also 42.23
cock before the c. crow, thou shalt deny me 42.164
cold the love of many shall wax c. 42.145
neither c. nor hot 67.14
colours a coat of many c. 1.64
colt a c. the foal of an ass 42.128
come rise up, my love ... and c. away 20.6
Gentiles shall c. to thy light 21.94
that thou wouldest c. down 21.99
the Lord ... shall suddenly c. to his temple 34.2
the wrath to c. 42.6
c., and he cometh 42.46
art thou he that should c.? 42.70
neither in the world to c. 42.78
if any man will c. after me 42.106
Elias truly shall first c. 42.108
can there any good thing c. out of Nazareth? 45.5
mine hour is not yet c. 45.6
no man can c. to me, except the Father ... draw him 45.31
if I will that he tarry till I c., what is that to thee? 45.96
this same Jesus ... shall so c. in like manner 46.3
when the day of Pentecost was fully c. 46.6
gods are c. down ... in the likeness of men 46.34

the more part knew not wherefore they were c. together 46.44
let us do evil, that good may c. 47.12
nor things present, nor things to c. 47.31
when that which is perfect is c. 48.35
hold fast till I c. 67.9
which was, and is, and is to c. 67.16
the devil is c. . . . having great wrath 67.39
I c. as a thief 67.52
behold, I c. quickly 67.70
the Spirit and the bride say, c. 67.71
comeliness no form nor c. 21.81
comely I am black, but c. 20.1
comest whence c. thou, Gehazi? 12.7
cometh the day of the Lord c. 27.2
he that c. after me is mightier than I 42.7
that which c. out of the mouth . . . defileth 42.101
woe to that man by whom the offence c. 42.113
him that c. to me I will in no wise cast out 45.30
the night c., when no man can work 45.43
the day of the Lord so c. as a thief in the night 54.4
he c. with clouds 67.2
comfort let me alone, that I may take c. 16.25
the waters of c. 17.45
thy rod and thy staff c. me 17.45
neither found I any to c. me 17.148
c. me with apples 20.4
c. ye, comfort ye my people 21.59
the Lord shall c. Zion 21.79
comfortably speak ye c. to Jerusalem 21.59
comforted he refused to be c. 1.66
Rachel weeping . . . and would not be c. 42.4
Comforter another C., that he may abide 45.59
if I go not . . . the C. will not come 45.68
comforters miserable c. are ye all 16.32
coming who may abide the day of his c.? 34.2
the Son of man c. . . . with power 42.148
lest c. suddenly he find you sleeping 43.22
he . . . c. after me is preferred before me 45.3
command c. that these stones be made bread 42.9
commandment thy c. is exceeding broad 17.248
the first and great c. 42.136
speak this by permission, and not of c. 48.17
commandments fear God, and keep his c. 19.42
if ye love me, keep my c. 45.59
blessed are they that do his c. 67.71
commend into thy hands I c. my spirit 17.68, 44.75
common all that believed . . . had all things c. 46.9
what God hath cleansed, that call not thou c. 46.29
no temptation . . . but such as is c. to man 48.28
commotions their secret plots, and popular persuasions and c. 35.8
commune c. with your own heart 17.8
communicate willing to c. 56.14
communication let your c. be, yea, yea 42.22
evil c. corrupt good manners 48.42
companion brother, and c. in tribulation 67.2
compassed c. about with so great a cloud of witnesses 60.16
compassion he had c. on him 44.32
shutteth up his bowels of c. 64.5
compassions his c. fail not 23.4
compel whosoever shall c. thee to go a mile, go with him twain 42.23
complainers murmurers, c. 66.4
complaining my daily c. 17.71
no c. in our streets 17.290
complaint let thine ears consider well . . . my c. 17.271
comprehend c. . . . what is the breadth 51.5
comprehended the darkness c. it not 45.1
conceal the glory of God to c. a thing 18.80
conceit a man wise in his own c. 18.86
conceits be not wise in your own c. 47.37
conclusion let us hear the c. of the whole matter 19.42
concupiscence c. doth undermine the simple mind 38.5
condemn neither do I c. thee 45.37
condemnation thou art in the same c. 44.74
the c. . . . men loved darkness 45.13
condemned by thy words thou shalt be c. 42.80
condescend c. to men of low estate 47.37
confess every tongue . . . c. . . . Christ is Lord 52.4
confessed c. the name of God 36.2
confidence his c. shall be rooted out 16.34
c. in an unfaithful man in time of trouble is like a broken tooth 18.81
put ye not c. in a guide 30.5
confound the foolish things of the world to c. the wise 48.3
the weak things of the world to c. the . . . mighty 48.3
confounded mine enemies shall be c. 17.13
confusion let me never be put to c. 17.66
congregations the c. of naughty men 17.179
conquer went forth conquering, and to c. 67.22
conquerors we are more than c. 47.31
conscience a c. void of offence toward God 46.56
subject . . . for c. sake 47.41
why is my liberty judged of another man's c.? 48.31
the testimony of our c. 49.1
holding faith, and a good c. 56.3
consent if sinners entice thee, c. thou not 18.2
they all with one c. began to make excuse 44.44
consenting Saul was c. unto his death 46.21

consider an unwise man doth not well c. 17.189
let thine ears c. well . . . my complaint 17.271
c. her ways, and be wise 18.14
c. your ways 32.1
c. the lilies of the field 42.31
considered hast thou c. my servant Job? 16.1
I have c. the days of old 17.160
consolation ye have received your c. 44.21
Barnabas . . . the son of c. 46.13
the God of patience and c. 47.47
constraineth the love of Christ c. us 49.10
consummatum c. est 45.83
contemned all the substance of his house for love . . . would be utterly c. 20.26
content be c. with your wages 44.16
contention a man of c. 22.12
contentious a continual dropping . . . and a c. woman 18.93
contentment better a little . . . than great treasure and trouble therewith 18.42
food convenient for me 18.105
better is an handful with quietness 19.11
continue they think that their houses shall c. for ever 17.110
let brotherly love c. 60.20
continuing c. instant in prayer 47.37
no c. city 60.22
convert lest they see with their eyes . . . and c. 21.18
converteth he which c. the sinner from the error of his way 61.17
conviction fully persuaded in his own mind 47.45
the same calling wherein he was called 48.19
cool the c. of the day 1.14
cord a threefold c. is not quickly broken 19.13
or ever the silver c. be loosed 19.40
cords I drew them with c. of a man 26.3
corn the valleys also shall stand so thick with c. 17.140
corner the head-stone in the c. 17.242
she . . . lieth in wait at every c. 18.17
this thing was not done in a c. 46.60
corners lurking in the thievish c. of the streets 17.17
corner stone who laid the c.? 16.54
a precious c. 21.42
correcteth whom the Lord loveth he c. 18.7
corrupt where moth and rust doth c. 42.28
a c. tree bringeth forth evil fruit 42.41
evil communications c. good manners 48.42
corruptible a c. crown 48.27
this c. must put on incorruption 48.45
born again, not of c. seed 62.4
corruption I have said to c., thou art my father 16.33
the bondage of c. 47.26
sown in c. 48.43
he that soweth to his flesh shall . . . reap c. 50.13
cost counteth the c. 44.46
cottage as a c. in a vineyard 21.2
counsel who . . . darkeneth c.? 16.54
who . . . hideth c. without knowledge? 16.62
the c. of the ungodly 17.1
we took sweet c. together 17.120
where no c. is, the people fall 18.28
c. in the heart of man is like deep water 18.60
the spirit of c. and might 21.25
if this c. . . . be of men 46.15
Counsellor Wonderful, C. 21.23
counsellors in the multitude of c. there is safety 18.28
counsels leaders of the people by their c. 39.28
counted he c. it to him for righteousness 1.42
c. as sheep . . . to be slain 17.98
countenance his c. fell 1.20
the Lord lift up his c. upon thee 4.3
ruddy, and withal of a beautiful c. 9.18
the light of thy c. 17.9
a merry heart maketh a cheerful c. 18.41
his c. was as the sun 67.2
counteth c. the cost 44.46
country get thee out of thy c. 1.39
good news from a far c. 18.83
they departed into their own c. 42.3
prophet . . . not without honour, save in his own c. 42.95
courage be strong and of a good c. 5.14
only be strong and of a good c. 6.2
every one said to his brother, be of good c. 21.65
course finish my c. with joy 46.49
I have finished my c. 57.7
court a c. for owls 21.51
courts my soul hath a desire and longing to enter into the c. of the Lord 17.173
covenant a c. between me and the earth 1.34
your c. with death shall be disannulled 21.42
cover I . . . will c. thee with my hand 2.44
to the hills, c. us 44.71
covered they c. him with clothes, but he gat no heat 11.1
thou hast c. my head 17.284
nothing c., that shall not be revealed 42.64
covereth but love c. all sins 18.25
he that c. a transgression seeketh love 18.50
covet thou shalt not c. 2.29
crackling the c. of thorns under a pot, so is the laughter of the fool 19.19
craftiness the wise in their own c. 16.15
cunning c. 51.7
create I c. new heavens and a new earth 21.103
created God c. . . . the earth 1.1
hath not one God c. us? 34.1
for thy pleasure they are and were c. 67.17
creation the whole c. groaneth . . . in pain 47.26
Creator remember now thy C. in the days of thy youth 19.40
worshipped . . . the creature more than the C. 47.7

creature God created ... every living c. 1.5
preach the gospel to every c. 43.23
worshipped ... the c. more than the Creator 47.7
the earnest expectation of the c. 47.26
the c. was made subject to vanity 47.26
every c. of God is good 56.5
creatures their houses shall be full of doleful c. 21.28
creeping cattle and c. thing 1.6
things c. innumerable 17.215
Cretians the C. are alway liars 58.1
cried some therefore c. one thing, and some another 46.44
crieth thy brother's blood c. unto me 1.21
wisdom c. without 18.5
the voice of him that c. in the wilderness 21.59
crooked leviathan that c. serpent 21.40
the c. shall be made straight 21.59
cross take up his c. 42.106
the preaching of the c. 48.1
even the death of the c. 52.4
crow before the cock c., thou shalt deny me 42.164
crown a virtuous woman is a c. to her husband 18.30
the hoary head is a c. of glory 18.46
children's children are the c. of old men 18.49
one that was never thought of hath worn the c. 39.11
a corruptible c. 48.27
a c. of righteousness 57.7
the c. of life 61.2
I will give thee a c. of life 67.7
crowned c., and receive palms 36.2
not c., except he strive lawfully 57.3
crowns cast their c. before the throne 67.17
crucified preach Christ c. 48.2
save Jesus Christ, and him c. 48.4
cruel c. bondage 2.12
the tender mercies of the wicked are c. 18.31
jealousy is c. as the grave 20.26
crumbs dogs eat of the c. 42.103
c. which fall from their masters' table 42.103
c. which fell from the rich man's table 44.55
cry a great c. in Egypt 2.20
the voice of them that c. 2.40
let them ... be soon brought to shame, that c. over me, there, there 17.150
the c. of him that ruleth among fools 19.30
he looked for ... righteousness, but behold a c. 21.14
c. unto her, that her warfare is accomplished 21.59
the voice said, c. ... what shall I cry? 21.59
the stones would immediately c. out 44.64
whereby we c., Abba, Father 47.25
crying the voice of one c. in the wilderness 42.5
neither sorrow, nor c. 67.65
crystal sea of glass like unto c. 67.16
cucumbers as a lodge in a garden of c. 21.2
cud clovenfooted, and cheweth the c. 3.1
cumbered Martha was c. about much serving 44.34
cumbereth why c. it the ground? 44.42
cunning c. works 2.36
let my right hand forget her c. 17.276
the c. artificer 21.10
c. craftiness 51.7
cup my c. shall be full 17.45
my c. runneth over 17.47
there is a c., and the wine is red 17.158
give to drink ... a c. of cold water 42.69
are ye able to drink of the c.? 42.127
let this c. pass from me 42.166
remove this c. from me 44.70
the c. which my Father hath given me 45.73
cups in their c., they forget their love 35.2
curious be not c. in unnecessary matters 39.4
curse I will ... c. him that curseth thee 1.39
c. me this people 4.12
he will c. thee to thy face 16.3
c. God, and die 16.4
the c. causeless shall not come 18.84
c. not the king, no not in thy thought 19.35
c. not the rich in thy bedchamber 19.35
bless them that c. you 42.24
cursed thou art c. above all cattle 1.17
c. is the ground for thy sake 1.17
Job ... c. his day 16.5
cursing blessing and c. 5.13
their mouth is full of c. 17.22
his delight was in c., and it shall happen unto him 17.226
out of the same mouth proceedeth blessing and c. 61.9
curtain that stretcheth out the heavens as a c. 21.62
custom sitting at the receipt of c. 42.51
c. to whom custom 47.42
cut they shall soon be c. down like the grass 17.82
in the evening ... c. down 17.182
c. off out of the land of the living 21.81
an everlasting sign that shall not be c. off 21.87
an everlasting name, that shall not be c. off 21.88
I am c. off 23.6
c. to the heart 46.18
cymbal a tinkling c. 48.35
cymbals praise him in the c. and dances 17.300

D

Dagon only the stump of D. was left to him 9.11
daily our d. bread 42.27
exhort one another d. 60.4

Damascus Abana and Pharpar, rivers of D. 12.6
near D. ... there shined round about him a light from heaven 46.25
damnation whose d. is just 47.12
dance a time to mourn, and a time to d. 19.9
danced David d. before the Lord 10.4
we have piped unto you, and ye have not d. 42.73
the daughter of Herodias d. 42.96
danger in d. of hell fire 42.19
in d. to be called in question for this day's uproar 46.46
Daniel brought D., and cast him into the den 25.11
dark they grope in the d. 16.29
d. sayings 18.1
darkened the sun and the moon shall be d. 27.7
darkeneth who ... d. counsel? 16.54
darkly through a glass, d. 48.35
darkness d. was upon the face of the deep 1.1
God divided the light from the d. 1.1
an horror of great d. 1.43
d. which may be felt 2.17
the thick d. where God was 2.30
the land of d. and the shadow of death 16.25
he made d. his secret place 17.31
God shall make my d. to be light 17.32
the pestilence that walketh in d. 17.186
peradventure the d. shall cover me 17.279
d. is no darkness with thee 17.279
d. and light to thee are both alike 17.279
that put d. for light 21.16
the people that walked in d. 21.22
thy d. be as the noonday 21.92
gross d. 21.94
if ... the light that is in thee be d., how great is that darkness 42.29
outer d. 42.47
the d. comprehended it not 45.1
men loved d. ... because their deeds were evil 45.13
cast off the works of d. 47.43
against the rulers of the d. of this world 51.14
darling deliver ... my d. from the power of the dog 17.44
darts the fiery d. of the wicked 51.14
daughter the king's d. is all glorious within 17.101
as is the mother, so is her d. 24.5
thy mother's d. 24.5
the d. of Herodias danced 42.96
the d. against the mother 44.41
daughters the d. of men 1.27
kings' d. were among thy honourable women 17.100
the horseleach hath two d., crying, give, give 18.106
all the d. of musick shall be brought low 19.40
my d. from the ends of the earth 21.67
a place and a name better than ... of d. 21.88
David D. his ten thousands 9.22
the root and the offspring of D. 67.71
David and Goliath 9.20
David and Jonathan 10.3
day God called the light D. 1.1
a d. of trouble ... rebuke, and blasphemy 12.15
Job ... cursed his d. 16.5
let the d. perish wherein I was born 16.6
one d. telleth another 17.35
killed all the d. long 17.98
one d. in thy courts is better than a thousand 17.175
the arrow that flieth by d. 17.186
then shall my night be turned to d. 17.279
thou knowest not what a d. may bring forth 18.90
until the d. break, and the shadows flee away 20.8
at that d. shall a man look to his Maker 21.33
the d. of the Lord cometh 27.2
the d. of the Lord ... is nigh at hand 27.2
the d. of the Lord is great and very terrible 27.3
the d. of the Lord ... who can abide it? 27.3
put far away the evil d. 28.5
who hath despised the d. of small things? 33.4
who may abide the d. of his coming? 34.2
the d. cometh, that shall burn as an oven 34.3
sufficient unto the d. is the evil thereof 42.32
the d. is far spent 44.79
when the d. of Pentecost was fully come 46.6
d. is at hand 47.43
he that regardeth the d. 47.45
the d. of the Lord so cometh as a thief in the night 54.4
in the spirit on the Lord's d. 67.2
days his d. shall be an hundred and twenty years 1.27
my d. are swifter than a weaver's shuttle 16.19
the number of my d. 17.88
the d. of our age are threescore years and ten 17.183
the d. of man are but as grass 17.210
length of d. is in her right hand 18.8
the d. are prolonged, and every vision faileth 24.4
the Ancient of d. 25.13
in the d. of Herod the king 42.2
forty d. and forty nights 42.9
redeeming the time, because the d. are evil 51.11
love life, and see good d. 62.13
dayspring the d. from on high 44.5
day star until ... the d. arise in your hearts 63.1
dead not a house where there was not one d. 2.20
we be all d. men 2.21
the Lord deal kindly with you, as ye have dealt with the d. 8.1
forgotten, as a d. man out of mind 17.70
I praised the d. ... more than the living 19.10
the d. know not any thing 19.26

for the living to the d. 21.21
vain to pray for the d. 41.1
let the d. bury their dead 42.49
not d., but sleepeth 42.55
this my son was d. 44.50
though one rose from the d. 44.57
why seek ye the living among the d.? 44.77
the d. shall hear the voice of the Son of God 45.23
your fathers did eat manna ... and are d. 45.32
the patriarch David ... is both d. and buried 46.8
Christ being raised from the d. 47.20
reckon ... yourselves to be d. indeed unto sin 47.20
now is Christ risen from the d. 48.40
the d. shall be raised incorruptible 48.45
d. in trespasses and sins 51.2
faith, if it hath not works, is d. 61.6
he that liveth, and was d. 67.3
blessed are the d. which die in the Lord 67.47
the sea gave up the d. 67.64

deaf the ears of the d. shall be unstopped 21.54

deal the Lord d. kindly with you, as ye have dealt with the dead 8.1

death thou shalt go to thy fathers 1.44
the d. of the righteous 4.14
life and d. 5.13
their latter end 5.18
going the way of all the earth 6.7
the Lord do so to me ... if ought but d. part thee and me 8.2
surely the bitterness of d. is past 9.16
in their d. they were not divided 10.2
slept with his fathers 11.2
which long for d., but it cometh not 16.9
neither shall his place know him any more 16.21
the land of darkness and the shadow of d. 16.25
to d., and to the house appointed for all living 16.46
in d. no man remembereth thee 17.12
the snares of d. overtook me 17.30
the valley of the shadow of d. 17.45
the place thereof shall know it no more 17.210
at d.'s door 17.220
the snares of d. compassed me round 17.238
thou hast delivered my soul from d. 17.124, 17.239
he hath not given me over unto d. 17.241
he shall turn again to his earth 17.292
one event happeneth to them all 19.7
better ... the day of d. than the day of one's birth 19.18
man goeth to his long home 19.40
love is strong as d. 20.26
the land of the shadow of d. 21.22
your covenant with d. shall be disannulled 21.42
d. cannot celebrate thee 21.58
he hath poured out his soul unto d. 21.82
such as are for d., to death 22.11
a perpetual sleep 22.22
I am cut off 23.6
that ... turneth the shadow of d. into the morning 28.4
their departure is taken for misery 38.3
power of life and d. 38.13
judge none blessed before his d. 39.12
thou shalt die the d. 39.14
O d., how bitter is the remembrance of thee 39.26
O d., acceptable is thy sentence 39.26
my soul is exceeding sorrowful, even unto d. 42.165
lieth at the point of d. 43.10
passed from d. unto life 45.23
if a man keep my saying, he shall never see d. 45.42
he fell asleep 46.20
Saul was consenting unto his d. 46.21
d. hath no more dominion over him 47.20
the wages of sin is d. 47.21
who shall deliver me from the body of this d.? 47.23
to be carnally minded is d. 47.24
neither d., nor life, nor angels 47.31
the apostles ... as it were appointed to d. 48.10
by man came d. 48.40
the last enemy ... is d. 48.41
O d., where is thy sting? 48.45
even the d. of the cross 52.4
finished my course 57.7
the keys of hell and of d. 67.3
faithful unto d. 67.7
D., and Hell followed with him 67.24
men seek d., and shall not find it 67.34
on such the second d. hath no power 67.63
there shall be no more d. 67.65
–*See also* darkness, dead, die, grave.

Deborah I D. arose ... a mother in Israel 7.3

debt pay me that thou owest 42.118

debtor d. both to the Greeks, and to the Barbarians 47.4
d. both ... to the wise, and to the unwise 47.4

decay no d., no leading into captivity 17.290

deceit as a cage ... full of birds ... their houses full of d. 22.3
the holy spirit of discipline will flee d. 38.1
philosophy and vain d. 53.1

deceitful the Lord will abhor ... the blood-thirsty and d. man 17.10
men are d. upon the weights 17.135
the kisses of an enemy are d. 18.92
the heart is d. above all things 22.13

deceitfulness the d. of riches 42.88
the d. of sin 60.4

deceits prophesy d. 21.45

deceive if we say that we have no sin, we d. 64.2

deceived take heed ... that your heart be not d. 5.5
be not d. 50.13
deceivers as d., and yet true 49.13
deceiveth if a man think himself to be something ... he d. himself 50.12
deceiving d., and being deceived 57.4
decently done d. and in order 48.38
decision multitudes in the valley of d. 27.7
deck d. thyself ... with majesty and excellency 16.59
declare I will d. hard sentences 17.162
decree a d. from Caesar Augustus 44.7
deed blessed in his d. 61.4
deeds the due reward of our d. 44.74
deep one d. calleth another 17.96
thy thoughts are very d. 17.189
out of the d. have I called unto thee 17.271
counsel in the heart of man is like d. water 18.60
I never went down into the d. 36.3
a night and a day I have been in the d. 49.18
deeps ye dragons, and all d. 17.297
defamed being d., we intreat 48.10
defence my stony rock, and my d. 17.29
the Lord ... is the wholesome d. of his Anointed 17.60
be thou my strong rock, and house of d. 17.67
whoso dwelleth under the d. of the most High 17.185
the Lord is thy d. upon thy right hand 17.257
deferred hope d. maketh the heart sick 18.33
defiance we are not careful to answer thee 25.5
kick against the pricks 46.25
defiled he that toucheth pitch shall be d. 39.13
defileth that which cometh out of the mouth ... d. 42.101
delicate no more be called tender and d. 21.71
delicately Agag came unto him d. 9.16
deliciously lived d. 67.55
delight his d. is in the law of the Lord 17.1
d. ... in the Lord 17.83
let your soul d. itself in fatness 21.84
delighteth neither d. he in any man's legs 17.295
delights clothed ... in scarlet, with other d. 10.2
how fair ... art thou, O love, for d. 20.22
deliver he trusted in God, that he would d. him 17.41
d. ... my darling from the power of the dog 17.44
d. me from blood-guiltiness 17.115
d. me ... from the evil man 17.282
thy God whom thou servest ... will d. thee 25.11
d. us from evil 42.27
who shall d. me from the body of this death? 47.23
deliverance compass me about with songs of d. 17.72
delivered thou hast d. my soul from death 17.124, 17.239
d. out of the mouth of the lion 57.9
den cast him into the d. of lions 25.11
a d. of thieves 42.130
denied d. the Holy One and the Just 46.11
dens his lurking d. 17.17
deny let him d. himself 42.106
before the cock crow, thou shalt d. me 42.164
though I should die ... yet will I not d. thee 42.164
depart d. from me, ye that work iniquity 42.43
lettest thou thy servant d. in peace 44.12
a desire to d., and to be with Christ 52.3
departed he wist not that the Lord was d. from him 7.16
I-chabod ... the glory is d. 9.10
they d. ... another way 42.3
departure their d. is taken for misery 38.3
the time of my d. is at hand 57.7
depth nor height, nor d. ... able to separate us 47.31
the breadth, and length, and d. 51.5
derision they that are younger than I have me in d. 16.45
the Lord shall have them in d. 17.3
descended the Lord d. upon it in fire 2.28
descending angels of God ascending and d. 1.56
desert the d. shall rejoice, and blossom 21.52
make straight in the d. a highway for our God 21.59
her d. like the garden of the Lord 21.79
deserts wandered in d. ... dens and caves 60.15
desirable d. young men 24.9
desire thy d. shall be to thy husband 1.17
my d. is ... that mine adversary had written a book 16.47
thou hast given him his heart's d. 17.40
he shall give thee thy heart's d. 17.83
Lord, thou knowest all my d. 17.87
my soul hath a d. 17.173
when the d. cometh, it is a tree of life 18.33
the d. accomplished is sweet 18.34
better ... the sight of the eyes than the wandering of the d. 19.17
d. shall fail 19.40
I am my beloved's, and his d. is toward me 20.23
no beauty that we should d. him 21.81
d. not a multitude of unprofitable children 39.15
a d. to depart, and to be with Christ 52.3
desired a tree to be d. to make one wise 1.14
more to be d. ... than gold 17.36
desireth like as the hart d. the water-brooks 17.94
he d. a good work 56.4

desolation satyrs shall dance there 21.28
a possession for the bittern 21.31
thorns shall come up in her palaces 21.51
that which the palmerworm hath left hath the locust eaten 27.1
not ... one stone upon another 42.143
abomination of d. 42.146
despise take heed that ye d. not one of these little ones 42.114
despised d. and rejected of men 21.81
who hath d. the day of small things? 33.4
ye are honourable, but we are d. 48.10
destroy they that ... would d. me guiltless, are mighty 17.146
they shall not hurt nor d. in all my holy mountain 21.26
pastors that d. and scatter the sheep 22.15
able to d. both body and soul 42.64
destroyed Egypt is d. 2.16
the last enemy that shall be d. is death 48.41
destruction the d. of the poor is their poverty 18.26
hell and d. are never full 18.96
sweep it with the besom of d. 21.31
their going ... utter d. 38.3
broad is the way, that leadeth to d. 42.39
whose end is d. 52.9
destructions O thou enemy, d. are come to a perpetual end 17.15
devil tempted of the d. 42.9
he hath a d. 42.74
the enemy that sowed them is the d. 42.92
thou art a Samaritan, and hast a d. 45.41
neither give place to the d. 51.8
the wiles of the d. 51.14
resist the d., and he will flee 61.12
your adversary the d., as a roaring lion 62.16
serpent, called the d., and Satan 67.38
the d. is come ... having great wrath 67.39
devilish earthly, sensual, d. 61.10
devils casteth out d. through the prince of the devils 42.56
them that were possessed with d. 43.1
devour he shall d. the prey 1.81
d. widows' houses 43.20
seeking whom he may d. 62.16
devoured some evil beast hath d. him 1.65
dew the d. of heaven 1.54
my head is filled with d. 20.15
his body was wet with the d. of heaven 25.8
the remnant of Jacob shall be ... as a d. 30.3
Diana great is D. of the Ephesians 46.43
die thou shalt surely d. 1.10
let me d. the death of the righteous 4.14
all ... shall d. in the flower of their age 9.3
we must needs d. 10.8
curse God, and d. 16.4
ye are the people, and wisdom shall d. with you 16.27
I shall not d., but live 17.241
a time to be born, and a time to d. 19.9
the living know that they shall d. 19.26
in the sight of the unwise they seemed to d. 38.3
thou shalt d. the death 39.14
let us d. manfully for our brethren 40.2
though I should d. ... yet will I not deny thee 42.164
except ... wheat fall into the ground and d. 45.52
if it d., it bringeth forth much fruit 45.52
expedient that one man should d. for the people 45.74
as in Adam all d. 48.40
to d. is gain 52.2
died would God I had d. for thee 10.11
great favour laid up for those that d. godly 41.1
in that he d., he died unto sin once 47.20
dieth their worm d. not 43.17
Christ being raised from the dead d. no more 47.20
differeth one star d. from another ... in glory 48.43
dig I cannot d. 44.53
diggeth he that d. a pit shall fall into it 19.32
dignities not afraid to speak evil of d. 63.2
dim his eyes were d., that he could not see 9.8
dippeth he that d. his hand with me in the dish 42.162
disappointed let me not be d. of my hope 17.251
disappointeth he that sweareth unto his neighbour, and d. him not 17.24
discern d. the signs of the times 42.104
discerner a d. of the thoughts ... of the heart 60.5
discharge there is no d. in that war 19.24
disciple the d. is not above his master 42.63
disciples one of his d., whom Jesus loved 45.55
discipline bear the yoke in his youth 23.5
the holy spirit of d. 38.1
discouraged he shall not fail nor be d. 21.66
provoke not your children ... lest they be d. 53.6
discourse miss not the d. of the elders 39.8
discretion a fair woman ... without d. 18.29
he that covereth a transgression 18.50
if thou hast heard a word, let it die 39.18
disease the physician cutteth off a long d. 39.10
all manner of d. 42.14
diseased d. in his feet 11.13
dish butter in a lordly d. 7.6
he that dippeth his hand with me in the d. 42.162
dishonour another unto d. 47.33
disobedience a revolting ... heart 22.2
children of d. 51.2
cometh the wrath of God upon the children of d. 51.10
dispersed he hath d. abroad, and given to the poor 17.231

displeased they ... d. the most high God 17.165
disposing the lot is cast ... but the ... d. thereof is of the Lord 18.48
disputations doubtful d. 47.44
disquieted why art thou so d. within me? 17.95
disquieteth man ... d. himself in vain 17.88
dissemble they ... d. in their double heart 17.20
dissimulation let love be without d. 47.37
distress d. of nations, with perplexity 44.68
good for the present d. 48.20
distribute ready to d. 56.14
ditch both shall fall into the d. 42.102
diversities d. of gifts, but the same Spirit 48.34
divide he shall d. the spoil 1.81
d. him a portion with the great 21.82
divided have they not d. the prey? 7.7
in their death they were not d. 10.2
thy kingdon is d., and given to the Medes and Persians 25.10
if a kingdom be d. ... that kingdom cannot stand 43.6
five in one house d. 44.41
divideth as a shepherd d. his sheep from the goats 42.157
do I know that thou canst d. every thing 16.62
whatsoever thy hand findeth to d. 19.28
d. with me as seemeth good ... unto you 22.17
whatsoever ye would that men should d. to you 42.38
d. this, and he doeth it 42.46
is it not lawful for me to d. what I will with mine own? 42.126
go, and d. thou likewise 44.33
for they know not what they d. 44.73
my meat is to d. the will of him that sent me 45.19
what shall we d., that we might work the works of God? 45.28
the good that I would I d. not 47.22
d. all to the glory of God 48.32
able to d. exceeding abundantly 51.5
d. all things through Christ 52.13
whatsoever ye d., do it heartily 53.7
doctors sitting in the midst of the d. 44.13
doctrine my d. shall drop as the rain 5.15
every wind of d. 51.7
doers be ye d. of the word 61.4
doeth he that d. the will of my Father 42.42
whosoever heareth these sayings ... and d. them 42.44
dog am I a d., that thou comest to me with staves? 9.21
is thy servant a d.? 12.9
the power of the d. 17.44
grin like a d., and run about 17.130
as a d. returneth to his vomit 18.86
one that taketh a d. by the ears 18.88
a living d. is better than a dead lion 19.26
dogs d. shall eat Jezebel 11.28
not meet to ... cast it to d. 42.103
d. eat of the crumbs 42.103
doing the Lord's d. 17.242
patient continuance in well d. 47.8
let us not be weary in well d. 50.13
doings even a child is known by his d. 18.61
Domine non nobis, D. 17.236
dominion let them have d. 1.7
women have d. over you 35.5
death hath no more d. over him 47.20
Dominus D. illuminatio mea 17.56
nisi D. ... frustra 17.266
done d. it unto one of the least of these 42.159
not my will, but thine, be d. 44.70
what shall be d. in the dry? 44.71
this thing was not d. in a corner 46.60
d. decently and in order 48.38
door at death's d. 17.220
as the d. turneth upon his hinges, so doth the slothful upon his bed 18.87
the posts of the d. moved at the voice 21.17
I am the d. 45.47
the judge standeth before the d. 61.14
an open d., and no man can shut it 67.12
I stand at the d., and knock 67.15
a d. was opened in heaven 67.16
door-keeper I had rather be a d. in the house of my God 17.175
doors be ye lift up, ye everlasting d. 17.49
the d. shall be shut in the streets 19.40
Dorcas D.: this woman ... full of good works 46.28
double d. for all her sins 21.59
doubt O thou of little faith, wherefore didst thou d.? 42.98
doubtful d. disputations 47.44
doubting the Spirit bade me go ... nothing d. 46.32
dove wings like a d. 17.119
I did mourn as a d. 21.57
the Spirit of God descending like a d. 42.8
doves thou hast d.' eyes within thy locks 20.11
harmless as d. 42.61
down-sitting thou knowest my d. 17.277
dragon fought against the d. 67.38
laid hold on the d. ... and bound him 67.62
dragons ye d., and all deeps 17.297
d. in their pleasant palaces 21.28
an habitation of d. 21.51
draw d. me, we will run after thee 20.1
we ... as soon as we were born, began to d. to our end 38.6
no man can come to me, except the Father ... d. him 45.31
if I be lifted up ... d. all men unto me 45.53
d. nigh to God, and he will draw nigh to you 61.12
drawers d. of water 6.5

dream behold, it was a d. 1.69
your old men shall d. dreams 27.5
warned of God in a d. 42.3
suffered many things ... in a d. 42.171
dreamer this d. cometh 1.65
that prophet, or ... d. of dreams 5.7
dreamers filthy d. 66.2
dreams what will become of his d. 1.65
dregs as for the d. ... the ungodly of the earth shall drink them 17.158
drew a certain man d. a bow at a venture 11.33
I d. them with cords of a man 26.3
I d. them ... with bands of love 26.3
drink the people sat down to ... d. 2.38
wine and strong d. 4.1
a d. of deadly wine 17.132
all the beasts ... d. thereof 17.212
strong d. is raging 18.58
I commended mirth ... to eat ... to d., and to be merry 19.25
d. thy wine with a merry heart 19.27
woe unto them that ... follow strong d. 21.15
let us eat and d.; for tomorrow we ... die 21.35
they shall not d. wine with a song 21.39
stagger, but not with strong d. 21.43
ye d., but ye are not filled with drink 32.1
eat the fat, and d. the sweet 35.9
what shall we d.? 42.31
give to d. ... a cup of cold water 42.69
are ye able to d. of the cup? 42.127
thirsty, and ye gave me d. 42.158
d. ye all of it 42.163
take thine ease, eat, d., and be merry 44.38
the cup which my Father hath given ... shall I not d. it? 45.73
d. no longer water 56.9
drinketh whosoever d. of this water shall thirst again 45.16
drinking John came neither eating nor d. 42.74
eating and d., marrying 42.150
driven he that wavereth ... d. with the wind and tossed 61.1
driveth Jehu ... d. furiously 12.11
driving the d. of Jehu 12.11
drop a d. of a bucket 21.61
dropping a continual d. in a very rainy day 18.93
drowsiness d. shall clothe a man with rags 18.74
drunk when men have well d., then that which is worse 45.7
drunkard the d. and the glutton shall come to poverty 18.74
drunken they ... stagger like a d. man 16.29
d., but not with wine 21.43
d. with the blood of the saints 67.54
drunkenness strong drink is raging 18.58
woe unto them that ... follow strong drink 21.15
a labouring man ... given to d. 39.17
not in rioting and d. 47.43
dry the midst of the sea upon d. ground 2.23
a barren and d. land where no water is 17.136
lo, they were very d. 24.11
O ye d. bones 24.11
what shall be done in the d.? 44.71
due his fruit in d. season 17.1
one born out of d. time 48.39
dues render therefore to all their d. 47.42
dumb the tongue of the d. sing 21.54
as a sheep before her shearers is d. 21.81
dust God formed man of the d. of the ground 1.9
d. shalt thou eat 1.17
d. thou art 1.18
unto d. shalt thou return 1.18
I ... repent in d. and ashes 16.63
shall the d. give thanks unto thee? 17.65
his enemies shall lick the d. 17.154
then shall the d. return to the earth 19.40
the small d. of the balance 21.61
lick up the d. of thy feet 21.76
shake off the d. of your feet 42.60
duty this is the whole d. of man 19.42
dwell such as d. in tents 1.24
thou, Lord ... makest me d. in safety 17.9
Lord, who shall d. in thy tabernacle? 17.23
I will d. in the house of the Lord for ever 17.45
d. among scorpions 24.1
he that sitteth on the throne shall d. among them 67.28
he will d. with them 67.65
dwelleth whoso d. under the defence of the most High 17.185
God ... d. not in temples made with hands 46.38
dwelling the fir-trees are a d. for the stork 17.213
d. in the light which no man can approach 56.13
dwellings how amiable are thy d. 17.173
dwelt the word was made flesh, and d. among us 45.1
dying as d., and, behold, we live 49.13

E

eagle young and lusty as an e. 17.207
the way of an e. in the air 18.107
eagles mount up with wings as e. 21.64
wheresoever the carcase is, there will the e. be gathered 42.147
ear he that planted the e., shall he not hear? 17.194
the hearing e. ... the Lord hath made 18.62
nor the e. filled with hearing 19.2
the e. of jealousy heareth all things 38.2
nor e. heard 48.5

early God shall help her, and that right e. 17.104
I myself will awake right e. 17.128
e., when it was yet dark 45.87
earnest the e. expectation of the creature 47.26
earneth he ... e. wages to put it into a bag with holes 32.1
ears the seven thin e. 1.69
the e. of every one that heareth it shall tingle 9.6
e., and hear not 17.237
the e. of the deaf shall be unstopped 21.54
e. to hear, and hear not 24.3
hear with thine e. 24.13
e. to hear, let him hear 42.72
e. ... dull of hearing 42.86
blessed are your ... e., for they hear 42.86
earth the e. was without form 1.1
God called the dry land E. 1.3
let the e. bring forth grass 1.3
while the e. remaineth 1.32
a covenant between me and the e. 1.34
going the way of all the e. 6.7
from going to and fro in the e. 16.1
the e. is the Lord's 17.48
the e. is full of the goodness of the Lord 17.75
thou visitest the e., and blessest it 17.140
then shall the e. bring forth her increase 17.141
the e. is weak ... I bear up the pillars of it 17.157
the foundations of the e. are out of course 17.172
in his hand are all the corners of the e. 17.195
be the e. never so unquiet 17.201
food out of the e. 17.213
tremble, thou e., at the presence of the Lord 17.234
he shall turn again to his e. 17.292
the e. for depth 18.80
one generation passeth away ... but the e. abideth for ever 19.1
then shall the dust return to the e. 19.40
the whole e. is full of his glory 21.17
the e. shall be full of the knowledge of the Lord 21.26
he that sitteth upon the circle of the e. 21.62
let all the e. keep silence before him 31.2
we have walked to and fro through the e. 33.2
all the e. sitteth still, and is at rest 33.2
the eyes of the Lord, which run to and fro through the whole e. 33.4
the meek ... shall inherit the e. 42.15
the salt of the e. 42.16
neither by the e.; for it is his footstool 42.22
heaven and e. shall pass away 42.149
on e. peace, good will toward men 44.10
the e. is the Lord's, and the fulness thereof 48.30
of the e., earthy 48.44
strangers and pilgrims on the e. 60.12
woe to the inhabiters of the e. 67.39
redeemed from the e. 67.43
from whose face the e. and the heaven fled 67.64
a new heaven and a new e. 67.65
earthen treasure in e. vessels 49.6
earthly I have told you e. things, and ye believe not 45.10
our e. house 49.8
e., sensual, devilish 61.10
earthquake the Lord was not in the e. 11.23
ease his soul shall dwell at e. 17.51
eased I e. his shoulder from the burden 17.169
easier e. for a camel to go through the eye of a needle 42.122
east how wide also the e. is from the west 17.209
wise men from the e. 42.2
we have seen his star in the e. 42.2
east-wind thou shalt break the ships ... through the e. 17.108
easy my yoke is e. 42.76
eat of every tree ... thou mayest freely e. 1.10
and he did e. 1.14
in sorrow shalt thou e. of it 1.17
the people sat down to e. 2.38
arise and e. ... the journey is too great 11.22
thinkest thou that I will e. bulls' flesh 17.112
man did e. angels' food 17.164
the sleep of a labouring man is sweet, whether he e. little or much 19.16
I commended mirth ... to e. ... to drink, and to be merry 19.25
e. thy bread with joy 19.27
let my beloved ... e. his pleasant fruits 20.14
butter and honey shall he e. 21.19
let us e. and drink; for tomorrow we ... die 21.35
they shall not plant, and another e. 21.102
Nebuchadnezzar ... did e. grass as oxen 25.8
ye e., but ye have not enough 32.1
e. the fat, and drink the sweet 35.9
take no thought, saying, what shall we e.? 42.31
take, e.; this is my body 42.163
take thine ease, e., drink, and be merry 44.38
the husks that the swine did e. 44.49
your fathers did e. manna in the wilderness 45.32
if any would not work, neither should he e. 55.2
e. of the tree of life 67.6
e. of the hidden manna 67.8
eaten thou hast e. and art full 5.2
the fathers have e. sour grapes 24.6
that which the palmerworm hath left hath the locust e. 27.1
the years that the locust hath e. 27.4
e. of worms 46.33
eater out of the e. came forth meat 7.12

eaters be not among ... riotous e. of flesh 18.74
eating John came neither e. nor drinking 42.74
e. and drinking, marrying 42.150
ecce e. homo 45.79
Eden a garden eastward in E. 1.9
a river went out of E. 1.9
the garden of E. 1.10
east of E. 1.23
edge the children's teeth are set on e. 24.6
edifieth knowledge puffeth up, but charity e. 48.23
edify all things e. not 48.29
Edom over E. will I cast out my shoe 17.225
effectual the e. fervent prayer of a righteous man 61.16
elder the entrances of the e. world 36.5
rebuke not an e. 56.7
the e. unto the elect lady 65.1
elders miss not the discourse of the e. 39.8
four and twenty e. 67.16
elect mine e. shall long enjoy the work of their hands 21.102
gather together his e. 42.148
who shall lay any thing to the charge of God's e.? 47.30
the elder unto the e. lady 65.1
elements the weak and beggarly e. 50.6
Elias E. truly shall first come 42.108
Elijah E. went up by a whirlwind into heaven 12.1
the spirit of E. doth rest on Elisha 12.2
Elijah and the Ravens 11.14
eloquent I am not e. 2.9
the e. orator 21.10
embrace a time to e., and a time to refrain 19.9
his right hand doth e. me 20.4
empty e., swept, and garnished 42.83
sent e. away 44.3
end let my last e. be like his 4.14
that they would consider their latter e. 5.18
the Lord blessed the latter e. of Job 16.64
O thou enemy, destructions are come to a perpetual e. 17.15
Lord, let me know mine e. 17.88
at their wit's e. 17.221
her e. is bitter as wormwood 18.12
better ... the e. of a thing than the beginning 19.20
of making many books there is no e. 19.41
of the increase of his government ... there shall be no e. 21.23
at his e. shall be a fool 22.14
we ... as soon as we were born, began to draw to our e. 38.6
wisdom reacheth from one e. to another 38.9
he that endureth to the e. shall be saved 42.62
the harvest is the e. of the world 42.92
the e. is not yet 42.144
I am with you alway, even unto the e. of the world 42.177
whose e. is destruction 52.9
the e. of all things is at hand 62.14
endeavouring e. to keep the unity of the Spirit 51.6
ending the beginning and the e. 67.2
ends my daughters from the e. of the earth 21.67
endued e. with power from on high 44.82
endure they shall perish, but thou shalt e. 17.206
we count them happy which e. 61.15
endureth he that e. to the end shall be saved 42.62
hopeth all things, e. all things 48.35
blessed is the man that e. temptation 61.2
enemies mine e. shall be confounded 17.13
mine e. that trouble me 17.97
his e. shall lick the dust 17.154
until I make thine e. thy footstool 17.227
love your e. 42.24
till he hath put all e. under his feet 48.41
enemy hast thou found me, O mine e.? 11.27
O thou e., destructions are come to a perpetual end 17.15
the kisses of an e. are deceitful 18.92
his e. came and sowed tares 42.89
an e. hath done this 42.90
the last e. that shall be destroyed 48.41
enmity I will put e. between thee and the woman 1.17
enough four things say not, it is e. 18.106
entangleth no man that warreth e. himself with the affairs of this life 57.3
enter e. ye in at the strait gate 42.39
except ye ... become as little children, ye shall not e. into the kingdom 42.111
a rich man shall hardly e. into ... heaven 42.122
e. thou into the joy of thy lord 42.154
entered ye are e. into their labours 45.20
entereth he that e. in by the door is the shepherd 45.46
entertained e. angels unawares 60.20
entice if sinners e. thee, consent thou not 18.2
entrance all men have one e. into life 38.7
entrances the e. of this world made narrow 36.5
the e. of the elder world 36.5
envy who is able to stand before e.? 18.91
Ephesians great is Diana of the E. 46.43
Ephraim the children of E., who ... turned themselves back in the day of battle 17.163
E. ... is the strength of my head 17.225
err wine ... causeth all men to e. 35.1
error the last e. shall be worse than the first 42.176
the e. of his way 61.17
escape with the temptation ... a way to e. 48.28
escaped e. with the skin of my teeth 16.36
established in the last days ... the Lord's house shall be e. 21.6

estate condescend to men of low e. 47.37
eternal the gift of God is e. life 47.21
exceeding and e. weight of glory 49.7
Ethiopian can the E. change his skin? 22.9
Evangelistic Beasts 67.16
Eve E. . . . the mother of all living 1.18
evening in the e. . . . cut down, dried up 17.182
man goeth forth to his work . . . until the e. 17.214
in the e. withhold not thine hand 19.39
when it is e., ye say, it will be fair weather 42.104
toward e., and the day is far spent 44.79
event one e. happeneth to them all 19.7
ever son, thou art e. with me 44.52
everlasting underneath are the e. arms 5.21
God from e. 17.181
an e. sign that shall not be cut off 21.87
an e. name, that shall not be cut off 21.88
e. habitations 44.54
evermore I am alive for e. 67.3
evidence faith . . . the e. of things not seen 60.11
evil as gods, knowing good and e. 1.14
e. from his youth 1.32
few and e. have the days . . . of my life been 1.75
an e. report 4.7
eschew e., and do good 17.79
all that they imagine is to do me e. 17.122
there shall no e. happen unto thee 17.187
deliver me . . . from the e. man 17.282
devise not e. against thy neighbour 18.9
whoso rewardeth e. for good, evil shall not depart from his house 18.51
better is he . . . who hath not seen the e. work 19.10
woe unto them that call e. good 21.16
refuse the e., and choose the good 21.19
the righteous is taken away from the e. to come 21.89
their feet run to e. 21.93
I will bring e. upon all flesh 22.19
shall there be e. in a city? 28.2
put far away the e. day 28.5
cast lots, that we may know for whose cause this e. is upon us 29.1
they are but few and e. 36.5
he maketh his sun to rise on the e. and on the good 42.24
deliver us from e. 42.27
sufficient unto the day is the e. thereof 42.32
ye . . . being e. . . . give good gifts 42.38
a corrupt tree bringeth forth e. fruit 42.41
how can ye, being e., speak good? 42.79
an e. and adulterous generation 42.81
is thine eye e., because I am good? 42.126
men loved darkness . . . because their deeds were e. 45.13
let us do e., that good may come 47.12
the e. which I would not, that I do 47.22
e. is present with me 47.22
recompense to no man e. for evil 47.37
be not overcome of e. 47.38
e. communications corrupt good manners 48.42
redeeming the time, because the days are e. 51.11
able to withstand in the e. day 51.14
love of money is the root of all e. 56.11
e. men and seducers 57.4
e. beasts, slow bellies 58.1
the tongue . . . an unruly e. 61.8
not rendering e. for evil 62.13
not afraid to speak e. of dignities 63.2
–*See also* darkness, wickedness.
ewe one little e. lamb 10.6
exalt whosoever shall e. himself shall be abased 42.138
example a publick e. 42.1
exceed e. the righteousness of the scribes 42.18
exceeding e. and eternal weight of glory 49.7
excellency the e. of the power may be of God 49.6
excellent very e. things are spoken of thee, thou city of God 17.180
by inheritance obtained a more e. name 60.1
exchange what shall a man give in e. for his soul? 43.15
excuse they all with one consent began to make e. 44.44
exercise bodily e. profiteth little 56.6
exhort e. one another daily, while it is called To day 60.4
expectation the earnest e. of the creature 47.26
expedient it is e. for you that I go away 45.68
e. that one man should die for the people 45.74
all things are not e. 48.29
experience tribulation worketh patience; and patience, e. 47.17
expert they all hold swords, being e. in war 20.10
eye e. for eye 2.31
as the apple of his e. 5.16
the e. . . . shall see me no more 16.20
keep me as the apple of an e. 17.28
he that made the e., shall he not see? 17.194
the seeing e., the Lord hath made 18.62
the e. is not satisfied with seeing 19.2
they shall see e. to eye 21.80
if thy right e. offend thee, pluck it out 42.21
the light of the body is the e. 42.29
the mote that is in thy brother's e. 42.34
is thine e. evil, because I am good? 42.126
e. hath not seen 48.5
every e. shall see him 67.2
eyes your e. shall be opened 1.14
his e. were dim, that he could not see 9.8
I was e. to the blind 16.44
e. . . . and see not 17.237

thou hast delivered ... mine e. from tears 17.239
turn away mine e., lest they behold vanity 17.246
I will lift up mine e. unto the hills 17.255
be not wise in thine own e. 18.6
the e. of man are never satisfied 18.96
thou hast doves' e. within thy locks 20.11
the e. of the blind shall be opened 21.54
e. to see, and see not 24.3
behold with thine e. 24.13
the e. of the Lord, which run to and fro 33.4
blessed are your e., for they see 42.86
mine e. have seen thy salvation 44.12
the e. of your understanding being enlightened 51.1
the lust of the e. 64.4
e. were as a flame of fire 67.2
full of e. before and behind 67.16
God shall wipe away all tears from their e. 67.28

F

fables f. and endless genealogies 56.1
old wives' f. 56.6
face I have seen God f. to face 1.62
the Lord make his f. shine upon thee 4.3
whom the Lord knew f. to face 5.23
Jezebel ... painted her f. 12.12
he turned his f. to the wall 12.16
a spirit passed before my f. 16.12
hide not thy f. from me 17.57
in water f. answereth to face 18.95
with twain he covered his f. 21.17
I hid not my f. from shame and spitting 21.78
in a little wrath I hid my f. from thee 21.83
before the f. of all people 44.12
as it had been the f. of an angel 46.17
but then f. to face 48.35
from whose f. the earth and the heaven fled 67.64
they shall see his f. 67.69
faces grind the f. of the poor 21.11
fade we all do f. as a leaf 21.100
fadeth the flower f. 21.59
fail he will not f. thee, nor forsake thee 5.14
I will not f. thee, nor forsake thee 6.1
thy years shall not f. 17.206
desire shall f. 19.40
he shall not f. nor be discouraged 21.66
prophecies, they shall f. 48.35
failed not one thing hath f. of all the good things 6.7
faileth every vision f. 24.4
charity never f. 48.35
faint f., yet pursuing 7.10
if thou f. in ... adversity, thy strength is small 18.77
they shall walk, and not f. 21.64
in due season we shall reap, if we f. not 50.13
fainted hast laboured, and hast not f. 67.5
fair the lot is fallen unto me in a f. ground 17.25
thou art all f. ... there is no spot in thee 20.11
f. as the moon 20.19
how f. ... art thou, O love, for delights 20.22
fairest thou f. among women 20.1
faith ye of little f. 42.31
I have not found so great f. 42.46
O thou of little f., wherefore didst thou doubt? 42.98
f. as a grain of mustard seed 42.109
thy f. hath saved thee 44.26
the just shall live by f. 47.5
by the law of f. 47.14
f. cometh by hearing 47.35
though I have all f. 48.35
now abideth f., hope, charity 48.35
by f. ye stand 49.2
we walk by f., not by sight 49.9
after that f. is come, we are no longer under a schoolmaster 50.4
the shield of f. 51.14
work of f. 54.1
some ... concerning f. have made shipwreck 56.3
fight the good fight of f. 56.12
f. is the substance of things hoped for 60.11
f. ... the evidence of things not seen 60.11
by f. the walls of Jericho fell down 60.14
Jesus the author and finisher of our f. 60.16
ask in f., nothing wavering 61.1
f., if it hath not works, is dead 61.6
stedfast in the f. 62.16
faithful f. are the wounds of a friend 18.92
a f. man shall abound with blessings 18.100
how is the f. city become an harlot 21.5
a f. friend is the medicine of life 39.7
thou good and f. servant 42.154
f. in that which is least ... faithful also in much 44.54
a f. saying 56.2
f. and just to forgive 64.2
f. unto death 67.7
called f. and true 67.60
faithfulness no f. in his mouth 17.11
his f. and truth shall be thy shield and buckler 17.186
great is thy f. 23.4
faithless be not f., but believing 45.92
fall see that ye f. not out 1.74
there shall not one hair ... f. to the ground 9.14
whose mouths must be held ... lest they f. upon thee 17.73
a thousand shall f. beside thee 17.186
let the ungodly f. into their own nets 17.287
and an haughty spirit before a f. 18.45
if they f., the one will lift up his fellow 19.12
he that diggeth a pit shall f. into it 19.32
if the tree f. ... there it shall be 19.37
we will f. into the hands of the Lord 39.3

great was the f. of it 42.44
one ... shall not f. on the ground without your Father 42.65
both shall f. into the ditch 42.102
crumbs which f. from their masters' table 42.103
beheld Satan as lightning f. from heaven 44.29
say to the mountains, f. on us 44.71
except ... wheat f. into the ground and die 45.52
take heed lest he f. 48.28
a fearful thing to f. into the hands of ... God 60.10
I saw a star f. from heaven 67.32

fallen how are the mighty f. 10.1
they have digged a pit ... and are f. into the midst of it 17.127
the Lord helpeth them that are f. 17.293
how art thou f. from heaven, O Lucifer 21.30
Babylon is f. 67.45

falleth woe to him that is alone when he f. 19.12

falling thou hast delivered ... my feet from f. 17.239
a f. away first 55.1

Fall of Man 1.14

false thou shalt not bear f. witness 2.29
beware of f. prophets 42.40

falsely science f. so called 56.15

familiar mine own f. friend 17.93
them that have f. spirits 21.21

famine f. was sore in the land 1.72
such as are for the f., to the famine 22.11

famous let us now praise f. men 39.27

far that be f. from thee to do 1.47
f. be it from God 16.51
peace to him that is f. off 21.90
their heart is f. from me 42.100

fared f. sumptuously every day 44.55

farthing paid the uttermost f. 42.20
two sparrows sold for a f. 42.65

farthings five sparrows sold for two f. 44.37

fashion the f. of this world passeth away 48.21

fasted f. forty days and forty nights 42.9

fasten f. him as a nail in a sure place 21.36

fastings in f. often 49.18

fat the f. of the land 1.73
but Jeshurun waxed f., and kicked 5.17
f. bulls of Basan 17.42
f. and well-liking 17.191
make the heart of this people f. 21.18
eat the f., and drink the sweet 35.9

father the God of thy f. 2.6
hath the rain a f.? 16.55
when my f. and my mother forsake me 17.58
F. of the fatherless 17.142
a wise son maketh a glad f. 18.23
a wise son heareth his f.'s instruction 18.32
have we not all one F.? 34.1
our F. 42.27
the f. shall be divided against the son 44.41
the F. ... hath given all things into his hand 45.15
no man can come to me, except the F. ... draw him 45.31
in my F.'s house are many mansions 45.56
he that hath seen me hath seen the F. 45.58
Abba, F. 47.25
the F. of lights 61.3
an advocate with the F. 64.3

Father of Lies 45.40

fatherless the judgment of the f. 5.4
visit the f. and widows 61.5

fathers thou shalt go to thy f. 1.44
I am a stranger with thee ... as all my f. were 17.90
instead of thy f. thou shalt have children 17.102
the glory of children are their f. 18.49
kings shall be thy nursing f. 21.76
the f. have eaten sour grapes 24.6
your f., where are they? 33.1
our f. that begat us 39.27
your f. did eat manna in the wilderness 45.32
f., provoke not your children 53.6

fatness the f. of the earth 1.54
thy clouds drop f. 17.140
let your soul delight itself in f. 21.84

fatted the f. calf 44.50

fault without f. before the throne of God 67.44

favour she obtained grace and f. 15.2
loving f. rather than silver and gold 18.69
great f. laid up for those that died godly 41.1
in f. with God and man 44.15

favoured children ... well f. 25.1
thou that art highly f. 44.1

fear doth Job f. God for nought? 16.1
f. came upon me, and trembling 16.12
the f. of the Lord ... endureth for ever 17.36
will we not f., though the earth be moved 17.103
f. came there upon them, and sorrow 17.108
afraid where no f. was 17.118
the f. of the Lord is the beginning of wisdom 17.229
the f. of the Lord is the beginning of knowledge 18.1
f. thou the Lord and the king 18.79
f. God, and keep his commandments 19.42
every man hath his sword ... because of f. in the night 20.10
f. not: for I am with thee 21.67
f. him which is able to destroy both body and soul 42.64
they cried out for f. 42.97
f. not, little flock 44.39
secretly for f. of the Jews 45.85
f. to whom fear 47.42
work out your own salvation with f. and trembling 52.5
f. God 62.7
perfect love casteth out f. 64.8
f. none of those things 67.7

feared the isles saw it, and f. 21.65
fearful a f. thing to fall into the hands of ... God 60.10
fears within were f. 49.14
feasting better ... the house of mourning, than ... the house of f. 19.18
feasts the uppermost rooms at f. 42.137
spots in your f. of charity 66.3
feathers thou shalt be safe under his f. 17.186
feeble confirm the f. knees 21.53
feed he shall f. me in a green pasture 17.45
f. me with food convenient for me 18.105
he shall f. his flock 21.60
f. my lambs 45.94
f. my sheep 45.95
feedest thou f. them with the bread of tears 17.167
feedeth he f. among the lilies 20.8
Feeding of the Five Thousand 45.26
feet diseased in his f. 11.13
f. was I to the lame 16.44
their f. are swift to shed blood 17.22
thou ... hast set my f. in a large room 17.69
f. ... and walk not 17.237
thou hast delivered ... my f. from falling 17.239
her f. abide not in her house 18.17
how beautiful are thy f. with shoes 20.21
with twain he covered his f. 21.17
how beautiful upon the mountains are the f. 21.80
the f. of him that bringeth good tidings 21.80
their f. run to evil 21.93
his f. ... part of clay 25.3
shake off the dust of your f. 42.60
to guide our f. into the way of peace 44.5
wash his f. with tears 44.24
laid down their clothes at a young man's f. 46.19
till he hath put all enemies under his f. 48.41
f. shod with ... the gospel of peace 51.14
fell his countenance f. 1.20
the wall f. down flat 6.4
at her feet he bowed, he f. 7.6
f. by the way side 42.85
f. among thieves 44.31
crumbs which f. from the rich man's table 44.55
by faith the walls of Jericho f. down 60.14
fellow a pestilent f. 46.55
fellows certain lewd f. of the baser sort 46.36
fellowship the right hands of f. 50.2
felt darkness which may be f. 2.17
female male and f. created he them 1.7
male and f. of all flesh 1.29
neither male nor f. 50.5
fervent f. in spirit 47.37
the effectual f. prayer of a righteous man 61.16
few f. and evil have the days ... of my life been 1.75
they are but f. and evil 36.5
but f. are chosen 42.133
fiat f. lux 1.2
field woe unto them that ... lay f. to field 21.14
consider the lilies of the f. 42.31
the f. is the world 42.92
two be in the f.; the one shall be taken 42.151
shepherds abiding in the f. 44.9
fields the f. ... white already to harvest 45.19
fiery a burning f. furnace 25.4
the f. darts of the wicked 51.14
fig every man under his vine and under his f. tree 30.1
under the f. tree, I saw thee 45.5
as a f. tree casteth her untimely figs 67.26
fig leaves they sewed f. together 1.14
fight quit yourselves like men, and f. 9.7
he teacheth mine hands to f. 17.33
who teacheth ... my fingers to f. 17.288
lest haply ye ... f. against God 46.15
so f. I, not as one that beateth the air 48.27
f. the good fight 56.12
fightings without were f. 49.14
figs do men gather ... f. of thistles? 42.41
fill till he f. thy mouth with laughing 16.22
let us take our f. of love 18.18
filled it f. all the house where they were sitting 46.6
f. with all the fulness of God 51.5
filleth whereof the mower f. not his hand 17.270
filth made as the f. of the world 48.10
filthiness f. and superfluity of naughtiness 61.4
filthy all our righteousnesses are as f. rags 21.100
f. lucre 56.4
f. dreamers 66.2
he which is f., let him be filthy still 67.70
find your sin will f. you out 4.17
canst thou by searching f. out God? 16.26
thou shalt f. it after many days 19.36
few there be that f. it 42.39
he that loseth his life for my sake shall f. it 42.68
men seek death, and shall not f. it 67.34
findeth he that seeketh f. 42.36
he that f. his life shall lose it 42.68
finger this is the f. of God 2.15
my little f. shall be thicker than my father's loins 11.12
fingers thy heavens, even the works of thy f. 17.14
who teacheth ... my f. to fight 17.288
f. of a man's hand, and wrote 25.9
finish f. my course with joy 46.49
finished God hath numbered thy kingdom, and f. it 25.10
it is f. 45.82
I have f. my course 57.7
finisher Jesus the author and f. of our faith 60.16
fire the bush burned with f. 2.5
a pillar of f. 2.22
the Lord descended upon it in f. 2.28

the Lord was not in the f. 11.23
a chariot ... and horses of f. 12.1
f. and brimstone, storm and tempest 17.19
his ministers a flaming f. 17.211
f. and hail, snow and vapours 17.297
can a man take f. in his bosom ... and ... not be burned? 18.16
coals of f. upon his head 18.82
where no wood is, there the f. goeth out 18.89
the f. that saith not, it is enough 18.106
aha, I am warm, I have seen the f. 21.68
four men ... walking in the midst of the f. 25.7
a brand plucked out of the f. 33.3
like a refiner's f. 34.2
the thought of the wood was in vain, for the f. ... consumed it 36.4
baptize ... with the Holy Ghost, and with f. 42.7
in danger of hell f. 42.19
tree ... hewn down, and cast into the f. 42.41
the f. is not quenched 43.17
cloven tongues like as of f. 46.6
the f. shall try every man's work 48.7
his ministers a flame of f. 60.2
how great a matter a little f. kindleth 61.7
tormented with f. and brimstone 67.46
sea of glass mingled with f. 67.50

firebrand a f. plucked out of the burning 28.3

first the f. day 1.1
seek ye f. the kingdom of God 42.32
the last state ... is worse than the f. 42.83
Elias truly shall f. come 42.108
many that are f. shall be last 42.123
the f. and great commandment 42.136
the last error shall be worse than the f. 42.176
a falling away f. 55.1
the f. and the last 67.2
thou hast left thy f. love 67.5

firstborn I ... will smite all the f. 2.19

firstfruits first of the f. 2.33
the f. of them that slept 48.40

fish a great f. to swallow up Jonah 29.2

fishers f. of men 42.13

fishes f. ... taken in an evil net 19.29
a great multitude of f. 44.19
five barley loaves, and two small f. 45.26

fishing I go a f. 45.93

fixed a great gulf f. 44.56

flagons stay me with f. 20.4

flame his ministers a f. of fire 60.2
eyes were as a f. of fire 67.2

flatter they f. with their tongue 17.11
they do but f. with their lips 17.20

flattery persons in admiration because of advantage 66.4

flax the smoking f. shall he not quench 21.66

fled he left his garment ... and f. 1.68

flee should such a man as I f.? 14.2
then would I f. away, and be at rest 17.119
at thy rebuke they f. 17.212
the wicked f. when no man pursueth 18.98
one thousand shall f. at the rebuke of one 21.47
f. from the wrath to come 42.6
resist the devil, and he will f. 61.12

fleeth my soul f. ... before the morning watch 17.273

flesh f. of my flesh 1.12
they shall be one f. 1.12
he also is f. 1.27
f. ... like unto the flesh of a little child 12.6
in my f. shall I see God 16.38
thinkest thou that I will eat bulls' f. 17.112
unto thee shall all f. come 17.139
be not among ... riotous eaters of f. 18.74
much study is a weariness of the f. 19.41
all f. shall see it together 21.59
all f. is grass 21.59
I will pour out my spirit upon all f. 27.5
no more twain, but one f. 42.119
the f. is weak 42.167
born, not of blood, nor of the will of the f. 45.1
the word was made f. 45.1
that which is born of the f. is flesh 45.9
my f., which I will give for the life of the world 45.32
the f. profiteth nothing 45.33
they that are after the f. 47.24
the f., to fulfil the lusts thereof 47.43
trouble in the f. 48.20
we do not war after the f. 49.16
a thorn in the f. 49.20
use not liberty for an occasion to the f. 50.9
the f. lusteth against the Spirit 50.10
he that soweth to his f. shall ... reap corruption 50.13
to abide in the f. is more needful for you 52.3
all f. is as grass 62.4
the lust of the f. 64.4

fleshly f. lusts, which war against the soul 62.6

flesh pots when we sat by the f. 2.26

fleshy f. tables of the heart 49.3

flies dead f. cause the ointment ... to send forth a stinking savour 19.31

flint-stone the f. into a springing well 17.234

flittings thou tellest my f. 17.123

flock he shall feed his f. 21.60
keeping watch over their f. by night 44.9
fear not, little f. 44.39

flood the f. was forty days upon the earth 1.29
knew not until the f. came 42.150

floods the f. have lift up their voice 17.193
let the f. clap their hands 17.200
who turneth the f. into a wilderness 17.223
neither can the f. drown ... love 20.26

flourishing the ungodly ... f. like a green bay-tree 17.86

flow all nations shall f. unto it 21.6

flower all ... shall die in the f. of their age 9.3
man ... flourisheth as a f. of the field 17.210

the goodliness thereof is as the f. of the field 21.59
the f. fadeth 21.59
the f. . . . falleth 62.4
fly with twain he did f. 21.17
flying f. upon the wings of the wind 17.31
foal a colt the f. of an ass 42.128
foes a man's f. shall be they of his own household 42.67
fold other sheep I have . . . not of this f. 45.49
one f., and one shepherd 45.49
folding a little f. of the hands to sleep 18.15
follow take up his cross, and f. me 42.106
following intreat me not . . . to return from f. after thee 8.2
folly answer a fool according to his f. 18.85
one that taketh a dog by the ears 18.88
food man did eat angels' f. 17.164
f. out of the earth 17.213
fool I have played the f. 9.23
the f. hath said in his heart 17.21
as a f. to the correction of the stocks 18.19
he that begetteth a f. doeth it to his sorrow 18.52
every f. will be meddling 18.59
honour is not seemly for a f. 18.84
a rod for the f.'s back 18.84
answer a f. according to his folly 18.85
as a dog returneth to his vomit, so a f. . . . to his folly 18.86
though thou shouldest bray a f. in a mortar . . . yet will not his foolishness depart 18.97
a f. uttereth all his mind 18.102
a man that is hasty in his words . . . more hope of a f. than of him 18.104
who knoweth whether he shall be a wise man or a f.? 19.8
the crackling of thorns under a pot, so is the laughter of the f. 19.19
at his end shall be a f. 22.14
whosoever shall say, thou f. 42.19
thou f., this night thy soul shall be required 44.38
I speak as a f. 49.18
foolish if a wise man contendeth with a f. . . . there is no rest 18.101
a f. man, which built his house upon the sand 42.44
the f. things of the world 48.3
O f. Galatians 50.3
foolishly nor charged God f. 16.2
foolishness though thou shouldest bray a fool in a mortar . . . yet will not his f. depart 18.97
the preaching of the cross is to them that perish f. 48.1
by the f. of preaching 48.2
Christ crucified . . . unto the Greeks f. 48.2
the wisdom of this world is f. with God 48.8
fools f., deal not so madly 17.157
professing themselves to be wise, they became f. 47.6
f. for Christ's sake 48.10
suffer f. gladly 49.17
walk circumspectly, not as f. 51.11
foot no rest for the sole of her f. 1.30
f. for foot 2.31
thou hurt not thy f. against a stone 17.187
he will not suffer thy f. to be moved 17.256
footstool until I make thine enemies thy f. 17.227
forbearing f. one another in love 51.6
forbid suffer the little children . . . and f. them not 43.18
forcible how f. are right words 16.16
forefront the f. of the hottest battle 10.5
foreheads his name shall be in their f. 67.69
foreknowledge suffered many things . . . in a dream 42.171
under the fig tree, I saw thee 45.5
forgers f. of lies 16.30
forget f. also thine own people, and thy father's house 17.100
if I f. thee, O Jerusalem 17.276
can a woman f. her sucking child? 21.75
they may f., yet will I not forget thee 21.75
forgetteth f. what manner of man he was 61.4
forgetting f. those things which are behind 52.8
forgive how oft shall . . . I f. him? 42.116
Father, f. them 44.73
faithful and just to f. us our sins 64.2
forgiven blessed is he whose unrighteousness is f. 17.71
blasphemy against the Holy Ghost shall not be f. 42.78
not be f. . . . neither in this world 42.78
her sins, which are many, are f. 44.25
forgotten for the poor shall not alway be f. 17.16
I am clean f., as a dead man 17.70
hath God f. to be gracious? 17.161
thou harlot that hast been f. 21.38
five sparrows . . . not one of them is f. 44.37
form no f. nor comeliness 21.81
the f. of a servant 52.4
the f. of sound words 57.2
formed God f. man of the dust of the ground 1.9
former there is no remembrance of f. things 19.3
the f. things are passed away 67.65
fornication the wine of the wrath of her f. 67.45
forsake he will not fail thee, nor f. thee 5.14
I will not fail thee, nor f. thee 6.1
when my father and my mother f. me 17.58
f. me not . . . in mine old age 17.152
f. not an old friend 39.9
forsaken yet saw I never the righteous f. 17.85
for a small moment have I f. thee 21.83
my God, why hast thou f. me? 42.174
forsook no man stood with me, but all men f. me 57.9

forty f. days and forty nights 42.9
f. stripes save one 49.18
fought they f. from heaven 7.5
after the manner of men I have f. with beasts 48.42
I have f. a good fight 57.7
f. against the dragon 67.38
found hast thou f. me, O mine enemy? 11.27
they f. no more of her than . . . the palms of her hands 12.14
where shall wisdom be f.? 16.42
in a time when thou mayest be f. 17.72
his place could no where be f. 17.86
seek ye the Lord while he may be f. 21.85
f. wanting 25.10
I have f. my sheep which was lost 44.47
he was lost, and is f. 44.50
foundation a sure f. 21.42
prepared for you from the f. of the world 42.158
from the f. of the world 67.41
the first f. was jasper 67.67
foundations where wast thou when I laid the f. of the earth? 16.54
the f. of the earth are out of course 17.172
her f. are upon the holy hills 17.180
fountain a f. sealed 20.12
a f. of gardens 20.13
fountains living f. of waters 67.28
four f. men . . . walking in the midst of the fire 25.7
fowl God created . . . every winged f. 1.5
fowler as a bird out of the snare of the f. 17.262
fowls worms and feathered f. 17.297
the f. of the air . . . sow not 42.31
foxes a portion for f. 17.138
the little f., that spoil the vines 20.7
the f. have holes 42.48
fragments gather up the f. that remain 45.27
frankincense the hill of f. 20.11
gold, and f., and myrrh 42.3
free then are the children f. 42.110
the truth shall make you f. 45.39
I was f. born 46.52
neither bond nor f. 50.5
Jerusalem which is above is f. 50.8
freedom thou . . . hast set my feet in a large room 17.69
God that . . . bringeth the prisoners out of captivity 17.142
how hath the oppressor ceased 21.29
with a great sum obtained I this f. 46.52
freely f. ye have received, freely give 42.59
take the water of life f. 67.71
frequent in prisons more f. 49.18
fret f. not thyself because of the ungodly 17.82
fretting a moth f. a garment 17.89
friend thy f., which is as thine own soul 5.8
mine own familiar f. 17.93
a f. that sticketh closer than a brother 18.56
faithful are the wounds of a f. 18.92
a man sharpeneth the countenance of his f. 18.94
trust ye not in a f. 30.5
a faithful f. is the medicine of life 39.7
forsake not an old f. 39.9
a new f. is as new wine 39.9
a f. of publicans and sinners 42.74
f., wherefore art thou come? 42.168
f., go up higher 44.43
the f. of the bridegroom . . . rejoiceth 45.14
friendly let the righteous . . . smite me f. 17.286
friends we . . . walked in the house of God as f. 17.120
he that repeateth a matter separateth very f. 18.50
a man that hath f. must shew himself friendly 18.56
wealth maketh many f. 18.57
I was wounded in the house of my f. 33.6
entering into holy souls, she maketh them f. of God 38.8
f. of the mammon of unrighteousness 44.54
that a man lay down his life for his f. 45.63
friendship Mizpah . . . the Lord watch 1.60
see that ye fall not out 1.74
love . . . passing the love of women 10.3
face answereth to face; so the heart of man to man 18.95
can two walk together? 28.1
–*See also* friend.
frost who is able to abide his f.? 17.296
fruit fruit tree yielding f. 1.3
she took of the f. thereof 1.14
his f. in due season 17.1
bring forth more f. in their age 17.191
the f. of the lips 21.90
they shall plant vineyards, and eat the f. 21.102
the entrances of the elder world . . . brought immortal f. 36.5
every tree which bringeth not forth good f. 42.7
every good tree bringeth forth good f. 42.41
brought forth f., some an hundredfold 42.85
if it die, it bringeth forth much f. 45.52
the f. of the Spirit is love, joy, peace 50.11
fruitful be f. and multiply 1.7
a f. land maketh he barren 17.223
fruits let my beloved . . . eat his pleasant f. 20.14
by their f. ye shall know them 42.41
frustra nisi Dominus . . . f. 17.266
fugitive a f. and a vagabond 1.22
fulfil to f. all righteousness 42.8
fulfilled f. a long time 38.5
he that loveth . . . hath f. the law 47.42
fulfilling love is the f. of the law 47.43
full thou hast eaten and art f. 5.2
f. of matter 16.49
my cup shall be f. 17.45

all the rivers run into the sea; yet the sea is not f. 19.2
both the hands f. with travail and vexation 19.11
the earth shall be f. of the knowledge of the Lord 21.26
the earth shall be f. . . . as the waters cover the sea 21.26
the press is f. 27.7
woe unto you that are f. 44.21
f. of new wine 46.7
f. of good works 46.28
that your joy may be f. 64.1
f. of eyes before and behind 67.16
fullers f.' soap 34.2
fulness in thy presence is the f. of joy 17.27
the earth is the Lord's, and the f. 48.30
filled with all the f. of God 51.5
furiously Jehu . . . driveth f. 12.11
furnace the f. of affliction 21.72
a burning fiery f. 25.4
heat the f. one seven times more 25.6
the f. of adversity 39.2
furnished throughly f. unto all good works 57.5
furrows the plowers . . . made long f. 17.269

G

Gadarene Swine 43.8
gain what shall it profit a man, if he . . . g. 43.15
to die is g. 52.2
g. . . . I counted loss for Christ 52.7
Galatians O foolish G. 50.3
Galilee men of G., why stand ye gazing up into heaven? 46.3
gall the wormwood and the g. 23.3
Gallio G. cared for none of those things 46.40
garden God planted a g. 1.9
the g. of Eden 1.10
a g. of herbs 11.26
a g. inclosed is my sister, my spouse 20.12
blow upon my g., that the spices thereof may flow 20.14
let my beloved come into his g. 20.14
as a lodge in a g. of cucumbers 21.2
her desert like the g. of the Lord 21.79
gardener supposing him to be the g. 45.89
gardens a fountain of g. 20.13
my beloved is gone down . . . to feed in the g. 20.18
garment a moth fretting a g. 17.89
wax old as doth a g. 17.206
thou deckest thyself with light as it were with a g. 17.211
only touch the hem of his g. 42.99
garments a very great multitude spread their g. 42.129
garnished empty, swept, and g. 42.83
gate the g. of heaven 1.57
strait is the g. 42.39
gates lift up your heads, O ye g. 17.49
thou leadest to the g. of hell 38.13
the g. of hell shall not prevail 42.105
the twelve g. were twelve pearls 67.67
Gath tell it not in G. 10.1
gather the Lord doth . . . g. together the outcasts of Israel 17.294
he shall g. the lambs with his arm 21.60
with great mercies will I g. thee 21.83
lest while ye g. up the tares 42.90
g. together his elect 42.148
g. up the fragments that remain 45.27
gathered the kings of the earth are g., and gone by 17.108
there shall the vultures also be g. 21.51
where two or three are g. together 42.115
wheresoever the carcase is, there will the eagles be g. 42.147
gathereth he that g. not . . . scattereth abroad 42.77
gathering g. where thou hast not strawed 42.155
gave the Lord g., and the Lord hath taken away 16.2
the spirit shall return unto God who g. it 19.40
God . . . g. his only begotten Son 45.12
I have planted . . . but God g. the increase 48.6
gazing men of Galilee, why stand ye g. up into heaven? 46.3
Gehazi whence comest thou, G.? 12.7
genealogies fables and endless g. 56.1
generation one g. passeth away . . . but the earth abideth for ever 19.1
O g. of vipers 42.6
an evil and adulterous g. 42.81
the children of this world . . . in their g. 44.54
generations honoured in their g. 39.28
all g. shall call me blessed 44.2
generosity God loveth a cheerful giver 49.15
Gentiles G. shall come to thy light 21.94
a light to lighten the G. 44.12
get a time to g., and a time to lose 19.9
getting with all thy g. get understanding 18.10
ghost oh that I had given up the g. 16.24
yielded up the g. 42.175
–*See also* Holy Ghost.
giant the sun . . . rejoiceth as a g. 17.35
like a g. refreshed with wine 17.166
arrows in the hand of the g. . . . are the young children 17.265
giants there were g. in the earth 1.27
the g., the sons of Anak 4.7
Gideon the sword of the Lord, and of G. 7.9
gift children . . . are an heritage and g. . . . of the Lord 17.265
thought that the g. of God may be purchased 46.22

impart unto you some spiritual g. 47.3
the g. of God is eternal life 47.21
every good g. and every perfect gift 61.3
gifts their right hand is full of g. 17.54
ye . . . being evil . . . give good g. 42.38
diversities of g., but the same Spirit 48.34
Gilead G. is mine 17.225
is there no balm in G.? 22.7
triacle (treacle) in G. 22.8
gird g. up now thy loins like a man 16.54
g. up the loins of your mind 62.3
girded let your loins be g. about 44.40
girdeth let not him that g. on his harness boast . . . as he that putteth it off 11.25
give g. all the substance of his house for love 20.26
g. us this day our daily bread 42.27
freely ye have received, freely g. 42.59
g. to the poor 42.121
not mine to g. 42.127
g., and it shall be given unto you 44.22
my peace I g. unto you 45.61
not as the world giveth, g. I unto you 45.61
such as I have g. I thee 46.10
more blessed to g. than to receive 46.50
given oh that I had g. up the ghost 16.24
ask, and it shall be g. 42.36
unto every one that hath shall be g. 42.156
the Father . . . hath g. all things into his hand 45.15
g. to hospitality 47.37
giver God loveth a cheerful g. 49.15
giveth God, that g. to all men liberally 61.1
glad the multitude of the isles may be g. 17.198
wine that maketh g. the heart of man 17.213
g., because they are at rest 17.222
I was g. when they said unto me 17.258
a wise son maketh a g. father 18.23
Jonah was exceeding g. of the gourd 29.4
gladly suffer fools g. 49.17
gladness thou hast put g. in my heart 17.9
serve the Lord with g. 17.202
glass through a g., darkly 48.35
beholding his natural façe in a g. 61.4
sea of g. like unto crystal 67.16
sea of g. mingled with fire 67.50
pure gold, like unto clear g. 67.67
glorious the king's daughter is all g. within 17.101
the Lord . . . hath put on g. apparel 17.192
the g. liberty of the children of God 47.26
much more that which remaineth is g. 49.5
glory while my g. passeth by 2.44
I-chabod . . . the g. is departed 9.10
array thyself with g. and beauty 16.59
the heavens declare the g. of God 17.35
who is the King of g.? 17.49
let the saints be joyful with g. 17.298
the hoary head is a crown of g. 18.46
the g. of children are their fathers 18.49
the g. of God to conceal a thing 18.80
the whole earth is full of his g. 21.17
the g. of the Lord shall be revealed 21.59
the g. of the Lord shall be thy rereward 21.91
the g. of the Lord is risen upon thee 21.94
all the kingdoms of the world, and the g. of them 42.10
even Solomon in all his g. was not arrayed 42.31
the Son of man coming . . . with power and great g. 42.148
the g. of the Lord shone round about them 44.9
g. to God in the highest 44.10
not . . . returned to give g. to God 44.58
because he gave not God the g. 46.33
all have sinned, and come short of the g. of God 47.13
we g. in tribulations 47.17
do all to the g. of God 48.32
if a woman have long hair, it is a g. 48.33
one star differeth from another . . . in g. 48.43
exceeding and eternal weight of g. 49.7
worthy . . . to receive g. and honour and power 67.17
the g. of God did lighten it 67.67
glorying your g. is not good 48.13
glutton the drunkard and the g. shall come to poverty 18.74
gluttonous a man g. 42.74
gnashed g. on him with their teeth 46.18
gnashing g. of teeth 42.47
gnat strain at a g., and swallow a camel 42.140
go I will not let thee g., except thou bless me 1.61
neither will I let Israel g. 2.10
before I g. whence I shall not return 16.25
before I g. hence, and be no more seen 17.90
thou shalt g. upon the lion and adder 17.187
whosoever shall compel thee to g. a mile 42.23
g., and he goeth 42.46
g., and do thou likewise 44.33
g. out into the highways and hedges 44.45
if I g. not . . . the Comforter will not come 45.68
the Spirit bade me g. . . . nothing doubting 46.32
I g. bound in the spirit 46.48
goats as a shepherd divideth his sheep from the g. 42.157
god cry aloud: for he is a g. 11.18
the multitude . . . took him now for a g. 38.12
the voice of a g. . . . not of a man 46.33
to the unknown g. 46.38
God thy G. my God 8.2
neither doth G. respect any person 10.8
the wisdom of G. . . . to do judgment 11.5
doth Job fear G. for nought? 16.1
nor charged G. foolishly 16.2
canst thou by searching find out G.? 16.26
G., even our own God 17.141
hath G. forgotten to be gracious? 17.161
G. from everlasting 17.181
a G. at hand . . . not a God afar off 22.16

the word was G. 45.1
it is G. that justifieth 47.30
fear G. 62.7
godliness g. is profitable 56.6
godly great favour laid up for those that died g. 41.1
gods ye shall be as g. 1.14
no other g. before me 2.29
these be thy g., O Israel 2.37
a great king above all g. 17.195
g. are come down ... in the likeness of men 46.34
a setter forth of strange g. 46.37
goeth not that which g. into the mouth defileth 42.101
Gog G. and Magog 67.63
going from g. to and fro ... walking up and down 16.1
he shall direct his g. 17.178
thy g. out, and thy coming in 17.257
their g. ... utter destruction 38.3
all men have one entrance into life, and the like g. out 38.7
goings he ... ordered my g. 17.91
gold more to be desired ... than g. 17.36
as a jewel of g. in a swine's snout 18.29
loving favour rather than silver and g. 18.69
g., and frankincense, and myrrh 42.3
silver and g. have I none 46.10
the city was pure g. 67.67
golden or ever ... the g. bowl be broken 19.40
Gomorrah Sodom and ... G. 1.48
gone they are all g. out of the way 17.21
lo, he was g. 17.86
thou art g. up on high 17.143
it is g.; and the place thereof shall know it no more 17.210
virtue had g. out of him 43.12
good God saw that it was g. 1.3, 1.5
it is not g. that man should be alone 1.11
as gods, knowing g. and evil 1.14
rest was g. 1.78
a g. land and a large 2.7
shall he not make it g.? 4.15
not one thing hath failed of all the g. things 6.7
who will shew us any g.? 17.9
there is none that doeth g. 17.21
what man is he ... would fain see g. days? 17.78
eschew evil, and do g. 17.79
a g. man is merciful, and lendeth 17.230
how g. and joyful ... brethren, to dwell together in unity 17.275
a word spoken in due season, how g. is it 18.44
g. news from a far country 18.83
she will do him g. ... all the days of her life 18.109
her merchandise is g. 18.110
wisdom is g. with an inheritance 19.21
refuse the evil, and choose the g. 21.19
we looked for peace, but no g. came 22.5
do with me as seemeth g. ... unto you 22.17
g. for a man that he bear the yoke in his youth 23.5
an holy and g. thought 41.1
that they may see your g. works 42.16
he maketh his sun to rise on the evil and on the g. 42.24
ye ... being evil ... give g. gifts 42.38
a g. tree cannot bring forth evil fruit 42.41
neither can a corrupt tree bring forth g. fruit 42.41
how can ye, being evil, speak g.? 42.79
it is g. for us to be here 42.107
it is not g. to marry 42.120
thou g. and faithful servant 42.154
it had been g. for that man if he had not been born 42.162
g. tidings of great joy 44.9
on earth peace, g. will toward men 44.10
g. measure, pressed down 44.22
Mary hath chosen that g. part 44.34
a g. man, and a just 44.76
any g. thing come out of Nazareth 45.5
every man at the beginning doth set forth g. wine 45.7
g. shepherd giveth his life for the sheep 45.48
full of g. works 46.28
let us do evil, that g. may come 47.12
the g. that I would I do not 47.22
all things work together for g. 47.28
cleave to that which is g. 47.37
overcome evil with g. 47.38
rulers are not a terror to g. works 47.40
your glorying is not g. 48.13
g. for the present distress 48.20
evil communications corrupt g. manners 48.42
the thing which is g. 51.8
whatsoever things are of g. report 52.12
hold fast that which is g. 54.5
he desireth a g. work 56.4
every creature of God is g. 56.5
rich in g. works 56.14
throughly furnished unto all g. works 57.5
I have fought a g. fight 57.7
every g. gift and every perfect gift 61.3
see g. days 62.13
this world's g. 64.5
goodliness the g. thereof is as the flower of the field 21.59
goodman the g. is not at home 18.18
goodness the blessings of g. 17.40
surely g. and mercy shall follow me 17.47
the earth is full of the g. of the Lord 17.75
thou crownest the year with thy g. 17.140
long-suffering, and of great g. 17.291
goods his g. are in peace 44.35
soul, thou hast much g. laid up 44.38
bestow all my g. to feed the poor 48.35
Good Samaritan 44.32
gospel preaching the g. of the kingdom 42.14
preach the g. to every creature 43.23
separated unto the g. of God 47.1
the preparation of the g. of peace 51.14

gourd Jonah was exceeding glad of the g. 29.4
it smote the g. that it withered 29.4
government the g. shall be upon his shoulder 21.23
of the increase of his g. . . . there shall be no end 21.23
grace she obtained g. and favour 15.2
allured by the g. of the work 38.12
the word . . . full of g. and truth 45.1
through the g. of . . . Christ we shall be saved 46.35
g. did much more abound 47.18
by the g. of God I am what I am 48.39
g. of our Lord Jesus Christ be with you 48.46
my g. is sufficient for thee 49.21
speech be alway with g. 53.8
gracious hath God forgotten to be g.? 17.161
O give thanks unto the Lord, for he is g. 17.217
grain a g. of mustard seed 42.91
grapes any liquor of g. 4.1
it brought forth wild g. 21.13
the fathers have eaten sour g. 24.6
do men gather g. of thorns? 42.41
grass let the earth bring forth g. 1.3
the days of man are but as g. 17.210
the g. growing upon the house-tops 17.270
all flesh is g. 21.59
the g. withereth 21.59
the people is g. 21.59
Nebuchadnezzar . . . did eat g. as oxen 25.8
much g. in the place 45.26
all flesh is as g. 62.4
they should not hurt the g. 67.33
grasshopper the g. shall be a burden 19.40
grasshoppers we were . . . as g. . . . in their sight 4.7
the inhabitants thereof are as g. 21.62
grave my gray hairs with sorrow to the g. 1.71
no work, nor device, nor knowledge . . . in the g. 19.28
thy pomp is brought down to the g. 21.30
the g. cannot praise thee 21.58
O g., where is thy victory? 48.45
graven any g. image 2.29
gray bring down my g. hairs with sorrow to the grave 1.71
in mine old age, when I am g.-headed 17.152
great the journey is too g. for thee 11.22
g. men are not always wise 16.48
divide him a portion with the g. 21.82
seekest thou g. things for thyself? 22.19
the day of the Lord is g. and very terrible 27.3
g. is truth, and mighty above all things 35.6
be not ignorant of any thing in a g. matter 39.6
for he had g. possessions 42.121
good tidings of g. joy 44.9
a g. gulf fixed 44.56
g. is Diana of the Ephesians 46.43
compassed about with so g. a cloud of witnesses 60.16
how g. a matter a little fire kindleth 61.7
a g. voice, as of a trumpet 67.2
so g. riches is come to nought 67.56
greater a g. than Solomon is here 42.82
g. love hath no man 45.63
greatest he that is g. . . . shall be your servant 42.138
the g. of these is charity 48.35
greed the horseleach hath two daughters . . . give, give 18.106
greedy be not g. to add money to money 37.1
not g. of filthy lucre 56.4
Greek neither Jew nor G. 50.5
Greeks debtor both to the G., and to the Barbarians 47.4
G. seek after wisdom 48.2
green in the morning it is g. 17.182
if they do these things in a g. tree 44.71
they should not hurt . . . any g. thing 67.33
greetings g. in the markets 42.137
grief I will go down into the grave . . . mourning 1.66
my gray hairs with sorrow to the grave 1.71
would God I had died for thee, O Absalom, my son 10.11
it was pain and g. to me 17.88
by the waters of Babylon 17.276
in much wisdom is much g. 19.5
acquainted with g. 21.81
I perish through great g. in a strange land 40.1
lamentation, and weeping 42.4
griefs he hath borne our g. 21.81
grieve g. not the holy Spirit of God 51.9
grin g. like a dog, and run about 17.130
grind g. the faces of the poor 21.11
grinders the g. cease because they are few 19.40
grinding the sound of the g. is low 19.40
groaned he g. in the spirit 45.51
groaneth the whole creation g. . . . in pain 47.26
groaning weary of my g. 17.12
my g. is not hid from thee 17.87
groanings g. which cannot be uttered 47.27
grope they g. in the dark 16.29
gross g. darkness 21.94
this people's heart is waxed g. 42.86
ground blood crieth unto me from the g. 1.21
the place . . . is holy g. 2.6
we . . . are as water spilt on the g. 10.8
the lot is fallen unto me in a fair g. 17.25
water-springs of a dry g. 17.223
the parched g. shall become a pool 21.54
as a root out of a dry g. 21.81
fell into good g. 42.85
why cumbereth it the g.? 44.42
except . . . wheat fall into the g. and die 45.52
grounded rooted and g. in love 51.5
grow he shall g. up . . . as a tender plant 21.81

consider the lilies of the field, how they g. 42.31
let both g. together until the harvest 42.90
grudge they will . . . g. if they be not satisfied 17.131
g. not one against another 61.14
grudging use hospitality . . . without g. 62.15
guide having no g., overseer, or ruler 18.14
put ye not confidence in a g. 30.5
to g. our feet into the way of peace 44.5
how can I, except some man should g. me? 46.23
guides blind g. 42.140
guile in whose spirit there is no g. 17.71
an Israelite . . . in whom is no g. 45.5
neither was g. found in his mouth 62.9
guiltless they that . . . would destroy me g., are mighty 17.146
gulf a great g. fixed 44.56

H

ha he saith among the trumpets, h., ha 16.58
habitation an h. of dragons 21.51
habitations everlasting h. 44.54
hail h. shall sweep away the refuge of lies 21.42
h., thou that art highly favoured 44.1
hair there shall not one h. of his head fall 9.14
the h. of my flesh stood up 16.12
thy h. is as a flock of goats 20.11
thou canst not make one h. white or black 42.22
if a woman have long h. 48.33
hairs the very h. of your head are all numbered 42.65
wipe them with the h. of her head 44.24
hairy a h. man 1.53
half the h. was not told me 11.9
hallowed h. be thy name 42.27
halt how long h. ye between two opinions? 11.17
the h., and the blind 44.44
hammer her right hand to the workmen's h. 7.6
hand his h. will be against every man 1.45
h. for hand 2.31
I . . . will cover thee with my h. 2.44
kill me . . . out of h. 4.4
her right h. to the workmen's hammer 7.6
a little cloud . . . like a man's h. 11.20
every one . . . with the other h. held a weapon 14.1
their right h. is full of gifts 17.54
the sheep of his h. 17.197
with his own right h. . . . hath he gotten himself the victory 17.199
my soul is alway in my h. 17.250
let my right h. forget her cunning 17.276
even there also shall thy h. lead me 17.279
whatsoever thy h. findeth to do 19.28
in the evening withhold not thine h. 19.39
his left h. is under my head 20.4
a God at h. . . . not a God afar off 22.16
behold, I am in your h. 22.17
fingers of a man's h., and wrote 25.9
the day of the Lord . . . is nigh at h. 27.2
the souls of the righteous are in the h. of God 38.3
repent: for the kingdom of heaven is at h. 42.12
let not thy left h. know what thy right hand doeth 42.26
he that dippeth his h. with me in the dish 42.162
having put his h. to the plough 44.27
the Father . . . hath given all things into his h. 45.15
day is at h. 47.43
how large a letter . . . with mine own h. 50.14
the time of my departure is at h. 57.7
the end of all things is at h. 62.14
humble yourselves . . . under the mighty h. of God 62.16
in his right h. seven stars 67.2
handful an h. of meal in a barrel 11.15
better is an h. with quietness 19.11
handle such as h. the harp and organ 1.24
touch not; taste not; h. not 53.2
handmaiden the low estate of his h. 44.2
hands every one with one of his h. wrought in the work 14.1
into thy h. I commend my spirit 17.68
they shall bear thee in their h. 17.187
his h. prepared the dry land 17.195
their idols are . . . the work of men's h. 17.237
h., and handle not 17.237
who teacheth my h. to war 17.288
a two-edged sword in their h. 17.298
a little folding of the h. to sleep 18.15
both the h. full with travail and vexation 19.11
strengthen . . . the weak h., and confirm the feeble knees 21.53
we will fall into the h. of the Lord 39.3
Pilate . . . washed his h. 42.172
lay thy h. on her, that she may be healed 43.10
into thy h. I commend my spirit 44.75
temples made with h. 46.38
labour, working with our own h. 48.10
an house not made with h. 49.8
the right h. of fellowship 50.2
working with his h. 51.8
a fearful thing to fall into the h. of . . . God 60.10
palms in their h. 67.27
handy-work prosper thou our h. 17.184
hanged our harps, we h. . . . up 17.276
happy h. is the man that hath his quiver full of them 17.265
we count them h. which endure 61.15

hard is any thing too h. for the Lord? 1.46
I knew thee that thou art an h. man 42.155
h. for thee to kick against the pricks 46.25
harden I will h. Pharaoh's heart 2.13
hardened Pharaoh's heart was h. 2.15
h. through the deceitfulness of sin 60.4
harlot how is the faithful city become an h. 21.5
thou h. that hast been forgotten 21.38
harlots the mother of h. 67.54
harmless h. as doves 42.61
harness let not him that girdeth on his h. boast ... as he that putteth it off 11.25
harnessed the children of Ephraim ... being h. 17.163
harp such as handle the h. and organ 1.24
praise the Lord with h. 17.74
awake, lute and h. 17.128
harpers the voice of h. harping 67.43
harps our h., we hanged ... up 17.276
having every one of them h. 67.20
hart like as the h. desireth the water-brooks 17.94
a young h. upon the mountains of spices 20.27
harvest seedtime and h. 1.32
gathereth her food in the h. 18.14
according to the joy in h. 21.22
the h. is past ... and we are not saved 22.6
put ye in the sickle, for the h. is ripe 27.7
the h. truly is plenteous 42.57
let both grow together until the h. 42.90
the h. is the end of the world 42.92
the fields ... white already to h. 45.19
the h. of the earth is ripe 67.48
haste he that maketh h. to be rich shall not be innocent 18.100
make h., my beloved 20.27
they make h. to shed innocent blood 21.93
hasty a man that is h. in his words ... more hope of a fool than of him 18.104
hate they that h. me without a cause are more than the hairs of my head 17.146
a time to love, and a time to h. 19.9
hated I h. all my labour 19.8
h. of all men for my name's sake 42.62
hateth love God, and h. his brother 64.9
hatred h. stirreth up strifes 18.25
a stalled ox and h. therewith 18.42
haven the h. where they would be 17.222
head it shall bruise thy h. 1.17
there shall not one hair of his h. fall 9.14
go up, thou bald h. 12.3
thou hast covered my h. in the day of battle 17.284
the hoary h. is a crown of glory 18.46
heap coals of fire upon his h. 18.82
his left hand is under my h. 20.4
waters flowed over mine h. 23.6
neither shalt thou swear by thy h. 42.22
the Son of man hath not where to lay his h. 42.48
the very hairs of your h. are all numbered 42.65
John Baptist's h. in a charger 42.96
head-stone the h. in the corner 17.242
heal a time to kill, and a time to h. 19.9
physician, h. thyself 44.18
healed lest they see with their eyes ... and be h. 21.18
with his stripes we are h. 21.81
healeth he h. those that are broken in heart 17.294
healing shall ... arise with h. in his wings 34.3
of the most High cometh h. 39.24
h. all manner of sickness 42.14
the leaves ... were for the h. of the nations 67.68
health the voice of joy and h. is in the dwellings of the righteous 17.240
O Lord God, thou strength of my h. 17.284
thine h. shall spring forth speedily 21.91
we looked ... for a time of h., and behold trouble 22.5
heap h. coals of fire 18.82
heaps h. upon heaps 7.15
hear the Lord h. thee in the day of trouble 17.38
he that planted the ear, shall he not h.? 17.194
to-day if ye will h. his voice 17.197
ears, and h. not 17.237
out of the deep have I called ... Lord, h. my voice 17.271
lest they ... h. with their ears 21.18
ears to h., and hear not 24.3
h. with thine ears 24.13
what ye h. in the ear ... preach ye upon the housetops 42.64
ears to h., let him hear 42.72
by hearing ye shall h. 42.86
desired ... to hear those things which ye h. 44.30
if they h. not Moses and the prophets 44.57
they that h. shall live 45.23
to tell, or to h. some new thing 46.38
swift to h. 61.4
heard I have h. of thee ... but now mine eye seeth 16.63
we have not so much as h. whether there be any Holy Ghost 46.41
nor ear h. 48.5
hearers be ye doers of the word, and not h. only 61.4
heareth whosoever h. these sayings ... and doeth them 42.44
hearing nor the ear filled with h. 19.2
ears ... dull of h. 42.86
both h. them, and asking them questions 44.13
faith cometh by h. 47.35
heart I will harden Pharaoh's h. 2.13
Pharaoh's h. was hardened 2.15
take heed ... that your h. be not deceived 5.5
lay up these my words in your h. 5.6
there were great searchings of h. 7.4
a man after his own h. 9.13
the Lord looketh on the h. 9.17

give . . . an understanding h. 11.4
which hath put such a thing as this in the king's h. 13.2
his h. is as firm as a stone 16.61
his h. is . . . as hard as a . . . millstone 16.61
commune with your own h. 17.8
thou hast put gladness in my h. 17.9
them which are true of h. 17.18
they . . . dissemble in their double h. 17.20
the fool hath said in his h. 17.21
my h. . . . is even like melting wax 17.43
the sorrows of my h. are enlarged 17.52
try out my reins and my h. 17.53
my h. was hot within me 17.88
my h. is inditing of a good matter 17.99
a broken and contrite h. . . . shalt thou not despise 17.116
if riches increase, set not your h. upon them 17.135
thy rebuke hath broken my h. 17.148
I commune with mine own h. 17.160
wine that maketh glad the h. of man 17.213
those that are broken in h. 17.294
hope deferred maketh the h. sick 18.33
the h. knoweth his own bitterness 18.36
even in laughter the h. is sorrowful 18.37
a merry h. maketh a cheerful countenance 18.41
a merry h. doeth good like a medicine 18.53
counsel in the h. of man is like deep water 18.60
apply thine h. unto instruction 18.73
the h. of kings is unsearchable 18.80
face answereth to face; so the h. of man to man 18.95
I gave my h. to . . . search out . . . all things 19.4
I sleep, but my h. waketh 20.15
set me as a seal upon thine h. 20.26
the righteous perisheth, and no man layeth it to h. 21.89
a revolting and a rebellious h. 22.2
the h. is deceitful above all things 22.13
the h. is deceitful . . . who can know it? 22.13
give them one h. 24.2
take the stony h. out of their flesh 24.2
give them an h. of flesh 24.2
set thine h. upon all that I shall shew 24.13
a candle of understanding in thine h. 36.7
the pure in h. 42.15
where your treasure is, there will your h. be also 42.28
meek and lowly in h. 42.76
out of the abundance of the h. the mouth speaketh 42.79
this people's h. is waxed gross 42.86
catcheth away that which was sown in his h. 42.87
their h. is far from me 42.100
love the Lord thy God with all thy h. 42.136
Mary . . . pondered them in her h. 44.11
did not our h. burn within us? 44.80
let not your h. be troubled 45.61
cut to the h. 46.18
thy h. is not right in the sight of God 46.22
fleshy tables of the h. 49.3
a discerner of the thoughts . . . of the h. 60.5

heartily whatsoever ye do, do it h. 53.7

hearts so I gave them up unto their own h.' lusts 17.171
if ye will hear his voice, harden not your h. 17.197
who imagine mischief in their h. 17.282
the Lord pondereth the h. 18.66
scattered the proud in the imagination of their h. 44.3
settle it . . . in your h. 44.66
the love of God is shed abroad in our h. 47.17
until . . . the day star arise in your h. 63.1

heat they covered him with clothes, but he gat no h. 11.1
the sun . . . there is nothing hid from the h. thereof 17.35
h. the furnace one seven times more 25.6
borne the burden and h. of the day 42.125

heathen the h. so furiously rage together 17.2
the h. may know themselves to be but men 17.16
the h. make much ado 17.104

heaven God created the h. 1.1
whose top may reach unto h. 1.37
h. and earth, the sea, and all that in them is 2.29
h. . . . cannot contain thee 11.6
the Lord looked down from h. 17.21
look how high the h. is in comparison of the earth 17.209
if I climb up into h., thou art there 17.279
the h. for height 18.80
how art thou fallen from h., O Lucifer 21.30
neither did I . . . climb up into h. 36.3
repent: for the kingdom of h. is at hand 42.12
neither by h.; for it is God's throne 42.22
which art in h. 42.27
treasures in h. 42.28
a rich man shall hardly enter into . . . h. 42.122
h. and earth shall pass away 42.149
beheld Satan as lightning fall from h. 44.29
caught up to the third h. 49.19
a door was opened in h. 67.16
a throne was set in h. 67.16
the h. departed as a scroll 67.26
silence in h. 67.29
there was war in h. 67.38
neither was their place found any more in h. 67.38
from whose face the earth and the h. fled 67.64
a new h. and a new earth 67.65

heavenly how shall ye believe, if I tell you of h. things? 45.10

heavens he bowed the h. also 17.31
the h. declare the glory of God 17.35
him that rideth upon the h. 17.142
thou . . . spreadest out the h. like a curtain 17.211
that stretcheth out the h. as a curtain 21.62

as the h. are higher than the earth, so are my ways higher than your ways 21.86
oh that thou wouldest rend the h. 21.99
I create new h. and a new earth 21.103
heaviness the end of that mirth is h. 18.37
garment of praise for the spirit of h. 21.96
in h. through manifold temptations 62.1
heavy it is too h. for me 4.4
an old man, and h. 9.9
thy father made our yoke h. 11.12
all ye that labour and are h. laden 42.76
Hebrew an H. of the Hebrews 52.6
Hebrews are they H.? so am I 49.18
hedge whoso breaketh an h., a serpent shall bite 19.32
hedges go out into the highways and h. 44.45
heed I will take h. to my ways 17.88
let him that thinketh he standeth take h. 48.28
heel thou shalt bruise his h. 1.17
heifer plowed with my h. 7.13
height nor h., nor depth ... able to separate us 47.31
length, and depth, and h. 51.5
heir h. of all things 60.1
heirs and if children, then h. 47.25
hell thou shalt not leave my soul in h. 17.27
the pains of h. came about me 17.30
thou ... hast brought my soul out of h. 17.63
the pains of h. gat hold upon me 17.238
if I go down to h., thou art there 17.279
h. and destruction are never full 18.96
your agreement with h. shall not stand 21.42
thou leadest to the gates of h. 38.13
in danger of h. fire 42.19
the gates of h. shall not prevail 42.105
twofold more the child of h. 42.139
their worm dieth not 43.17
the keys of h. and of death 67.3
Death, and H. followed with him 67.24
the bottomless pit 67.32
helmet the h. of salvation 51.14
help a very present h. in trouble 17.103
God shall h. her, and that right early 17.104
vain is the h. of man 17.133
the hills, from whence cometh my h. 17.255
there is no h. in them 17.292
h. thou mine unbelief 43.16
helped they h. every one his neighbour 21.65
helpers h. of your joy 49.2
helpeth the Spirit also h. our infirmities 47.27
help meet I will make him an h. 1.11
hem only touch the h. of his garment 42.99
hen even as a h. gathereth her chickens 42.142
herb the h. yielding seed 1.3
withered even as the green h. 17.82
green h. for the service of men 17.213
herbs a garden of h. 11.26
a dinner of h. where love is 18.42
another, who is weak, eateth h. 47.44
here Samuel ... answered, h. am I 9.4
heritage I have a goodly h. 17.25
children ... are an h. and gift ... of the Lord 17.265
Herod in the days of H. the king 42.2
hewers h. of wood 6.5
hid I h. not my face from shame and spitting 21.78
in a little wrath I h. my face from thee 21.83
the noise of murmurings is not h. 38.2
a city ... set on an hill cannot be h. 42.16
h., that shall not be known 42.64
h. these things from the wise and prudent 42.75
your life is h. with Christ in God 53.3
hide h. me under the shadow of thy wings 17.28
h. not thy face from me 17.57
h. a multitude of sins 61.17
hidest a God that h. thyself 21.70
hideth who ... h. counsel without knowledge? 16.62
high thou art gone up on h. 17.143
the dayspring from on h. 44.5
endued with power from on h. 44.82
h. time to awake out of sleep 47.43
against spiritual wickedness in h. places 51.14
a great h. priest 60.6
higher the rock that is h. than I 17.134
as the heavens are h. than the earth, so are my ways higher than your ways 21.86
friend, go up h. 44.43
subject unto the h. powers 47.39
highest sit not down in the h. room 44.43
high-minded I am not h. 17.274
highway make straight in the desert a h. for our God 21.59
highways go out into the h. and hedges 44.45
hill thou ... hast made my h. so strong 17.64
the h. of Sion is ... the joy of the whole earth 17.108
as the h. of Basan, so is God's hill 17.143
the h. of frankincense 20.11
a city ... set on an h. cannot be hid 42.16
hills unto the utmost bound of the everlasting h. 1.80
the little h. shall rejoice on every side 17.140
why hop ye so, ye high h.? 17.143
her foundations are upon the holy h. 17.180
let the h. be joyful together 17.200
the waters stand in the h. 17.212
the high h. are a refuge for the wild goats 17.213
the little h. like young sheep 17.233
I will lift up mine eyes unto the h. 17.255
the h. stand about Jerusalem 17.263
to the h., cover us 44.71
hinds the voice of the Lord maketh the h. to bring forth 17.62
hip he smote them h. and thigh 7.14
hire the labourer is worthy of his h. 44.28
hireling he that is an h. 45.48
hoar-frost he ... scattereth the h. like ashes 17.296

hold h. fast that which is good 54.5
lay h. on eternal life 56.12
that which ye have already h. fast 67.9
laid h. on the dragon . . . and bound him 67.62
holes he . . . earneth wages to put it into a bag with h. 32.1
the foxes have h. 42.48
holier h. than thou 21.101
holiness this is none other but the house of God 1.57
put off thy shoes from off thy feet 2.6
h. becometh thine house for ever 17.193
your body is the temple 48.15
–*See also* holy.
hollow the h. of his thigh 1.61
holy h., holy, holy, is the Lord of hosts 21.17
they shall not hurt nor destroy in all my h. mountain 21.26
entering into h. souls, she maketh them friends of God 38.8
an h. and good thought 41.1
denied the H. One and the Just 46.11
a living sacrifice, h., acceptable 47.36
salute one another with an h. kiss 47.48
h., holy, holy, Lord God Almighty 67.16
O Lord, h. and true 67.25
blessed and h. is he that hath part in the first resurrection 67.63
he that is h., let him be holy still 67.70
Holy Ghost baptize . . . with the H., and with fire 42.7
blasphemy against the H. shall not be forgiven 42.78
filled with the H. 46.6
we have not so much as heard whether there be any H. 46.41
your body is the temple of the H. 48.15
home the city where they dwelt 17.219
the goodman is not at h. 18.18
man goeth to his long h. 19.40
homelessness hath not where to lay his head 42.48
no certain dwellingplace 48.10
homo ecce h. 45.79
honest seven men of h. report 46.16
provide things h. in the sight of all men 47.37
whatsoever things are h. 52.12
honestly walk h., as in the day 47.43
honey a land flowing with milk and h. 2.7
a land of oil olive, and h. 5.2
what is sweeter than h.? 7.13
sweeter also than h. 17.36
butter and h. shall he eat 21.19
locusts and wild h. 42.5
honeycomb eaten my h. with my honey 20.15
honour h. thy father and thy mother 2.29
what shall be done unto the man whom the king delighteth to h.? 15.4
man being in h. hath no understanding 17.111
in her left hand riches and h. 18.8
the h. of kings is to search out a matter 18.80
h. is not seemly for a fool 18.84
strength and h. are her clothing 18.111
the Lord will bring you to h. 35.9
h. a physician 39.24
let us not stain our h. 40.2
a prophet is not without h. 42.95
to make one vessel unto h. 47.33
in h. preferring one another 47.37
h. to whom honour 47.42
h. all men 62.7
h. the king 62.7
honourable whose traffickers are the h. of the earth 21.37
ye are h., but we are despised 48.10
honoured was but h. as a man 38.12
h. in their generations 39.28
honoureth this people . . . h. me with their lips 42.100
hook canst thou draw out leviathan with an h.? 16.60
hop why h. ye so, ye high hills? 17.143
hope my days are . . . spent without h. 16.19
the h. of all the ends of the earth 17.140
let me not be disappointed of my h. 17.251
h. deferred maketh the heart sick 18.33
to him that is joined to all the living there is h. 19.26
they that go down into the pit cannot h. for thy truth 21.58
my strength and my h. is perished from the Lord 23.3
ye prisoners of h. 33.5
their h. full of immortality 38.3
who against h. believed in hope 47.16
h. maketh not ashamed 47.17
rejoicing in h. 47.37
now abideth faith, h., charity 48.35
the h. of his calling 51.1
patience of h. 54.1
hoped faith is the substance of things h. for 60.11
hopeth h. all things, endureth all things 48.35
horn set not up your h. on high 17.157
horror an h. of great darkness 1.43
horse the h. and his rider hath he thrown into the sea 2.24
hast thou given the h. strength? 16.57
be ye not like to h. and mule 17.73
a h. is counted but a vain thing 17.76
at thy rebuke . . . both the chariot and h. are fallen 17.159
no pleasure in the strength of an h. 17.295
the h. is prepared against . . . battle 18.68
a whip for the h. 18.84
behold a white h. 67.22
a pale h. 67.24
horseleach the h. hath two daughters, crying, give, give 18.106
horsemen the chariot of Israel, and the h. thereof 12.1
h. riding upon horses 24.9
horses a chariot . . . and h. of fire 12.1
some put their trust . . . in h. 17.39

I have compared thee ... to a company of h. 20.1
as fed h. in the morning 22.1
horsemen riding upon h. 24.9
hosanna h. to the Son of David 42.129
h. in the highest 42.129
hospitality given to h. 47.37, 56.4
use h. ... without grudging 62.15
hosts the Lord of h. is with us 17.105
hot my heart was h. within me 17.88
neither cold nor h. 67.14
hour mine h. is not yet come 45.6
house get thee out ... from thy father's h. 1.39
the h. of God 1.57
how much less this h. that I have builded? 11.6
set thine h. in order 12.16
to beautify the h. of the Lord 13.2
to death, and to the h. appointed for all living 16.46
I have loved the habitation of thy h. 17.54
the sparrow hath found her an h. 17.173
I had rather be a door-keeper in the h. of my God 17.175
holiness becometh thine h. for ever 17.193
he maketh the barren woman to keep h. 17.232
the h. of my pilgrimage 17.247
we will go into the h. of the Lord 17.258
except the Lord build the h. 17.265
her feet abide not in her h. 18.17
wisdom hath builded her h. 18.21
better to dwell in a corner ... than with a brawling woman in a wide h. 18.67
in the last days ... the Lord's h. shall be established 21.6
woe unto them that join h. to house 21.14
I was wounded in the h. of my friends 33.6
a foolish man, which built his h. upon the sand 42.44
my h. shall be called the house of prayer 42.130
a h. ... divided against itself 43.6
peace be to this h. 44.28
in my Father's h. are many mansions 45.56
an h. not made with hands 49.8
household a man's foes shall be they of his own h. 42.67
houses they think that their h. shall continue for ever 17.110
they shall build h., and inhabit them 21.102
housetops what ye hear in the ear ... preach ye upon the h. 42.64
howling in the waste h. wilderness 5.16
humble he that shall h. himself shall be exalted 42.138
h. yourselves ... under the mighty hand of God 62.16
humbled h. himself, and became obedient unto death 52.4
humbly walk h. with thy God 30.4
humility serving the Lord with all h. of mind 46.47
hundredfold brought forth fruit, some an h. 42.85
hunger blessed are they which do h. and thirst after righteousness 42.15
they shall h. no more 67.28
hungred h., and ye gave me meat 42.158
hungry h. and thirsty, their soul fainted in them 17.218
hunter Nimrod the mighty h. 1.35
the snare of the h. 17.186
hurt they shall not h. nor destroy in all my holy mountain 21.26
h. not the oil and the wine 67.23
they should not h. the grass 67.33
h. ... only those men which have not the seal of God 67.33
power was to h. men 67.35
husband thy desire shall be to thy h. 1.17
a virtuous woman is a crown to her h. 18.30
the heart of her h. doth safely trust in her 18.109
he whom thou now hast is not thy h. 45.17
h. render unto the wife due benevolence 48.16
the wife see that she reverence her h. 51.12
h. of one wife 56.4
husbandman my Father is the h. 45.62
husbands h., love your wives 53.5
husks the h. that the swine did eat 44.49
hypocrisy considerest not the beam ... in thine own eye 42.34
works ... for to be seen of men 42.137
whited sepulchres 42.141
for a pretence make long prayers 43.20
hypocrites scribes and Pharisees, h. 42.139
hyssop purge me with h. 17.114

I

ice he casteth forth his i. like morsels 17.296
I-chabod I. ... the glory is departed 9.10
idle every i. word ... they shall give account thereof 42.80
others standing i. in the marketplace 42.124
seemed ... i. tales, and they believed them not 44.78
idleness she ... eateth not the bread of i. 18.111
through i. of the hands the house droppeth 19.33
if any would not work 55.2
–*See also* sloth.
idols their i. are silver and gold 17.237
little children, keep yourselves from i. 64.10
ignorant be not i. of any thing in a great matter 39.6
unlearned and i. men 46.12
I would not have you to be i. 54.3
ignorantly whom therefore ye i. worship 46.38

ill love worketh no i. to his neighbour 47.43
illuminatio Dominus i. mea 17.56
image make man in our own i. 1.7
in the i. of God 1.7
any graven i. 2.29
fall down and worship the golden i. 25.4
whose is this i.? 42.134
the express i. of his person 60.1
imagination the i. of man's heart 1.32
scattered the proud in the i. of their hearts 44.3
imagine why do the people i. a vain thing? 17.2
Immanuel call his name I. 21.19
immortal they that have put off the mortal clothing, and put on the i. 36.2
immortality their hope full of i. 38.3
this mortal must put on i. 48.45
impart i. unto you some spiritual gift 47.3
impatient be the people never so i. 17.201
impossible nothing shall be i. unto you 42.109
incense i. is an abomination 21.3
the smoke of the i. ... prayers of the saints 67.30
inclosed a garden i. is my sister, my spouse 20.12
incommunicable ascribe unto stones and stocks the i. name 38.12
incorruptible thine i. spirit is in all things 38.11
they ... obtain a corruptible crown ... we an i. 48.27
the dead shall be raised i. 48.45
incorruption raised in i. 48.43
this corruptible must put on i. 48.45
increase if riches i., set not your heart upon them 17.135
then shall the earth bring forth her i. 17.141
of the i. of his government ... there shall be no end 21.23
he must i., but I must decrease 45.14
I have planted ... but God gave the i. 48.6
increased the waters i. 1.29
how are they i. that trouble me 17.6
i. in wisdom and stature 44.15
indecision how long halt ye between two opinions? 11.17
inditing my heart is i. of a good matter 17.99
infirmities the Spirit also helpeth our i. 47.27
strong ought to bear the i. of the weak 47.46
use a little wine for ... thine often i. 56.9
infirmity the spirit of a man will sustain his i. 18.55
inflame that continue ... till wine i. them 21.15
influence wisdom ... a pure i. flowing from the ... Almighty 38.8
ingratitude were there not ten cleansed? 44.58
inhabit they shall not build, and another i. 21.102
inhabitant until the cities be wasted without i. 21.18
inhabitants the i. thereof are as grasshoppers 21.62
inhabiters woe to the i. of the earth 67.39
inherit his seed shall i. the land 17.51
the meek ... shall i. the earth 42.15
i. the kingdom 42.158
i. a blessing 62.13
inheritance an i. may be gotten hastily 18.64
wisdom is good with an i. 19.21
by i. obtained a more excellent name 60.1
iniquity thine i. is taken away 21.17
plowed wickedness ... reaped i. 26.2
depart from me, ye that work i. 42.43
i. shall abound 42.145
the reward of i. 46.4
ink written not with i., but with the Spirit 49.3
inn no room for them in the i. 44.8
inner strengthened ... in the i. man 51.5
innocency keep i. 17.86
i. was found in me 25.12
innocent who ever perished, being i.? 16.11
he that maketh haste to be rich shall not be i. 18.100
they make haste to shed i. blood 21.93
i. of the blood of this just person 42.172
instant be i. in season, out of season 57.6
instructer an i. of every artificer 1.24
instruction a wise son heareth his father's i. 18.32
apply thine heart unto i. 18.73
instrument i. of ten strings 17.74
intreat i. me not to leave thee 8.2
i. me not ... to return from following after thee 8.2
being defamed, we i. 48.10
inventions knowledge of witty i. 18.20
they have sought out many i. 19.23
inward truth in the i. parts 17.114
iron a land whose stones are i. 5.2
the i. entered into his soul 17.216
to bind ... their nobles with links of i. 17.299
i. sharpeneth iron 18.94
rule them with a rod of i. 67.10
Isaac the God of I. 2.6
isles the multitude of the i. 17.198
he taketh up the i. as a very little thing 21.61
the i. saw it, and feared 21.65
the i. shall wait for his law 21.66
Israel I Deborah arose ... a mother in I. 7.3
peace upon I. 17.268
the Lord doth ... gather together the out-casts of I. 17.294
the vineyard of the Lord ... is ... I. 21.14
the lost sheep of the house of I. 42.58
art thou a master of I.? 45.10
Israelite an I. ... in whom is no guile 45.5
Israelites are they I.? so am I 49.18
ivory i., and apes, and peacocks 11.10

J

Jacob the God of J. 2.6
Jacob's Ladder 1.56
Jael J. the wife of Heber 7.6
jasper a j. and a sardine stone 67.16
the first foundation was j. 67.67
jawbone with the j. of an ass 7.15
jealous a j. God 2.29
jealousy j. is cruel as the grave 20.26
the ear of j. heareth all things 38.2
Jehu J. . . . driveth furiously 12.11
jeopardy went in j. of their lives 10.12
Jericho by faith the walls of J. fell down 60.14
Jerusalem J. is built as a city . . . at unity 17.259
pray for the peace of J. 17.260
the hills stand about J. 17.263
if I forget thee, O J. 17.276
the Lord doth build up J. 17.294
J. which is above is free 50.8
the holy city, new J. 67.65
that great city, the holy J. 67.66
Jesse a rod out of the stem of J. 21.25
Jesus when J. was born in Bethlehem of Judaea 42.2
at the name of J. every knee should bow 52.4
J. the author and finisher of our faith 60.16
Jew neither J. nor Greek 50.5
jewel as a j. of gold in a swine's snout 18.29
Jews King of the J. 42.2
J. require a sign 48.2
Jezebel dogs shall eat J. 11.28
J. . . . painted her face 12.12
Job hast thou considered my servant J.? 16.1
what man is like J., who drinketh up scorning 16.50
the Lord answered J. out of the whirlwind 16.54
the Lord blessed the latter end of J. 16.64
the patience of J. 61.15
Job's Comforters 16.32
John the Baptist 45.3
joined what . . . God hath j. together, let not man put asunder 42.119
joint-heirs j. with Christ 47.25
jollity wine . . . turneth . . . every thought into j. 35.1
Jonah and the lot fell upon J. 29.1
a great fish to swallow up J. 29.2
Jonah and the Whale 29.2
Jordan the people were passed clean over J. 6.3
dipped himself seven times in J. 12.6
J. was driven back 17.233
jot one j. or one tittle 42.17
journey arise and eat . . . the j. is too great 11.22
a sabbath day's j. 46.3
journeyings in j. often 49.18
joy the noise of the shout of j. 13.1
all the sons of God shouted for j. 16.54
in thy presence is the fulness of j. 17.27
j. cometh in the morning 17.64
the hill of Sion is . . . the j. of the whole earth 17.108
the voice of j. and health is in the dwellings of the righteous 17.240
they that sow in tears shall reap in j. 17.264
hast put gladness in my heart 17.9
a stranger doth not intermeddle with his j. 18.36
eat thy bread with j. 19.27
according to the j. in harvest 21.22
with j. shall ye draw water out of the wells of salvation 21.27
oil of j. for mourning 21.96
the Lord . . . give thee j. for this thy sorrow 37.2
enter thou into the j. of thy lord 42.154
good tidings of great j. 44.9
j. . . . in heaven over one sinner that repenteth 44.47
my j. . . . is fulfilled 45.14
j. that a man is born into the world 45.71
finish my course with j. 46.49
helpers of your j. 49.2
in every prayer . . . making request with j. 52.1
rejoice with j. unspeakable 62.2
that your j. may be full 64.1
–*See also* rejoice.
joyful O be j. in the Lord 17.202
a j. mother of children 17.232
how good and j. . . . brethren, to dwell together in unity 17.275
let the saints be j. with glory 17.298
in the day of prosperity be j. 19.22
jubilate j. Deo 17.203
Judah J. is my law-giver 17.225
the men of J. his pleasant plant 21.14
judge the J. of all the earth 1.47
a prince and a j. over us 2.3
who is able to j. this . . . people? 11.4
j. . . . the people with equity 17.200
j. none blessed before his death 39.12
j. not, that ye be not judged 42.33
out of thine own mouth will I j. thee 44.63
j. not according to the appearance 45.34
the j. standeth before the door 61.14
j. and avenge our blood 67.25
in righteousness he doth j. and make war 67.60
judged why is my liberty j. of another man's conscience? 48.31
judges princes and all j. of the world 17.297
judgment cursed be he that perverteth the j. 5.11
ye may know there is a j. 16.39
he looked for j., but behold oppression 21.14
establish it with j. and with justice 21.23
j. also will I lay to the line 21.42
the j. of the great whore 67.53

Judgment of Solomon 11.5
judgments the j. of the Lord are true 17.36
juniper he . . . sat down under a j. tree 11.21
just shall mortal man be more j. than God? 16.13
it becometh well the j. to be thankful 17.74
thy j. dealing as the noon-day 17.84
the path of the j. is as the shining light 18.11
the memory of the j. is blessed 18.24
a j. man . . . perisheth in his righteousness 19.22
rain on the j. and on the unjust 42.24
have thou nothing to do with that j. man 42.171
ninety and nine j. persons, which need no repentance 44.47
a good man, and a j. 44.76
denied the Holy One and the J. 46.11
the j. shall live by faith 47.5
whose damnation is j. 47.12
whatsoever things are j. 52.12
the spirits of j. men made perfect 60.19
faithful and j. to forgive 64.2
justice shall not the Judge of all the earth do right? 1.47
eye for eye, tooth for tooth 2.31
thy just dealing as the noon-day 17.84
remove not the old landmark 18.72
establish it with judgment and with j. 21.23
–*See also* just.
justified wisdom is j. of her children 42.74
by thy words thou shalt be j. 42.80
justifieth it is God that j. 47.30
justly what doth the Lord require of thee, but to do j.? 30.4

K

keep k. me as the apple of an eye 17.28
his angels . . . to k. thee in all thy ways 17.187
k. the door of my lips 17.285
a time to k., and a time to cast away 19.9
if a man k. my saying, he shall never see death 45.42
if ye love me, k. my commandments 45.59
endeavouring to k. the unity of the Spirit 51.6
k. himself unspotted from the world 61.5
keeper a k. of sheep 1.19
am I my brother's k.? 1.21
keepers the day when the k. of the house shall tremble 19.40
keepeth he that k. thee will not sleep 17.256
keeping in k. of them there is great reward 17.36
kept Mary k. all these things 44.11
key lawyers . . . have taken away the k. of knowledge 44.36
the k. of the bottomless pit 67.32
keys the k. of the kingdom of heaven 42.105
the k. of hell and of death 67.3
kick to k. against the pricks 46.25
kicked but Jeshurun waxed fat, and k. 5.17
kid a k. in his mother's milk 2.33
kill thou shalt not k. 2.29
k. me . . . out of hand 4.4
a time to k., and a time to heal 19.9
killed hast thou k., and also taken possession? 11.27
k. all the day long 17.98
k. the Prince of life 46.11
killeth whosoever k. you will think that he doeth God service 45.65
the letter k. 49.4
kind charity suffereth long, and is k. 48.35
kindly he . . . spake k. unto the damsel 1.63
the Lord deal k. with you, as ye have dealt with the dead 8.1
be k. affectioned 47.37
kindness in her tongue is the law of k. 18.111
the barbarous people shewed us no little k. 46.62
kindred get thee out . . . from thy k. 1.39
kindreds all k. of the earth shall wail 67.2
all nations, and k., and people 67.27
king a new k. over Egypt 2.1
the k. of terrors 16.34
who is the K. of glory? 17.49
the Lord remaineth a K. for ever 17.62
a great k. above all gods 17.195
fear thou the Lord and the k. 18.79
better . . . a poor and a wise child than an old and foolish k. 19.14
curse not the k., no not in thy thought 19.35
K. of the Jews 42.2
thy K. cometh unto thee 42.128
honour the k. 62.7
k. of kings 67.61
kingdom thy k. is divided, and given to the Medes and Persians 25.10
repent: for the k. of heaven is at hand 42.12
the gospel of the k. 42.14
thy k. come 42.27
seek ye first the k. of God 42.32
k. against kingdom 42.144
if a k. be divided . . . that kingdom cannot stand 43.6
the k. of God cometh not with observation 44.59
the k. of God is within you 44.59
remember me when thou comest into thy k. 44.74
the k. of God is not in word 48.11
the k. and patience of Jesus Christ 67.2
kingdoms such as did bear rule in their k. 39.28
all the k. of the world 42.10
kings the k. of the earth are gathered, and gone by 17.108
k. of the earth and all people 17.297
to bind their k. in chains 17.299
the honour of k. is to search out a matter 18.80

the heart of k. is unsearchable 18.80
k. shall be thy nursing fathers 21.76
k. to the brightness of thy rising 21.94
he removeth k., and setteth up kings 25.2
of whom do the k. . . . take custom or tribute? 42.110
many prophets and k. have desired to see 44.30

kiss k. the Son, lest he be angry 17.5
let him k. me with the kisses of his mouth 20.1
salute one another with an holy k. 47.48

kissed hail, master; and k. him 42.168
fell on his neck, and k. him 44.49

kisses the k. of an enemy are deceitful 18.92

knee at the name of Jesus every k. should bow 52.4

knees strengthen . . . the weak hands, and confirm the feeble k. 21.53

knew Joseph k. his brethren 1.70
a new king . . . which k. not Joseph 2.1
whom the Lord k. face to face 5.23
I never k. you 42.43
the more part k. not wherefore they were come 46.44

knock k., and it shall be opened unto you 42.36
I stand at the door, and k. 67.15

know I k. not the Lord 2.10
he shall k. that there is a prophet in Israel 12.5
neither shall his place k. him any more 16.21
I k. that my redeemer liveth 16.38
the heathen may k. themselves to be but men 17.16
Lord, let me k. mine end 17.88
be still then, and k. that I am God 17.105
the heart is deceitful . . . who can k. it? 22.13
let not thy left hand k. what thy right hand doeth 42.26
by their fruits ye shall k. them 42.41
ye k. not when the master of the house cometh 43.22
for they k. not what they do 44.73
we speak that we do k. 45.10
the sheep . . . k. his voice 45.46
we k. not where they have laid him 45.87
not for you to k. the times or the seasons 46.1
Jesus I k., and Paul I know 46.42
we k. in part, and we prophesy in part 48.35
then shall I k. even as also I am known 48.35
k. the love of Christ, which passeth knowledge 51.5

knowest not a word in my tongue, but thou . . . k. it 17.277
O Lord God, thou k. 24.11
a master of Israel, and k. not these things 45.10
thou k. all things 45.95

knoweth that my soul k. right well 17.280
who k. whether he shall be a wise man or a fool? 19.8
the ox k. his owner 21.1
your Father k. what things ye have need of 42.27

knowledge the tree of the k. of good and evil 1.9
Job . . . multiplieth words without k. 16.52
I will fetch my k. from afar 16.53
he that is perfect in k. 16.53
counsel without k. 16.62
is there k. in the most High? 17.155
such k. is too wonderful . . . for me 17.278
the fear of the Lord is the beginning of k. 18.1
k. of witty inventions 18.20
a man of k. increaseth strength 18.76
he that increaseth k. increaseth sorrow 19.5
the earth shall be full of the k. of the Lord 21.26
he giveth . . . k. to them that know understanding 25.2
k. shall be increased 25.14
lawyers . . . have taken away the key of k. 44.36
a zeal of God, but not according to k. 47.34
k. puffeth up 48.23
k., it shall vanish away 48.35

known surely this thing is k. 2.3
a people whom I have not k. shall serve me 17.34
hid, that shall not be k. 42.64
if thou hadst k. . . . the things which belong unto thy peace 44.65
k. of them in breaking of bread 44.81
have I been so long . . . and yet hast thou not k. me? 45.58

L

labour six days shalt thou l. 2.29
man goeth forth to his work, and to his l. 17.214
but lost l. that ye . . . rise up early 17.265
that our oxen may be strong to l. 17.290
in all l. there is profit 18.38
what profit hath a man of all his l.? 19.1
all things are full of l. 19.2
I hated all my l. which I had taken 19.8
two . . . have a good reward for their l. 19.12
your l. for that which satisfieth not 21.84
do ye not l. . . . and bring all to the woman? 35.5
all ye that l. and are heavy laden 42.76
l., working with our own hands 48.10
steal no more: but rather let him l. 51.8
l. of love 54.1
–*See also* work.

laboured l. more abundantly 48.39
hast l., and hast not fainted 67.5

labourer the l. is worthy of his hire 44.28

labourers but the l. are few 42.57

labouring the sleep of a l. man is sweet 19.16
a l. man . . . given to drunkenness 39.17

l. . . . to support the weak 46.50
labours ye are entered into their l. 45.20
in l. more abundant 49.18
they may rest from their l. 67.47
lack therefore can I l. nothing 17.45
ladder behold a l. set up on earth 1.56
lady the elder unto the elect l. 65.1
laid we know not where they have l. him 45.87
l. down their clothes at a young man's feet 46.19
lamb God will provide . . . a l. 1.50
l. . . . without blemish 2.18
one little ewe l. 10.6
the wolf also shall dwell with the l. 21.26
as a l. to the slaughter 21.81
the L. of God 45.4
a L. as it had been slain 67.19
worthy is the L. that was slain 67.21
washed . . . in the blood of the L. 67.28
the L. slain from the foundation of the world 67.41
the marriage of the L. 67.58
the L. is the light thereof 67.67
lambs he shall gather the l. with his arm 21.60
l. out of the flock 28.5
send you forth as l. among wolves 44.28
feed my l. 45.94
lame feet was I to the l. 16.44
lamentation a voice heard, l., and weeping 42.4
lamented we have mourned . . . and ye have not l. 42.73
lamps trimmed their l. 42.152
our l. are gone out 42.152
seven l. of fire burning before the throne 67.16
land unto a l. that I will shew thee 1.39
the fat of the l. 1.73
a stranger in a strange l. 2.4
a l. flowing with milk and honey 2.7
the l. of darkness and the shadow of death 16.25
his seed shall inherit the l. 17.51
a barren and dry l. where no water is 17.136
his hands prepared the dry l. 17.195
a fruitful l. maketh he barren 17.223
the voice of the turtle is heard in our l. 20.6
the l. of the shadow of death 21.22
the shadow of a great rock in a weary l. 21.50
the thirsty l. springs of water 21.54
cut off out of the l. of the living 21.81
I perish through great grief in a strange l. 40.1
landmark cursed be he that removeth his neighbour's l. 5.11
remove not the old l. 18.72
lands they . . . call the l. after their own names 17.110
language the whole earth was of one l. 1.36
Babel; because the Lord did there confound the l. 1.38
lantern thy word is a l. unto my feet 17.249
Laodicean 67.14
large thou . . . hast set my feet in a l. room 17.69
how l. a letter I have written 50.14
last bring . . . peace at the l. 17.86
in the l. days . . . the Lord's house shall be established 21.6
the l. state . . . is worse than the first 42.83
many that are first shall be l. 42.123
the l. shall be first 42.123
the l. error shall be worse than the first 42.176
I will raise him up at the l. day 45.31
the l. enemy that shall be destroyed 48.41
at the l. trump 48.45
the first and the l. 67.2
the seven l. plagues 67.50
Last Judgment 67.64
Last Supper 42.163
laugh he that dwelleth in heaven shall l. them to scorn 17.3
a time to weep, and a time to l. 19.9
woe unto you that l. now 44.21
laughing till he fill thy mouth with l. 16.22
laughter even in l. the heart is sorrowful 18.37
I said of l., it is mad 19.6
the crackling of thorns under a pot, so is the l. of the fool 19.19
law tables of stone, and a l. 2.34
his delight is in the l. of the Lord 17.1
the l. of the Lord is an undefiled law 17.35
blessed are those that . . . walk in the l. of the Lord 17.244
the isles shall wait for his l. 21.66
the l. and the prophets 42.38
all the l. and the prophets 42.136
a l. unto themselves 47.10
by the l. of faith 47.14
the l. worketh wrath 47.15
where no l. is, there is no transgression 47.15
the l. entered, that the offence might abound 47.18
a l., that . . . evil is present with me 47.22
he that loveth . . . hath fulfilled the l. 47.42
love is the fulfilling of the l. 47.43
the l. was our schoolmaster 50.4
against such there is no l. 50.11
as touching the l., a Pharisee 52.6
the perfect l. of liberty 61.4
lawful is it not l. for me to do what I will with mine own? 42.126
all things are l. 48.29
lawfully not crowned, except he strive l. 57.3
law-giver Judah is my l. 17.225
laws the l. of the Persians and the Medes 15.1
lawyers woe unto you, l. 44.36
lay l. up for yourselves treasures in heaven 42.28
layeth no man l. it to heart 21.89
Lazarus L. . . . laid at his gate, full of sores 44.55
lead who will l. me into the strong city? 17.225
gently l. those that are with young 21.60

l. us not into temptation 42.27
leaders l. of the people by their counsels 39.28
blind l. of the blind 42.102
leadership if the trumpet give an uncertain sound 48.36
leadest thou l. to the gates of hell, and bringest up again 38.13
leadeth he l. me beside the still waters 17.46
leaf his l. also shall not wither 17.1
we all do fade as a l. 21.100
leaning who is this ... l. upon her beloved? 20.25
leap I shall l. over the wall 17.32
leaping l. upon the mountains, skipping upon the hills 20.5
learned they will not be l. nor understand 17.172
God hath given me the tongue of the l. 21.77
learning a wise man will hear, and will increase l. 18.1
much l. doth make thee mad 46.60
least the l. of these my brethren 42.159
faithful in that which is l. 44.54
unjust in the l. ... unjust also in much 44.54
the l. of the apostles 48.39
the l. of all saints 51.4
leave intreat me not to l. thee 8.2
l. off first for manners' sake 39.21
l. the ninety and nine in the wilderness 44.47
not reason that we should l. the word of God 46.16
leaven a little l. leaveneth the whole lump 48.13
the l. of malice and wickedness 48.13
leaves the l. ... were for the healing of the nations 67.68
Lebanon streams from L. 20.13
led he l. them forth by the right way 17.219
as many as are l. by the Spirit of God 47.25
left let not thy l. hand know what thy right hand doeth 42.26
not be l. here one stone upon another 42.143
one shall be taken, and the other l. 42.151
the goats on the l. 42.157
the armour of righteousness on the right hand and on the l. 49.13
thou hast l. thy first love 67.5
Legion my name is L.: for we are many 43.7
leisure tarry thou the Lord's l. 17.59
wisdom ... cometh by opportunity of l. 39.25
lendeth a good man is merciful, and l. 17.230
length l. of days is in her right hand 18.8
the breadth, and l., and depth 51.5
leopard the l. shall lie down with the kid 21.26
or the l. his spots 22.9
leper recover the l. 12.6
a l. as white as snow 12.8
less l. than the least of all saints 51.4
the l. is blessed of the better 60.8
letter the l. killeth 49.4
how large a l. I have written 50.14
leviathan canst thou draw out l. with an hook? 16.60
l. ... made to take his pastime 17.215
l. the piercing serpent 21.40
l. that crooked serpent 21.40
lewd certain l. fellows of the baser sort 46.36
liar a l., and the father of it 45.40
let God be true, but every man a l. 47.11
love God ... hateth his brother, he is a l. 64.9
liars all men are l. 17.239
the Cretians are alway l. 58.1
liberty to proclaim l. to the captives 21.96
the glorious l. of the children of God 47.26
lest ... this l. of yours become a stumbling-block 48.24
why is my l. judged of another man's conscience? 48.31
use not l. for an occasion to the flesh 50.9
the perfect law of l. 61.4
lick his enemies shall l. the dust 17.154
l. up the dust of thy feet 21.76
lie I called not; l. down again 9.4
let her cherish him, and ... l. in thy bosom 11.1
he maketh me to l. down in green pastures 17.46
l. in wait for thine own life 39.16
lie God is not a man, that he should l. 4.15
who changed the truth of God into a l. 47.7
whosoever loveth and maketh a l. 67.71
lies forgers of l. 16.30
remove far from me vanity and l. 18.105
the refuge of l. 21.42
lieth she ... l. in wait at every corner 18.17
lieth l. at the point of death 43.10
life the breath of l. 1.9
the tree of l. 1.9
my l. is preserved 1.62
few and evil have the days ... of my l. been 1.75
l. for life 2.31
l. and death 5.13
therefore choose l. 5.13
take away my l.; for I am not better than my fathers 11.21
who is there ... would go into the temple to save his l.? 14.2
all that a man hath will he give for his l. 16.3
my soul is weary of my l. 16.23
the path of l. 17.27
a long l., even for ever and ever 17.40
thou hast kept my l. from them that go down to the pit 17.63
in his pleasure is l. 17.64
the well of l. 17.81
with long l. will I satisfy him 17.188
when the desire cometh, it is a tree of l. 18.33
a wicked man that prolongeth his l. 19.22
all men have one entrance into l. 38.7
power of l. and death 38.13
a faithful friend is the medicine of l. 39.7
lie in wait for thine own l. 39.16
take no thought for your l. 42.30

is not the l. more than meat? 42.30
he that loseth his l. for my sake 42.68
in him was l. . . . the light of men 45.1
should not perish, but have everlasting l. 45.12
he that believeth not the Son shall not see l. 45.15
well of water springing up into everlasting l. 45.16
passed from death unto l. 45.23
the scriptures . . . in them . . . ye have eternal l. 45.25
I am the bread of l. 45.29
give for the l. of the world 45.32
good shepherd giveth his l. for the sheep 45.48
I am the resurrection, and the l. 45.50
I am the way, the truth, and the l. 45.57
that a man lay down his l. for his friends 45.63
killed the Prince of l. 46.11
walk in newness of l. 47.19
the gift of God is eternal l. 47.21
to be spiritually minded is l. and peace 47.24
neither death, nor l., nor angels 47.31
the spirit giveth l. 49.4
he that soweth to the Spirit shall . . . reap l. everlasting 50.13
your l. is hid with Christ in God 53.3
lay hold on eternal l. 56.12
the crown of l. 61.2
what is your l. . . . a vapour 61.13
he that will love l., and see good days 62.13
the pride of l. 64.4
eat of the tree of l. 67.6
I will give thee a crown of l. 67.7
out of the book of l. 67.11
a pure river of water of l. 67.68
take the water of l. freely 67.71
–*See also* live, living.

lift l. up your heads, O ye gates 17.49
I will l. up mine eyes unto the hills 17.255
if they fall, the one will l. up his fellow 19.12
as if the staff should l. up itself 21.24
thy watchmen shall l. up the voice 21.80

lifted a throne, high and l. up 21.17
even so must the Son of man be l. up 45.11
if I be l. up . . . draw all men unto me 45.53

light let there be l. 1.1
God divided the l. from the darkness 1.1
wherefore is l. given 16.9
where the l. is as darkness 16.25
the l. of thy countenance 17.9
thou . . . shalt l. my candle 17.32
God shall make my darkness to be l. 17.32
in thy l. shall we see light 17.81
thy righteousness as clear as the l. 17.84
the l. of the living 17.124
thou deckest thyself with l. 17.211
thy word is . . . a l. unto my paths 17.249
darkness and l. to thee are both alike 17.279
the path of the just is as the shining l. 18.11
wisdom excelleth folly, as . . . l. excelleth darkness 19.7
that put darkness for l. 21.16
the people . . . have seen a great l. 21.22
then shall thy l. break forth 21.91
then shall thy l. rise in obscurity 21.92
for thy l. is come 21.94
Gentiles shall come to thy l. 21.94
l. dwelleth with him 25.2
l. a candle of understanding 36.7
the l. of the world 42.16
l. a candle, and put it under a bushel 42.16
let your l. so shine before men 42.16
the l. of the body is the eye 42.29
to give l. to them that sit in darkness 44.5
a l. to lighten the Gentiles 44.12
the children of l. 44.54
the l. shineth in darkness 45.1
the true l., which lighteth every man 45.1
a burning and a shining l. 45.24
I am the l. of the world 45.38
yet a little while is the l. with you 45.54
walk while ye have the l. 45.54
put on the armour of l. 47.43
our l. affliction . . . is but for a moment 49.7
the l. which no man can approach 56.13
her l. was like unto a stone most precious 67.66
the Lamb is the l. thereof 67.67
the Lord God giveth them l. 67.69

lightning l. cometh out of the east 42.147
beheld Satan as l. fall from heaven 44.29

lightnings l. and thunderings and voices 67.16

lights God made two great l. 1.4
your l. burning 44.40
the Father of l. 61.3

likeminded l. one toward another 47.47

likeness after our l. 1.7
any l. of any thing 2.29
gods are come down . . . in the l. of men 46.34

lilies he feedeth among the l. 20.8
my beloved is gone down . . . to gather l. 20.18
consider the l. of the field 42.31

lily the l. of the valleys 20.3
the l. among thorns 20.3

line who hath stretched the l. upon it? 16.54
l. upon line 21.41
judgment also will I lay to the l. 21.42

lines the l. are fallen unto me in pleasant places 17.26

lion what is stronger than a l.? 7.13
thou shalt go upon the l. and adder 17.187
a living dog is better than a dead l. 19.26
the l. shall eat straw like the ox 21.26
will a l. roar . . . when he hath no prey? 28.1
delivered out of the mouth of the l. 57.9
your adversary the devil, as a roaring l. 62.16

lions my soul is among l. 17.126
the l. roaring after their prey . . . seek 17.214
cast him into the den of l. 25.11
God . . . hath shut the l.' mouths 25.12

lips they do but flatter with their l. 17.20
they shoot out their l. 17.41
keep the door of my l. 17.285
the l. of a strange woman drop as an honeycomb 18.12

thy l. are like a thread of scarlet 20.11
a man of unclean l. 21.17
the fruit of the l. 21.90
this people ... honoureth me with their l. 42.100
listeth the wind bloweth where it l. 45.10
little better is l. with the fear of the Lord 18.42
here a l., and there a little 21.41
he taketh up the isles as a very l. thing 21.61
a l. one shall become a thousand 21.95
Beth-lehem Ephratah, though thou be l. 30.2
ye have sown much, and bring in l. 32.1
give to drink unto one of these l. ones 42.69
no l. kindness 46.62
a l. leaven leaveneth the whole lump 48.13
bodily exercise profiteth l. 56.6
live there shall no man see me, and l. 2.43
I shall not die, but l. 17.241
stablish me ... that I may l. 17.251
can these bones l.? 24.11
man shall not l. by bread alone 42.9
they that hear shall l. 45.23
because I l., ye shall live also 45.60
in him we l., and move, and have our being 46.39
the just shall l. by faith 47.5
l. peaceably with all men 47.37
as dying, and, behold, we l. 49.13
to l. is Christ 52.2
lived I l. a Pharisee 46.59
l. deliciously 67.55
lives went in jeopardy of their l. 10.12
liveth I know that my redeemer l. 16.38
their name l. for evermore 39.29
in that he l., he liveth unto God 47.20
the word of God, which l. and abideth 62.4
he that l., and was dead 67.3
worship him that l. for ever and ever 67.17
living let the earth bring forth the l. creature 1.6
man became a l. soul 1.9
to death, and to the house appointed for all l. 16.46
let them be wiped out of the book of the l. 17.149
walk before the Lord in the land of the l. 17.239
I praised the dead ... more than the l. 19.10
a well of l. waters 20.13
for the l. to the dead 21.21
cut off out of the land of the l. 21.81
l. peaceably in their habitations 39.28
riotous l. 44.48
why seek ye the l. among the dead? 44.77
the l. bread 45.32
a l. sacrifice, holy, acceptable 47.36
fall into the hands of the l. God 60.10
l. fountains of waters 67.28
Loaves and Fishes 45.26
locust that which the palmerworm hath left hath the l. eaten 27.1
the years that the l. hath eaten 27.4
locusts l. and wild honey 42.5
lodge as a l. in a garden of cucumbers 21.2
loins your l. girded 2.19
my little finger shall be thicker than my father's l. 11.12
let your l. be girded about 44.40
l. girt about with truth 51.14
gird up the l. of your mind 62.3
long which l. for death, but it cometh not 16.9
make no l. tarrying, O my God 17.92
Lord, how l.? 21.18
fulfilled a l. time 38.5
the physician cutteth off a l. disease 39.10
have I been so l. ... and yet hast thou not known me? 45.58
how l., O Lord, holy and true? 67.25
longer no l. under a schoolmaster 50.4
longeth so l. my soul after thee, O God 17.94
longing my soul hath a desire and l. to enter into the courts of the Lord 17.173
long-suffering l., and of great goodness 17.291
l. to us-ward 63.3
look afraid to l. upon God 2.6
a proud l. and a high stomach 17.204
at that day shall a man l. to his Maker 21.33
do we l. for another? 42.70
looked the mother of Sisera l. out 7.6
the Lord l. down from heaven 17.21
he l. for judgment, but behold oppression 21.14
looketh man l. on the outward appearance 9.17
the Lord l. on the heart 9.17
who is she that l. forth as the morning? 20.19
loose canst thou ... l. the bands of Orion? 16.56
whatsoever thou shalt l. on earth shall be loosed in heaven 42.105
loosed the string of his tongue was l. 43.13
Satan shall be l. out of his prison 67.63
Lord the sword of the L., and of Gideon 7.9
he wist not that the L. was departed from him 7.16
the L. is my shepherd 17.45
the L. ... is the wholesome defence of his Anointed 17.60
the voice of the L. breaketh the cedar-trees 17.61
the L. remaineth a King for ever 17.62
I waited patiently for the L. 17.91
except the L. build the house 17.265
the spirit of man is the candle of the L. 18.65
the L. pondereth the hearts 18.66
safety is of the L. 18.68
fear thou the L. and the king 18.79
the vineyard of the L. ... is ... Israel 21.14
the L. sitting upon a throne, high and lifted up 21.17
the L. is his name 28.4
the L. ... shall suddenly come to his temple 34.2

O L., thou lover of souls 38.10
thou shalt not tempt the L. thy God 42.10
my L. and my God 45.92
L. of lords 67.61
Lord's Prayer 42.27
lose a time to get, and a time to l. 19.9
he that findeth his life shall l. it 42.68
gain the whole world, and l. his ... soul 43.15
loss gain ... I counted l. for Christ 52.7
lost the l. sheep of the house of Israel 42.58
I have found my sheep which was l. 44.47
he was l., and is found 44.50
gather up the fragments ... that nothing be l. 45.27
lot the l. is fallen unto me in a fair ground 17.25
the rod of the ungodly cometh not into the l. of the righteous 17.263
cast in thy l. among us 18.3
the l. is cast into the lap 18.48
and the l. fell upon Jonah 29.1
neither part nor l. 46.22
Lot remember L.'s wife 44.60
lots cast l., that we may know for whose cause this evil is upon us 29.1
they parted his raiment, and cast l. 44.73
Lot's Wife 1.49
loud the l. cymbals 17.300
she is l. and stubborn 18.17
love they seemed ... but a few days, for the l. he had to her 1.59
thy l. ... passing the love of women 10.3
they shall prosper that l. thee 17.260
be thou ravished always with her l. 18.13
let us take our fill of l. 18.18
but l. covereth all sins 18.25
a dinner of herbs where l. is 18.42
he that covereth a transgression seeketh l. 18.50
open rebuke is better than secret l. 18.92
a time to l., and a time to hate 19.9
their l., and their hatred ... is now perished 19.26
thy l. is better than wine 20.1
the lily among thorns, so is my l. among the daughters 20.3
his banner over me was l. 20.4
I am sick of l. 20.4
rise up, my l. ... and come away 20.6
thou art all fair, my l. 20.11
how fair ... art thou, O l., for delights 20.22
stir not up, nor awake my l. 20.24
l. is strong as death 20.26
many waters cannot quench l. 20.26
neither can the floods drown ... l. 20.26
all the substance of his house for l. 20.26
I drew them ... with bands of l. 26.3
in their cups, they forget their l. 35.2
if men have gathered together gold and silver ... do they not l. a woman? 35.4
when he hath ... robbed, he bringeth it to his l. 35.5
l. your enemies 42.24
if ye l. them which love you, what reward have ye? 42.24
l. the Lord thy God with all thy heart 42.136
l. thy neighbour as thyself 42.136
the l. of many shall wax cold 42.145
if ye l. me, keep my commandments 45.59
greater l. hath no man 45.63
thou knowest that I l. thee 45.95
the l. of God is shed abroad in our hearts 47.17
all things work ... for good to them that l. God 47.28
nor height, nor depth ... able to separate us from the l. of God 47.31
let l. be without dissimulation 47.37
l. worketh no ill to his neighbour 47.43
l. is the fulfilling of the law 47.43
the things which God hath prepared for them that l. him 48.5
the l. of Christ constraineth us 49.10
the fruit of the Spirit is l., joy, peace 50.11
rooted and grounded in l. 51.5
know the l. of Christ, which passeth knowledge 51.5
forbearing one another in l. 51.6
l. his wife even as himself 51.12
husbands, l. your wives 53.5
labour of l. 54.1
l. of money is the root of all evil 56.11
spirit ... of power, and of l. 57.1
let brotherly l. continue 60.20
whom having not seen, ye l. 62.2
l. the brotherhood 62.7
l. life 62.13
beloved, let us l. one another 64.7
l. is of God 64.7
God is l. 64.7
perfect l. casteth out fear 64.8
l. God, and hateth his brother 64.9
mercy unto you ... and l., be multiplied 66.1
thou hast left thy first l. 67.5
loved he l. the damsel 1.63
Solomon l. many strange women 11.11
I have l. the habitation of thy house 17.54
for she l. much 44.25
God so l. the world 45.12
the condemnation ... men l. darkness 45.13
one of his disciples, whom Jesus l. 45.55
having l. this present world 57.8
lovely l. and pleasant in their lives 10.2
whatsoever things are l. 52.12
lover thou l. of souls 38.10
loveth whom the Lord l. he correcteth 18.7
he that l. him chasteneth him betimes 18.35
thou whom my soul l. 20.1
God l. none but him that dwelleth with wisdom 38.8
he that l. ... hath fulfilled the law 47.42
God l. a cheerful giver 49.15
whom the Lord l. he chasteneth 60.17
whosoever l. and maketh a lie 67.71

loving thy l.-kindness and mercy shall follow me 17.45
l. favour rather than silver and gold 18.69
wisdom is a l. spirit 38.1
low every mountain and hill shall be made l. 21.59
condescend to men of l. estate 47.37
lower thou madest him l. than the angels 17.14
lowest begin with shame to take the l. room 44.43
lowly he that ... is l. in his own eyes 17.24
meek and l. in heart 42.76
Lucifer how art thou fallen from heaven, O L. 21.30
L., son of the morning 21.30
luck we wish you good l. in the name of the Lord 17.270
lucre not greedy of filthy l. 56.4
Luke L., the beloved physician 53.9
lukewarm thou art l. 67.14
lump a little leaven leaveneth the whole l. 48.13
lurking l. in the thievish corners of the streets 17.17
lust the l. of the flesh 64.4
lusteth the flesh l. against the Spirit 50.10
lusts so I gave them up unto their own hearts' l. 17.171
the flesh, to fulfil the l. thereof 47.43
fleshly l., which war against the soul 62.6
murmurers, complainers, walking after their own l. 66.4
lute l., and instrument of ten strings 17.74
awake, l. and harp 17.128
lux fiat l. 1.2
lying a l. spirit 11.31
which befell me by the l. in wait of the Jews 46.47

M

mad I said of laughter, it is m. 19.6
much learning doth make thee m. 46.60
made it is he that hath m. us, and not we 17.202
fearfully and wonderfully m. 17.280
without him was not any thing m. 45.1
madly fools, deal not so m. 17.157
madness who stilleth ... the m. of the people 17.140
Magi 42.3
magna m. est veritas 35.7
Magnificat 44.2
magnify shall the saw m. itself? 21.24
my soul doth m. the Lord 44.2
Magog Gog and M. 67.63
maid the way of a man with a m. 18.107
maidens young men and m. 17.297
maimed the poor, and the m. 44.44
majesty deck thyself ... with m. and excellency 16.59
for fear of the Lord, and for the glory of his m. 21.8
as his m. is, so is his mercy 39.3
make much learning doth m. thee mad 46.60
behold, I m. all things new 67.65
maker the rich and poor meet together: the Lord is the m. of them all 18.69
at that day shall a man look to his M. 21.33
woe unto him that striveth with his m. 21.69
makest shall the clay say to him that fashioneth it, what m. thou? 21.69
maketh whosoever loveth and m. a lie 67.71
male m. and female created he them 1.7
m. and female of all flesh 1.29
neither m. nor female 50.5
malice the leaven of m. and wickedness 48.13
in m. be ye children 48.37
mammon ye cannot serve God and m. 42.30
friends of the m. of unrighteousness 44.54
man make m. in our own image 1.7
m. became a living soul 1.9
it is not good that m. should be alone 1.11
by m. shall his blood be shed 1.33
his hand will be against every m. 1.45
the Lord is a m. of war 2.25
God is not a m., that he should lie 4.15
thou mighty m. of valour 7.8
every m. did that which was right in his own eyes 7.17
the people arose as one m. 7.18
a m. after his own heart 9.13
the Lord seeth not as m. seeth 9.17
thou art the m. 10.7
thou bloody m. 10.9
m. of Belial 10.9
should such a m. as I flee? 14.2
what shall be done unto the m. whom the king delighteth to honour? 15.4
a perfect and an upright m. 16.1
shall mortal m. be more just than God? 16.13
m. is born unto trouble, as the sparks fly upward 16.14
is there not an appointed time to m. upon earth? 16.17
God will not cast away a perfect m. 16.22
m. that is born of a woman 16.31
m. ... is of few days 16.31
there is a spirit in m. 16.48
m. that hath not walked in the counsel of the ungodly 17.1
the Lord will abhor ... the bloodthirsty and deceitful m. 17.10
what is m., that thou art mindful of him? 17.14
up, Lord, and let not m. have the upper hand 17.16
a worm, and no m. 17.41
what m. is he ... would fain see good days? 17.78
m. walketh in a vain shadow 17.88
m. being in honour hath no understanding 17.111

vain is the help of m. 17.133
m. did eat angels' food 17.164
m. ... flourisheth as a flower of the field 17.210
happy is the m. that hath his quiver full of them 17.265
m. is like a thing of nought 17.289
when the breath of m. goeth forth 17.292
the spirit of m. is the candle of the Lord 18.65
face answereth to face; so the heart of man to m. 18.95
the eyes of m. are never satisfied 18.96
the way of a m. with a maid 18.107
this sore travail hath God given to ... m. 19.4
leave it unto the m. that shall be after me 19.8
God hath made m. upright 19.23
no m. ... hath power over the spirit to retain the spirit 19.24
this is the whole duty of m. 19.42
cease ye from m., whose breath is in his nostrils 21.9
the mighty m., and the man of war 21.10
seven women shall take hold of one m. 21.12
a m. of sorrows 21.81
a m. of strife 22.12
a m. of contention 22.12
good for a m. that he bear the yoke in his youth 23.5
every m. under his vine and under his fig tree 30.1
a m. ... goeth his way to rob 35.5
was but honoured as a m. 38.12
m. shall not live by bread alone 42.9
what manner of m. is this 42.50
the sabbath was made for m. 43.4
what shall it profit a m., if he ... gain 43.15
a m. sent from God 45.1
no m. hath seen God at any time 45.2
never m. spake like this man 45.35
greater love hath no m. 45.63
joy that a m. is born into the world 45.71
behold the m. 45.78
I myself also am a m. 46.30
the voice of a god ... not of a m. 46.33
let every m. be fully persuaded in his own mind 47.45
when I became a m., I put away childish things 48.35
strengthened ... in the inner m. 51.5
the m. of God may be perfect 57.5
the number of the beast ... is the number of a m. 67.42

Manasses M. is mine 17.225

manger laid him in a m. 44.8

manifest every man's work shall be made m. 48.7

manifold in heaviness through m. temptations 62.1

manna it is m. 2.27
gave you m. ... angels' bread 36.1
your fathers did eat m. ... and are dead 45.32
eat of the hidden m. 67.8

manner what m. of man is this 42.50
after what m. I have been with you at all seasons 46.47
after the m. of men I have fought with beasts 48.42

manners leave off first for m.' sake 39.21
evil communications corrupt good m. 48.42

mansions in my Father's house are many m. 45.56

mantle Elijah ... cast his m. upon him 11.24

many there be m. that say, who will shew us any good? 17.9
a monster unto m. 17.151
m. shall run to and fro 25.14
m. are called 42.133
my name is Legion: for we are m. 43.7
her sins, which are m. 44.25
what are they among so m.? 45.26
as m. as are led by the Spirit of God 47.25

mark the Lord set a m. upon Cain 1.23
they ... m. my steps, when they lay wait for my soul 17.122
press toward the m. for the prize 52.8
the m. ... of the beast 67.42

marketplace others standing idle in the m. 42.124

Mark of Cain 1.23

marriage who can find a virtuous woman? 18.109
no more twain, but one flesh 42.119
neither marry, nor are given in m. 42.135
render ... due benevolence 48.16
have trouble in the flesh 48.20
love his wife 51.12
love your wives, and be not bitter 53.5
the m. of the Lamb 67.58
—See also husband, wife.

married I have m. a wife 44.44
he that is m. careth ... how he may please his wife 48.22

marry it is not good to m. 42.120
neither m., nor are given in marriage 42.135
better to m. than to burn 48.18

marrying m. and giving in marriage 42.150

martyrs drunken with the blood of the ... m. 67.54

marvellous the Lord's doing, and ... m. in our eyes 17.242

master the disciple is not above his m. 42.63
m., is it I? 42.162
ye know not when the m. of the house cometh 43.22
art thou a m. of Israel? 45.10
Rabboni; which is to say, M. 45.89

masteries strive for m. 57.3

masters no man can serve two m. 42.30

mastery man that striveth for the m. 48.27

materialism treasures upon earth 42.28
ye cannot serve God and mammon 42.30
the care of this world 42.88
much goods laid up 44.38

matter the root of the m. 16.39
full of m. 16.49
meal an handful of m. in a barrel 11.15
mean no m. city 46.51
measure good m., pressed down 44.22
a m. of wheat for a penny 67.23
meat out of the eater came forth m. 7.12
the lions ... seek their m. from God 17.214
m. in due season 17.215
m. in the summer 18.14
I laid m. unto them 26.3
is not the life more than m.? 42.30
hungred, and ye gave me m. 42.158
my m. is to do the will of him that sent me 45.19
need of milk, and not of strong m. 60.7
meats m. for the belly 48.14
meddle m. not with them that are given to change 18.79
meddleth he that ... m. with strife 18.88
meddling every fool will be m. 18.59
Medes the laws of the Persians and the M. 15.1
thy kingdom is ... given to the M. and Persians 25.10
medicine a merry heart doeth good like a m. 18.53
a faithful friend is the m. of life 39.7
meditation think on these things 52.12
meek Moses was very m. 4.6
the patient abiding of the m. 17.16
blessed are the m. 42.15
m. and lowly in heart 42.76
m., and sitting upon an ass 42.128
the ornament of a m. and quiet spirit 62.11
Melchisedech a priest for ever after the order of M. 17.228
melody the voice of m. 21.79
melteth he sendeth out his word, and m. them 17.296
member the tongue is a little m. 61.7
members it is profitable for thee that one of thy m. should perish 42.21
m. one of another 51.8
memorial their m. is perished with them 17.15
some there be, which have no m. 39.28
memory the m. of the just is blessed 18.24
men mighty m. which were of old 1.27
m. of renown 1.27
m. of a great stature 4.7
quit yourselves like m. 9.7
the heathen may know themselves to be but m. 17.16
m. are deceitful upon the weights 17.135
green herb for the service of m. 17.213
all m. are liars 17.239
young m. and maidens 17.297
mighty and strong m. for the war 22.20
desirable young m. 24.9
without women cannot m. be 35.4
all m. have one entrance into life 38.7
let us now praise famous m. 39.27
fishers of m. 42.13
m. as trees, walking 43.14
if I be lifted up ... draw all m. unto me 45.53
these m. are full of new wine 46.7
if this counsel ... be of m. 46.15
all things to all m. 48.26
the tongues of m. and of angels 48.35
of all m. most miserable 48.40
after the manner of m. I have fought with beasts 48.42
honour all m. 62.7
mene m., mene, tekel, upharsin 25.10
mention I make m. of you always in my prayers 47.2
merchandise her m. is good 18.110
merchant a m. man, seeking goodly pearls 42.93
merchants Tyre ... whose m. are princes 21.37
mercies the tender m. of the wicked are cruel 18.31
with great m. will I gather thee 21.83
it is of the Lord's m. that we are not consumed 23.4
merciful a good man is m., and lendeth 17.230
blessed are the m. 42.15
God be m. to me a sinner 44.62
mercy shewing m. unto thousands 2.29
thy loving-kindness and m. shall follow me 17.45
surely goodness and m. shall follow me 17.47
my trust is in the tender m. of God 17.117
m. and truth are met together 17.177
his m. is everlasting 17.202
how high the heaven is ... so great is his m. 17.209
in m. shall the throne be established 21.32
sow ... in righteousness, reap in m. 26.2
as his majesty is, so is his m. 39.3
but of God that sheweth m. 47.32
m. unto you ... be multiplied 66.1
merry God is gone up with a m. noise 17.106
a m. heart maketh a cheerful countenance 18.41
a m. heart doeth good like a medicine 18.53
I commended mirth ... to eat ... to drink, and to be m. 19.25
drink thy wine with a m. heart 19.27
take thine ease, eat, drink, and be m. 44.38
messenger the m. ... cometh not again 12.10
Methuselah all the days of M. 1.26
midst there am I in the m. of them 42.115
might the m. of mine hand hath gotten me this wealth 5.3
David danced ... with all his m. 10.4
whatsoever thy hand findeth to do, do it with thy m. 19.28
in the power of his m. 51.14
mightier he that cometh after me is m. than I 42.7

mighty m. men which were of old 1.27
they are too m. for me 4.12
how are the m. fallen 10.1
the waves of the sea are m. 17.193
m. and strong men for the war 22.20
great is truth, and m. above all things 35.6
put down the m. 44.3
the weak things of the world to confound the ... m. 48.3
humble yourselves ... under the m. hand of God 62.16
mile whosoever shall compel thee to go a m. 42.23
milk his teeth white with m. 1.77
a land flowing with m. and honey 2.7
a kid in his mother's m. 2.33
need of m., and not of strong meat 60.7
the sincere m. of the word 62.5
millstone his heart is ... as hard as a ... m. 16.61
a m. ... hanged about his neck 42.112
a stone like a great m. 67.57
mind forgotten, as a dead man out of m. 17.70
God that maketh men to be of one m. in an house 17.142
a fool uttereth all his m. 18.102
concupiscence doth undermine the simple m. 38.5
a man's m. is sometime wont to tell him more than seven watchmen 39.23
in his right m. 43.9
serving the Lord with all humility of m. 46.47
be of the same m. 47.37
let every man be fully persuaded in his own m. 47.45
spirit ... of a sound m. 57.1
gird up the loins of your m. 62.3
minded to be carnally m. is death 47.24
mindful what is man, that thou art m. of him? 17.14
minister which m. questions 56.1
ministered Samuel m. before the Lord 9.2
angels came and m. unto him 42.11
ministering m. spirits 60.3
ministers his m. a flaming fire 17.211
his m. a flame of fire 60.2
mirror wisdom ... the unspotted m. ... of God 38.8
mirth if I prefer not Jerusalem in my m. 17.276
the end of that m. is heaviness 18.37
and of m., what doeth it? 19.6
I commended m. ... to eat ... to drink, and to be merry 19.25
mischief if m. befall him 1.71
who imagine m. in their hearts 17.282
misdeeds put out all my m. 17.114
miserable of all men most m. 48.40
misery going through the vale of m. 17.174
their departure is taken for m. 38.3
–*See also* woe.

mission here am I; send me 21.17
fishers of men 42.13
send forth labourers into his harvest 42.57
go ye into all the world 43.23
send you forth as lambs 44.28
a setter forth of strange gods 46.37
instant in season, out of season 57.6
mist there went up a m. from the earth 1.9
mistake they daily m. my words 17.122
mixture the wrath of God ... poured out without m. 67.46
Mizpah M. ... the Lord watch between me and thee 1.60
Moab M. is my wash-pot 17.225
mocked God is not m. 50.13
moment for a small m. have I forsaken thee 21.83
in a m. of time 44.17
in a m., in the twinkling of an eye 48.45
our light affliction ... is but for a m. 49.7
money m. answereth all things 19.34
buy ... without m. and without price 21.84
be not greedy to add m. to money 37.1
thy m. perish with thee 46.22
love of m. is the root of all evil 56.11
monster a m. unto many 17.151
months m. of vanity 16.18
moon neither the m. by night 17.257
fair as the m. 20.19
the sun and the m. shall be darkened 27.7
the m. became as blood 67.26
more light ... shineth m. and more 18.11
morning joy cometh in the m. 17.64
in the m. it is green 17.182
my soul fleeth ... before the m. watch 17.273
take the wings of the m. 17.279
in the m. sow thy seed 19.39
who is she that looketh forth as the m.? 20.19
Lucifer, son of the m. 21.30
the m. cometh, and also the night 21.34
then shall thy light break forth as the m. 21.91
his compassions ... are new every m. 23.4
that ... turneth the shadow of death into the m. 28.4
the bright and m. star 67.71
morrow take ... no thought for the m. 42.32
mortal they that have put off the m. clothing 36.2
this m. must put on immortality 48.45
mortar though thou shouldest bray a fool in a m. ... yet will not his foolishness depart 18.97
Moses M. was very meek 4.6
there arose not a prophet ... like unto M. 5.23
as I was with M., so I will be with thee 6.1
Moses in the Bulrushes 2.2
mote the m. that is in thy brother's eye 42.34
moth a m. fretting a garment 17.89
where m. and rust doth corrupt 42.28
mother Eve ... the m. of all living 1.18
I Deborah arose ... a m. in Israel 7.3
when my father and my m. forsake me 17.58
a joyful m. of children 17.232
as is the m., so is her daughter 24.5

thy m.'s daughter 24.5
the same is my ... m. 42.84
the m. against the daughter 44.41
behold thy m. 45.81
Jerusalem ... the m. of us all 50.8
the m. of harlots 67.54
mothers queens thy nursing m. 21.76
motion wisdom is more moving than any m. 38.8
mount the whole m. quaked greatly 2.28
the m. called Olivet 46.3
mountain the m. of myrrh 20.11
they shall not hurt nor destroy in all my holy m. 21.26
get thee up into the high m. 21.59
say unto this m., remove 42.109
a great and high m. 67.66
mountains the m. shake at the tempest 17.103
the m. skipped like rams 17.233
a young hart upon the m. of spices 20.27
how beautiful upon the m. are the feet 21.80
say to the m., fall on us 44.71
all faith, so that I could remove m. 48.35
mourn a time to m., and a time to dance 19.9
I did m. as a dove 21.57
blessed are they that m. 42.15
mourned we have m. ... and ye have not lamented 42.73
mourning I will go down into the grave ... m. 1.66
better ... the house of m., than ... the house of feasting 19.18
oil of joy for m. 21.96
mouth out of the m. of ... babes and sucklings 17.14
their m. is full of cursing 17.22
a consuming fire out of his m. 17.31
I will keep my m. as it were with a bridle 17.88
set a watch ... before my m. 17.285
the praises of God be in their m. 17.298
he was oppressed ... yet he opened not his m. 21.81
out of the abundance of the heart the m. speaketh 42.79
not that which goeth into the m. defileth 42.101
out of thine own m. will I judge thee 44.63
I will give you a m. and wisdom 44.66
in the m. of two or three witnesses 49.22
delivered out of the m. of the lion 57.9
out of the same m. proceedeth blessing and cursing 61.9
neither was guile found in his m. 62.9
out of his m. went a sharp twoedged sword 67.2
in thy m. sweet as honey 67.36
mouths m., and speak not 17.237
God ... hath shut the lions' m. 25.12
move in him we live, and m., and have our being 46.39
moved he hath made the round world so sure that it cannot be m. 17.192
mover a m. of sedition 46.55
mower whereof the m. filleth not his hand 17.270
much ye have sown m., and bring in little 32.1
faithful also in m. 44.54
unjust in the least ... unjust also in m. 44.54
mule be ye not like to horse and m. 17.73
multiplied mercy unto you ... be m. 66.1
multiplieth Job ... m. words without knowledge 16.52
multiply be fruitful and m. 1.7
multitude in the m. of counsellors there is safety 18.28
the m. ... took him now for a god 38.12
desire not a m. of unprofitable children 39.15
a very great m. spread their garments 42.129
a m. of sins 61.17
a great m., which no man could number 67.27
multitudes m. in the valley of decision 27.7
murderer a m. from the beginning 45.40
desired a m. to be granted 46.11
murmurers m., complainers, walking after their own lusts 66.4
murmurings the noise of m. is not hid 38.2
musical such as found out m. tunes 39.28
musick all the daughters of m. shall be brought low 19.40
mustard a grain of m. seed 42.91
faith as a grain of m. seed 42.109
mutter wizards that peep, and that m. 21.21
muzzle thou shalt not m. the ox 5.10
myrrh a bundle of m. is my wellbeloved 20.2
the mountain of m. 20.11
gathered my m. with my spice 20.15
gold, and frankincense, and m. 42.3
myrtle the angel of the Lord that stood among the m. trees 33.2
mysteries stewards of the m. of God 48.9
mystery I shew you a m. 48.45
the m. of the seven stars 67.4

N

Naboth's Vineyard 11.26
nail fasten him as a n. in a sure place 21.36
naked they were both n. 1.12
they knew that they were n. 1.14
who told thee that thou wast n.? 1.16
n. came I out of my mother's womb 16.2
n., and ye clothed me 42.158
nakedness spies; to see the n. of the land 1.70
name that was the n. thereof 1.11
thou shalt not take the n. of ... God in vain 2.29
he shall have no n. in the street 16.35
sing praises unto his n. 17.142
unto thy n. give the praise 17.235
blessed be he that cometh in the n. of the Lord 17.243

his n. only is excellent 17.297
the n. of the wicked shall rot 18.24
a good n. is rather ... than great riches 18.69
a good n. is better than precious ointment 19.18
thy n. is as ointment 20.1
only let us be called by thy n. 21.12
call his n. Immanuel 21.19
his n. shall be called, Wonderful, Counsellor 21.23
a place and a n. better than of sons and of daughters 21.88
an everlasting n., that shall not be cut off 21.88
the Lord is his n. 28.4
confessed the n. of God 36.2
them that stood so stiffly for the n. of the Lord 36.2
ascribe unto stones and stocks the incommunicable n. 38.12
them, that have left a n. behind them 39.28
their n. liveth for evermore 39.29
hallowed be thy n. 42.27
receive one such little child in my n. 42.112
two or three ... gathered together in my n. 42.115
my n. is Legion 43.7
in the n. of Jesus Christ of Nazareth 46.10
a n. which is above every name 52.4
at the n. of Jesus every knee should bow 52.4
by inheritance obtained a more excellent n. 60.1
in the stone a new n. written 67.8
not blot out his n. 67.11
write upon him my new n. 67.13
the n. of the star is called Wormwood 67.31
his n. shall be in their foreheads 67.69
names they ... call the lands after their own n. 17.110
he telleth the number of the stars, and calleth them all by their n. 17.294
whose n. are not written in the book of life 67.41
narrow the entrances of this world made n. 36.5
n. is the way, which leadeth unto life 42.39
nation I will make of thee a great n. 1.39
righteousness exalteth a n. 18.39
n. shall not lift up sword against nation 21.7
a small one a strong n. 21.95
the wealthy n., that dwelleth without care 22.21
n. shall rise against nation 42.144
nations all n. shall flow unto it 21.6
distress of n., with perplexity 44.68
all n., and kindreds, and people 67.27
the healing of the n. 67.68
naught it is n., saith the buyer 18.63
naughtiness I know thy pride, and the n. of thine heart 9.19
the bewitching of n. 38.5
filthiness and superfluity of n. 61.4
naughty the congregations of n. men 17.179
navel thy n. is like a round goblet 20.21
nay yea, yea; n., nay 42.22
your n., nay 61.15
Nazareth can ... any good thing come out of N.? 45.5
in the name of Jesus Christ of N. 46.10
near peace to him ... that is n. 21.90
Nebuchadnezzar N. ... did eat grass as oxen 25.8
neck hast thou clothed his n. with thunder? 16.57
thy n. is like the tower of David 20.11
a millstone ... hanged about his n. 42.112
fell on his n., and kissed him 44.49
necks the n. of them that take the spoil 7.7
need your Father knoweth what things ye have n. of 42.27
n. of milk, and not of strong meat 60.7
the city had no n. of the sun 67.67
needful but one thing is n. 44.34
to abide in the flesh is more n. for you 52.3
needle easier for a camel to go through the eye of a n. 42.122
needle-work raiment of n. 17.101
needs it must n. be that offences come 42.113
needy as for me, I am poor and n. 17.92
O death, acceptable is thy sentence unto the n. 39.26
neighbour devise not evil against thy n. 18.9
thy n. ... dwelleth securely by thee 18.9
they helped every one his n. 21.65
love thy n. as thyself 42.136
love worketh no ill to his n. 47.43
neighed every one n. after his neighbour's wife 22.1
nests the birds of the air have n. 42.48
net the proud have ... spread a n. 17.283
in vain the n. is spread in the sight of any bird 18.4
nets let the ungodly fall into their own n. 17.287
a place for the spreading of n. 24.10
new sing unto the Lord a n. song 17.74
there is no n. thing under the sun 19.2
I create n. heavens and a new earth 21.103
his compassions ... are n. every morning 23.4
a n. friend is as new wine 39.9
n. wine into old bottles 42.54
out of his treasure things n. and old 42.94
my blood of the n. testament 42.163
to tell, or to hear some n. thing 46.38
all things are become n. 49.11
in the stone a n. name written 67.8
write upon him my n. name 67.13
a n. heaven and a new earth 67.65
I make all things n. 67.65
newness walk in n. of life 47.19
news good n. from a far country 18.83
nigh the day of the Lord ... is n. at hand 27.2
peace to ... them that were n. 51.3
draw n. to God 61.12

night   the darkness he called N. 1.1
that is past as a watch in the n. 17.182
afraid for any terror by n. 17.186
neither the moon by n. 17.257
then shall my n. be turned to day 17.279
her candle goeth not out by n. 18.110
by n. on my bed I sought him whom my soul loveth 20.9
every man hath his sword . . . because of fear in the n. 20.10
my locks with the drops of the n. 20.15
watchman, what of the n.? 21.34
the morning cometh, and also the n. 21.34
toiled all the n., and . . . taken nothing 44.19
the n. cometh, when no man can work 45.43
n. is far spent 47.43
as a thief in the n. 54.4
nights   wearisome n. are appointed to me 16.18
forty days and forty n. 42.9
Nimrod   N. the mighty hunter 1.35
Noah's Ark   1.29
nobis   non n., Domine 17.236
nobles   to bind . . . their n. with links of iron 17.299
Nod   the land of N. 1.23
noise   the n. of them that sing 2.40
the n. of the shout of joy 13.1
God is gone up with a merry n. 17.106
make a cheerful n. unto . . . God 17.168
let the sea make a n., and all that therein is 17.200
the n. of murmurings is not hid 38.2
noisome   the n. pestilence 17.186
noli   n. me tangere 45.90
non   n. nobis, Domine 17.236
none   silver and gold have I n. 46.10
Gallio cared for n. of those things 46.40
noon-day   thy just dealing as the n. 17.84
the sickness that destroyeth in the n. 17.186
nose   a smoke in my n. 21.101
noses   n. . . . and smell not 17.237
nostrils   God . . . breathed into his n. 1.9
not   he was n. 1.25
thine eyes are upon me, and I am n. 16.20
nothing   if thou hast gathered n. in thy youth 39.19
toiled all the night, and . . . taken n. 44.19
circumcision is n. 48.19
as having n., and yet possessing all things 49.13
certain we can carry n. out 56.10
nought   man is like a thing of n. 17.289
a thing of n. 22.10
the thought of . . . the sea came likewise to n. 36.4
if this counsel . . . be of men, it will come to n. 46.15
so great riches is come to n. 67.56
nourisher   a n. of thine old age 8.3
now   n. is the accepted time 49.12
number   the n. of my days 17.88
a great multitude, which no man could n. 67.27
the n. of the beast . . . is the number of a man 67.42
numbered   n. with the transgressors 21.82
God hath n. thy kingdom, and finished it 25.10
the very hairs of your head are all n. 42.65
Nunc Dimittis   44.12

O

oak   Absalom hanged in an o. 10.10
obedient   o. unto death 52.4
obey   to o. is better than sacrifice 9.15
even the winds and the sea o. him 42.50
ought to o. God rather than men 46.14
children, o. your parents 51.13
oblations   vain o. 21.3
oblivion   forgotten, as a dead man 17.70
no remembrance of former things 19.3
your fathers, where are they? 33.1
obscurity   then shall thy light rise in o. 21.92
observation   the kingdom of God cometh not with o. 44.59
observeth   he that o. the wind shall not sow 19.38
obtain   so run, that ye may o. 48.27
odours   golden vials full of o. 67.20
offence   rock of o. 21.20
woe to that man by whom the o. cometh 42.113
a conscience void of o. toward God 46.56
the law entered, that the o. might abound 47.18
offences   remember not the sins and o. of my youth 17.50
offend   if thy right eye o. thee, pluck it out 42.21
whoso shall o. one of these little ones 42.112
offendeth   who can tell how oft he o.? 17.36
offering   a lamb for a burnt o. 1.50
office   if a man desire the o. of a bishop 56.4
offscouring   the o. of all things 48.10
offspring   the root and the o. of David 67.71
oil   a little o. in a cruse 11.15
a land of o. olive, and honey 5.2
ointment   dead flies cause the o. . . . to send forth a stinking savour 19.31
thy name is as o. 20.1
an alabaster box of very precious o. 42.160
old   o., and well stricken in age 1.52
a nourisher of thine o. age 8.3
an o. man, and heavy 9.9
o. and stricken in years 11.1
I have been young, and now am o. 17.85
I have considered the days of o. 17.160
wax o. as doth a garment 17.206
children's children are the crown of o. men 18.49

when he is o., he will not depart from it 18.70
your o. men shall dream dreams 27.5
the times begin to wax o. 36.6
new wine into o. bottles 42.54
out of his treasure things new and o. 42.94
the o. is better 44.20
the o. leaven 48.13
o. things are passed away 49.11
that o. serpent 67.38
old wives o.' fables 56.6
olive an o. leaf pluckt off 1.31
I am like a green o.-tree in the house of God 17.117
thy children like the o.-branches 17.267
Olivet the mount called O. 46.3
Omega Alpha and O. 67.2
omnipotent the Lord God o. reigneth 67.58
Onan O. knew that the seed should not be his 1.67
one two are better than o. 19.12
one thousand shall flee at the rebuke of o. 21.47
have we not all o. father? 34.1
wisdom ... being but o. ... can do all things 38.8
no more twain, but o. flesh 42.119
two be in the field; the o. shall be taken 42.151
but o. thing is needful 44.34
five in o. house divided 44.41
expedient that o. man should die for the people 45.74
some therefore cried o. thing, and some another 46.44
open o. to me, my sister, my love 20.15
he shall o., and none shall shut 21.36
an o. door, and no man can shut it 67.12
opened your eyes shall be o. 1.14
the eyes of the blind shall be o. 21.54
he was oppressed ... yet he o. not his mouth 21.81
knock, and it shall be o. unto you 42.36
a door was o. in heaven 67.16
when he had o. the seventh seal 67.29
openeth to him the porter o. 45.46
opinions how long halt ye between two o.? 11.17
opportunity wisdom ... cometh by o. of leisure 39.25
oppositions o. of science 56.15
oppressed he was o., and ... afflicted 21.81
oppression he looked for judgment, but behold o. 21.14
oppressor the rod of his o. 21.22
how hath the o. ceased 21.29
orator the eloquent o. 21.10
ordained the powers that be are o. of God 47.39
order set thine house in o. 12.16
wisdom ... sweetly doth ... o. all things 38.9
done decently and in o. 48.38
ordered he ... o. my goings 17.91
organ such as handle the harp and o. 1.24
Orion canst thou ... loose the bands of O.? 16.56
seek him that maketh the seven stars and O. 28.4
ornament the o. of a meek and quiet spirit 62.11
other I thank thee, that I am not as o. men 44.61
out-casts the Lord doth ... gather together the o. of Israel 17.294
outer o. darkness 42.47
outgoings the o. of the morning and evening 17.140
the o. of paradise 36.3
overcome I have o. the world 45.72
be not o. of evil 47.38
overcometh to him that o. 67.6
overconfidence be not righteous over much 19.22
let him that thinketh he standeth take heed 48.28
over-past until this tyranny be o. 17.125
overthrow if it be of God, ye cannot o. it 46.15
owe o. no man any thing 47.42
owl an o. ... in the desert 17.205
owls o. shall dwell there 21.28
a court for o. 21.51
own came unto his o., and his own received him not 45.1
ox thou shalt not muzzle the o. 5.10
as an o. goeth to the slaughter 18.19
a stalled o. and hatred therewith 18.42
the o. knoweth his owner, and the ass his master's crib 21.1
the lion shall eat straw like the o. 21.26
oxen that our o. may be strong to labour 17.290

P

paid I p. them the things that I never took 17.146
p. the uttermost farthing 42.20
pain it was p. and grief to me 17.88
the whole creation groaneth ... in p. 47.26
pains the p. of hell came about me 17.30
the p. of hell gat hold upon me 17.238
painted Jezebel ... p. her face 12.12
palaces plenteousness within thy p. 17.260
pale a p. horse 67.24
palmerworm that which the p. hath left hath the locust eaten 27.1
palms crowned, and receive p. 36.2
p. in their hands 67.27
palm-tree the righteous shall flourish like a p. 17.190
palsy sick of the p. 43.3
parable I will open my mouth in a p. 17.162

paradise the outgoings of p. 36.3
to day shalt thou be with me in p. 44.74
in the midst of the p. of God 67.6
parents children, obey your p. 51.13
part the Lord do so to me ... if ought but death p. thee and me 8.2
neither p. nor lot 46.22
we know in part, and we prophesy in p. 48.35
parting stood at the p. of the way 24.8
partridge as the p. sitteth on eggs 22.14
parts truth in the inward p. 17.114
pass I will p. through the land of Egypt 2.19
I will not again p. by them any more 28.6
heaven and earth shall p. away 42.149
let this cup p. from me 42.166
passed the people were p. clean over Jordan 6.3
p. by on the other side 44.31
p. from death unto life 45.23
old things are p. away 49.11
a great high priest, that is p. into the heavens 60.6
the former things are p. away 67.65
passeth the fashion of this world p. away 48.21
know the love of Christ, which p. knowledge 51.5
the peace of God, which p. all understanding 52.11
passover it is the Lord's p. 2.19
Christ our p. is sacrificed for us 48.13
past that is p. as a watch in the night 17.182
pastime leviathan ... made to take his p. 17.215
pastors p. that destroy and scatter the sheep 22.15
pasture the people of his p. 17.197
pastures he maketh me to lie down in green p. 17.46
path the p. of life 17.27
thou art about my p. 17.277
the p. of the just is as the shining light 18.11
paths thy word is ... a light unto my p. 17.249
all her p. are peace 18.8
make his p. straight 42.5
patience have p. ... and I will pay thee all 42.117
in your p. possess ... your souls 44.67
tribulation worketh p. 47.17
the God of p. and consolation 47.47
suffer fools gladly 49.17
p. of hope 54.1
run with p. the race that is set 60.16
let p. have her perfect work 61.1
the p. of Job 61.15
the kingdom and p. of Jesus Christ 67.2
hast borne, and hast p. 67.5
–*See also* perseverance.
patient the p. abiding of the meek 17.16
the p. in spirit is better than the proud 19.20
p. continuance in well doing 47.8
patiently take it p. 62.8
Paul P. ... a prisoner of Jesus Christ 59.1
pay better ... not vow, than ... vow and not p. 19.15
have patience ... and I will p. thee all 42.117
p. me that thou owest 42.118
peace is it p.? 12.10
what hast thou to do with p.? 12.10
I will lay me down in p., and take my rest 17.9
seek p., and ensue it 17.79
bring ... p. at the last 17.86
God that maketh men to be of one mind in an house 17.142
righteousness and p. have kissed each other 17.177
I labour for p., but ... they make them ready for battle 17.254
pray for the p. of Jerusalem 17.260
p. be within thy walls 17.260
p. upon Israel 17.268
all her paths are p. 18.8
a time of war, and a time of p. 19.9
beat their swords into plowshares 21.7
the Prince of P. 21.23
of the increase of his government and p. 21.23
the wolf ... shall dwell with the lamb 21.26
then had thy p. been as a river 21.73
no p. ... unto the wicked 21.74
that publisheth p. 21.80
the chastisement of our p. was upon him 21.81
p. to him that is far off 21.90
p. to him ... that is near 21.90
saying, p., peace; when there is no peace 22.4
we looked for p., but no good came 22.5
all the earth sitteth still, and is at rest 33.2
their bodies are buried in p. 39.29
not to send p., but a sword 42.66
to guide our feet into the way of p. 44.5
on earth p., good will toward men 44.10
depart in p. 44.12
p. be to this house 44.28
his goods are in p. 44.35
the things which belong unto thy p. 44.65
p. I leave with you 45.61
my p. I give unto you 45.61
these things I have spoken ... that in me ye might have p. 45.72
to be spiritually minded is life and p. 47.24
p. to you which were afar off 51.3
the bond of p. 51.6
the preparation of the gospel of p. 51.14
the p. of God, which passeth all understanding 52.11
mercy unto you, and p. ... be multiplied 66.1
peaceable wisdom ... from above is first pure, then p. 61.11
peaceably living p. in their habitations 39.28
live p. with all men 47.37
peacemakers blessed are the p. 42.15
p. ... shall be called the children of God 42.15
peacocks ivory, and apes, and p. 11.10

pearl one p. of great price 42.93
pearls p. before swine 42.35
a merchant man, seeking goodly p. 42.93
the twelve gates were twelve p. 67.67
peculiar a p. people 5.9
pelican a p. in the wilderness 17.205
pen my tongue is the p. of a ready writer 17.99
penny a measure of wheat for a p. 67.23
Pentecost when the day of P. was fully come 46.6
penury talk of the lips tendeth only to p. 18.38
people the p. arose as one man 7.18
thy p. shall be my people 8.2
ye are the p., and wisdom shall die with you 16.27
why do the p. imagine a vain thing? 17.2
a p. whom I have not known shall serve me 17.34
the p. of his pasture 17.197
judge ... the p. with equity 17.200
be the p. never so impatient 17.201
even so standeth the Lord round about his p. 17.263
kings of the earth and all p. 17.297
where no counsel is, the p. fall 18.28
where there is no vision, the p. perish 18.103
a p. of unclean lips 21.17
should not a p. seek unto their God? 21.21
the p. that walked in darkness 21.22
the p. is grass 21.59
how doth the city sit solitary, that was full of p. 23.1
expedient that one man should die for the p. 45.74
they shall be his p. 67.65
perceive how should God p. it? 17.155
see, and shall not p. 42.86
perception discern the signs of the times 42.104
perdition the son of p. 55.1
perfect God will not cast away a p. man 16.22
he that is p. in knowledge 16.53
that shineth more and more unto the p. day 18.11
p. in a short time 38.5
be ye therefore p. 42.25
when that which is p. is come 48.35
my strength is made p. in weakness 49.21
the man of God may be p. 57.5
the spirits of just men made p. 60.19
let patience have her p. work 61.1
every good gift and every p. gift 61.3
the p. law of liberty 61.4
p. love casteth out fear 64.8
perform the zeal of the Lord ... will p. this 21.23
perils in p. of waters 49.18
in p. of robbers 49.18
in p. in the sea 49.18
perish ye shall soon utterly p. from off the land 5.1
if I p., I perish 15.3
lest ... ye p. from the right way 17.5
they shall p., but thou shalt endure 17.206
then all his thoughts p. 17.292
where there is no vision, the people p. 18.103
if so be that God will think upon us, that we p. not 29.1
I p. through great grief in a strange land 40.1
Lord, save us: we p. 42.50
they that take the sword shall p. with the sword 42.169
that whosoever believeth ... should not p. 45.12
thy money p. with thee 46.22
the preaching of the cross is to them that p. foolishness 48.1
perished they p. from among the congregation 4.9
how are ... the weapons of war p. 10.3
their memorial is p. with them 17.15
my strength and my hope is p. from the Lord 23.3
p., as though they had never been 39.28
permission by p., and not of commandment 48.17
permitted p. to speak for thyself 46.58
perplexity distress of nations, with p. 44.68
persecute bless them which p. you 47.37
persecuted princes have p. me without a cause 17.253
blessed are they which are p. for righteousness' sake 42.15
being p., we suffer it 48.10
persecutest Saul, why p. thou me? 46.25
perseverance patient continuance in well doing 47.8
in due season ... reap, if we faint not 50.13
hast laboured, and hast not fainted 67.5
–*See also* patience.
Persians the laws of the P. and the Medes 15.1
thy kingdom is ... given to the Medes and P. 25.10
person God accepteth no man's p. 50.1
the express image of his p. 60.1
persons God is no respecter of p. 46.31
no respect of p. with God 47.9
having men's p. in admiration 66.4
persuaded neither will they be p., though one rose from the dead 44.57
let every man be fully p. in his own mind 47.45
persuadest almost thou p. me to be a Christian 46.61
persuasions their secret plots, and popular p. and commotions 35.8
pestilence the noisome p. 17.186
the p. that walketh in darkness 17.186
pestilent a p. fellow 46.55

Peter thou art P. 42.105
Pharisee a P., the son of a Pharisee 46.54
I lived a P. 46.59
as touching the law, a P. 52.6
Pharisees the scribes and P. 42.18
Philistines the P. be upon thee, Samson 7.16
philosophy p. and vain deceit 53.1
physician the p. cutteth off a long disease 39.10
honour a p. 39.24
they that be whole need not a p. 42.52
p., heal thyself 44.18
Luke, the beloved p. 53.9
physicians p. of no value 16.30
suffered many things of many p. 43.11
pieces thirty p. of silver 42.170
Pilate P. . . . washed his hands 42.172
pilgrimage the days of the years of my p. 1.75
the house of my p. 17.247
pilgrims strangers and p. on the earth 60.12
pillar a p. of salt 1.49
a p. of a cloud 2.22
a p. in the temple of my God 67.13
pillars the earth is weak . . . I bear up the p. of it 17.157
wisdom . . . hath hewn out her seven p. 18.21
Pillars of the Church 50.2
pipe praise him upon the strings and p. 17.300
piped we have p. unto you, and ye have not danced 42.73
pit cast him into some p. 1.65
alive into the p. 4.9
thou hast kept my life from them that go down to the p. 17.63
they have digged a p. . . . and are fallen into the midst of it 17.127
he that diggeth a p. shall fall into it 19.32
they that go down into the p. cannot hope for thy truth 21.58
the bottomless p. 67.32
pitch he that toucheth p. shall be defiled 39.13
pitcher the p. . . . broken at the fountain 19.40
pity I looked for some to have p. on me 17.148
place the Lord is in this p. 1.57
the p. whereon thou standest 2.6
neither shall his p. know him any more 16.21
he made darkness his secret p. 17.31
the p. where thine honour dwelleth 17.54
his p. could no where be found 17.86
the hill of Sion is a fair p. 17.108
the p. which thou hast appointed for them 17.212
as a nail in a sure p. 21.36
a p. and a name better than of sons and of daughters 21.88
I go to prepare a p. for you 45.56
neither was their p. found any more in heaven 67.38
places the lines are fallen unto me in pleasant p. 17.26
plague neither shall any p. come nigh thy dwelling 17.187
plagues the seven last p. 67.50
plain the rough places p. 21.59
plainness great p. of speech 49.5
plant a time to p., and a time to pluck up 19.9
the men of Judah his pleasant p. 21.14
he shall grow up . . . as a tender p. 21.81
they shall not p., and another eat 21.102
every p. . . . shall be rooted up 42.102
planted God p. a garden 1.9
like a tree p. by the water-side 17.1
p. . . . with the choicest vine 21.13
I have p., Apollos watered 48.6
planting trees of righteousness, the p. of the Lord 21.96
play the people . . . rose up to p. 2.38
played I have p. the fool 9.23
plead p. thou my cause, O Lord 17.80
pleasant every tree that is p. to the sight 1.9
lovely and p. in their lives 10.2
the lines are fallen unto me in p. places 17.26
bread eaten in secret is p. 18.22
how p. art thou, O love, for delights 20.22
the men of Judah his p. plant 21.14
pleasantness her ways are ways of p. 18.8
please he that is married careth . . . how he may p. his wife 48.22
pleased in whom I am well p. 42.8
pleasure at thy right hand . . . p. for evermore 17.27
in his p. is life 17.64
so shall the King have p. in thy beauty 17.100
he hath no p. in the strength of an horse 17.295
for thy p. they are and were created 67.17
pleasures he shall . . . be satisfied with the p. of thy house 17.140
Pleiades canst thou bind the sweet influences of P.? 16.56
plenteousness p. within thy palaces 17.260
plenty p. of corn and wine 1.54
the fat of the land 1.73
a land flowing with milk and honey 2.7
a land of brooks of water 5.2
thou visitest the earth, and blessest it 17.140
plots their secret p., and popular persuasions and commotions 35.8
plough having put his hand to the p. 44.27
plowed p. with my heifer 7.13
the plowers p. upon my back 17.269
p. wickedness . . . reaped iniquity 26.2
plowers the p. plowed upon my back 17.269
plowshares beat their swords into p. 21.7
beat your p. into swords 27.6
pluck if thy right eye offend thee, p. it out 42.21
plucked a firebrand p. out of the burning 28.3
a brand p. out of the fire 33.3

plumbline the Lord ... with a p. in his hand 28.6
point lieth at the p. of death 43.10
poison adder's p. is under their lips 17.282
pomp thy p. is brought down to the grave 21.30
ponder whoso is wise will p. these things 17.224
pondered Mary ... p. them in her heart 44.11
pool the parched ground shall become a p. 21.54
poor for the p. shall not alway be forgotten 17.16
as for me, I am p. and needy 17.92
he hath dispersed abroad, and given to the p. 17.231
the rich and p. meet together 18.69
a poor man that oppresseth the p. is like a sweeping rain 18.99
grind the faces of the p. 21.11
blessed are the p. in spirit 42.15
give to the p. 42.121
ye have the p. always with you 42.161
this p. widow hath cast more in 43.21
the p., and the maimed 44.44
bestow all my goods to feed the p. 48.35
as p., yet making many rich 49.13
popular p. persuasions and commotions 35.8
porter to him the p. openeth 45.46
portion a p. for foxes 17.138
neither have they any more a p. 19.26
divide him a p. with the great 21.82
possess in your patience p. ... your souls 44.67
possessed them that were p. with devils 43.1
possessing as having nothing, and yet p. all things 49.13
possession hast thou killed, and also taken p.? 11.27
possessions a man ... at rest in his p. 39.26
for he had great p. 42.121
possible with God all things are p. 43.19
potter hath not the p. power over the clay? 47.33
pour I will p. out my spirit upon all flesh 27.5
p. out the vials of the wrath of God 67.51
poured he hath p. out his soul unto death 21.82
poverty thy p. ... as one that travelleth 18.15
the destruction of the poor is their p. 18.26
talk of the lips tendeth only to penury 18.38
the drunkard and the glutton shall come to p. 18.74
give me neither p. nor riches 18.105
–*See also* poor.
power the p. of the dog 17.44
girded about with p. 17.140
p. of life and death 38.13
men renowned for their p. 39.28
endued with p. from on high 44.82
p. to become the sons of God 45.1
hath not the potter p. over the clay? 47.33
the kingdom of God is not in word, but in p. 48.11
put down all rule ... and p. 48.41
the excellency of the p. may be of God 49.6
the prince of the p. of the air 51.2
according to the p. that worketh in us 51.5
in the p. of his might 51.14
spirit ... of p., and of love 57.1
the word of his p. 60.1
p. was given unto them over the fourth part of the earth 67.24
p. was to hurt men 67.35
on such the second death hath no p. 67.63
powers the p. of the heavens ... shaken 42.148
nor principalities, nor p. 47.31
subject unto the higher p. 47.39
the p. that be 47.39
praise p. the Lord with harp 17.74
his p. shall ever be in my mouth 17.77
go ... into his courts with p. 17.202
unto thy name give the p. 17.235
his p. above heaven and earth 17.297
p. him in the cymbals and dances 17.300
p. him upon the strings and pipe 17.300
the grave cannot p. thee 21.58
let us now p. famous men 39.27
praised thou, O God, art p. in Sion 17.139
I p. the dead ... more than the living 19.10
praises sing ... p. with understanding 17.107
sing p. unto his name 17.142
the p. of God be in their mouth, and a two-edged sword in their hands 17.298
pray p. for the peace of Jerusalem 17.260
vain to p. for the dead 41.1
p. for them which despitefully use you 42.24
when ye p., use not vain repetitions 42.27
watch and p. 42.167
prayer the house of p. 42.130
whatsoever ye shall ask in p., believing 42.131
give ourselves continually to p. 46.16
continuing instant in p. 47.37
in every p. ... making request with joy 52.1
the effectual fervent p. of a righteous man 61.16
watch unto p. 62.14
–*See also* pray, praise.
prayers for a pretence make long p. 43.20
I make mention of you always in my p. 47.2
golden vials full of odours, which are the p. of saints 67.20
the smoke of the incense ... p. of the saints 67.30
preach what ye hear in the ear ... p. ye upon the housetops 42.64
p. the gospel to every creature 43.23
p. Christ crucified 48.2
preaching p. the gospel of the kingdom 42.14
the p. of the cross 48.1
by the foolishness of p. 48.2
precept for p. must be upon precept 21.41

precious let not their p. balms break my head 17.286
a stone most p. 67.66
preferred he ... coming after me is p. before me 45.3
preparation the p. of the gospel of peace 51.14
prepare p. ye the way of the Lord 21.59, 42.5
p. thy soul for temptation 39.1
I go to p. a place for you 45.56
who shall p. himself to the battle? 48.36
prepared the horse is p. against ... battle 18.68
p. for you from the foundation of the world 42.158
p. before the face of all people 44.12
eye hath not seen ... the things which God hath p. 48.5
presence come before his p. with thanksgiving 17.195
the angel of his p. 21.98
present evil is p. with me 47.22
nor things p., nor things to come 47.31
p. in spirit 48.12
good for the p. distress 48.20
having loved this p. world 57.8
preserve the Lord shall p. thee from all evil 17.257
p. me from the wicked man 17.282
preserved my life is p. 1.62
press the p. is full 27.7
p. toward the mark for the prize 52.8
pressed good measure, p. down 44.22
pretence for a p. make long prayers 43.20
prevail if one p. ... two shall withstand 19.13
the gates of hell shall not p. 42.105
prevailed he p. not against him 1.61
the blessings of thy father have p. 1.80
prey he shall devour the p. 1.81
have they not divided the p.? 7.7
the lions roaring after their p. ... seek 17.214
will a lion roar ... when he hath no p.? 28.1
price the p. of wisdom is above rubies 16.43
her p. is far above rubies 18.109
buy ... without money and without p. 21.84
one pearl of great p. 42.93
pricks to kick against the p. 46.25
pride ye shall be as gods 1.14
my power ... hath gotten me this wealth 5.3
I know thy p., and the naughtiness of thine heart 9.19
set not up your horn on high 17.157
p. goeth before destruction 18.45
I am not as other men are 44.61
the p. of life 64.4
priest a p. for ever after the order of Melchisedech 17.228
answerest thou the high p. so? 45.75
a great high p. 60.6
prince a p. and a judge over us 2.3
altogether a p. over us 4.8
the P. of Peace 21.23
casteth out devils through the p. of the devils 42.56
now shall the p. of this world be cast out 45.53
the p. of the power of the air 51.2
princes p. also did sit and speak against me 17.245
p. have persecuted me without a cause 17.253
put not your trust in p. 17.292
p. and all judges of the world 17.297
give children to be their p. 21.10
Tyre ... whose merchants are p. 21.37
principalities nor p., nor powers 47.31
printed oh that they were p. in a book 16.37
prison the Lord looseth men out of p. 17.293
the opening of the p. to them that are bound 21.96
in p., and ye came unto me 42.158
Satan shall be loosed out of his p. 67.63
prisoner the p. of the Lord 51.6
Paul ... a p. of Jesus Christ 59.1
prisoners God that ... bringeth the p. out of captivity 17.142
ye p. of hope 33.5
prisons in p. more frequent 49.18
prize in a race run all, but one receiveth the p. 48.27
press toward the mark for the p. 52.8
the p. of the high calling of God 52.8
Prodigal Son 44.48
profane p. and old wives' fables 56.6
p. and vain babblings 56.15
professed p. a good profession 56.12
professing p. themselves to be wise 47.6
profession hold fast our p. 60.6
profit what p. is there in my blood? 17.65
in all labour there is p. 18.38
what p. hath a man of all his labour? 19.1
wisdom ... with an inheritance ... is p. 19.21
what shall it p. a man, if he ... gain the whole world 43.15
profitable it is p. for thee that one of thy members should perish 42.21
godliness is p. 56.6
profiteth the flesh p. nothing 45.33
bodily exercise p. little 56.6
profundis de p. 17.272
prolonged the days are p., and every vision faileth 24.4
promotion p. cometh neither from the east, nor from the west 17.157
prophecies p., they shall fail 48.35
prophecy a more sure word of p. 63.1
prophesy p. not unto us right things 21.45
we know in part, and we p. in part 48.35
prophet there arose not a p. ... like unto Moses 5.23
he shall know that there is a p. in Israel 12.5
a p. ... and more than a prophet 42.71
a p. is not without honour 42.95
prophets would God that all the Lord's people were p. 4.5
is Saul also among the p.? 9.12

entering into holy souls, she maketh them ... p. 38.8
the law and the p. 42.38
beware of false p. 42.40
all the law and the p. 42.136
many p. and kings have desired to see 44.30
if they hear not Moses and the p. 44.57
propitiation the p. for our sins 64.3
proselyte compass sea and land to make one p. 42.139
prosper whatsoever he doeth, it shall p. 17.1
p. thou our handy-work 17.184
they shall p. that love thee 17.260
the Lord p. you 17.270
thou knowest not whether shall p., either this or that 19.39
prosperity in the day of p. be joyful 19.22
p. ... adversity ... God also hath set the one over against the other 19.22
proud the p. are risen against me 17.179
a p. look and a high stomach 17.204
the deep waters of the p. 17.261
the p. have ... spread a net 17.283
scattered the p. 44.3
proudly the child shall behave himself p. 21.10
prove she came to p. him with hard questions 11.8
I go to p. them 44.44
p. all things 54.5
proved I p. thee also at the waters of strife 17.170
proverb a p. and a byword 11.7
proverbs every one that useth p. 24.5
provide God will p. ... a lamb 1.50
provision make not p. for the flesh 47.43
provoke p. not your children 53.6
prudence I wisdom dwell with p. 18.20
which ... sitteth not down first, and counteth the cost? 44.46
prudent the p., and the ancient 21.10
hid these things from the wise and p. 42.75
pruning-hooks their spears into p. 21.7
publicans do not even the p. the same? 42.24
a friend of p. and sinners 42.74
publick a p. example 42.1
publish p. it not in the streets of Askelon 10.1
puffed charity ... is not p. up 48.35
puffeth knowledge p. up, but charity edifieth 48.23
pulling the p. down of strong holds 49.16
punishment my p. is greater than I can bear 1.22
purchased thought that the gift of God may be p. 46.22
pure the p. in heart 42.15
whatsoever things are p. 52.12
unto the p. all things are pure 58.2
p. religion and undefiled 61.5
wisdom ... from above is first p. 61.11
a p. river of water of life 67.68
purge p. me with hyssop 17.114
p. out ... the old leaven 48.13
purged thy sin p. 21.17
purpose a time to every p. under the heaven 19.9
to what p. is this waste? 42.160
purse let us all have one p. 18.3
carry neither p., nor scrip 44.28
pursueth the wicked flee when no man p. 18.98
pursuing faint, yet p. 7.10
put p. her away privily 42.1
p. down the mighty 44.3
p. on the armour of light 47.43
p. ye on the Lord Jesus Christ 47.43
I p. away childish things 48.35
p. down all rule and all authority 48.41

Q

quaked the whole mount q. greatly 2.28
queen the q. of Sheba 11.8
q. of the south 42.82
I sit a q. 67.55
queens q. thy nursing mothers 21.76
quench many waters cannot q. love 20.26
the smoking flax shall he not q. 21.66
q. all the fiery darts of the wicked 51.14
quenched the fire is not q. 43.17
question called in q. for this day's uproar 46.46
questions she came to prove him with hard q. 11.8
both hearing them, and asking them q. 44.13
which minister q. 56.1
quicken q. thou me in thy way 17.246
quickeneth the spirit that q. 45.33
quickly agree with thine adversary q. 42.20
behold, I come q. 67.70
quiet the words of wise men are heard in q. 19.30
a wife full of words to a q. man 39.20
be q., and ... do nothing rashly 46.45
study to be q. 54.2
the ornament of a meek and q. spirit 62.11
quietness better is an handful with q. 19.11
quit q. yourselves like men 9.7
quiver happy is the man that hath his q. full of them 17.265
quo q. vadis? 45.67

R

Rabboni R.; which is to say, Master 45.89
race the r. is not to the swift 19.29
in a r. run all, but one receiveth the prize 48.27
run with patience the r. that is set 60.16

Rachel R. weeping for her children 42.4
rage the heathen so furiously r. together 17.2
the waters thereof r. and swell 17.103
raging who stilleth the r. of the sea 17.140
strong drink is r. 18.58
r. waves of the sea 66.3
rags all our righteousnesses are as filthy r. 21.100
railing a r. accusation 66.2
raiment r. of needle-work 17.101
the body than r. 42.30
a man clothed in soft r. 42.71
they parted his r., and cast lots 44.73
rain sound of abundance of r. 11.19
hath the r. a father? 16.55
thou sendest r. into the little valleys thereof 17.140
he shall come down like the r. 17.153
the r. is over and gone 20.6
he . . . sendeth r. on the just and on the unjust 42.24
the r. descended 42.44
raise I will r. him up at the last day 45.31
raised Christ being r. from the dead 47.20
r. in incorruption 48.43
ram a r. caught in a thicket 1.51
Rama in R. was there a voice heard 42.4
rams the mountains skipped like r. 17.233
ran the swine . . . r. violently down a steep place 43.8
they r. both together 45.88
r. upon him with one accord 46.19
ransomed the r. of the Lord shall return 21.55
rashly be quiet, and . . . do nothing r. 46.45
ravens I have commanded the r. to feed thee 11.14
razor there shall no r. come upon his head 4.2
reaching r. forth unto those things which are before 52.8
readest understandest thou what thou r.? 46.23
readeth that he may run that r. it 31.1
whoso r., let him understand 42.146
readiness your loins girded 2.19
here am I 9.4
every one had his sword girded by his side, and so builded 14.1
beat your plowshares into swords 27.6
when the master of the house cometh 43.22
ready r. to distribute 56.14
reap they that sow in tears shall r. in joy 17.264
he that regardeth the clouds shall not r. 19.38
sown the wind . . . r. the whirlwind 26.1
sow . . . in righteousness, r. in mercy 26.2
the fowls of the air . . . sow not, neither do they r. 42.31
to r. that whereon ye bestowed no labour 45.20
whatsoever a man soweth, that shall he also r. 50.13
reaped plowed wickedness . . . r. iniquity 26.2
reapers the r. are the angels 42.92
reaping r. where thou hast not sown 42.155
reason I desire to r. with God 16.30
the sluggard is wiser . . . than seven men that can render a r. 18.87
let us r. together, saith the Lord 21.4
not r. that we should leave the word of God 46.16
not r. that we should . . . serve tables 46.16
rebellion r. is as the sin of witchcraft 9.15
rebellious a revolting and a r. heart 22.2
rebuke thy r. hath broken my heart 17.148
at thy r. . . . both the chariot and horse are fallen 17.159
at thy r. they flee 17.212
open r. is better than secret love 18.92
one thousand shall flee at the r. of one 21.47
the Lord r. thee, O Satan 33.3
r. not an elder 56.7
the Lord r. thee 66.2
rebuked he . . . r. the winds and the sea 42.50
receipt sitting at the r. of custom 42.51
receive whoso shall r. one such little child 42.112
believing, ye shall r. 42.131
received freely ye have r., freely give 42.59
his own r. him not 45.1
a cloud r. him out of their sight 46.2
receiveth every one that asketh r. 42.36
scourgeth every son whom he r. 60.17
Rechabites sons of the house of the R. 22.18
recompence to me belongeth vengeance, and r. 5.19
recompense r. to no man evil for evil 47.37
recover r. the leper 12.6
red his eyes shall be r. with wine 1.77
the wine when it is r. 18.75
fair weather: for the sky is r. 42.104
redeemed he hath visited and r. his people 44.4
r. from the earth 67.43
redeemer I know that my r. liveth 16.38
O Lord, my strength, and my r. 17.37
redeeming r. the time 51.11
redemption thou shalt not leave my soul in hell 17.27
he shall save his soul alive 24.7
God . . . hath shut the lions' mouths 25.12
should not perish, but have everlasting life 45.12
sealed unto the day of r. 51.9
reed thou trustest in . . . this broken r. 21.56
a bruised r. shall he not break 21.66
a r. shaken with the wind 42.71
reel they r. to and fro 17.221
refined I have r. thee, but not with silver 21.72
refiner like a r.'s fire 34.2
refrain r. from these men 46.15
refreshed like a giant r. with wine 17.166
refuge the eternal God is thy r. 5.21
the God of Jacob is our r. 17.105

Lord ... our r. from one generation to another 17.181
the high hills are a r. for the wild goats 17.213
the r. of lies 21.42
refuse r. the evil, and choose the good 21.19
refused nothing to be r. 56.5
regardeth he that r. the day 47.45
reign r., till he hath put all enemies under his feet 48.41
reigneth thy God r. 21.80
the Lord God omnipotent r. 67.58
rejected despised and r. of men 21.81
rejoice the bones which thou hast broken may r. 17.114
the little hills shall r. on every side 17.140
let us heartily r. in the strength of our salvation 17.195
let the saints ... r. in their beds 17.298
r. with the wife of thy youth 18.13
she shall r. in time to come 18.111
as men r. when they divide the spoil 21.22
the desert shall r., and blossom 21.52
rejoice with them that do r. 47.37
r. in the Lord alway 52.10
again I say, r. 52.10
r. with joy unspeakable 62.2
rejoiced my spirit hath r. in God my Saviour 44.2
rejoicing he layeth it on his shoulders, r. 44.47
r. in hope 47.37
religion pure r. and undefiled 61.5
remain gather up the fragments that r. 45.27
remaineth much more that which r. is glorious 49.5
remember r. now thy Creator 19.40
when they are from the wine, they r. not what they have done 35.2
r. Lot's wife 44.60
r. me when thou comest into thy kingdom 44.74
remembered have I not r. thee in my bed? 17.137
remembereth in death no man r. thee 17.12
remembrance his r. shall perish from the earth 16.35
the righteous shall be had in everlasting r. 17.230
there is no r. of former things 19.3
O death, how bitter is the r. of thee 39.26
I thank my God upon every r. of you 52.1
remission without shedding of blood is no r. 60.9
remnant the r. of Jacob shall be ... as a dew 30.3
remove r. not the old landmark 18.72
say unto this mountain, r. 42.109
r. this cup from me 44.70
all faith, so that I could r. mountains 48.35
removeth cursed be he that r. his neighbour's landmark 5.11
he r. kings, and setteth up kings 25.2
rend a time to r., and a time to sew 19.9
oh that thou wouldest r. the heavens 21.99
render r. ... unto Caesar 42.134
r. therefore to all their dues 47.42
husband r. unto the wife due benevolence 48.16
rendering not r. evil for evil 62.13
renew r. a right spirit within me 17.114
they that wait upon the Lord shall r. their strength 21.64
renewal I will put a new spirit within you 24.2
walk in newness of life 47.19
renown men of r. 1.27
renowned men r. for their power 39.28
repay whatsoever thou spendest more ... I will r. 44.32
vengeance is mine; I will r. 47.37
repeateth he that r. a matter separateth very friends 18.50
repent I ... r. in dust and ashes 16.63
r.: for the kingdom of heaven is at hand 42.12
repentance Ahab ... went softly 11.29
baptize ... with water unto r. 42.7
but sinners to r. 42.52
found no place of r. 60.18
repented it r. the Lord that he had made man 1.28
repenteth joy ... over one sinner that r. 44.47
repetitions vain r. 42.27
report who hath believed our r.? 21.81
whatsoever things are of good r. 52.12
reproach let us be called by thy name, to take away our r. 21.12
the r. of Christ greater riches 60.13
reputation a little folly ... in r. for wisdom and honour 19.31
made himself of no r. 52.4
request in every prayer ... making r. with joy 52.1
require what doth the Lord r. of thee? 30.4
required thy soul shall be r. of thee 44.38
resist r. the devil, and he will flee 61.12
whom r. stedfast in the faith 62.16
respect neither doth God r. any person 10.8
no r. of persons with God 47.9
respecter God is no r. of persons 46.31
rest no r. for the sole of her foot 1.30
r. was good 1.78
I should have slept: then had I been at r. 16.7
there the weary be at r. 16.8
I was not in safety, neither had I r. 16.10
I will lay me down in peace, and take my r. 17.9
who shall r. upon thy holy hill? 17.23
then would I flee away, and be at r. 17.119
glad, because they are at r. 17.222
if a wise man contendeth with a foolish ... there is no r. 18.101
all the earth sitteth still, and is at r. 33.2
a man ... at r. in his possessions 39.26
all ye that labour ... and I will give you r. 42.76
r. not day and night 67.16

they may r. from their labours 67.47
rested God . . . r. on the seventh day 1.8
restore I will r. to you the years that the locust hath eaten 27.4
Elias truly shall . . . r. all things 42.108
resurrection I am the r., and the life 45.50
by man came also the r. of the dead 48.40
part in the first r. 67.63
return unto dust shalt thou r. 1.18
before I go whence I shall not r. 16.25
the spirit shall r. unto God who gave it 19.40
r., return, O Shulamite 20.20
the ransomed of the Lord shall r. 21.55
returned r. to give glory to God 44.58
revealed nothing covered, that shall not be r. 42.64
things . . . r. . . . unto babes 42.75
the righteousness of God r. from faith 47.5
revealeth he r. the deep and secret things 25.2
revenge eye for eye 2.31
to be belongeth vengeance 5.19
vengeance is mine 47.37
reverence the wife see that she r. her husband 51.12
reviled being r., we bless 48.10
revolting a r. and a rebellious heart 22.2
reward thy exceeding great r. 1.41
in keeping of them there is great r. 17.36
two . . . have a good r. for their labour 19.12
what r. have ye? 42.24
they have their r. 42.26
thy Father which seeth in secret . . . shall r. thee openly 42.26
the due r. of our deeds 44.74
the r. of iniquity 46.4
respect unto the recompence of the r. 60.13
my r. is with me 67.70
rewarded having been a little chastised, they shall be greatly r. 38.3
rib the r. . . . made he a woman 1.12
ribs God . . . took one of his r. 1.12
rich the r. man's wealth is his strong city 18.26
the r. and poor meet together 18.69
he that maketh haste to be r. shall not be innocent 18.100
the abundance of the r. will not suffer him to sleep 19.16
curse not the r. in thy bedchamber 19.35
a labouring man . . . given to drunkenness shall not be r. 39.17
r. men furnished with ability 39.28
a r. man shall hardly enter into . . . heaven 42.122
the r. he hath sent empty away 44.3
woe unto you that are r. 44.21
he that . . . is not r. toward God 44.38
a certain r. man . . . fared sumptuously every day 44.55
as poor, yet making many r. 49.13
r. in good works 56.14
riches he hath swallowed down r., and he shall vomit them up again 16.40
if r. increase, set not your heart upon them 17.135
in her left hand r. and honour 18.8
r. profit not in the day of wrath 18.27
a good name is rather . . . than great r. 18.69
r. certainly make themselves wings 18.71
give me neither poverty nor r. 18.105
nor yet r. to men of understanding 19.29
he that getteth r., and not by right 22.14
the deceitfulness of r. 42.88
the unsearchable r. of Christ 51.4
the reproach of Christ greater r. 60.13
so great r. is come to nought 67.56
–*See also* rich, wealth.
riding horsemen r. upon horses 24.9
right every man did that which was r. in his own eyes 7.17
the thing which is r. 17.23
every way of a man is r. in his own eyes 18.66
he that getteth riches, and not by r. 22.14
in his r. mind 43.9
thy heart is not r. in the sight of God 46.22
the armour of righteousness on the r. hand 49.13
right hand sit thou on my r. 17.227
let not thy left hand know what thy r. doeth 42.26
to sit on my r. . . . is not mine to give 42.127
the sheep on his r. 42.157
righteous to slay the r. with the wicked 1.47
yet saw I never the r. forsaken 17.85
let them . . . not be written among the r. 17.149
the r. shall flourish like a palm-tree 17.190
the r. shall be had in everlasting remembrance 17.230
the voice of joy and health is in the dwellings of the r. 17.240
the rod of the ungodly cometh not into the lot of the r. 17.263
let the r. . . . smite me friendly 17.286
a r. man regardeth the life of his beast 18.31
the r. are bold as a lion 18.98
be not r. over much 19.22
the r. perisheth, and no man layeth it to heart 21.89
the r. is taken away from the evil to come 21.89
the souls of the r. are in the hand of God 38.3
not come to call the r. 42.52
the effectual fervent prayer of a r. man 61.16
he that is r., let him be righteous still 67.70
righteousness he counted it to him for r. 1.42
I will . . . ascribe r. to my Maker 16.53
the paths of r. 17.45
thy r. as clear as the light 17.84
r. and peace have kissed each other 17.177
r. hath looked down from heaven 17.177
r. shall go before him 17.178
with r. shall he judge the world 17.200
r. exalteth a nation 18.39

a just man ... perisheth in his r. 19.22
he looked for ... r., but behold a cry 21.14
r. to the plummet 21.42
thy r. as the waves of the sea 21.73
trees of r. 21.96
sow ... in r., reap in mercy 26.2
the Sun of r. 34.3
to fulfil all r. 42.8
blessed are they which do hunger and thirst after r. 42.15
the r. of the scribes and Pharisees 42.18
seek ye first the kingdom of God, and his r. 42.32
the r. of God revealed from faith 47.5
the armour of r. 49.13
the breastplate of r. 51.14
a crown of r. 57.7
the wrath of man worketh not the r. of God 61.4
in r. he doth judge and make war 67.60
–*See also* righteous.
righteousnesses all our r. are as filthy rags 21.100
rioting not in r. and drunkenness 47.43
riotous r. living 44.48
ripe the harvest is r. 27.7
the harvest of the earth is r. 67.48
rise r. up, my love ... and come away 20.6
he maketh his sun to r. on the evil and on the good 42.24
in the name of Jesus ... r. up and walk 46.10
risen we are r., and stand upright 17.39
the glory of the Lord is r. upon thee 21.94
the Lord is r. indeed 44.81
now is Christ r. from the dead 48.40
rising kings to the brightness of thy r. 21.94
river a r. went out of Eden 1.9
the r. of God is full of water 17.140
a pure r. of water of life 67.68
a pure r. ... proceeding out of the throne of God 67.68
rivers Abana and Pharpar, r. of Damascus 12.6
he sendeth the springs into the r. 17.212
turn our captivity ... as the r. in the south 17.264
all the r. run into the sea; yet the sea is not full 19.2
rob a man ... goeth his way to r. 35.5
robbed when he hath ... r., he bringeth it to his love 35.5
robber a thief and a r. 45.46
now Barabbas was a r. 45.77
robbers in perils of r. 49.18
robes clothed with white r. 67.27
washed their r. ... in the blood of the Lamb 67.28
rock he smote the r. twice 4.11
the r. of his salvation 5.17
my stony r., and my defence 17.29
be thou my strong r., and house of defence 17.67
the r. that is higher than I 17.134
who turned the hard r. into a standing water 17.234
r. of offence 21.20
the shadow of a great r. in a weary land 21.50
a wise man, which built his house upon a r. 42.44
upon this r. I will build my church 42.105
rocks go into the holes of the r. 21.8
rod Aaron's r. 2.14
the r. of Aaron ... was budded 4.10
bruise them with a r. of iron 17.4
thy r. and thy staff comfort me 17.45
the r. of the ungodly cometh not into the lot of the righteous 17.263
he that spareth his r. hateth his son 18.35
a r. for the fool's back 18.84
the r. of his oppressor 21.22
as if the r. should shake itself 21.24
a r. out of the stem of Jesse 21.25
rule them with a r. of iron 67.10
room no r. for them in the inn 44.8
rooms the uppermost r. at feasts 42.137
root the r. of the matter 16.39
their stock shall not take r. 21.63
as a r. out of a dry ground 21.81
leave them neither r. nor branch 34.3
the axe is laid unto the r. of the trees 42.7
because they had no r., they withered away 42.85
ye r. up also the wheat 42.90
love of money is the r. of all evil 56.11
the r. and the offspring of David 67.71
rooted every plant ... shall be r. up 42.102
r. and grounded in love 51.5
roots his r. shall be dried up beneath 16.35
a branch shall grow out of his r. 21.25
rose the r. of Sharon 20.3
the desert shall ... blossom as the r. 21.52
neither will they be persuaded, though one r. from the dead 44.57
rot the name of the wicked shall r. 18.24
rough the r. places plain 21.59
rubies the price of wisdom is above r. 16.43
wisdom is better than r. 18.20
her price is far above r. 18.109
ruddy r., and withal of a beautiful countenance 9.18
my beloved is white and r. 20.17
rudiments after the r. of the world 53.1
rule he shall r. over thee 1.17
babes shall r. over them 21.10
do not men excel in strength, that bear r.? 35.3
such as did bear r. in their kingdoms 39.28
put down all r. and all authority 48.41
r. them with a rod of iron 67.10
ruler out of thee shall he come forth ... r. in Israel 30.2
rulers r. are not a terror to good works 47.40
against the r. of the darkness of this world 51.14

ruleth the cry of him that r. among fools 19.30
rumours wars and r. of wars 42.144
run grin like a dog, and r. about 17.130
they will r. here and there for meat 17.131
draw me, we will r. after thee 20.1
they shall r., and not be weary 21.64
their feet r. to evil 21.93
many shall r. to and fro 25.14
that he may r. that readeth it 31.1
the eyes of the Lord, which r. to and fro 33.4
r. to and fro like sparks 38.4
in a race r. all, but one receiveth the prize 48.27
so r., that ye may obtain 48.27
r. with patience the race that is set 60.16
runneth my cup r. over 17.47
nor of him that r. 47.32
running good measure ... r. over 44.22
rushing a r. mighty wind 46.6
rust where moth and r. doth corrupt 42.28
Ruth and Naomi 8.2

S

sabbath the s. day, to keep it holy 2.29
the s. was made for man 43.4
the Son of man is Lord also of the s. 43.4
a s. day's journey 46.3
sabbaths the new moons and s. ... I cannot away with 21.3
sackcloth Ahab ... lay in s., and went softly 11.29
sacrifice to obey is better than s. 9.15
thou desirest no s., else would I give it thee 17.116
a living s., holy, acceptable 47.36
sacrificed Christ our passover is s. for us 48.13
safe thou shalt be s. under his feathers 17.186
s. and sound 44.51
safety I was not in s., neither had I rest 16.10
thou, Lord ... makest me dwell in s. 17.9
thou hast covered my head in ... battle 17.284
in the multitude of counsellors there is s. 18.28
s. is of the Lord 18.68
when a strong man armed keepeth 44.35
delivered out of the mouth of the lion 57.9
said the fool hath s. in his heart 17.21
I was glad when they s. unto me 17.258
thou hast s. 42.162
saints let the s. be joyful with glory 17.298
many bodies of the s. which slept arose 42.175
less than the least of all s. 51.4
golden vials full of odours, which are the prayers of s. 67.20
saith not every one that s. ... Lord, Lord 42.42
sake for thy s. also are we killed 17.98
salt a pillar of s. 1.49
the s. of the earth 42.16
if the s. have lost his savour 42.16
speech ... seasoned with s. 53.8
salutation what manner of s. this should be 44.1
salute s. no man by the way 44.28
s. one another with an holy kiss 47.48
salvation I have waited for thy s. 1.79
the rock of his s. 5.17
s. belongeth unto the Lord 17.7
exceeding glad shall he be of thy s. 17.40
the Lord is my light, and my s. 17.55
let us heartily rejoice in the strength of our s. 17.195
water out of the wells of s. 21.27
s. is of the Lord 29.3
mine eyes have seen thy s. 44.12
our s. nearer 47.43
the helmet of s. 51.14
work out your own s. 52.5
Samaritan but a certain S. ... had compassion on him 44.32
thou art a S., and hast a devil 45.41
same the s. is my brother 42.84
the s. yesterday, and to day, and for ever 60.21
Samson the Philistines be upon thee, S. 7.16
Samuel S. ministered before the Lord 9.2
S. ... answered, here am I 9.4
sand the s. stood up and stopped them 36.4
a foolish man, which built his house upon the s. 42.44
sang when the morning stars s. together 16.54
sardine a jasper and a s. stone 67.16
sat by the waters of Babylon we s. down and wept 17.276
Satan the Lord rebuke thee, O S. 33.3
how can S. cast out Satan? 43.6
beheld S. as lightning fall from heaven 44.29
serpent, called the devil, and S. 67.38
S. shall be loosed out of his prison 67.63
satisfied he shall ... be s. with the pleasures of thy house 17.140
the eyes of man are never s. 18.96
three things that are never s. 18.106
the eye is not s. with seeing 19.2
satisfieth your labour for that which s. not 21.84
satisfy with long life will I s. him 17.188
let her breasts s. thee 18.13
satyrs s. shall dance there 21.28
Saul is S. also among the prophets? 9.12
S. hath slain his thousands 9.22
S. was consenting unto his death 46.21
save a horse is counted but a vain thing to s. a man 17.76
he shall s. his soul alive 24.7
Lord, s. us: we perish 42.50
Christ Jesus came into the world to s. sinners 56.2
saved the angel of his presence s. them 21.98
the harvest is past ... and we are not s. 22.6
the summer is ended, and we are not s. 22.6

he that endureth to the end shall be s. 42.62
he s. others; himself he cannot save 42.173
who then can be s.? 43.19
thy faith hath s. thee 44.26
by me if any man enter in, he shall be s. 45.47
through the grace of ... Christ we shall be s. 46.35
Saviour my spirit hath rejoiced in God my S. 44.2
savour the Lord smelled a sweet s. 1.32
if the salt have lost his s. 42.16
saw shall the s. magnify itself? 21.24
under the fig tree, I s. thee 45.5
I s. the dead, small and great, stand before God 67.64
say s. now Shibboleth 7.11
I have somewhat to s. 11.3
s. on 11.3
I have yet many things to s. ... but ye cannot bear them 45.69
if we s. that we have no sin, we deceive 64.2
saying if a man keep my s., he shall never see death 45.42
a faithful s. 56.2
sayings the words of the wise, and their dark s. 18.1
whosoever heareth these s. 42.44
scalp the hairy s. of such ... as goeth on still in his wickedness 17.144
scapegoat a s. into the wilderness 3.2
scarlet though your sins be as s. 21.4
Scarlet Woman 67.54
scatter pastors that destroy and s. the sheep 22.15
scattered s. ... as sheep that have not a shepherd 11.30
s. abroad, as sheep having no shepherd 42.57
s. the proud 44.3
scattereth he that gathereth not ... s. abroad 42.77
sceptre the s. shall not depart 1.76
schoolmaster the law was our s. 50.4
no longer under a s. 50.4
science oppositions of s. falsely so called 56.15
scorn he ... shall laugh them to s. 17.3
scornful the seat of the s. 17.1
scorning Job ... drinketh up s. 16.50
scorpions I will chastise you with s. 11.12
dwell among s. 24.1
scourgeth s. every son whom he receiveth 60.17
scribes as one having authority, and not as the s. 42.45
scrip carry neither purse, nor s. 44.28
scriptures search the s. 45.25
scroll the heaven departed as a s. 67.26
sea the midst of the s. upon dry ground 2.23
them that remain in the broad s. 17.140
the s. is his 17.195
let the s. make a noise, and all that therein is 17.200
the great and wide s. 17.215
they that go down to the s. in ships 17.221
the s. saw that, and fled 17.233
all the rivers run into the s.; yet the sea is not full 19.2
the earth shall be full ... as the waters cover the s. 21.26
the spreading of nets in the midst of the s. 24.10
the thought of ... the s. came likewise to nought 36.4
even the winds and the s. obey him 42.50
Jesus ... walking on the s. 42.97
in perils in the s. 49.18
s. of glass like unto crystal 67.16
s. of glass mingled with fire 67.50
the s. gave up the dead 67.64
there was no more s. 67.65
seal set me as a s. upon thine heart 20.26
shut up the words, and s. the book 25.14
the seventh s. 67.29
hurt ... only those men which have not the s. of God 67.33
sealed a fountain s. 20.12
s. unto the day of redemption 51.9
seals sealed with seven s. 67.18
search the honour of kings is to s. out a matter 18.80
I gave my heart to ... s. out ... all things 19.4
s. the scriptures 45.25
searched O Lord, thou hast s. me out 17.277
searching canst thou by s. find out God? 16.26
searchings there were great s. of heart 7.4
Seas the waters called he S. 1.3
season meat in due s. 17.215
a word spoken in due s., how good is it 18.44
to every thing there is a s. 19.9
a word in s. to him that is weary 21.77
in due s. we shall reap, if we faint not 50.13
be instant in s., out of season 57.6
seasoned speech ... s. with salt 53.8
seasons he changeth the times and the s. 25.2
not for you to know the times or the s. 46.1
after what manner I have been with you at all s. 46.47
second on such the s. death hath no power 67.63
secret s. things belong unto the Lord 5.12
he made darkness his s. place 17.31
bread eaten in s. is pleasant 18.22
he revealeth the deep and s. things 25.2
thy Father which seeth in s. ... shall reward thee openly 42.26
secretly s. for fear of the Jews 45.85
sect this s. ... every where it is spoken against 46.63
securely thy neighbour ... dwelleth s. by thee 18.9
sedition a mover of s. 46.55
seducers evil men and s. 57.4
see there shall no man s. me, and live 2.43
he that made the eye, shall he not s.? 17.194
these men s. the works of the Lord 17.221

eyes . . . and s. not 17.237
I s. that all things come to an end 17.248
thou shalt s. thy children's children 17.268
what will ye s. in the Shulamite? 20.20
lest they s. with their eyes 21.18
they shall s. eye to eye 21.80
eyes to s., and see not 24.3
seeing ye shall s. 42.86
what is that to us? s. thou to that 42.170
desired to see those things which ye s. 44.30
except a man be born again, he cannot s. the kingdom of God 45.8
whereas I was blind, now I s. 45.45
a little while, and ye shall not s. me 45.70
except I shall s. in his hands the print of the nails 45.91
s. through a glass, darkly 48.35
every eye shall s. him 67.2
they shall s. his face 67.69
seed Onan knew that the s. should not be his 1.67
a grain of mustard s. 42.91
seeds the least of all s. 42.91
seedtime s. and harvest 1.32
seeing the eye is not satisfied with s. 19.2
seek s. peace, and ensue it 17.79
s. unto them that have familiar spirits 21.21
should not a people s. unto their God? 21.21
s. ye the Lord while he may be found 21.85
s. him that maketh the seven stars 28.4
the Lord, whom ye s. 34.2
s. ye first the kingdom of God 42.32
s., and ye shall find 42.36
why s. ye the living among the dead? 44.77
men s. death, and shall not find it 67.34
seekest s. thou great things for thyself? 22.19
seeketh an evil . . . generation s. after a sign 42.81
charity . . . s. not her own 48.35
seeking s. whom he may devour 62.16
seen before I go hence, and be no more s. 17.90
no man hath s. God at any time 45.2
he that hath s. me hath seen the Father 45.58
blessed are they that have not s., and yet have believed 45.92
eye hath not s. 48.5
faith . . . the evidence of things not s. 60.11
whom having not s., ye love 62.2
seeth the Lord s. not as man seeth 9.17
I have heard of thee . . . but now mine eye s. 16.63
the world s. me no more 45.60
sell go and s. that thou hast 42.121
send whom shall I s.? 21.17
here am I; s. me 21.17
sensual earthly, s., devilish 61.10
sent I AM hath s. me unto you 2.8
s. empty away 44.3
a man s. from God 45.1
sentence O death, acceptable is thy s. 39.26
sentences I will declare hard s. 17.162
separate he shall s. them one from another 42.157
nor height, nor depth . . . able to s. us 47.31
separated s. unto the gospel of God 47.1
separation the Lord watch between me and thee 1.60
good news from a far country 18.83
sepulchre no man knoweth of his s. 5.22
their throat is an open s. 17.11
a new s., wherein was never man yet laid 45.86
the stone taken away from the s. 45.87
his s. is with us unto this day 46.8
sepulchres whited s. 42.141
seraphims the s.: each one had six wings 21.17
Sermon on the Mount 42.15
serpent the s. was more subtil 1.13
the s. beguiled me 1.17
a s. by the way 1.79
sharpened their tongues like a s. 17.282
wine . . . biteth like a s. 18.75
the way of a s. upon a rock 18.107
whoso breaketh an hedge, a s. shall bite 19.32
leviathan the piercing s. 21.40
as Moses lifted up the s. in the wilderness 45.11
that old s. 67.38
serpents wise as s. 42.61
servant a s. unto tribute 1.78
speak, Lord; for thy s. heareth 9.5
is thy s. a dog? 12.9
my righteous s. . . . shall bear their iniquities 21.82
he that is greatest . . . shall be your s. 42.138
thou good and faithful s. 42.154
the unprofitable s. 42.156
lettest thou thy s. depart 44.12
the form of a s. 52.4
servants how many hired s. of my father's have bread enough 44.49
serve a people whom I have not known shall s. me 17.34
s. the Lord with gladness 17.202
if thou . . . s. the Lord, prepare . . . for temptation 39.1
no man can s. two masters 42.30
not reason that we should . . . s. tables 46.16
served worshipped and s. the creature more than the Creator 47.7
servest thy God whom thou s. continually, he will deliver thee 25.11
serveth I am among you as he that s. 44.69
service whosoever killeth you will think that he doeth God s. 45.65
–See also serve.
serving s. either calamity or tyranny 38.12
Martha was cumbered about much s. 44.34
s. the Lord with all humility of mind 46.47
set s. thine house in order 12.16
s. not up your horn on high 17.157
s. me as a seal upon thine heart 20.26
s. thine heart upon all that I shall shew 24.13
a city . . . s. on an hill cannot be hid 42.16

setter a s. forth of strange gods 46.37
setteth he that s. not by himself 17.24
he removeth kings, and s. up kings 25.2
settle s. it ... in your hearts 44.66
seven Jacob served s. years for Rachel 1.59
wisdom ... hath hewn out her s. pillars 18.21
heat the furnace one s. times more 25.6
till s. times? 42.116
s. men of honest report 46.16
s. golden candlesticks 67.2
in his right hand s. stars 67.2
the s. spirits of God 67.16
sealed with s. seals 67.18
the s. last plagues 67.50
seventh God ... rested on the s. day 1.8
the s. seal 67.29
seventy until s. times seven 42.116
sew a time to rend, and a time to s. 19.9
shadow the land of darkness and the s. of death 16.25
hide me under the s. of thy wings 17.28
the valley of the s. of death 17.45
man walketh in a vain s. 17.88
abide under the s. of the Almighty 17.185
the s. of a great rock in a weary land 21.50
that ... turneth the s. of death into the morning 28.4
neither s. of turning 61.3
shadows until the day break, and the s. flee away 20.8
shake I will go out ... and s. myself 7.16
as if the rod should s. itself 21.24
s. off the dust of your feet 42.60
shaken a reed s. with the wind 42.71
the powers of the heavens ... s. 42.148
good measure ... s. together 44.22
shaking behold a s. 24.12
shame they were both naked ... and were not ashamed 1.12
put to s. suddenly 17.13
I hid not my face from s. and spitting 21.78
begin with s. to take the lowest room 44.43
–*See also* ashamed.
shapen I was s. in wickedness 17.114
Sharon the rose of S. 20.3
sharp s. as a two-edged sword 18.12
sharpeneth iron s. iron 18.94
sharper the word of God is ... s. than any two-edged sword 60.5
sheaves shall ... bring his s. with him 17.264
neither he that bindeth up the s. 17.270
Sheba the queen of S. 11.8
shed s. ... for the remission of sins 42.163
the love of God is s. abroad in our hearts 47.17
shedding without s. of blood is no remission 60.9
sheep scattered ... as s. that have not a shepherd 11.30
counted as s. ... to be slain 17.98
the folds shall be full of s. 17.140
the s. of his hand 17.197
the s. of his pasture 17.202
the little hills like young s. 17.233
all we like s. have gone astray 21.81
as a s. before her shearers is dumb 21.81
pastors that destroy and scatter the s. 22.15
s.'s clothing 42.40
scattered abroad, as s. having no shepherd 42.57
the lost s. of the house of Israel 42.58
as s. in the midst of wolves 42.61
as a shepherd divideth his s. from the goats 42.157
I have found my s. which was lost 44.47
the s. ... know his voice 45.46
good shepherd giveth his life for the s. 45.48
other s. I have ... not of this fold 45.49
feed my s. 45.95
shepherd the Lord is my s. 17.45
scattered abroad, as sheep having no s. 42.57
as a s. divideth his sheep from the goats 42.157
he that entereth in by the door is the s. 45.46
I am the good s. 45.48
one fold, and one s. 45.49
the s. and bishop of your souls 62.10
shepherds s. abiding in the field 44.9
Shibboleth 7.11
shield I am thy s. 1.41
his faithfulness and truth shall be thy s. and buckler 17.186
the s. of faith 51.14
Shiloh until S. come 1.76
shine arise, s. 21.94
let your light so s. before men 42.16
shined upon them hath the light s. 21.22
shineth that s. more and more unto the perfect day 18.11
s. even unto the west 42.147
shining the stars shall withdraw their s. 27.7
a burning and a s. light 45.24
ship the way of a s. in the midst of the sea 18.107
as a s. that passeth over the waves 38.6
ships thou shalt break the s. of the sea 17.108
they that go down to the sea in s. 17.221
shipwreck some ... concerning faith have made s. 56.3
shoe over Edom will I cast out my s. 17.225
whose s.'s latchet I am not worthy to unloose 45.3
shoes put off thy s. from off thy feet 2.6
your s. on your feet 2.19
how beautiful are thy feet with s. 20.21
shoot the ungodly ... privily s. at them which are true of heart 17.18
they s. out their lips 17.41
short perfect in a s. time 38.5
let thy speech be s. 39.22
all have sinned, and come s. of the glory of God 47.13
he hath but a s. time 67.39
shout the voice of them that s. for mastery 2.40
the people shouted with a loud s. 13.1

shouted all the sons of God s. for joy 16.54
showers as the s. upon the grass, that tarrieth not for man 30.3
Shulamite return, return, O S. 20.20
shut the doors shall be s. in the streets 19.40
  a spring s. up 20.12
  he shall open, and none shall s. 21.36
  an open door, and no man can s. it 67.12
shutteth s. up his bowels of compassion 64.5
Sichem I will . . . divide S. 17.225
sick hope deferred maketh the heart s. 18.33
  I am s. of love 20.4
  s., and ye visited me 42.158
  s. of the palsy 43.3
sickle put ye in the s. 27.7
  thrust in thy s. 67.48
sickness the s. that destroyeth in the noon-day 17.186
  healing all manner of s. 42.14
side who is on the Lord's s.? 2.41
  who is on my s.? who? 12.13
  passed by on the other s. 44.31
  with a spear pierced his s. 45.84
sighing sorrow and s. shall flee away 21.55
sight better . . . the s. of the eyes than the wandering of the desire 19.17
  a cloud received him out of their s. 46.2
  thy heart is not right in the s. of God 46.22
  we walk by faith, not by s. 49.9
sign bind them for a s. upon your hand 5.6
  an everlasting s. that shall not be cut off 21.87
  an evil . . . generation seeketh after a s. 42.81
  Jews require a s. 48.2
signs s. and . . . wonders in . . . Egypt 2.13
  discern the s. of the times 42.104
  s. in the sun 44.68
silence a time to keep s., and a time to speak 19.9
  let all the earth keep s. before him 31.2
  s. in heaven 67.29
silver or ever the s. cord be loosed 19.40
  I have refined thee, but not with s. 21.72
  thirty pieces of s. 42.170
  s. and gold have I none 46.10
sin your s. will find you out 4.17
  stand in awe, and s. not 17.8
  my s. is ever before me 17.113
  s. is a reproach to any people 18.39
  thy s. purged 21.17
  how oft shall my brother s. against me 42.116
  which taketh away the s. of the world 45.4
  s. no more, lest a worse thing come unto thee 45.22
  he that is without s. . . . let him first cast a stone 45.36
  go, and s. no more 45.37
  lay not this s. to their charge 46.20
  where s. abounded, grace did much more 47.18
  in that he died, he died unto s. once 47.20
  the wages of s. is death 47.21
  it is no more I that do it, but s. 47.22
  be ye angry, and s. not 51.8
  hardened through the deceitfulness of s. 60.4
  who did no s., neither was guile found 62.9
  if we say that we have no s., we deceive 64.2
  –*See also* sinner, sins.
sincere the s. milk of the word 62.5
sincerity the unleavened bread of s. and truth 48.13
sing the noise of them that s. 2.40
  s. unto the Lord a new song 17.74
  s. praises unto his Name 17.142
  s. we merrily unto God 17.168
  O come, let us s. unto the Lord 17.195
  s. unto the Lord a new song 17.199
  s. us one of the songs of Sion 17.276
  the tongue of the dumb s. 21.54
singing the time of the s. of birds 20.6
sinned father, I have s. against heaven 44.49
  all have s., and come short of the glory of God 47.13
sinner one s. that repenteth 44.47
  God be merciful to me a s. 44.62
  converteth the s. from the error of his way 61.17
sinners s. before the Lord exceedingly 1.40
  the way of s. 17.1
  not come to call the righteous, but s. 42.52
  a friend of publicans and s. 42.74
  Christ Jesus came into the world to save s. 56.2
sins remember not the s. . . . of my youth 17.50
  how wide also the east is . . . so far hath he set our s. from us 17.209
  but love covereth all s. 18.25
  though your s. be as scarlet 21.4
  double for all her s. 21.59
  shed . . . for the remission of s. 42.163
  her s., which are many, are forgiven 44.25
  dead in trespasses and s. 51.2
  hide a multitude of s. 61.17
  the propitiation for our s. 64.3
  –*See also* sin.
Sion the Lord . . . strengthen thee out of S. 17.38
  the hill of S. is a fair place 17.108
  walk about S., and go round about her 17.109
  thou, O God, art praised in S. 17.139
  the Lord loveth the gates of S. 17.180
  sing us one of the songs of S. 17.276
Sisera the stars . . . fought against S. 7.5
sister the same is my . . . s. 42.84
sit s. thou on my right hand 17.227
  their strength is to s. still 21.44
  O virgin daughter of Babylon, s. on the ground 21.71
  to s. on my right hand . . . is not mine to give 42.127
  s. not down in the highest room 44.43
sitteth he that s. upon the circle of the earth 21.62
sitting s. at the receipt of custom 42.51

skin skin for s. 16.3
escaped with the s. of my teeth 16.36
can the Ethiopian change his s.? 22.9
skipped the mountains s. like rams 17.233
skipping leaping upon the mountains, s. upon the hills 20.5
slain Saul hath s. his thousands 9.22
the beauty of Israel is s. 10.1
counted as sheep . . . to be s. 17.98
a Lamb as it had been s. 67.19
s. from the foundation of the world 67.41
slander adder's poison is under their lips 17.282
speak evil of dignities 63.2
slaughter as an ox goeth to the s. 18.19
as a lamb to the s. 21.81
yet breathing out threatenings and s. 46.24
slay to s. the righteous with the wicked 1.47
sleep they are even as a s. 17.182
he that keepeth thee will not s. 17.256
yet a little s., a little slumber 18.15
a little folding of the hands to s. 18.15
the s. of a labouring man is sweet 19.16
I s., but my heart waketh 20.15
s. a perpetual sleep 22.22
we shall not all s. 48.45
sleeper what meanest thou, O s.? 29.1
sleepeth peradventure he s., and must be awaked 11.18
not dead, but s. 42.55
sleeping lest coming suddenly he find you s. 43.22
sleight the s. of men 51.7
slept David s. with his fathers 11.2
I should have s.: then had I been at rest 16.7
many bodies of the saints which s. arose 42.175
the firstfruits of them that s. 48.40
sling his s. was in his hand 9.20
sloth yet a little sleep, a little slumber 18.15
slothful the way of the s. man is . . . an hedge of thorns 18.43
he . . . that is s. . . . is brother to . . . a great waster 18.54
as the door turneth upon his hinges, so doth the s. upon his bed 18.87
the s. hideth his hand in his bosom 18.87
not s. in business 47.37
slothfulness by much s. the building decayeth 19.33
slow s. of speech 2.9
of a s. tongue 2.9
evil beasts, s. bellies 58.1
s. to speak 61.4
s. to wrath 61.4
sluggard go to the ant, thou s. 18.14
the s. is wiser . . . than seven men that can render a reason 18.87
slumber yet a little sleep, a little s. 18.15
small is it a s. thing? 4.8
for a s. moment have I forsaken thee 21.83
a s. one a strong nation 21.95
the day of s. things 33.4
be not ignorant of any thing in a great matter or a s. 39.6
smell the s. of a field which the Lord hath blessed 1.54
noses . . . and s. not 17.237
smelled the Lord s. a sweet savour 1.32
he s. the smell of his raiment 1.54
smelleth he s. the battle afar off 16.58
smite let the righteous . . . s. me friendly 17.286
whosoever shall s. thee on thy right cheek 42.23
God shall s. thee, thou whited wall 46.53
smiters I gave my back to the s. 21.78
smitten s. of God, and afflicted 21.81
smoke Sinai was . . . on a s. 2.28
there went a s. out in his presence 17.31
a s. in my nose 21.101
the s. of the incense 67.30
the s. of their torment ascendeth 67.46
smoking the s. flax shall he not quench 21.66
smooth a s. man 1.53
speak unto us s. things 21.45
smoother words s. than oil 17.121
smote they s. the city with the edge of the sword 7.1
he s. them hip and thigh 7.14
snare this man be a s. unto us 2.16
the s. of the hunter 17.186
as a bird out of the s. of the fowler 17.262
snares the s. of death overtook me 17.30
the s. of death compassed me round 17.238
snow he giveth s. like wool 17.296
fire and hail, s. and vapours 17.297
as white as s. 67.2
soap fullers' s. 34.2
sober be s., be vigilant 62.16
soberness words of truth and s. 46.60
Sodom the men of S. were wicked 1.40
S. and . . . Gomorrah 1.48
soft a s. answer turneth away wrath 18.40
softer the words of his mouth were s. than butter 17.121
softly Ahab . . . lay in sackcloth, and went s. 11.29
I shall go s. all my years 21.57
sojourner I am a stranger with thee, and a s. 17.90
soldier a good s. of Jesus Christ 57.3
sole no rest for the s. of her foot 1.30
solitary how doth the city sit s. 23.1
Solomon S. loved many strange women 11.11
black . . . as the curtains of S. 20.1
even S. in all his glory was not arrayed 42.31
a greater than S. is here 42.82
somewhat I have s. to say 11.3
I have s. against thee 67.5
son the s. of his old age 1.64
O Absalom, my s. 10.11
a wise s. maketh a glad father 18.23
a wise s. heareth his father's instruction 18.32
a virgin shall conceive, and bear a s. 21.19
unto us a s. is given 21.23

Lucifer, s. of the morning 21.30
the form of the fourth is like the S. of God 25.7
this is my beloved S. 42.8
if his s. ask bread, will he give him a stone? 42.37
the S. of man hath not where to lay his head 42.48
the S. of man coming ... with power 42.148
the S. of man is Lord also of the sabbath 43.4
the only s. of his mother ... a widow 44.23
the s. of peace 44.28
the s. against the father 44.41
no more worthy to be called thy s. 44.49
this my s. was dead 44.50
s., thou art ever with me 44.52
he that believeth not the S. 45.15
woman, behold thy s. 45.81
Barnabas ... the s. of consolation 46.13
a Pharisee, the s. of a Pharisee 46.54
the s. of perdition 55.1
scourgeth every s. whom he receiveth 60.17
the S. of man, clothed ... down to the foot 67.2

song sing unto the Lord a new s. 17.74
they that led us away captive required ... a s. 17.276
the s. of songs, which is Solomon's 20.1
they shall not drink wine with a s. 21.39
a new s. before the throne 67.43

songs compass me about with s. of deliverance 17.72
thy statutes have been my s. 17.247

sons the s. of God 1.27
s. of Belial 9.1
all the s. of God shouted for joy 16.54
bring my s. from far 21.67
a place and a name better than of s. 21.88
Boanerges ... s. of thunder 43.5
power to become the s. of God 45.1

sores Lazarus ... laid at his gate, full of s. 44.55

sorrow in s. thou shalt bring forth children 1.17
in s. shalt thou eat of it 1.17
fear came there upon them, and s. 17.108
by s. of the heart the spirit is broken 18.41
he that increaseth knowledge increaseth s. 19.5
s. and sighing shall flee away 21.55
see if there be any s. like unto my sorrow 23.2
the Lord ... give thee joy for this thy s. 37.2
there shall be no more death, neither s. 67.65
–See also tears.

sorrowful even in laughter the heart is s. 18.37
went away s.: for he had great possessions 42.121
my soul is exceeding s., even unto death 42.165

sorrows the s. of my heart are enlarged 17.52
a man of s. 21.81
the beginning of s. 42.144

sort certain lewd fellows of the baser s. 46.36

sought they have s. out many inventions 19.23
by night on my bed I s. him whom my soul loveth 20.9

soul man became a living s. 1.9
my s. is weary of my life 16.23
my s. ... should flee as a bird 17.18
thou shalt not leave my s. in hell 17.27
he shall convert my s. 17.45
his s. shall dwell at ease 17.51
shut not up my s. with the sinners 17.54
thou ... hast brought my s. out of hell 17.63
my s. is athirst for God 17.94
why art thou so full of heaviness, O my s.? 17.95
they ... mark my steps, when they lay wait for my s. 17.122
my s. is among lions 17.126
my s. hath a desire 17.173
the iron entered into his s. 17.216
hungry and thirsty, their s. fainted in them 17.218
their s. melteth away because of the trouble 17.221
thou hast delivered my s. from death 17.239
my s. is alway in my hand 17.250
our s. is escaped ... as a bird 17.262
my s. fleeth unto the Lord 17.273
that my s. knoweth right well 17.280
thou whom my s. loveth 20.1
I shall go softly ... in the bitterness of my s. 21.57
the travail of his s. 21.82
he shall save his s. alive 24.7
prepare thy s. for temptation 39.1
destroy both body and s. in hell 42.64
my s. is exceeding sorrowful 42.165
gain the whole world, and lose his ... s. 43.15
what shall a man give in exchange for his s.? 43.15
my s. doth magnify the Lord 44.2
s., thou hast much goods laid up 44.38
thou fool, this night thy s. shall be required 44.38
let every s. be subject unto the higher powers 47.39
fleshly lusts, which war against the s. 62.6

souls the s. of the righteous are in the hand of God 38.3
entering into holy s., she maketh them friends of God 38.8
thou lover of s. 38.10
in your patience possess ... your s. 44.67
the shepherd and bishop of your s. 62.10

sound s. of abundance of rain 11.19
do not s. a trumpet before thee 42.26
a great s. of a trumpet 42.148
safe and s. 44.51
a s. ... as of a rushing mighty wind 46.6
if the trumpet give an uncertain s. 48.36
the trumpet shall s. 48.45
of a s. mind 57.1

the form of s. words 57.2
the s. of many waters 67.2
sounding s. brass 48.35
sour the fathers have eaten s. grapes 24.6
south thou hast given me a s. land 6.6
queen of the s. 42.82
sow they that s. in tears shall reap in joy 17.264
he that observeth the wind shall not s. 19.38
in the morning s. thy seed 19.39
s. ... in righteousness, reap in mercy 26.2
the fowls of the air ... s. not 42.31
sower a s. went forth to sow 42.85
soweth whatsoever a man s., that shall he also reap 50.13
sown s. the wind ... reap the whirlwind 26.1
ye have s. much, and bring in little 32.1
reaping where thou hast not s. 42.155
s. in corruption 48.43
spake never man s. like this man 45.35
God, who ... in divers manners s. 60.1
spare s. me a little, that I may recover my strength 17.90
bread enough and to s. 44.49
spareth he that s. his rod hateth his son 18.35
sparks man is born unto trouble, as the s. fly upward 16.14
run to and fro like s. 38.4
sparrow the s. hath found her an house 17.173
a s., that sitteth alone 17.205
sparrows two s. sold for a farthing 42.65
five s. sold for two farthings 44.37
speak s., Lord; for thy servant heareth 9.5
I have yet to s. on God's behalf 16.53
s. not with a stiff neck 17.157
mouths, and s. not 17.237
neither s. they through their throat 17.237
princes also did sit and s. against me 17.245
a time to keep silence, and a time to s. 19.9
s. unto us smooth things 21.45
s. ye comfortably to Jerusalem 21.59
s. the word only 42.46
woe unto you when all men shall s. well of you 44.21
we s. that we do know 45.10
he shall s. for himself 45.44
permitted to s. for thyself 46.58
s. this by permission 48.17
though I s. with the tongues of men 48.35
I s. as a fool 49.18
I may s. boldly, as I ought 51.15
slow to s. 61.4
speaketh out of the abundance of the heart the mouth s. 42.79
speaking their much s. 42.27
tattlers ... s. things which they ought not 56.8
spear with a s. pierced his side 45.84
spears their s. into pruning-hooks 21.7
spectacle made a s. unto the world 48.10
speech the whole earth was ... of one s. 1.36
slow of s. 2.9
my s. shall distil as the dew 5.15
I am full of matter 16.49
there is neither s. nor language 17.35
thy s. is comely 20.11
let thy s. be short 39.22
great plainness of s. 49.5
s. be alway with grace 53.8
s. ... seasoned with salt 53.8
spendest whatsoever thou s. more ... I will repay 44.32
spent the day is far s. 44.79
night is far s. 47.43
spices blow upon my garden, that the s. thereof may flow 20.14
my beloved is gone down ... to the beds of s. 20.18
the mountains of s. 20.27
spies s.; to see the nakedness of the land 1.70
spilled seed ... Onan ... s. it on the ground 1.67
spin neither do they s. 42.31
spirit the S. of God moved upon ... the waters 1.1
my s. shall not always strive with man 1.27
anguish of s. 2.12
a lying s. 11.31
the s. of Elijah doth rest on Elisha 12.2
a s. passed before my face 16.12
there is a s. in man 16.48
into thy hands I commend my s. 17.68
in whose s. there is no guile 17.71
renew a right s. within me 17.114
the sacrifice of God is a troubled s. 17.116
by sorrow of the heart the s. is broken 18.41
and an haughty s. before a fall 18.45
a broken s. drieth the bones 18.53
the s. of a man will sustain his infirmity 18.55
a wounded s. who can bear? 18.55
the s. of man is the candle of the Lord 18.65
vanity and vexation of s. 19.4
the patient in s. is better than the proud 19.20
no man ... hath power over the s. to retain the spirit 19.24
the s. shall return unto God who gave it 19.40
the s. of wisdom and understanding 21.25
the s. of counsel and might 21.25
garment of praise for the s. of heaviness 21.96
put a new s. within you 24.2
I will pour out my s. upon all flesh 27.5
the holy s. of discipline 38.1
wisdom is a loving s. 38.1
thine incorruptible s. is in all things 38.11
the S. of God descending like a dove 42.8
blessed are the poor in s. 42.15
the unclean s. is gone out 42.83
it is a s. 42.97
the s. ... is willing 42.167
my s. hath rejoiced in God my Saviour 44.2
waxed strong in s. 44.6
into thy hands I commend my s. 44.75
born of water and of the S. 45.9
that which is born of the Spirit is s. 45.9
God is a S. 45.18
worship ... in s. and in truth 45.18

the s. that quickeneth 45.33
he groaned in the s. 45.51
the S. of truth 45.59
as the S. gave them utterance 46.6
the S. bade me go ... nothing doubting 46.32
bound in the s. 46.48
they that are after the S. 47.24
as many as are led by the S. of God 47.25
the S. also helpeth our infirmities 47.27
fervent in s. 47.37
present in s. 48.12
diversities of gifts, but the same S. 48.34
written ... with the S. of the living God 49.3
the s. giveth life 49.4
the flesh lusteth against the S. 50.10
the fruit of the S. is love, joy, peace 50.11
he that soweth to the S. shall ... reap life everlasting 50.13
the s. that ... worketh in the children of disobedience 51.2
the unity of the S. 51.6
the sword of the S. 51.14
s. ... of power, and of love, and of a sound mind 57.1
the ornament of a meek and quiet s. 62.11
believe not every s. 64.6
in the s. on the Lord's day 67.2
immediately I was in the s. 67.16
carried me away in the s. 67.66
the S. and the bride say, come 67.71

spirits I ... search out my s. 17.160
he maketh his angels s. 17.211
them that have familiar s. 21.21
who maketh his angels s. 60.2
ministering s. 60.3
the s. of just men made perfect 60.19
try the s. whether they are of God 64.6
the seven s. ... before his throne 67.1
the seven s. of God 67.16

spiritual impart unto you some s. gift 47.3
against s. wickedness in high places 51.14

spiritually to be s. minded is life and peace 47.24

spoil he shall divide the s. 1.81
the necks of them that take the s. 7.7
as men rejoice when they divide the s. 21.22
beware lest any man s. you through philosophy 53.1

spoilers s. that spoiled them 7.2

spoken very excellent things are s. of thee 17.180
these things cannot be s. against 46.45
every where it is s. against 46.63

spot thou art all fair ... there is no s. in thee 20.11

spots or the leopard his s. 22.9
s. in your feasts of charity 66.3

spouse a garden inclosed is my sister, my s. 20.12

spreading a place for the s. of nets 24.10

spring a s. shut up 20.12
thine health shall s. forth speedily 21.91

springs the upper s. and the nether springs 6.6
he sendeth the s. into the rivers 17.212
the thirsty land s. of water 21.54

staff your s. in your hand 2.19
the stay and the s. 21.10
as if the s. should lift up itself 21.24
thou trustest in the s. of this broken reed 21.56

stagger they ... s. like a drunken man 16.29, 17.221
s., but not with strong drink 21.43

stand he shall s. at the latter day upon the earth 16.38
s. in awe, and sin not 17.8
we are risen, and s. upright 17.39
who is able to s. before envy? 18.91
who shall s. when he appeareth? 34.2
if Satan rise up against himself ... he cannot s. 43.6
men of Galilee, why s. ye gazing up into heaven? 46.3
by faith ye s. 49.2
having done all, to s. 51.14
I s. at the door, and knock 67.15
the dead, small and great, s. before God 67.64

standeth let him that thinketh he s. take heed 48.28

star we have seen his s. in the east 42.2
one s. differeth from another ... in glory 48.43
the name of the s. is called Wormwood 67.31
I saw a s. fall from heaven 67.32
the bright and morning s. 67.71

stars he made the s. also 1.4
the s. in their courses 7.5
when the morning s. sang together 16.54
he telleth the number of the s. 17.294
the s. shall withdraw their shining 27.7
seek him that maketh the seven s. 28.4
wandering s. 66.3
in his right hand seven s. 67.2
the s. ... fell unto the earth 67.26

starting s. aside like a broken bow 17.165

state the last s. ... is worse than the first 42.83

stature one cubit unto his s. 42.31
increased in wisdom and s. 44.15

statutes thy s. have been my songs 17.247

staves am I a dog, that thou comest to me with s.? 9.21

stay s. me with flagons 20.4
the s. and the staff 21.10

steal thou shalt not s. 2.29
where thieves break through and s. 42.28
let him that stole s. no more 51.8

stedfast whom resist s. in the faith 62.16

steep the swine ... ran violently down a s. place 43.8

stem a rod out of the s. of Jesse 21.25

steward the unjust s. 44.54

stewards s. of the mysteries of God 48.9

stiffly them that stood so s. for the name of the Lord 36.2

stiff neck speak not with a s. 17.157
stiffnecked a s. people 2.39
still a s. small voice 11.23
be s. then, and know that I am God 17.105
their strength is to sit s. 21.44
all the earth sitteth s., and is at rest 33.2
sting O death, where is thy s.? 48.45
stings s. in their tails 67.35
stir s. up strife all the day long 17.282
s. not up, nor awake my love 20.24
stock their s. shall not take root 21.63
stocks ascribe unto stones and s. the incommunicable name 38.12
stolen s. waters are sweet 18.22
stomach a proud look and a high s. 17.204
use a little wine for thy s.'s sake 56.9
stone tables of s., and a law 2.34
his heart is as firm as a s. 16.61
thou hurt not thy foot against a s. 17.187
the same s. which the builders refused 17.242
s. of stumbling 21.20
if his son ask bread, will he give him a s.? 42.37
not be left here one s. upon another 42.143
he that is without sin ... let him first cast a s. 45.36
the s. taken away from the sepulchre 45.87
not in tables of s. 49.3
in the s. a new name written 67.8
a s. like a great millstone 67.57
a s. most precious 67.66
stones five smooth s. out of the brook 9.20
ascribe unto s. and stocks the incommunicable name 38.12
God is able of these s. to raise up children unto Abraham 42.7
command that these s. be made bread 42.9
the s. would immediately cry out 44.64
stony take the s. heart out of their flesh 24.2
fell upon s. places 42.85
stood the hair of my flesh s. up 16.12
s. at the parting of the way 24.8
no man s. with me, but all men forsook me 57.9
stork the fir-trees are a dwelling for the s. 17.213
storm fire and brimstone, s. and tempest 17.19
wind and s., fulfilling his word 17.297
storms all thy waves and s. are gone over me 17.96
straight make s. in the desert a highway for our God 21.59
the crooked shall be made s. 21.59
make his paths s. 42.5
the street which is called S. 46.26
strain s. at a gnat, and swallow a camel 42.140
strait s. is the gate 42.39
strange Solomon loved many s. women 11.11
how shall we sing the Lord's song in a s. land? 17.276
the lips of a s. woman drop as an honeycomb 18.12
I perish through great grief in a s. land 40.1
a setter forth of s. gods 46.37
stranger a s. in a strange land 2.4
thy s. that is within thy gates 2.29
I am a s. with thee ... as all my fathers were 17.90
a s. doth not intermeddle with his joy 18.36
a s., and ye took me in 42.158
not ... returned to give glory to God, save this s. 44.58
strangers the Lord careth for the s. 17.293
s. and pilgrims on the earth 60.12
straw s. to make brick 2.11
streams s. from Lebanon 20.13
street the s. which is called Straight 46.26
streets publish it not in the s. of Askelon 10.1
lurking in the thievish corners of the s. 17.17
no complaining in our s. 17.290
wisdom ... uttereth her voice in the s. 18.5
strength as thy days, so shall thy s. be 5.20
children are come to the birth, and there is not s. to bring forth 12.15
hast thou given the horse s.? 16.57
O Lord, my s. 17.37
the king shall rejoice in thy s. 17.40
the Lord is the s. of my life 17.55
spare me a little, that I may recover my s. 17.90
go from s. to strength 17.174
their s. then but labour and sorrow 17.183
O Lord God, thou s. of my health 17.284
he hath no pleasure in the s. of an horse 17.295
a man of knowledge increaseth s. 18.76
if thou faint in ... adversity, thy s. is small 18.77
s. and honour are her clothing 18.111
their s. is to sit still 21.44
they that wait upon the Lord shall renew their s. 21.64
my s. and my hope is perished from the Lord 23.3
do not men excel in s., that bear rule? 35.3
my s. is made perfect in weakness 49.21
as the sun shineth in his s. 67.2
thou hast a little s. 67.12
–*See also* strong.
strengthen the Lord ... s. thee out of Sion 17.38
bread to s. man's heart 17.213
s. ... the weak hands, and confirm the feeble knees 21.53
strengthened s. ... in the inner man 51.5
strengtheneth do all things through Christ which s. me 52.13
stricken old, and well s. in age 1.52
old and s. in years 11.1
s., smitten of God, and afflicted 21.81
strife I proved thee also at the waters of s. 17.170
stir up s. all the day long 17.282

he that ... meddleth with s. belonging not to him 18.88
where there is no talebearer, the s. ceaseth 18.89
the forcing of wrath bringeth forth s. 18.108
a man of s. 22.12
strifes hatred stirreth up s. 18.25
striker no s. 56.4
string the s. of his tongue was loosed 43.13
strings instrument of ten s. 17.74
praise him upon the s. and pipe 17.300
stripe s. for stripe 2.31
stripes with his s. we are healed 21.81
in s. above measure 49.18
strive my spirit shall not always s. with man 1.27
not crowned, except he s. lawfully 57.3
striveth woe unto him that s. with his maker 21.69
man that s. for the mastery 48.27
strong a s. ass 1.78
be s. and of a good courage 5.14
only be s. and of a good courage 6.2
out of the s. came forth sweetness 7.12
thou ... hast made my hill so s. 17.64
that our oxen may be s. to labour 17.290
the rich man's wealth is his s. city 18.26
nor the battle to the s. 19.29
the s. men shall bow themselves 19.40
love is s. as death 20.26
woe unto them that ... follow s. drink 21.15
a small one a s. nation 21.95
mighty and s. men for the war 22.20
how exceeding s. is wine 35.1
except he ... first bind the s. man 43.6
waxed s. in spirit 44.6
a s. man armed keepeth his palace 44.35
s. ought to bear the infirmities of the weak 47.46
we are weak, but ye are s. 48.10
the pulling down of s. holds 49.16
be s. in the Lord 51.14
s. meat 60.7
stronger what is s. than a lion? 7.13
stubble the whirlwind shall take them away as s. 21.63
run to and fro like sparks among the s. 38.4
stubborn she is loud and s. 18.17
stubbornness I will harden Pharaoh's heart 2.13
Pharaoh's heart was hardened 2.15
s. is as iniquity 9.15
like the deaf adder that stoppeth her ears 17.129
speak not with a stiff neck 17.157
study much s. is a weariness of the flesh 19.41
s. to be quiet 54.2
stumbling stone of s. 21.20
stumblingblock Christ crucified, unto the Jews a s. 48.2
lest ... this liberty of yours become a s. 48.24
stump only the s. of Dagon was left to him 9.11
subdue let us ... s. the woods of the plain 36.4
subject the creature was made s. to vanity 47.26
s. unto the higher powers 47.39
s., not only for wrath, but also for conscience sake 47.41
subjection keep under my body, and bring it into s. 48.27
substance all the s. of his house for love 20.26
wasted his s. with riotous living 44.48
faith is the s. of things hoped for 60.11
subtil the serpent was more s. 1.13
subtilty thy brother came with s. 1.55
Succoth mete out the valley of S. 17.225
suck thereout s. they no small advantage 17.155
sucklings out of the mouth of ... babes and s. 17.14
suddenly lest coming s. he find you sleeping 43.22
suffer s. the little children to come 43.18
being persecuted, we s. it 48.10
s. fools gladly 49.17
suffered s. many things of many physicians 43.11
sufficient s. unto the day is the evil thereof 42.32
my grace is s. for thee 49.21
sum with a great s. obtained I this freedom 46.52
summer meat in the s. 18.14
the s. is ended, and we are not saved 22.6
sumptuously fared s. every day 44.55
sun the s. ... cometh forth as a bridegroom 17.35
the s. ... rejoiceth as a giant 17.35
the s. ariseth, and they get them away together 17.214
the s. shall not burn thee by day 17.257
there is no new thing under the s. 19.2
while the s. ... be not darkened 19.40
black, because the s. hath looked upon me 20.1
clear as the s. 20.19
the s. and the moon shall be darkened 27.7
the S. of righteousness 34.3
he maketh his s. to rise on the evil and on the good 42.24
let not the s. go down upon your wrath 51.8
his countenance was as the s. 67.2
as the s. shineth in his strength 67.2
the s. became black 67.26
neither shall the s. light on them 67.28
a woman clothed with the s. 67.37
the city had no need of the s. 67.67
sundry God, who at s. times ... spake 60.1
superscription whose is this image and s.? 42.134
superstitious men of Athens ... ye are too s. 46.38

support labouring . . . to s. the weak 46.50
supposing s. him to be the gardener 45.89
sure the round world so s. 17.192
be ye s. that the Lord he is God 17.202
as a nail in a s. place 21.36
a more s. word of prophecy 63.1
swallow the s. a nest where she may lay her young 17.173
strain at a gnat, and s. a camel 42.140
swallowed death is s. up in victory 48.45
swalloweth he s. the ground 16.58
swear s. not at all 42.22
sweareth he that s. unto his neighbour 17.24
sweat the s. of thy face 1.18
sweep s. it with the besom of destruction 21.31
hail shall s. away the refuge of lies 21.42
sweet stolen waters are s. 18.22
the desire accomplished is s. 18.34
that put bitter for s. 21.16
eat the fat, and drink the s. 35.9
s. water and bitter 61.9
in thy mouth s. as honey 67.36
sweeter what is s. than honey? 7.13
s. also than honey 17.36
sweetness out of the strong came forth s. 7.12
swelling great s. words 66.4
swept empty, s., and garnished 42.83
swift their feet are s. to shed blood 17.22
the race is not to the s. 19.29
s. to hear 61.4
swine as a jewel . . . in a s.'s snout, so is a fair woman . . . without discretion 18.29
pearls before s. 42.35
the s. . . . ran violently down a steep place 43.8
the husks that the s. did eat 44.49
sword they smote the city with the edge of the s. 7.1
the s. of the Lord, and of Gideon 7.9
thy s. hath made women childless 9.16
the praises of God be in their mouth, and a two-edged s. in their hands 17.298
sharp as a two-edged s. 18.12
every man hath his s. . . . because of fear in the night 20.10
nation shall not lift up s. against nation 21.7
his sore and great and strong s. 21.40
such as are for the s., to the sword 22.11
not to send peace, but a s. 42.66
they that take the s. shall perish with the sword 42.169
the s. of the Spirit 51.14
the word of God is . . . sharper than any two-edged s. 60.5
out of his mouth went a sharp twoedged s. 67.2
swords they all hold s., being expert in war 20.10
beat their s. into plowshares 21.7
in their cups, they . . . draw out s. 35.2

T

tabernacle our earthly house of this t. 49.8
the t. of God is with men 67.65
tabernacles let us make here three t. 42.107
table crumbs which fall from their masters' t. 42.103
crumbs which fell from the rich man's t. 44.55
tables t. of stone, and a law 2.34
not in t. of stone 49.3
fleshy t. of the heart 49.3
tails stings in their t. 67.35
take thou shalt not t. the name of . . . God in vain 2.29
t. up his cross 42.106
t. up thy bed, and walk 43.3
t. it patiently 62.8
taken the Lord gave, and the Lord hath t. away 16.2
one shall be t., and the other left 42.151
from him that hath not shall be t. away 42.156
t. away the Lord out of the sepulchre 45.87
while they beheld, he was t. up 46.2
taketh the Lord t. me up 17.58
the Lamb of God, which t. away the sin 45.4
tale a t. that is told 17.183
talebearer where there is no t., the strife ceaseth 18.89
talents unto one he gave five t. 42.153
tales seemed . . . idle t., and they believed them not 44.78
talk t. of the lips tendeth only to penury 18.38
how can he get wisdom . . . whose t. is of bullocks? 39.25
tame the tongue can no man t. 61.8
tangere noli me t. 45.90
tares his enemy came and sowed t. 42.89
t. are the children of the wicked one 42.92
tarrieth as the showers upon the grass, that t. not for man 30.3
tarry t. thou the Lord's leisure 17.59
t. ye here, and watch with me 42.165
if I will that he t. till I come, what is that to thee? 45.96
tarrying make no long t., O my God 17.92
taskmasters the t. of the people 2.11
taste touch not; t. not; handle not 53.2
tattlers t. . . . and busybodies 56.8
taught thou, O God, hast t. me from my youth up 17.152
he t. them as one having authority 42.45
taxed all the world should be t. 44.7
teach apt to t. 56.4
teacheth he t. mine hands to fight 17.33
tears every night wash I my bed . . . with my t. 17.12
put my t. into thy bottle 17.123
the bread of t. 17.167
thou hast delivered . . . mine eyes from t. 17.239
they that sow in t. shall reap in joy 17.264

wash his feet with t. 44.24
sought it carefully with t. 60.18
God shall wipe away all t. 67.28
teeth mine enemies that trouble me cast me in the t. 17.97
whose t. are spears and arrows 17.126
thy t. are like a flock of sheep 20.11
the children's t. are set on edge 24.6
gnashing of t. 42.47
gnashed on him with their t. 46.18
tekel mene, mene, t., upharsin 25.10
tell t. it not in Gath 10.1
who can t. how oft he offendeth? 17.36
that ye may t. them that come after 17.109
a man's mind is sometime wont to t. him more than seven watchmen 39.23
to t., or to hear some new thing 46.38
tellest thou t. my flittings 17.123
telleth he t. the number of the stars 17.294
temperate man that striveth for the mastery is t. 48.27
temple who is there . . . would go into the t. to save his life? 14.2
his train filled the t. 21.17
the Lord . . . shall suddenly come to his t. 34.2
the veil of the t. was rent in twain 42.175
your body is the t. of the Holy Ghost 48.15
a pillar in the t. of my God 67.13
the Lord God Almighty and the Lamb are the t. 67.67
temples t. made with hands 46.38
tempt thou shalt not t. the Lord thy God 42.10
temptation the day of t. in the wilderness 17.197
prepare thy soul for t. 39.1
lead us not into t. 42.27
watch and pray, that ye enter not into t. 42.167
no t. . . . but such as is common to man 48.28
with the t. . . . a way to escape 48.28
Temptation in the Wilderness 42.9
temptations in heaviness through manifold t. 62.1
tempted they t. . . . the most high God 17.165
ten David his t. thousands 9.22
were there not t. cleansed? 44.58
Ten Commandments 2.29
tender Leah was t. eyed 1.58
the t. mercies of the wicked 18.31
no more be called t. and delicate 21.71
tents such as dwell in t. 1.24
how goodly are thy t., O Jacob 4.16
the t. of ungodliness 17.175
black . . . as the t. of Kedar 20.1
terrible t. as an army with banners 20.19
the day of the Lord is great and very t. 27.3
terror afraid for any t. by night 17.186
rulers are not a t. to good works 47.40
terrors the king of t. 16.34
testament my blood of the new t. 42.163
testify the scriptures . . . t. of me 45.25
testimony the t. of the Lord is sure 17.35
the t. of our conscience 49.1
thank I t. thee, that I am not as other men 44.61
I t. my God upon every remembrance of you 52.1
thankful it becometh well the just to be t. 17.74
thanks who will give thee t. in the pit? 17.12
shall the dust give t. unto thee? 17.65
O give t. unto the Lord, for he is gracious 17.217
thanksgiving come before his presence with t. 17.195
go your way . . . with t. 17.202
t., and the voice of melody 21.79
sacrifice . . . with the voice of t. 29.3
thief a t. and a robber 45.46
as a t. in the night 54.4
I come as a t. 67.52
thieves where t. break through and steal 42.28
a den of t. 42.130
fell among t. 44.31
thigh Jacob's t. was out of joint 1.61
he smote them hip and t. 7.14
thighs thy t. are like jewels 20.21
thing which hath put such a t. as this in the king's heart 13.2
I know that thou canst do every t. 16.62
a t. of nought 22.10
the t. which is good 51.8
things secret t. belong unto the Lord 5.12
t. too wonderful for me 16.62
t. creeping innumerable 17.215
out of his treasure t. new and old 42.94
all t. were made by him 45.1
how can these t. be? 45.10
these t. cannot be spoken against 46.45
all t. to all men 48.26
all t. are become new 49.11
think on these t. 52.12
set your affection on t. above 53.3
prove all t. 54.5
speaking t. which they ought not 56.8
unto the pure all t. are pure 58.2
upholding all t. by the word of his power 60.1
the end of all t. is at hand 62.14
t. which must be hereafter 67.16
I make all t. new 67.65
think if so be that God will t. upon us, that we perish not 29.1
if a man t. himself to be something . . . he deceiveth himself 50.12
above all that we ask or t. 51.5
t. on these things 52.12
third caught up to the t. heaven 49.19
thirst whosoever drinketh of this water shall t. again 45.16
thirsteth ho, every one that t. 21.84
thirsty hungry and t., their soul fainted in them 17.218
t., and ye gave me drink 42.158

thirty t. pieces of silver 42.170
thistles do men gather ... figs of t.? 42.41
thorn a t. in the flesh 49.20
thorns the way of the slothful man is ... an hedge of t. 18.43
the lily among t. 20.3
t. shall come up in her palaces 21.51
do men gather grapes of t.? 42.41
fell among t. 42.85
thought no t. can be withholden from thee 16.62
curse not the king, no not in thy t. 19.35
wine ... turneth ... every t. into jollity 35.1
one that was never t. of hath worn the crown 39.11
an holy and good t. 41.1
take no t. for your life 42.30
which ... by taking t. can add one cubit unto his stature? 42.31
take ... no t. for the morrow 42.32
thoughts thy t. are very deep 17.189
thou understandest my t. long before 17.277
then all his t. perish 17.292
my t. are not your thoughts 21.86
thousand one day in thy courts is better than a t. 17.175
a t. years ... are but as yesterday 17.182
a t. shall fall beside thee 17.186
one t. shall flee at the rebuke of one 21.47
a little one shall become a t. 21.95
bound him a t. years 67.62
thousands Saul hath slain his t. 9.22
threatenings yet breathing out t. and slaughter 46.24
three where two or t. are gathered together 42.115
faith, hope, charity, these t. 48.35
threefold a t. cord is not quickly broken 19.13
threescore the days of our age are t. years and ten 17.183
throat neither speak they through their t. 17.237
throne the Lord sitting upon a t., high and lifted up 21.17
in mercy shall the t. be established 21.32
the seven spirits ... before his t. 67.1
a t. was set in heaven 67.16
cast their crowns before the t. 67.17
a new song before the t. 67.43
without fault before the t. of God 67.44
a pure river ... proceeding out of the t. of God 67.68
thrones the t. were cast down 25.13
thrust t. in thy sickle 67.48
Thummim Urim and ... T. 2.35
thunder Boanerges ... sons of t. 43.5
the voice of a great t. 67.43
thunderings lightnings and t. and voices 67.16
tidings that bringest good t. 21.59
that bringeth good t. 21.80
good t. of great joy 44.9
tiller a t. of the ground 1.19
time in a t. when thou mayest be found 17.72
his t. passeth away like a shadow 17.289
a t. to be born, and a time to die 19.9
t. and chance happeneth to them all 19.29
man also knoweth not his t. 19.29
the t. of the singing of birds 20.6
perfect in a short t. 38.5
fulfilled a long t. 38.5
in a moment of t. 44.17
high t. to awake out of sleep 47.43
one born out of due t. 48.39
now is the accepted t. 49.12
redeeming the t. 51.11
the t. of my departure is at hand 57.7
he hath but a short t. 67.39
times he changeth the t. and the seasons 25.2
the t. begin to wax old 36.6
discern the signs of the t. 42.104
not for you to know the t. or the seasons 46.1
tingle the ears of every one that heareth it shall t. 9.6
tinkling a t. cymbal 48.35
tittle one jot or one t. 42.17
to day while it is called T. 60.4
the same yesterday, and t., and for ever 60.21
toil they t. not 42.31
toiled we have t. all the night 44.19
token a t. of a covenant 1.34
told the half was not t. me 11.9
hath it not been t. you from the beginning? 21.62
tomorrow boast not thyself of t. 18.90
let us eat and drink; for t. we ... die 21.35
tongue my t. is the pen of a ready writer 17.99
their t. a sharp sword 17.126
let my t. cleave to the roof of my mouth 17.276
not a word in my t., but thou ... knowest it 17.277
in her t. is the law of kindness 18.111
the t. of the dumb sing 21.54
God hath given me the t. of the learned 21.77
the string of his t. was loosed 43.13
every t. ... confess ... Christ is Lord 52.4
the t. is a little member 61.7
the t. can no man tame 61.8
tongues sharpened their t. like a serpent 17.282
cloven t. like as of fire 46.6
though I speak with the t. of men 48.35
t., they shall cease 48.35
took God t. him 1.25
I paid them the things that I never t. 17.146
a stranger, and ye t. me in 42.158
tooth t. for tooth 2.31
top a tower, whose t. may reach unto heaven 1.37
torment the smoke of their t. ascendeth 67.46
tormented t. with fire and brimstone 67.46

tossed he that wavereth ... driven with the wind and t. 61.1
tossings I am full of t. to and fro 16.18
touch only t. the hem of his garment 42.99
t. me not 45.89
t. not; taste not; handle not 53.2
toucheth he that t. pitch shall be defiled 39.13
tower a t., whose top may reach unto heaven 1.37
Tower of Babel 1.38
towers walk about Sion ... and tell the t. 17.109
train t. up a child in the way he should go 18.70
transgression he that covereth a t. seeketh love 18.50
where no law is, there is no t. 47.15
transgressors numbered with the t. 21.82
travail this sore t. hath God given to ... man 19.4
both the hands full with t. and vexation 19.11
the t. of his soul 21.82
travaileth the whole creation ... t. in pain 47.26
treachery mine own familiar friend ... hath laid great wait for me 17.93
sheep's clothing 42.40
and kissed him 42.168
treacle triacle (t.) in Gilead
treasure better is little ... than great t. and trouble therewith 18.42
where your t. is, there will your heart be also 42.28
out of his t. things new and old 42.94
t. in earthen vessels 49.6
treasures t. in heaven 42.28
greater riches than the t. in Egypt 60.13
tree every t. that is pleasant to the sight 1.9
every t. ... that is good for food 1.9
the t. of life 1.9
the t. of the knowledge of good and evil 1.9
of every t. ... thou mayest freely eat 1.10
like a t. planted by the water-side 17.1
if the t. fall ... there it shall be 19.37
every t. which bringeth not forth good fruit 42.7
every good t. bringeth forth good fruit 42.41
if they do these things in a green t. 44.71
eat of the t. of life 67.6
the leaves of the t. were for the healing of the nations 67.68
trees the t. of the Lord ... are full of sap 17.213
fruitful t. and all cedars 17.297
t. of righteousness 21.96
the t. ... said ... make war against the sea 36.4
the axe is laid unto the root of the t. 42.7
men as t., walking 43.14
tremble t., thou earth, at the presence of the Lord 17.234
trembling fear came upon me, and t. 16.12
work out your own salvation with fear and t. 52.5
trespasses dead in t. and sins 51.2
tribulation companion in t. 67.2
ye shall have t. ten days 67.7
came out of great t. 67.28
tribulations we glory in t. 47.17
tribute a servant unto t. 1.78
of whom do the kings ... take ... t.? 42.110
t. to whom tribute is due 47.42
tried thy word is t. to the uttermost 17.252
trimmed t. their lamps 42.152
triumphed he hath t. gloriously 2.24
trodden I have t. the winepress alone 21.97
trouble yet t. came 16.10
man is born unto t., as the sparks fly upward 16.14
man ... is ... full of t. 16.31
how are they increased that t. me 17.6
my beauty is gone for very t. 17.12
the Lord hear thee in the day of t. 17.38
a very present help in t. 17.103
their soul melteth away because of the t. 17.221
better is little ... than great treasure and t. therewith 18.42
confidence in an unfaithful man in time of t. is like a broken tooth 18.81
behold t. 22.5
t. in the flesh 48.20
troubled he was t., and all Jerusalem with him 42.2
see that ye be not t. 42.144
careful and t. about many things 44.34
an angel ... t. the water 45.21
let not your heart be t. 45.61
troubling the wicked cease from t. 16.8
true them which are t. of heart 17.18
the t. light 45.1
t. worshippers shall worship ... in spirit and in truth 45.18
the t. vine 45.62
let God be t., but every man a liar 47.11
as deceivers, and yet t. 49.13
whatsoever things are t. 52.12
O Lord, holy and t. 67.25
called faithful and t. 67.60
trump at the last t. 48.45
trumpet shall a t. be blown ... and the people not be afraid? 28.2
do not sound a t. before thee 42.26
a great sound of a t. 42.148
if the t. give an uncertain sound 48.36
the t. shall sound 48.45
a great voice, as of a t. 67.2
the first voice ... as it were of a t. 67.16
trumpets he saith among the t., ha, ha 16.58
trust some put their t. in chariots 17.39
in thee, O Lord, have I put my t. 17.66
my t. is in the tender mercy of God 17.117
my t. shall be under the covering of thy wings 17.134
put not your t. in princes 17.292

the heart of her husband doth safely t. in her 18.109
t. ye not in a friend 30.5
trusted he t. in God, that he would deliver him 17.41
trustest thou t. in ... this broken reed 21.56
truth the word of the Lord in thy mouth is t. 11.16
t. in the inward parts 17.114
mercy and t. are met together 17.177
t. shall flourish out of the earth 17.177
his faithfulness and t. shall be thy shield and buckler 17.186
his t. endureth from generation to generation 17.202
for thy t.'s sake 17.235
they that go down into the pit cannot hope for thy t. 21.58
great is t., and mighty above all things 35.6
the word ... full of grace and t. 45.1
worship ... in spirit and in t. 45.18
the t. shall make you free 45.39
I am the way, the t., and the life 45.57
the Spirit of t. 45.59
what is t.? 45.76
words of t. and soberness 46.60
who changed the t. of God into a lie 47.7
the unleavened bread of sincerity and t. 48.13
loins girt about with t. 51.14
the t. is not in us 64.2
–*See also* true.
try t. out my reins and my heart 17.53
the fire shall t. every man's work 48.7
t. the spirits whether they are of God 64.6
tunes such as found out musical t. 39.28
turn whosoever shall smite thee on thy right cheek, t. to him the other also 42.23
turned he t. his face to the wall 12.16
mine enemies ... shall be t. back 17.13
the children of Ephraim, who ... t. themselves back in the day of battle 17.163
thou hast t. away the captivity of Jacob 17.176
these that have t. the world upside down 46.36
turtle the voice of the t. is heard 20.6
twinkling his wrath endureth but the t. of an eye 17.64
in the t. of an eye 48.45
two into the ark, t. and two 1.29
t. are better than one 19.12
if one prevail ... t. shall withstand 19.13
can t. walk together, except they be agreed? 28.1
no man can serve t. masters 42.30
where t. or three are gathered together 42.115
t. be in the field; the one shall be taken 42.151
twofold t. more the child of hell 42.139
tyranny until this t. be over-past 17.125
serving either calamity or t. 38.12
Tyre T. ... whose merchants are princes 21.37

U

unawares entertained angels u. 60.20
unbelief help thou mine u. 43.16
uncertain if the trumpet give an u. sound 48.36
uncircumcision u. is nothing 48.19
unclean a man of u. lips 21.17
the u. spirit is gone out 42.83
undefiled blessed are those that are u. in the way 17.244
pure religion and u. 61.5
understand then thought I to u. this 17.156
they will not be learned nor u. 17.172
lest they ... u. with their heart 21.18
hear, and shall not u. 42.86
whoso readeth, let him u. 42.146
understandest thou u. my thoughts long before 17.277
u. thou what thou readest? 46.23
understanding give ... an u. heart 11.4
in length of days u. 16.28
where is the place of u.? 16.42
horse and mule, which have no u. 17.73
sing ... praises with u. 17.107
man being in honour hath no u. 17.111
a good u. have all they that do thereafter 17.229
a man of u. 18.1
with all thy getting get u. 18.10
nor yet riches to men of u. 19.29
a candle of u. 36.7
astonished at his u. 44.13
be not children in u. 48.37
the eyes of your u. being enlightened 51.1
the peace of God, which passeth all u. 52.11
understood I uttered that I u. not 16.62
undone woe is me! for I am u. 21.17
unemployment standing idle in the market-place 42.124
unfaithful confidence in an u. man in time of trouble is like a broken tooth 18.81
ungodliness the tents of u. 17.175
ungodly the u. ... privily shoot at them which are true of heart 17.18
fret not thyself because of the u. 17.82
the u. ... flourishing like a green bay-tree 17.86
the rod of the u. cometh not into the lot of the righteous 17.263
let the u. fall into their own nets 17.287
the way of the u., he turneth it upside down 17.293
unity Jerusalem is built as a city ... at u. 17.259
how good and joyful ... brethren, to dwell together in u. 17.275
he that is not with me is against me 42.77
the u. of the Spirit 51.6
unjust rain on the just and on the u. 42.24
the u. steward 44.54
u. in the least ... unjust also in much 44.54

he that is u., let him be unjust still 67.70
unknown to the u. god 46.38
unlearned u. and ignorant men 46.12
unleavened the u. bread of sincerity and truth 48.13
unnecessary be not curious in u. matters 39.4
unproductiveness why cumbereth it the ground? 44.42
unprofitable desire not a multitude of u. children 39.15
the u. servant 42.156
unquenchable u. fire 42.7
unquiet be the earth never so u. 17.201
unrighteousness friends of the mammon of u. 44.54
to cleanse us from all u. 64.2
unsearchable the heart of kings is u. 18.80
the u. riches of Christ 51.4
unspotted u. from the world 61.5
unwise an u. man doth not well consider 17.189
debtor both ... to the wise, and to the u. 47.4
upharsin mene, mene, tekel, u. 25.10
upholding u. all things by the word of his power 60.1
upper up, Lord, and let not man have the u. hand 17.16
up-rising thou knowest ... mine u. 17.277
uproar called in question for this day's u. 46.46
upside the way of the ungodly, he turneth it u. down 17.293
these that have turned the world u. down 46.36
Uriah set ... U. in the forefront of the hottest battle 10.5
Urim U. and ... Thummim 2.35
utter man cannot u. it 19.2
utterance as the Spirit gave them u. 46.6
uttered I u. that I understood not 16.62
groanings which cannot be u. 47.27
uttermost the u. part of the heaven 17.35
thy word is tried to the u. 17.252
paid the u. farthing 42.20

V

vadis quo v.? 45.67
vagabond a fugitive and a v. 1.22
vain thou shalt not take the name of ... God in v. 2.29
why do the people imagine a v. thing? 17.2
a horse is counted but a v. thing 17.76
man ... disquieteth himself in v. 17.88
v. is the help of man 17.133
the watchman waketh but in v. 17.265
in v. the net is spread in the sight of any bird 18.4
v. oblations 21.3
v. to pray for the dead 41.1
v. repetitions 42.27
v. babblings 56.15
vale going through the v. of misery 17.174
valley the v. of the shadow of death 17.45
mete out the v. of Succoth 17.225
every v. shall be exalted 21.59
the v. which was full of bones 24.11
multitudes in the v. of decision 27.7
valleys the v. also shall stand so thick with corn 17.140
the lily of the v. 20.3
valour thou mighty man of v. 7.8
value ye are of more v. than many sparrows 42.65
vanish knowledge, it shall v. away 48.35
vanity months of v. 16.18
away from me, all ye that work v. 17.12
altogether lighter than v. 17.135
turn away mine eyes, lest they behold v. 17.246
remove far from me v. and lies 18.105
v. of vanities 19.1
all is v. and vexation of spirit 19.4
the creature was made subject to v. 47.26
–*See also* vain.
vapour what is your life ... a v. 61.13
variableness the Father of lights, with whom is no v. 61.3
veil the v. of the temple was rent in twain 42.175
vengeance to me belongeth v., and recompence 5.19
v. is mine; I will repay 47.37
venite v., exultemus 17.196
veritas magna est v. 35.7
verses such as ... recited v. in writing 39.28
vessel break them ... like a potter's v. 17.4
break it as ... the potter's v. 21.46
a chosen v. 46.27
to make one v. unto honour 47.33
the weaker v. 62.12
vessels treasure in earthen v. 49.6
vexation all is vanity and v. of spirit 19.4
both the hands full with travail and v. 19.11
vials golden v. full of odours 67.20
the v. of the wrath of God 67.51
victory with his own right hand ... hath he gotten himself the v. 17.199
death is swallowed up in v. 48.45
vigilant be sober, be v. 62.16
vine thy wife shall be as the fruitful v. 17.267
planted ... with the choicest v. 21.13
every man under his v. and under his fig tree 30.1
I am the true v. 45.62
vines the little foxes, that spoil the v. 20.7
vineyard mine own v. have I not kept 20.1
as a cottage in a v. 21.2
my wellbeloved hath a v. 21.13
the v. of the Lord ... is ... Israel 21.14

vineyards they shall plant v., and eat the fruit 21.102
violence the seat of v. 28.5
they that take the sword ... perish with the sword 42.169
do v. to no man 44.16
thus with v. shall ... Babylon be thrown down 67.57
violently the swine ... ran v. down a steep place 43.8
viols the noise of thy v. 21.30
vipers O generation of v. 42.6
virgin a v. shall conceive 21.19
O v. daughter of Babylon 21.71
virgins therefore do the v. love thee 20.1
those v. arose, and trimmed their lamps 42.152
virtue v. had gone out of him 43.12
virtuous a v. woman is a crown to her husband 18.30
who can find a v. woman? 18.109
vision where there is no v., the people perish 18.103
every v. faileth 24.4
visions your young men shall see v. 27.5
visit v. the fatherless and widows 61.5
visited sick, and ye v. me 42.158
he hath v. and redeemed his people 44.4
vocation walk worthy of the v. 51.6
voice I heard thy v. in the garden 1.16
the v. of thy brother's blood 1.21
the v. of them that shout for mastery 2.40
a still small v. 11.23
the v. of the Lord breaketh the cedar-trees 17.61
the deaf adder ... which refuseth to hear the v. of the charmer 17.129
he doth send out his v., yea, and that a mighty voice 17.145
the floods have lift up their v. 17.193
to-day if ye will hear his v. 17.197
a bird of the air shall carry the v. 19.35
the v. of my beloved 20.5
the v. of the turtle is heard 20.6
the posts of the door moved at the v. 21.17
the v. of him that crieth in the wilderness 21.59
the v. of melody 21.79
thy watchmen shall lift up the v. 21.80
in Rama was there a v. heard 42.4
the v. of one crying in the wilderness 42.5
the dead shall hear the v. of the Son of God 45.23
the sheep ... know his v. 45.46
the v. of a god ... not of a man 46.33
a great v., as of a trumpet 67.2
his v. as the sound of many waters 67.2
the first v. ... as it were of a trumpet 67.16
the v. of a great thunder 67.43
voices lightnings and thunderings and v. 67.16
void a conscience v. of offence toward God 46.56
vomit he hath swallowed down riches, and he shall v. them up again 16.40
as a dog returneth to his v. 18.86
vow better ... not v., than ... vow and not pay 19.15
vultures there shall the v. also be gathered 21.51

W

wages he ... earneth w. to put it into a bag with holes 32.1
be content with your w. 44.16
the w. of sin is death 47.21
wail all kindreds of the earth shall w. 67.2
wait they that w. upon the Lord shall renew their strength 21.64
waited I w. patiently for the Lord 17.91
wake sleep a perpetual sleep, and not w. 22.22
waketh I sleep, but my heart w. 20.15
walk w. about Sion, and go round about her 17.109
w. before God in the light of the living 17.124
feet ... and w. not 17.237
w. before the Lord in the land of the living 17.239
this is the way, w. ye in it 21.49
they shall w., and not faint 21.64
can two w. together, except they be agreed? 28.1
w. humbly with thy God 30.4
take up thy bed, and w. 43.3
w. while ye have the light 45.54
in the name of Jesus ... rise up and w. 46.10
w. in newness of life 47.19
w. worthy of the vocation 51.6
walked Enoch w. with God 1.25
man that hath not w. in the counsel of the ungodly 17.1
the people that w. in darkness 21.22
we have w. to and fro through the earth 33.2
walketh he w. in the circuit of heaven 16.41
walking w. in the garden 1.14
from going to and fro ... w. up and down 16.1
four men ... w. in the midst of the fire 25.7
Jesus ... w. on the sea 42.97
men as trees, w. 43.14
wall he turned his face to the w. 12.16
I shall leap over the w. 17.32
thou whited w. 46.53
walls by faith the w. of Jericho fell down 60.14
Walls of Jericho 6.4
wander cursed be he that maketh the blind to w. 5.11
wandered w. in deserts ... dens and caves 60.15
wandering w. stars 66.3

want the Lord is my shepherd; I shall not w. 17.46
thy w. as an armed man 18.15
she of her w. did cast in all that she had 43.21
wanting found w. 25.10
wantonness not in chambering and w. 47.43
war the Lord is a man of w. 2.25
words ... softer than butter, having w. in his heart 17.121
who teacheth my hands to w. 17.288
a time of w., and a time of peace 19.9
there is no discharge in that w. 19.24
they all hold swords, being expert in w. 20.10
neither shall they learn w. any more 21.7
mighty and strong men for the w. 22.20
make w. against the sea ... that we may make us more woods 36.4
we do not w. after the flesh 49.16
fleshly lusts, which w. against the soul 62.6
there was w. in heaven 67.38
in righteousness he doth judge and make w. 67.60
warfare her w. is accomplished 21.59
who goeth a w. ... at his own charges? 48.25
the weapons of our w. are not carnal 49.16
warm aha, I am w., I have seen the fire 21.68
ye clothe you, but there is none w. 32.1
warned w. of God in a dream 42.3
who hath w. you to flee from the wrath to come? 42.6
warreth no man that w. entangleth himself with the affairs of this life 57.3
wars he maketh w. to cease in all the world 17.105
w. and rumours of wars 42.144
wash w., and be clean 12.6
every night w. I my bed ... with my tears 17.12
w. me throughly from my wickedness 17.113
wash-pot Moab is my w. 17.225
washed Pilate ... w. his hands 42.172
w. their robes ... in the blood of the Lamb 67.28
waste to what purpose is this w.? 42.160
wasted w. his substance with riotous living 44.48
waster he ... that is slothful ... is brother to ... a great w. 18.54
watch the Lord w. between me and thee 1.60
set a w. ... before my mouth 17.285
tarry ye here, and w. with me 42.165
w. and pray 42.167
keeping w. over their flock by night 44.9
w. unto prayer 62.14
watchings in w. often 49.18
watchman the w. waketh but in vain 17.265
w., what of the night? 21.34
watchmen thy w. shall lift up the voice 21.80
a man's mind is sometime wont to tell him more than seven w. 39.23
water the w. came out abundantly 4.11
a land of brooks of w. 5.2
drawers of w. 6.5
we ... are as w. spilt on the ground 10.8
w. of affliction 11.32
I ... w. my couch with my tears 17.12
a barren and dry land where no w. is 17.136
the river of God is full of w. 17.140
he maketh the wilderness a standing w. 17.223
who turned the hard rock into a standing w. 17.234
the whole stay of w. 21.10
w. out of the wells of salvation 21.27
the w. of affliction 21.48
baptize ... with w. unto repentance 42.7
the w. that was made wine 45.7
born of w. and of the Spirit 45.9
well of w. springing up into everlasting life 45.16
an angel ... troubled the w. 45.21
forthwith came there out blood and w. 45.84
drink no longer w. 56.9
sweet w. and bitter 61.9
clouds ... without w. 66.3
a pure river of w. of life 67.68
let him take the w. of life freely 67.71
watered I have planted, Apollos w. 48.6
water-flood the Lord sitteth above the w. 17.62
waters the Spirit of God moved upon ... the w. 1.1
the w. increased 1.29
the w. were on the face of the whole earth 1.30
the w. were abated 1.31
the w. of comfort 17.45
he leadeth me beside the still w. 17.46
the w. thereof rage and swell 17.103
the w. of strife 17.170
the w. stand in the hills 17.212
they ... occupy their business in great w. 17.221
the deep w. of the proud 17.261
by the w. of Babylon 17.276
he bloweth with his wind, and the w. flow 17.296
stolen w. are sweet 18.22
cast thy bread upon the w. 19.36
many w. cannot quench love 20.26
the earth shall be full ... as the w. cover the sea 21.26
w. flowed over mine head 23.6
in perils of w. 49.18
the sound of many w. 67.2
living fountains of w. 67.28
water-springs w. of a dry ground 17.223
wavereth he that w. ... driven with the wind and tossed 61.1
wavering ask in faith, nothing w. 61.1
waves all thy w. and storms are gone over me 17.96
the w. of the sea are mighty 17.193
raging w. of the sea 66.3
way going the w. of all the earth 6.7
they are all gone out of the w. 17.21
he shall direct his going in the w. 17.178
he led them forth by the right w. 17.219

the w. of the ungodly, he turneth it upside down 17.293
train up a child in the w. he should go 18.70
this is the w., walk ye in it 21.49
prepare ye the w. of the Lord 21.59
every one to his own w. 21.81
stood at the parting of the w. 24.8
broad is the w., that leadeth to destruction 42.39
I am the w., the truth, and the life 45.57
I go my w. to him that sent me 45.66
the error of his w. 61.17
ways I will take heed to my w. 17.88
thou . . . spiest out all my w. 17.277
her w. are ways of pleasantness 18.8
neither are your w. my ways 21.86
consider your w. 32.1
way side fell by the w. 42.85
weak strengthen . . . the w. hands 21.53
the flesh is w. 42.167
labouring . . . to support the w. 46.50
another, who is w., eateth herbs 47.44
strong ought to bear the infirmities of the w. 47.46
the w. things of the world 48.3
we are w., but ye are strong 48.10
this liberty . . . a stumblingblock to them that are w. 48.24
the w. and beggarly elements 50.6
weaker the w. vessel 62.12
weakness my strength is made perfect in w. 49.21
wealth my power . . . hath gotten me this w. 5.3
the rich man's w. is his strong city 18.26
w. maketh many friends 18.57
wealthy the w. nation, that dwelleth without care 22.21
weapons how are . . . the w. of war perished 10.3
the w. of our warfare are not carnal 49.16
weariness much study is a w. of the flesh 19.41
wearisome w. nights are appointed to me 16.18
weary there the w. be at rest 16.8
my soul is w. of my life 16.23
I am w. of my groaning 17.12
neither be w. of his correction 18.7
the shadow of a great rock in a w. land 21.50
they shall run, and not be w. 21.64
a word in season to him that is w. 21.77
let us not be w. in well doing 50.13
weather fair w.: for the sky is red 42.104
weaver my days are swifter than a w.'s shuttle 16.19
weep a time to w., and a time to laugh 19.9
w. not for me, but . . . for yourselves 44.71
w. with them that weep 47.37
weeping a voice heard, lamentation, and w. 42.4
w. and gnashing of teeth 42.47
weighed thou art w. in the balances, and art found wanting 25.10
weight exceeding and eternal w. of glory 49.7
well is it w. with thee? 12.4
the w. of life 17.81
who going through the vale of misery use it for a w. 17.174
the flint-stone into a springing w. 17.234
a w. of living waters 20.13
w. done, thou good and faithful servant 42.154
woe unto you when all men shall speak w. of you 44.21
w. of water springing up into everlasting life 45.16
wellbeloved a bundle of myrrh is my w. 20.2
my w. hath a vineyard 21.13
well favoured Rachel was . . . w. 1.58
wells with joy shall ye draw water out of the w. 21.27
well-tuned the w. cymbals 17.300
wept by the waters of Babylon we . . . w. 17.276
Jesus w. 45.51
wet his body was w. with the dew of heaven 25.8
whale three days . . . in the w.'s belly 42.81
whales God created great w. 1.5
wheat a land of w., and barley 5.2
gather his w. into the garner 42.7
tares among the w. 42.89
gather the w. into my barn 42.90
except a corn of w. fall into the ground 45.52
a measure of w. for a penny 67.23
wheel the w. broken at the cistern 19.40
while a little w., and ye shall not see me 45.70
whips my father hath chastised you with w. 11.12
whirlwind Elijah went up by a w. into heaven 12.1
the w. shall take them away as stubble 21.63
sown the wind . . . reap the w. 26.1
white his teeth w. with milk 1.77
the fields . . . w. already to harvest 45.19
w. like wool, as white as snow 67.2
a w. stone 67.8
behold a w. horse 67.22
clothed with w. robes 67.27
arrayed in w. robes 67.28
whited w. sepulchres 42.141
thou w. wall 46.53
whole they that be w. need not a physician 42.52
whore the judgment of the great w. 67.53
Whore of Babylon 67.54
wicked the men of Sodom were w. 1.40
to slay the righteous with the w. 1.47
the w. cease from troubling 16.8
preserve me from the w. man 17.282
the name of the w. shall rot 18.24
the tender mercies of the w. 18.31
the candle of the w. shall be put out 18.78
the w. flee when no man pursueth 18.98
a w. man that prolongeth his life 19.22

no peace ... unto the w. 21.74
the heart is deceitful ... and desperately w. 22.13
then cometh the w. one 42.87
the fiery darts of the w. 51.14
wickedness far be it from God, that he should do w. 16.51
their inward parts are very w. 17.11
wash me throughly from my w. 17.113
I was shapen in w. 17.114
the hairy scalp of such ... as goeth on still in his w. 17.144
plowed w. ... reaped iniquity 26.2
the leaven of malice and w. 48.13
against spiritual w. in high places 51.14
–*See also* wicked, evil.
wide the great and w. sea 17.215
the entrances of the elder world were w. 36.5
widow the judgment of the ... w. 5.4
the only son of his mother ... a w. 44.23
widows devour w.' houses 43.20
visit the fatherless and w. 61.5
Widow's Cruse 11.15
Widow's Mite 43.21
wife man ... shall cleave unto his w. 1.12
the w. of thy bosom 5.8
thy w. shall be as the fruitful vine 17.267
rejoice with the w. of thy youth 18.13
every one neighed after his neighbour's w. 22.1
a w. full of words to a quiet man 39.20
I have married a w. 44.44
remember Lot's w. 44.60
husband render unto the w. due benevolence 48.16
art thou bound unto a w.? 48.20
seek not a w. 48.20
love his w. even as himself 51.12
the w. see that she reverence her husband 51.12
the w. ... the weaker vessel 62.12
wild a w. man 1.45
it brought forth w. grapes 21.13
wilderness in the waste howling w. 5.16
the day of temptation in the w. 17.197
who turneth the floods into a w. 17.223
who is this that cometh up from the w.? 20.25
the voice of him that crieth in the w. 21.59
the voice of one crying in the w. 42.5
what went ye out into the w. to see? 42.71
leave the ninety and nine in the w. 44.47
as Moses lifted up the serpent in the w. 45.11
wiles the w. of the devil 51.14
will thy w. be done 42.27
he that doeth the w. of my Father 42.42
not as I w., but as thou wilt 42.166
not my w., but thine, be done 44.70
the w. of the flesh 45.1
my meat is to do the w. of him that sent me 45.19
willeth not of him that w. 47.32
willing the spirit ... is w. 42.167
w. to communicate 56.14
wind the Lord was not in the w. 11.23
flying upon the wings of the w. 17.31
as soon as the w. goeth over it, it is gone 17.210
who ... walketh upon the wings of the w. 17.211
at his word the stormy w. ariseth 17.221
he bloweth with his w., and the waters flow 17.296
w. and storm, fulfilling his word 17.297
he that observeth the w. shall not sow 19.38
awake, O north w. 20.14
sown the w. ... reap the whirlwind 26.1
winnow not with every w. 39.5
a reed shaken with the w. 42.71
the w. bloweth where it listeth 45.10
a rushing mighty w. 46.6
carried about with every w. of doctrine 51.7
winds even the w. and the sea obey him 42.50
gather ... his elect from the four w. 42.148
wine his eyes shall be red with w. 1.77
w. and strong drink 4.1
a drink of deadly w. 17.132
there is a cup, and the w. is red 17.158
like a giant refreshed with w. 17.166
w. that maketh glad the heart of man 17.213
w. is a mocker 18.58
look not thou upon the w. when it is red 18.75
drink thy w. with a merry heart 19.27
drunk my w. with my milk 20.15
that continue ... till w. inflame them 21.15
they shall not drink w. with a song 21.39
drunken, but not with w. 21.43
we will drink no w. 22.18
how exceeding strong is w. 35.1
w. ... causeth all men to err 35.1
w. ... maketh the mind of the king and of the fatherless child to be all one 35.1
w. ... turneth ... every thought into jollity 35.1
when they are from the w., they remember not what they have done 35.2
new w. into old bottles 42.54
no man ... having drunk old w. straightway desireth new 44.20
the water that was made w. 45.7
full of new w. 46.7
not given to w. 56.4
use a little w. for thy stomach's sake 56.9
the w. of the wrath of her fornication 67.45
winebibber a man gluttonous, and a w. 42.74
winebibbers be not among w. 18.74
winepress I have trodden the w. alone 21.97
w. of the wrath of God 67.49
wings hide me under the shadow of thy w. 17.28
O that I had w. like a dove 17.119
my trust shall be under the covering of thy w. 17.134
take the w. of the morning 17.279
riches certainly make themselves w. 18.71
the seraphims: each one had six w. 21.17
mount up with w. as eagles 21.64

shall ... arise with healing in his w. 34.3
as a hen gathereth her chickens under her w. 42.142
winnow w. not with every wind 39.5
winter the w. is past 20.6
wipe God shall w. away all tears 67.28
wiped let them be w. out of the book of the living 17.149
wisdom the w. of God was in him 11.5
ye are the people, and w. shall die with you 16.27
with the ancient is w. 16.28
hold your peace! and it should be your w. 16.30
where shall w. be found? 16.42
the price of w. is above rubies 16.43
multitude of years should teach w. 16.48
the testimony of the Lord ... giveth w. unto the simple 17.35
the fear of the Lord is the beginning of w. 17.229
w. crieth without 18.5
w. ... uttereth her voice in the streets 18.5
w. is the principal thing 18.10
w. is better than rubies 18.20
I w. dwell with prudence 18.20
w. hath builded her house 18.21
she openeth her mouth with w. 18.111
in much w. is much grief 19.5
w. excelleth folly, as ... light excelleth darkness 19.7
w. is good with an inheritance 19.21
the spirit of w. and understanding 21.25
he giveth w. unto the wise 25.2
w. is a loving spirit 38.1
w. ... will not acquit a blasphemer 38.1
w. is more moving than any motion 38.8
w. ... the breath of the power of God 38.8
w. ... a pure influence flowing from the glory of the Almighty 38.8
w. ... the unspotted mirror ... of God 38.8
w. ... being but one ... can do all things 38.8
God loveth none but him that dwelleth with w. 38.8
w. reacheth from one end to another 38.9
w. ... sweetly doth ... order all things 38.9
w. ... cometh by opportunity of leisure 39.25
how can he get w. ... whose talk is of bullocks? 39.25
w. is justified of her children 42.74
increased in w. and stature 44.15
I will give you a mouth and w. 44.66
Greeks seek after w. 48.2
the w. of this world is foolishness with God 48.8
if any ... lack w., let him ask of God 61.1
w. ... from above is first pure 61.11
wise a tree to be desired to make one w. 1.14
the w. in their own craftiness 16.15
great men are not always w. 16.48
whoso is w. will ponder these things 17.224
a w. man will hear, and will increase learning 18.1
be not w. in thine own eyes 18.6
consider her ways, and be w. 18.14
a w. son maketh a glad father 18.23
a w. son heareth his father's instruction 18.32
a w. man is strong 18.76
a man w. in his own conceit 18.86
if a w. man contendeth with a foolish ... there is no rest 18.101
who knoweth whether he shall be a w. man or a fool? 19.8
the words of w. men are heard in quiet 19.30
he giveth wisdom unto the w. 25.2
w. men from the east 42.2
a w. man, which built his house upon a rock 42.44
w. as serpents 42.61
hid these things from the w. and prudent 42.75
debtor both ... to the w., and to the unwise 47.4
professing themselves to be w. 47.6
be not w. in your own conceits 47.37
the foolish things of the world to confound the w. 48.3
Wise and Foolish Virgins 42.152
wisely charm he never so w. 17.129
wiser w. than the children of light 44.54
wit at their w.'s end 17.221
witch thou shalt not suffer a w. to live 2.32
witchcraft rebellion is as the sin of w. 9.15
with he that is not w. me is against me 42.77
withdraw the stars shall w. their shining 27.7
wither his leaf also shall not w. 17.1
withered w. even as the green herb 17.82
it smote the gourd that it w. 29.4
withereth the grass w. 21.59, 62.4
within the kingdom of God is w. you 44.59
withstand if one prevail ... two shall w. 19.13
able to w. in the evil day 51.14
witness thou shalt not bear false w. 2.29
I call heaven and earth to w. against you 5.1
a w., to bear witness of the light 45.1
God is my w. 47.2
the Spirit itself beareth w. with our spirit 47.25
witnesses the w. laid down their clothes 46.19
in the mouth of two or three w. 49.22
professed a good profession before many w. 56.12
so great a cloud of w. 60.16
wives husbands, love your w. 53.5
wizards w. that peep, and that mutter 21.21
woe w. to him that is alone when he falleth 19.12
w. unto them that join house to house 21.14
w. unto them that ... lay field to field 21.14
w. unto them that ... follow strong drink 21.15
w. unto them that call evil good 21.16
w. is me! for I am undone 21.17
w. unto him that striveth with his maker 21.69
w. is me, my mother, that thou hast borne me 22.12
w. to the inhabiters of the earth 67.39

wolf the w. also shall dwell with the lamb 21.26
wolves inwardly they are ravening w. 42.40
as sheep in the midst of w. 42.61
send you forth as lambs among w. 44.28
woman the rib ... made he a w. 1.12
she shall be called W. 1.12
the w. whom thou gavest to be with me 1.17
fear came there upon them ... as upon a w. in her travail 17.108
he maketh the barren w. to keep house 17.232
the lips of a strange w. drop as an honeycomb 18.12
as a jewel ... in a swine's snout, so is a fair w. ... without discretion 18.29
a virtuous w. is a crown to her husband 18.30
better to dwell in a corner of the housetop, than with a brawling w. 18.67
a continual dropping ... and a contentious w. 18.93
who can find a virtuous w.? 18.109
can a w. forget her sucking child? 21.75
if men have gathered together gold and silver ... do they not love a w.? 35.4
do ye not labour ... and bring all to the w.? 35.5
w., behold thy son 45.81
Dorcas: this w. ... full of good works 46.28
if a w. have long hair 48.33
a w. clothed with the sun 67.37
women thy love ... passing the love of w. 10.3
Solomon loved many strange w. 11.11
kings' daughters were among thy honourable w. 17.100
thou fairest among w. 20.1
seven w. shall take hold of one man 21.12
without w. cannot men be 35.4
w. have dominion over you 35.5
wonderful things too w. for me 16.62
three things which are too w. for me 18.107
W., Counsellor 21.23
wonders signs and ... w. in ... Egypt 2.13
his w. in the deep 17.221
wood hewers of w. 6.5
the thought of the w. was in vain, for the fire ... consumed it 36.4
woods make war against the sea ... that we may make us more w. 36.4
let us ... subdue the w. of the plain 36.4
wool white like w. 67.2
word at his w. the stormy wind ariseth 17.221
thy w. is a lantern unto my feet 17.249
thy w. is tried to the uttermost 17.252
not a w. in my tongue, but thou ... knowest it 17.277
he sendeth out his w., and melteth them 17.296
wind and storm, fulfilling his w. 17.297
a w. spoken in due season, how good is it 18.44
a w. behind thee, saying, this is the way 21.49
a w. in season to him that is weary 21.77
if thou hast heard a w., let it die with thee 39.18
by every w. ... out of the mouth of God 42.9
speak the w. only 42.46
every idle w. ... they shall give account thereof 42.80
in the beginning was the w. 45.1
the w. was with God 45.1
the w. was made flesh 45.1
hearing by the w. of God 47.35
the kingdom of God is not in w. 48.11
in the mouth of ... witnesses shall every w. be established 49.22
upholding all things by the w. of his power 60.1
the w. of God is ... sharper than any two-edged sword 60.5
be ye doers of the w. 61.4
the w. of God, which liveth and abideth 62.4
the sincere milk of the w. 62.5
words lay up these my w. in your heart 5.6
how forcible are right w. 16.16
oh that my w. were now written 16.37
Job ... multiplieth w. without knowledge 16.52
w. without knowledge 16.54
let the w. of my mouth ... be alway acceptable in thy sight 17.37
the w. of his mouth were softer than butter 17.121
they daily mistake my w. 17.122
the w. of the wise, and their dark sayings 18.1
a man that is hasty in his w. ... more hope of a fool than of him 18.104
the w. of wise men are heard in quiet 19.30
shut up the w., and seal the book 25.14
wisdom ... will not acquit a blasphemer of his w. 38.1
a wife full of w. to a quiet man 39.20
let thy speech be short, comprehending much in few w. 39.22
by thy w. thou shalt be justified 42.80
by thy w. thou shalt be condemned 42.80
my w. shall not pass away 42.149
w. of truth and soberness 46.60
the form of sound w. 57.2
great swelling w. 66.4
these w. are true and faithful 67.65
work to w. in gold, and in silver 2.36
every one with one of his hands wrought in the w. 14.1
man goeth forth to his w., and to his labour 17.214
he ... that is slothful in his w. is brother to ... a great waster 18.54
no w., nor device, nor knowledge ... in the grave 19.28
thy thighs are like jewels, the w. ... of a cunning workman 20.21
allured by the grace of the w. 38.12
w. the works of God 45.28
the night cometh, when no man can w. 45.43
all things w. together for good 47.28

every man's w. shall be made manifest 48.7
the fire shall try every man's w. 48.7
w. out your own salvation 52.5
w. of faith 54.1
if any would not w., neither should he eat 55.2
–*See also* labour.

worketh according to the power that w. in us 51.5
the wrath of man w. not the righteousness of God 61.4

working w. with his hands the thing which is good 51.8

works thy heavens, even the w. of thy fingers 17.14
these men see the w. of the Lord 17.221
marvellous are thy w. 17.280
I have seen all the w. that are done under the sun 19.4
that they may see your good w. 42.16
w. they do for to be seen of men 42.137
full of good w. 46.28
rulers are not a terror to good w. 47.40
cast off the w. of darkness 47.43
faith, if it hath not w., is dead 61.6

world the compass of the w. 17.48
he hath made the round w. so sure that it cannot be moved 17.192
the round w., and they that dwell therein 17.200
with righteousness shall he judge the w. 17.200
the entrances of this w. made narrow 36.5
the entrances of the elder w. 36.5
the w. hath lost his youth 36.6
all the kingdoms of the w. 42.10
the light of the w. 42.16
the care of this w. 42.88
all the w. should be taxed 44.7
the children of this w. 44.54
in the w. . . . and the world knew him not 45.1
which taketh away the sin of the w. 45.4
God so loved the w. 45.12
give for the life of the w. 45.32
I am the light of the w. 45.38
now shall the prince of this w. be cast out 45.53
the w. seeth me no more 45.60
not as the w. giveth 45.61
joy that a man is born into the w. 45.71
I have overcome the w. 45.72
these that have turned the w. upside down 46.36
against the rulers of the darkness of this w. 51.14
after the rudiments of the w. 53.1
brought nothing into this w. 56.10
having loved this present w. 57.8
keep himself unspotted from the w. 61.5
this w.'s good 64.5
from the foundation of the w. 67.41

worm the w., thou art my mother 16.33
a w., and no man 17.41
the w. is spread under thee 21.30
their w. dieth not 43.17

worms w. and feathered fowls 17.297
eaten of w. 46.33

wormwood her end is bitter as w. 18.12
the w. and the gall 23.3
the name of the star is called W. 67.31

worse the last error shall be w. than the first 42.176
was nothing bettered, but rather grew w. 43.11
sin no more, lest a w. thing come unto thee 45.22
evil men and seducers shall wax w. 57.4

worship fall down and w. the golden image 25.4
true worshippers shall w. . . . in spirit and in truth 45.18
whom therefore ye ignorantly w. 46.38
w. him that liveth for ever and ever 67.17

worshipped w. and served the creature more than the Creator 47.7

worthy they which were bidden were not w. 42.132
the labourer is w. of his hire 44.28
no more w. to be called thy son 44.49
whose shoe's latchet I am not w. to unloose 45.3
walk w. of the vocation 51.6
w. . . . to receive glory and honour and power 67.17
who is w. to open the book? 67.18
w. is the Lamb that was slain 67.21

wound w. for wound 2.31

wounded w. for our transgressions 21.81
I was w. in the house of my friends 33.6

wounds bound up his w. 44.32

wrapped w. him in swaddling clothes 44.8

wrath his w. endureth but the twinkling of an eye 17.64
riches profit not in the day of w. 18.27
a soft answer turneth away w. 18.40
w. is cruel, and anger is outrageous 18.91
the forcing of w. bringeth forth strife 18.108
in a little w. I hid my face from thee 21.83
the w. to come 42.6
the w. of God abideth on him 45.15
the law worketh w. 47.15
give place unto w. 47.37
subject, not only for w. 47.41
let not the sun go down upon your w. 51.8
cometh the w. of God upon the children of disobedience 51.10
slow to w. 61.4
the w. of man worketh not the righteousness of God 61.4
the devil is come . . . having great w. 67.39
the wine of the w. of her fornication 67.45
the w. of God . . . poured out without mixture 67.46
winepress of the w. of God 67.49
the vials of the w. of God 67.51
–*See also* wrath.

wrestle we w. not against flesh and blood 51.14
wrestled there w. a man 1.61
wretchedness let me not see my w. 4.4
write w. upon him my new name 67.13
w.: for these words are true and faithful 67.65
writer my tongue is the pen of a ready w. 17.99
Writing on the Wall 25.9
written thy book which thou hast w. 2.42
oh that my words were now w. 16.37
in thy book were all my members w. 17.281
what I have w. I have written 45.80
w. not with ink, but with the Spirit 49.3
how large a letter I have w. 50.14
wrote w. . . . upon the plaister of the wall of the king's palace 25.9

Y

yea y., yea; nay, nay 42.22
let your y. be yea 61.15
year thou crownest the y. with thy goodness 17.140
to proclaim the acceptable y. of the Lord 21.96
years multitude of y. should teach wisdom 16.48
the y. that are past 17.160
a thousand y. . . . are but as yesterday 17.182
thy y. shall not fail 17.206
I shall go softly all my y. 21.57
the y. that the locust hath eaten 27.4
yesterday a thousand years . . . are but as y. 17.182
the same y., and to day, and for ever 60.21
yoke thy father made our y. heavy 11.12
broken the y. of his burden 21.22
good . . . that he bear the y. in his youth 23.5
take my y. upon you 42.76
my y. is easy 42.76
a y. . . . which neither our fathers nor we were able to bear 46.35
young I have been y., and now am old 17.85
y. and lusty as an eagle 17.207
gently lead those that are with y. 21.60
desirable y. men 24.9
your y. men shall see visions 27.5
laid down their clothes at a y. man's feet 46.19
younger they that are y. than I have me in derision 16.45
youth evil from his y. 1.32
remember not the sins . . . of my y. 17.50
thou, O God, hast taught me from my y. up 17.152
rejoice with the wife of thy y. 18.13
remember now thy Creator in the days of thy y. 19.40
good . . . that he bear the yoke in his y. 23.5
the world hath lost his y. 36.6
if thou hast gathered nothing in thy y. 39.19
–*See also* young.
you-ward more abundantly to y. 49.1

Z

zeal the z. of thine house 17.147
the z. of the Lord of hosts will perform this 21.23
a z. of God, but not according to knowledge 47.34